THE DECLINE
AND FALL OF
NAZI
GERMANY
AND
IMPERIAL
JAPAN

A Pictorial History of the Final Days
of World War II

HANS DOLLINGER

Technical Adviser
DR. HANS-ADOLF JACOBSEN

Translated from the German by
ARNOLD POMERANS

GRAMERCY BOOKS
New York • Avenel

This 1995 edition is published by Gramercy Books,
distributed by Random House Value Publishing, Inc.,
40 Engelhard Avenue, Avenel, New Jersey 07001.

Random House
New York • Toronto • London • Sydney • Auckland

Printed and bound in the United States of America

Library of Congress Cataloging-in-Publication Data
Dollinger, Hans.
    The decline and fall of Nazi Germany and imperial
Japan.
    Translation of: Die letzten hundert Tage.
    Bibliography: p.
    Includes index.
    ISBN 0-517-12399-1
    1. World War, 1939–1945—Campaigns—Germany.
2. World War, 1939–1945—Campaigns—East Asia.
3. Germany—History—1933–1945. 4. Japan—
History—1912–1945. I. Title
D755.7.D613   1982   82-4483
940.54´21   AACR2

10 9 8 7 6 5 4 3 2

FOREWORD

BY IRA C. EAKER, LIEUTENANT GENERAL USAF (RET.)

An introduction or foreword, I believe, should prepare the reader for what he will find in the book, a sort of road map for the journey ahead.

Having had the privilege of reading the manuscript for this book, and having seen the earlier German edition, *Die letzten Hundert Tage*, which created quite a stir in Europe, I welcome this opportunity to make some observations about it.

If the Chinese were right, and one picture is worth a thousand words, this book, if converted wholly to language, would contain well over one million words. In fact, it is so profusely illustrated with portraits of leaders and warriors at all levels, and with war scenes and campaign maps, that some may conclude hastily that it is just another picture book of World War II. But the patient reader will find that it is, instead, a significant history of the fall of two tyrannies.

I was surprised and relieved to find that Hans Dollinger is a remarkably nonpartisan, objective historian. Although German, he offers no apology for Nazism, and little sympathy for the German people seduced by it. He does not express personal views and convictions. Instead he tells what Hitler did and said. He thus holds the miserable maniac up for all to see as he led Germany to destruction and moved inexorably to his own last hours in the Berlin bunker. So it is with all the other politicians, generals, and admirals who parade these pages: their speeches, prophecies, exhortations, field orders, diaries, and messages to their troops, paint a truer picture of them and their defeats and triumphs than any I have seen elsewhere.

The treatment is necessarily kaleidoscopic as it moves swiftly from one battle to the next, from one front to the other. Its style is never plodding, tedious, or dull. It marches in double-time, and sometimes seems jet-propelled in its swift movement toward the final scenes, the capture of Berlin and the atomic bomb on Hiroshima.

The early chapters deal with the war in Europe from the days when the invading Allied armies reached and crossed the Rhine, and broke through the Eastern Front after Stalingrad, until the fall of Berlin, the unconditional surrender, and dismemberment of Germany.

Campaigns described and clarified by maps, orders of battle, and disposition of forces provide valuable material for students of military history and rewarding human-interest material for any reader. The battle plans, no longer top secret, and quotes from the correspondence, military diaries, and books of the commanders leave little doubt about who was responsible for victory or defeat.

Some readers will find many of the photographs of death, starvation, and destruction morbid. They are. But this war was like that.

One of the very valuable contributions of this book is the notice it takes of the political leaders and how their decisions impinged on the war. Here are such agreements as the Atlantic Charter and the pronouncements from the Cairo, Yalta, and Potsdam meetings of heads of state.

It is now clear from the historical records here presented that the political objectives and war aims of Churchill and Roosevelt were not the same as Stalin's. The Prime Minister and the President proposed only the destruction of two tyrannies, permitting the nations of the world to live, generally in their old boundaries, in peace. Stalin's immediate objective was to throw the invader out of the Motherland and make it impossible for Germany ever again to be a threat to Russia. But his long range objective, here clearly revealed, was to extend Communist rule to as many nations and peoples as possible. While Churchill appreciated Stalin's full purpose, his warning to his international partners went unheeded.

The second section of this book deals with the last few months of the war against Japan. Surprisingly, since the author is European, the description of the fall of the Japanese warlords is well covered and thoroughly documented. The campaigns are all here, from Leyte to the surrender. The Allied leaders in the Pacific war may no longer feel that they and their war have been neglected by historians. The decision to drop the atomic bomb, and its relation to the Japanese surrender, are confirmed by official documents and diaries.

It is interesting to compare the two wars, the European and the Pacific, as this book permits us to do. The objectives of the Nazis and the Japanese warlords were quite similar: one sought the conquest of Europe, and the other, control over Asia and the Pacific Ocean. Both were initially successful for the same reason: preparation of vast armaments, seizure of the initiative through cruel aggression, plus the fact that the opposition in each area failed to heed the signs of the coming conflict and was laggard in preparing adequate defenses.

I commend this book to my contemporaries who lived through those always dramatic and sometimes tragic years from 1939 to 1945. Especially do I feel that those who fought in these wars will be rewarded. Those whose outlook on World War II was from one headquarters, one army, one fleet, or one air force may now see the larger picture. The fog of war—and there was quite a bit of fog when we were there—has now cleared from the battlefields, and, thanks to the energy and capability of Hans Dollinger, we can all learn what happened.

There are some lessons from this account of World War II that are pertinent and applicable today.

Those miniwits who now prate about the ineffectiveness of air power obviously never saw Berlin or Tokyo and never served on a battlefield or a fleet under hostile aircraft. Here they can gain that experience.

The reader will be reminded that bad leaders, if followed too long, may lead a nation or a people to disaster.

Then there is the final conclusion that the Second World War, tragic as it was, and here revealed in stark reality, was not so bad as the alternative—living under the Nazi and Japanese tyrannies. Let any doubter, in all the generations to come, contemplate what it would be like to live in a world dominated by Hitler, the Japanese warlords, or any other cruel dictator or despot. Here he can gain some idea of what such a life would have been.

I hope this book finds its way into every public, high school, and college library so that it may be read by the prospective leaders of the future. Let them learn that so long as evil men roam the world, the arsenal of the peacekeepers must be as good as the arsenal of the badmen.

IRA C. EAKER
Lieutenant General USAF (Ret.)
(Commanding General, United States
Eighth Air Force in England, 1942 to
1944; Commanding General,
Mediterranean Allied Air Forces,
January 1944 to March 1945)

CONTENTS

5

THE STRUGGLE AGAINST COLONIALISM

ASIA AT THE END OF THE SECOND WORLD WAR

THE CONSEQUENCES OF THE SECOND WORLD WAR IN EUROPE AND ASIA

THE CATASTROPHE IN FIGURES

THE DECLINE AND FALL OF NAZI GERMANY AND IMPERIAL JAPAN

A Pictorial History of the Final Days of World War II

THE ROAD TO CATASTROPHE

There is no difficulty at all in deciding who started the Second World War. "The documents proving Hitler's dogged determination to wage a war of conquest are so many and so clear that whoever doubts them is either a liar or blind, either an extravagant controversialist like A. J. P. Taylor, or as misguided as poor Dr. Hoggan." (Golo Mann). It was Hitler and Hitler alone who unleashed this war, and who must bear the sole responsibility for it ... (Herzfeld). After the victories of 1939–1941 Hitler thought that nothing and nobody could stand in his way. The "greatest general of all time" accordingly attacked the Soviet Union, stupidly underestimated his new opponent, and made one strategic blunder after another. Most of his officers were content to shelter behind their oath of allegiance, consoling and excusing themselves with the Fuehrer's past infallibility. Only a handful of them were prepared for active resistance, and joined the "moral revolt" that led to the tragedy of 20 July 1944.

After Stalingrad and the landing in North Africa—the military turning-points of the war—the Western Allies and the Soviet Union resolutely set their sights at Hitler's "Fortress Europe". Fascist Italy floundered after the landing in Sicily. In the East, the German Front collapsed and, by 6 July 1944, when the Allies launched the greatest invasion in military history, the Red Army was already in Poland. Paris was liberated in August and the deadly ring round Germany closed—"the pendulum of power which had swung out so violently, hurling whole countries to destruction, now swept back and shattered Germany in her turn". (J. R. von Salis).

At the beginning of 1945, about ten million Allied and Soviet soldiers prepared for the decisive battle. On 3 January 1945, the Allied Expeditionary Forces under their Supreme Commander, General Dwight Eisenhower, launched a counter-attack on the Western Front, having just thrown back the last German offensive in the Ardennes. To the north, the Canadian 1st, the British 2nd and the U.S. 9th Armies (21st Army Group) were drawn up under Field-Marshal Montgomery. In Holland, Canadian and British troops engaged in Operation "Veritable", were advancing to the Lower Rhine, to strike southeastwards between the Maas and Rhine rivers.

Directly below them, the U.S. 9th Army in Operation "Grenade", was advancing northeast towards the Rhine, with its right flank on the Juelich–Neuss line. In the centre, the U.S. 1st and 3rd Armies (12th Army Group) under General Bradley, prepared to move north of the Moselle in Operation "Lumberjack". In the south, finally, the 6th Army Group, made up of the U.S. 7th Army and the French 1st Army, under the command of Lt.-General Devers converged south of the Moselle, closed in on the Rhine and joined the southern flank of the U.S. 3rd Army south of Coblenz (Operation "Overtone"). By March 1945, these operations had cleared the western banks of the Rhine. Once that river had been crossed on a very broad front, organized German resistance began to crumble: in Holland, the 25th Army of Army Group H under General Blaskowitz was completely encircled by the British; in the centre, the bulk of Army Group B under Field-Marshal Model was remorselessly driven into the Ruhr pocket, in the south, Army Group G under SS General Hausser gave way under pressure. Hitler, in a senseless fit of rage, removed Field-Marshal von Rundstedt from his post of Commander-in-Chief of the German Armies in the West, and had him replaced by Field-Marshal Kesselring.

On 12 January 1945, the First White Russian Front under Marshal Zhukov opened its great offensive from the Baranov bridgehead, and prepared to advance on Berlin. Meanwhile in the north, the First Baltic Front under Marshal Bagramyan, the Third White Russian Front under General Chernyakhovsky (killed on 18 February and replaced by Marshal Vassilevsky), and the Second White Russian Front under Marshal Rokossovsky were preparing to cut off East Prussia (4 March 1945). In the south, the four Ukrainian Fronts under Marshals Konev, Tolbukhin, Malinovsky and Petrov were pressing on towards Silesia, Czechoslovakia, Hungary and Austria. In the north, the Red Armies were opposed by German Army Group Courland (General Hilpert), Army Group North (General Weiss), Army Group Vistula (SS-Reichsfuehrer Himmler and from 20th March, General Heinrici), and Army Group Centre (Field-Marshal Schoerner). Until 28 March 1945, the Chief of the

German General Staff, General Guderian, was responsible for all German operations in the East. In spite of desperate German resistance, the Red Army, which was greatly superior in equipment and number—in January 1945, 1·8 million German troops opposed 5·3 million Soviet troops—smashed through the borders of the Reich and on 25 April, made contact with the Americans on the Elbe. In southeastern Europe, the Russians were opposed by Army Group Southeast (General Woehler), while Marshal Tito's forces were engaged by Army Group South (General Loehr). Finally, in Italy, Army Group Southwest (General von Vietinghoff and SS General Wolff) faced the British 8th as well as the U.S. 5th Armies under Field-Marshal Alexander.

So fieht die Blutbilanz aus!

Von Kriegsbeginn bis 1. Januar 1945:

Von 18 672 334 Soldaten sind gefallen, vermißt oder gefangen: 7 068 509 Mann.

Das kämpfende Volk verlor: 37.8%

Von 1 551 709 politischen Leitern sind gefallen, vermißt oder gefangen: 38 102 Mann.

Die Parteileitung verlor: 2½%

Die Verluste der gewöhnlichen Volksgenossen im wehrfähigen Alter sind prozentual 15 mal so groß wie die der politischen Leiter der NSDAP.

Allied Leaflet January 1945: While the German nation as a whole lost 37·8% of its fighting men, the party leadership lost a mere 2½%.

In this book we have tried to give a chronological account of the main military and political events during the last hundred days of the Second World War, amply supported with documents and photographs. As the story is unfolded, the reader will meet inhumanity on a scale without parallel in world history. The military operations, the criminal actions of both sides, the misery of the civilian population caught in the cross-fire and the hailstorm of bombs, the horrible sufferings of the refugees, and the discovery of the abominable mass murders in German concentration camps, all combined to turn the end of this "total war" into an apocalyptic inferno. Meanwhile "the chief culprit of this 'nightmare-turned-reality' sat in the air-raid shelter of the Reichs Chancel-lery in Berlin. Old before his time, worn out with fatigue, kept alive on drugs, trembling-ashen-faced and with blazing eyes, he held the last of his military conferences, now completely out of touch with reality." (Golo Mann). The collapse of the Third Reich was like the downfall of a gang of completely unscrupulous, contentious and reckless gamblers who had ventured everything on one last throw. Count Folke Bernadotte, who met Himmler and other SS leaders several times during the last days, and who had a ringside seat at the collapse of the Third Reich, wrote that the end tore the masks from the faces of the Nazi leaders. "My experience tells me that they were men lacking in all moral conceptions, in all loftiness of mind. In the last act there they were, with their hideous pasts, desperately intriguing among themselves, while at the same time trying to take shelter behind each other's backs, cowardly, undecided, irresolute." Or as Friedrich Meinecke put it, all this gang left behind in Germany was the spent crater of their ambition.

Alas, the military triumph of the Western Alliance proved to be a hollow victory; indeed, it amounted to political defeat. As early as February 1945, at the Yalta conference, it had become obvious that although West and East were fighting a common foe, their motives and objectives were far from identical. The Western Allies concentrated on military considerations. "Let us win the war first, and then talk politics," was their motto, and it was this attitude which explains General Eisenhower's misguided decision to march on Leipzig instead of Berlin (28 March 1945) or to halt at Pilsen instead of going on to Prague. The Western Allies were engaged in a "crusade for Europe": after defeating the aggressor militarily, they would implement the United Nations resolutions taken at the San Francisco Conference and then gradually withdraw their troops from Germany.

The Soviet Union, on the other hand, entered the struggle with clear political objectives. In all the areas it "liberated", the Red Army faced the world with a series of *faits accomplis* that changed not only the map of Europe but the balance of power of the whole world.

Thus the history of post-war Germany begins with the end of hostilities on the Elbe, when the social and political consequences of Hitler's "audacious policy", as Goebbels called it, found their tangible expression in the Berlin Wall and the no less fatal line running through the heart of Germany.

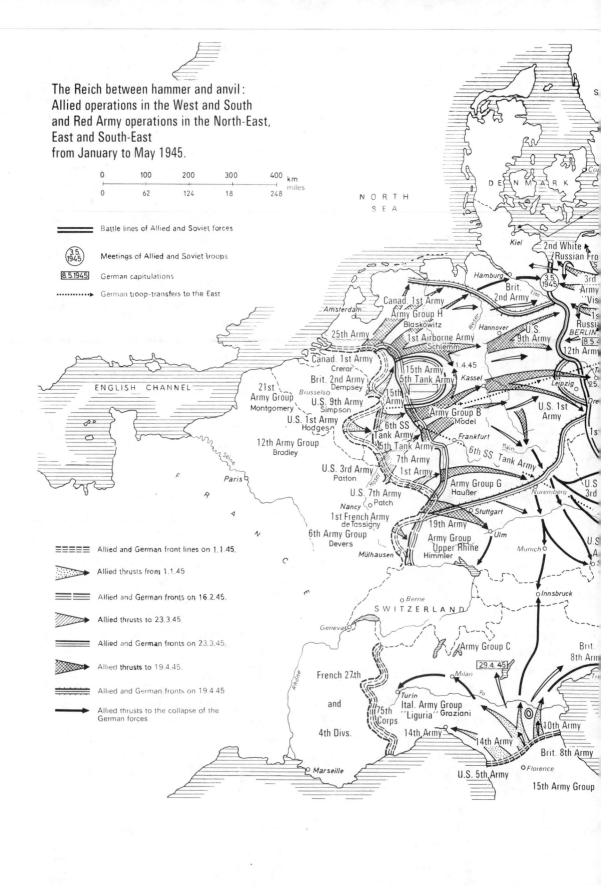

The Reich between hammer and anvil:
Allied operations in the West and South
and Red Army operations in the North-East,
East and South-East
from January to May 1945.

0	100	200	300	400	km
0	62	124	18	248	miles

Battle lines of Allied and Soviet forces

(3.5. 1945) Meetings of Allied and Soviet troops

8.5.1945 German capitulations

German troop-transfers to the East

Allied and German front lines on 1.1.45.

Allied thrusts from 1.1.45

Allied and German fronts on 16.2.45.

Allied thrusts to 23.3.45.

Allied and German fronts on 23.3.45.

Allied thrusts to 19.4.45.

Allied and German fronts on 19.4.45

Allied thrusts to the collapse of the German forces.

NORTH SEA

DENMARK

Kiel

2nd White Russian Fro

Hamburg

Brit. 2nd Army

3rd Army "Vis

Elbe

Amsterdam

Canad. 1st Army
Army Group H
Blaskowitz

Weser

Hannover

U.S. 9th Army

1st Russia

BERLIN

8.5.4

12th Army

25th Army

1st Airborne Army
Schlemm

1.4.45

15th Army
5th Tank Army

Kassel

Leipzig

25

Canad. 1st Army
Crerar
Brit. 2nd Army
Dempsey

Brusselso

21st Army Group
Montgomery

U.S. 9th Army
Simpson

15th Army

Army Group B
Model

U.S. 1st Army

1st

Dre

U.S. 1st Army
Hodges

6th SS Tank Army
5th Tank Army

Frankfurt

Main

6th SS Tank Army

12th Army Group
Bradley

7th Army
1st Army

Seine

Paris

U.S. 3rd Army
Patton

Mosel

Nuremberg

U.S. 3rd

F

R

A

N

C

E

U.S. 7th Army
Patch

Nancy

1st French Army
de Tassigny

6th Army Group
Devers

Mülhausen

19th Army

Army Group G
Haußer

Stuttgart

Army Group Upper Rhine
Himmler

Ulm

Munich

Innsbruck

Berne

SWITZERLAND

Geneva

Rhône

ENGLISH CHANNEL

Army Group C

Brit. 8th Arm

29.4.45

Milan

Po

French 27th

and

4th Divs.

Turin

75th Corps

Ital. Army Group "Liguria" Graziani

10th Army

14th Army

14th Army

Brit. 8th Army

Marseille

U.S. 5th Army

Florence

15th Army Group

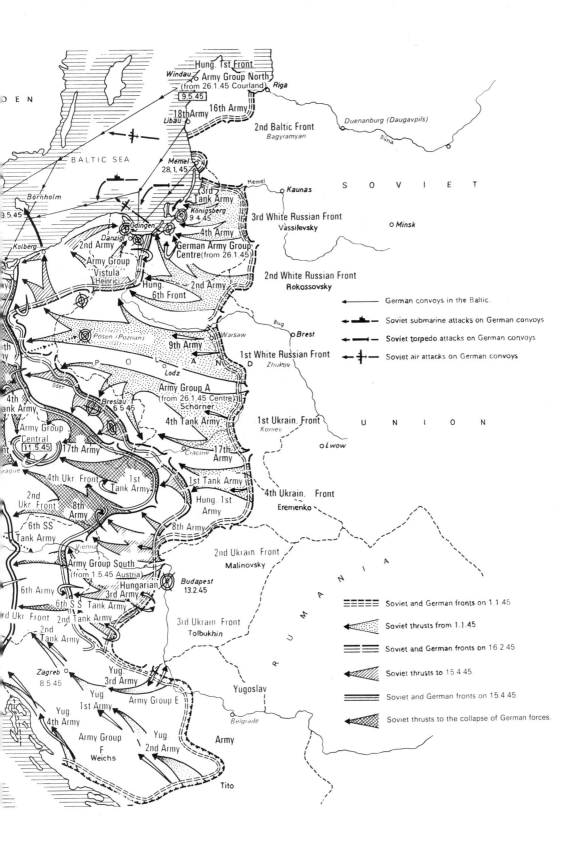

Hung. 1st Front
Windau ○ Army Group North
(from 26.1.45 Courland)
9.5.45
18th Army — 16th Army
Libau ○
Riga

2nd Baltic Front
Bagyramyan

Duenanburg (Daugavpils)

Düna

BALTIC SEA

Memel
28.1.45

Memel
Kaunas ○

S O V I E T

Bornholm

3rd Tank Army
Königsberg
9.4.45

3rd White Russian Front
Vassilevsky

○ Minsk

Kolberg

Gdingen
Danzig
2nd Army

4th Army

German Army Group Centre (from 26.1.45)

Army Group Vistula Heinrici
Hung. 2nd Army
6th Front

2nd White Russian Front
Rokossovsky

German convoys in the Baltic.

Soviet submarine attacks on German convoys

Soviet torpedo attacks on German convoys

Soviet air attacks on German convoys

Posen (Poznań)
Warsaw
9th Army
Lodz
Brest

Bug

1st White Russian Front
Zhukov

Army Group A
(from 26.1.45 Centre)
Schörner

P O L A N D

Oder

4th Tank Army
Breslau
6.5.45

4th Tank Army

Army Group Central
11.5.45
17th Army
Cracow
17th Army

1st Ukrain. Front
Koniev
○ Lwow

U N I O N

4th Ukr Front
1st Tank Army
1st Tank Army

2nd Ukr Front
8th Army
Hung. 1st Army

4th Ukrain. Front
Eremenko

6th SS Tank Army
8th Army

Vienna

Army Group South
(from 1.5.45 Austria)

6th Army
Hungarian 3rd Army
Budapest
13.2.45

2nd Ukrain Front
Malinovsky

R U M A N I A

6th SS Tank Army
2nd Tank Army

3rd Ukrain Front
Tolbukhin

2nd Tank Army

Zagreb ○
8.5.45
Yug. 3rd Army

Yug. 1st Army
Army Group E

Yugoslav
Army

Yug. 4th Army

Yug. 2nd Army

Army Group F
Weichs

Belgrade

Tito

═════ Soviet and German fronts on 1.1.45

◄▬▬ Soviet thrusts from 1.1.45

═══ Soviet and German fronts on 16.2.45

◄▬▬ Soviet thrusts to 15.4.45

═══ Soviet and German fronts on 15.4.45

◄▬▬ Soviet thrusts to the collapse of German forces.

THE CONQUEST OF GERMANY

The advance of the Western Allies from the Rhine and of the Red Army from the Vistula to the link-up on the Elbe and the fall of Berlin.

CHRONOLOGICAL TABLE: January

1/1 364 German aircraft brought down during low-level attacks on Allied harbours. Germans continue to exert heavy pressure on U.S. 7th Army in the Palatinate.

2/1 U.S. 3rd Army repulses counter attacks and broadens the Bastogne corridor in the Ardennes into a salient.

3/1 U.S. 1st Army attacks German northern flank in the Ardennes.

4/1 U.S. 1st Army advances further in the Ardennes.

7/1 Field-Marshal Montgomery reports that Allies have regained the initiative in the Ardennes Salient. 2,000 U.S. bombers and fighter-bombers make sorties into W. Germany.

8/1 Houffalize under Allied cross-fire.

9/1 Germans withdraw at various points along the Ardennes front.

10/1 German thrust towards Strasbourg. 1,100 U.S. bombers attack German positions in the rear of the Ardennes Salient.

11/1 German resistance in the Ardennes collapses. Laroche falls into Allied hands.

12/1 Troops of the U.S. 1st and 3rd Armies link up near Houffal-ize, the centre of the Ardennes Salient. German withdrawal continues. Allies exert heavy pressure in the direction of St. Vith.

Soviet forces launch offensive in Poland on a broad front from their bridgehead across the Vistula at Baranov, 120 miles S. of Warsaw.

13/1 The Houffalize–St. Vith road cut.

Soviet forces advancing on Koenigsberg attack the German 3rd Tank Army.

14/1 Soviet forces advancing on Elblag attack German 2nd Army.

Soviet armour enters Schlossberg.

15/1 Street fighting in Houffalize. U.S. Secretary of War announces that 40,000 Germans have been taken prisoner and an estimated 50,000 killed and wounded in the Ardennes.

Hitler refuses to withdraw Army Group Centre from the Warsaw sector. Soviet troops capture Kielce, an important administrative and communications centre, 32 miles N.E. of Cracow.

16/1 Allied troops capture Houffalize and Cherain in the Ardennes Salient. British 2nd Army launches attack on German salient between the rivers Maas and Roer.

Soviet forces capture Radom, 58 miles S. of Warsaw.

16/1–17/1 Germans evacuate Warsaw.

17/1 Soviet forces liberate 800 Jews in Czestochowa and 870 Jews in Lodz.

18/1 Soviet forces cross the German frontier in Silesia.

19/1 British continue to exert pressure east of the Maas.

Soviet troops capture Lodz, Kutno, Tomaszow, Gostynin and Leczyca, important centres of communication.

20/1 3rd White Russian Front storms the E. Prussian towns of Tilsit, Gross-Skaisgirren, Aulowohnen, Szillen and Kaukehmen.

21/1 3rd White Russian Front storms the E. Prussian town of Gumbinnen. 2nd White Russian Front occupies Tannenberg. Soviet forces are 68 miles from Danzig and 15 miles from Insterburg.

22/1 British troops engaged in heavy fighting N.E. of Echt. Hitler withdraws 28th Army Corps from the Memel bridgehead. 3rd White Russian Front captures Allenstein and Deutsch-Eylau in East Prussia, and advance on Bromberg (Bydgoszcz) (Silesia) and on Wolozyn and Strzelce in Poland.

23/1 Third White Russian Front captures Wehlau between Insterburg and Koenigsberg; 2nd White Russian Front captures Bromberg. Soviet forces reach the Oder some 24 miles W. of Breslau.

24/1 British 2nd Army enters Heinzberg.

First Ukrainian Front captures Oppeln (Opole), Gleiwitz (Gliwice), Trachenburg, Rawitsch (Rawicz) and Kalisch (Kalisz).

25/1 German counter-attack in the West between Hagenau and Kaltenhausen is thrown back. The *Aachener Nachrichten* becomes the first German newspaper to be published by the Allied military government.

Major-General Rendulic relieves Major-General Reinhardt as C.-in-C. East Prussia. German Army Group Vistula is formed. Army Group A becomes Army Group Centre; Army Group Centre (forced northwards by Soviet offensive) becomes Army Group North. German forces are withdrawn from Loetzen and the Masurian lakes. Soviet forces advance into E. Samland; other Soviet troops press on westwards, bypassing Posen (Poznan). Street fighting in Elblag, Krenau, Paslek and Liebstadt. First Ukrainian Front captures Ostrow in Poland, and Oels in Silesia.

26/1 British troops reach the Roer. The left bank of the Roer from Roermond to Dueren in Allied hands. Americans mop up the Ardennes Salient.

Second White Russian Front takes Marienburg. Soviet troops capture Talkemit, thus cutting off the German forces in East Prussia from Central Germany. Third White Russian Front lays siege to Koenigsberg. Poznan is surrounded. The Red Army crosses the Oder at several points, 120 miles S. of Breslau. Hindenburg in Upper Silesia is captured. Thorn is surrounded. Street fighting in Beuthen (Bytom). Soviet forces liberate 2,819 victims from Auschwitz.

27/1 U.S. 3rd Army reaches the German–Luxemburg frontier at several points.

Major General Rendulic recalled to East Prussia and given command of Army Group North. Major-General Vietinghoff-Scheel transferred to Courland from Italy. Third White Russian Front smashes powerful enemy defences in the Masurian Lakes area and closes in on Koenigsberg. Mass exodus from the city. Russian forces capture several places in Polish Upper Silesia.

28/1 The capture of the Baltic port of Memel (Klaipeda) and the liberation of Lithuania announced by Stalin.

American troops capture Bullange and three other towns North-East of St. Vith.

General Lasch appointed Town Commander of Koenigsberg.

29/1 Red Army enters Pomerania and takes Woldenberg, 95 miles from Berlin. Soviet forces mop up the Upper Silesia industrial region. Fall of Beuthen (Bytom) and Kattowitz (Katowice).

30/1 Hitler's last broadcast to the German nation.

French troops cross the Colmar canal in Alsace.

Red Army cuts communications between Koenigsberg and Pillau. General Hossbach, Commander of 4th Army, relieved of his post and replaced by General Mueller. Soviet forces occupy Marienwerder in East Prussia, cross the German–Polish frontier, and occupy Stolzenberg, 100 miles from Berlin.

31/1 U.S. 1st and 3rd Armies come to within three miles of the main West Wall (Siegfried Line) defences.

Soviet troops capture Landsberg, Heilsberg and Friedland in E. Prussia.

January: A Hitler Youth regiment is sent to relieve Breslau.

Total War on the "Home Front". A town in the Palatinate (March 1945).

EISENHOWER'S PLAN OF OPERATION OF 31 DECEMBER 1944

General George C. Marshall,
U.S. Chief of Staff.

Office of the Supreme Commander

31 December 1944

Outline Plan

My outline plan of operations, based on the current situation and prospects, is as follows:

Basic play—to destroy enemy forces west of Rhine, north of the Moselle, and to prepare for crossing the Rhine in force with the *main effort north of the Ruhr*. The several tasks are:

(a) To reduce the Ardennes salient by immediate attacks from north and south, with present command arrangements undisturbed until tactical victory within the salient has been assured and the Third Army and Collins' Corps have joined up for a drive to the north-east. Bradley then to resume command of the First U.S. Army. (Enemy action within the salient indicates his determination to make this battle an all-out effort with his mobile forces. *Therefore we must be prepared to use everything consistent with minimum security requirements to accomplish their destruction.*)

(b) Thereafter First and Third Armies to drive to northeast on general line Prum–Bonn, eventually to Rhine.

(c) When *a* is accomplished, 21st Army Group, with Ninth U.S. Army under operational command, to resume preparations for "VERITABLE".

(d) All priorities in building up strength of U.S. Armies in personnel, material and units, to go to 12th Army Group.

(e) The front south of Moselle to be strictly defensive for the present.

(f) I will build up a reserve (including refitting divisions) which will be available to reinforce success.

(g) As soon as reduction of Ardennes salient permits, H.Q. 12th Army Group will move north, in close proximity to 21st Army Group H.Q.

(h) From now on, any detailed or emergency co-ordination required along Army Group boundaries in the north will be effected by the two Army Group commanders with power of decision vested in C.G. 21st Army Group.

The one thing that must now be prevented is the stabilization of the enemy salient with infantry, permitting him the opportunity to use his Panzers at will on any part of the front. We must regain the initiative, and speed and energy are essential.

At conclusion of the battle for the salient, assignment of Divisions to Army Groups and changes in boundaries will be announced.

Dwight D. Eisenhower.

General Dwight D. Eisenhower, Supreme Commander of Allied Expeditionary Force.

◄

Allies counter-attacking in the Ardennes on 3 January 1945.

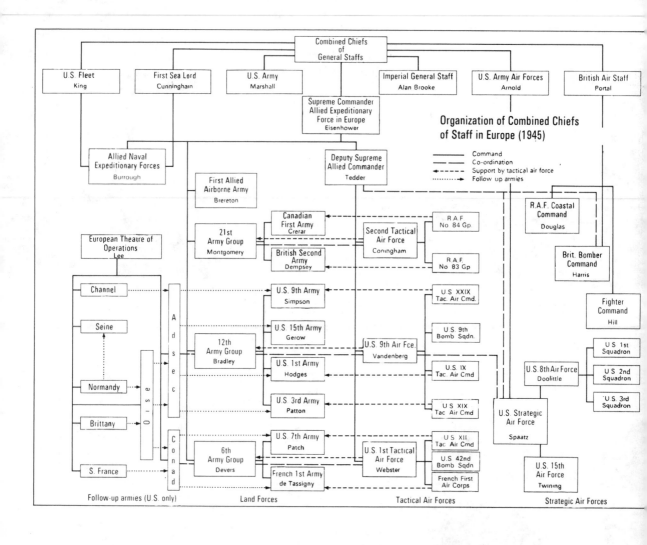

Organization of Combined Chiefs of Staff in Europe (1945)

Combined Chiefs of General Staffs

U.S. Fleet — King
First Sea Lord — Cunningham
U.S. Army — Marshall
Imperial General Staff — Alan Brooke
U.S. Army Air Forces — Arnold
British Air Staff — Portal

Supreme Commander Allied Expeditionary Force in Europe — Eisenhower

Allied Naval Expeditionary Forces — Burrough

First Allied Airborne Army — Brereton

Deputy Supreme Allied Commander — Tedder

Legend	
——	Command
——	Co-ordination
- - - ►	Support by tactical air force
······ ►	Follow up armies

European Theatre of Operations — Lee

Channel
Seine
Normandy
Brittany
S. France

Adsec — Base — Oise — Conad

Canadian First Army — Crerar
British Second Army — Dempsey

21st Army Group — Montgomery

Second Tactical Air Force — Coningham

R.A.F. No. 84 Gp.
R.A.F. No. 83 Gp.

R.A.F. Coastal Command — Douglas
Brit. Bomber Command — Harris
Fighter Command — Hill

U.S. 9th Army — Simpson
U.S. 15th Army — Gerow
12th Army Group — Bradley
U.S. 1st Army — Hodges
U.S. 3rd Army — Patton

U.S. 9th Air Fce. — Vandenberg

U.S. XXIX Tac. Air Cmd.
U.S. 9th Bomb. Sqdn.
U.S. IX Tac. Air Cmd.
U.S. XIX Tac. Air Cmd.

U.S. 8th Air Force — Doolittle

U.S. 1st Squadron
U.S. 2nd Squadron
U.S. 3rd Squadron

U.S. 7th Army — Patch
6th Army Group — Devers
French 1st Army — de Tassigny

U.S. 1st Tactical Air Force — Webster

U.S. XII Tac. Air Cmd
U.S. 42nd Bomb Sqdn
French First Air Corps

U.S. Strategic Air Force — Spaatz

U.S. 15th Air Force — Twining

Follow-up armies (U.S. only)   Land Forces   Tactical Air Forces   Strategic Air Forces

German salient in the Ardennes being reduced with "Long Toms".

ALLIED FORCES IN GERMANY

Field-Marshal von Rundstedt

Field-Marshal Model
(Army Group B)

SS Obergruppenfuehrer Hausser
(Army Group G)

	U.S.	British, Canadian, Polish	French
31 Dec. 1944 Armies	1st, 3rd, 7th, 9th, 15th.	2nd, 1st Canadian.	1st
Corps	3rd, 5th, 6th, 7th, 8th, 12th, 13th, 15th, 16th, 18th, 19th, 20th, 21st.	1st, 8th, 12th, 30th and 2nd Canadian.	1st, 2nd.
Divisions	1st, 2nd, 3rd, 4th, 5th, 8th, 9th, 26th, 28th, 29th, 30th, 35th, 36th, 44th, 45th, 75th, 78th, 79th, 80th, 83rd, 84th, 87th, 90th, 94th, 95th, 99th, 100th, 102nd, 103rd, 104th, 106th infantry: 17th, 82nd, 101st airborne: 2nd, 3rd, 4th, 5th, 6th, 7th, 9th, 10th, 11th, 12th, 14th armoured.	3rd, 15th, 43rd, 49th, 50th, 51st, 52nd, 53rd infantry: 6th airborne: 7th, 11th, 79th guards armoured: 4th Canadian armoured: 1st Pol. armoured.	1st, 2nd, 5th armoured: 1st motorized: 2nd Moroccan: 4th Mor. mtn.: 3rd Algerian: 9th Col.: 27th Alpine.
26 Mar. 1945 Armies	1st, 3rd, 7th, 9th, 15th; 1st airborne.	2nd and 1st Canadian.	1st.
Corps	3rd, 5th, 6th, 7th, 8th, 12th, 13th, 15th, 16th, 19th, 20th, 21st, 22nd, 23rd: 18th airborne.	1st, 8th, 12th, 30th: 1st and 2nd Can.	1st and 2nd.
Divisions	1st, 2nd, 3rd, 4th, 5th, 8th, 9th, 26th, 28th, 29th, 30th, 35th, 36th, 42nd, 44th, 45th, 63rd, 65th, 66th, 69th, 70th, 71st, 75th, 76th, 78th, 79th, 80th, 83rd, 84th, 86th, 87th, 89th, 90th, 94th, 95th, 97th, 99th, 100th, 102nd, 103rd, 104th, 106th infantry: 13th, 17th, 82nd, 101st airborne: 2nd, 3rd, 4th, 5th, 6th, 7th, 8th, 9th, 10th, 11th, 12th, 13th, 14th, 16th, 20th armoured.	3rd, 15th, 43rd, 49th, 51st, 52nd, 53rd infantry: 6th airborne: 7th, 11th, 79th guards armoured: 2nd and 3rd Can. infantry: 4th and 5th Can. armoured: 1st Polish armoured.	1st, 2nd and 5th armoured: 1st motorized: 2nd Moroccan: 4th Moroccan mtn.: 3rd Algerian: 9th Col.: 27th Alpine: Gironde.
8 May 1945 Armies	(Same as 26 Mar. 1945)	2nd and 1st Canad.	1st.
Corps	(Same as 26 Mar. 1945)	1st, 8th, 12th and 30th: 1st and 2nd Can.	1st and 2nd.
Divisions	(Same as 26 Mar. 1945)	3rd, 5th, 15th, 43rd, 49th, 51st, 52nd, 53rd infantry: 6th airborne: 7th, 11th, 79th guards armoured: 1st, 2nd and 3rd Can. infantry: 4th and 5th Can. armoured: 1st Polish armoured.	1st, 2nd and 5th armoured: 1st motorized: 2nd Moroccan: 4th Mor. mtn.: 3rd Algerian: 9th Col.: 27th Alpine: Gironde: 1st, 10th and 14th infantry (for occupation duty).

(From *Encyclopaedia Britannica*, Vol. 23)

ALLIED FIELD COMMANDERS IN NORTHWESTERN EUROPE

General Devers (6th Army Group)

Supreme Commander Allied Forces	*General Dwight D. Eisenhower (U.S.A.)*
Deputy Supreme Commander Allied Forces	*Marshal of the Royal Air Force, Sir Arthur Tedder (Britain)*
Commander-in-Chief Allied Naval Expeditionary Forces	*Admiral Sir Harold Burrough (Britain)*
Commander-in-Chief 21st Army Group (Canadian 1st, British 2nd and U.S. 9th Armies)	*Field-Marshal Sir Bernard Montgomery (Britain)*
Commander-in-Chief 12th Army Group (U.S. 1st and 3rd Armies)	*General Omar N. Bradley (U.S.A.)*
Commander-in-Chief 6th Army Group (U.S. 7th and French 1st Armies)	*General Jacob L. Devers (U.S.A.)*
Commander-in-Chief Allied Expeditionary Air Force	*Marshal of the Royal Air Force Sir Trafford Leigh-Mallory (Britain)*

MONTGOMERY'S PRESS CONFERENCE ON THE BATTLE OF THE ARDENNES

7 January 1945

1. I have asked you to come here today so that I can give you some information which may be of use to you, and also to ask you to help me in a certain matter.

2. The story of the present battle. Rundstedt attacked on 16 December; he obtained tactical surprise. He drove a deep wedge into the centre of the First U.S. Army and split the American forces in two. The situation looked as if it might become awkward; the Germans had broken right through a weak spot, and were heading for the Meuse.

3. As soon as I saw what was happening I took certain steps myself to ensure that *if* the Germans got to the Meuse they would certainly not get over the river. And I carried out certain movements so as to provide balanced dispositions to meet the threatened danger; these were, at the time, merely precautions, i.e. I was thinking ahead.

4. Then the situation began to deteriorate. But the whole allied team rallied to meet the danger; national considerations were thrown overboard; General Eisenhower placed me in command of the whole northern front . . .

5. The battle has been most interesting; I think possibly one of the most interesting and tricky battles I have ever handled, with great issues at stake. The first thing to be done was to "head off" the enemy from the tender spots and vital places. Having done that successfully, the next thing to do was to "see him off", i.e. rope him in and make quite certain that he could not get to the places he wanted, *and also* that he was slowly but surely removed away from those places. he was therefore "headed off", and then "seen off".

He is now being "written off", and heavy toll is being taken of his divisions by ground and air action. You must not imagine that the battle is over yet; it is by no means over and a great deal still remains to be done . . .

On 3 January, Allied Headquarters reported gains of up to 3,000 yards on a 12-mile front between Grandmenil and

General Bradley (12th Army Group)

Field-Marshal Montgomery (21st Army Group) and General Hodges (U.S. 1st Army).

6. What was Rundstedt trying to achieve? No one can tell for certain. The only guide we have is the message he issued to his soldiers before the battle began; he told them it was the last great effort to try and win the war, that everything depended on it; that they must go "all out".

On the map you see his gains; *that* will not win the war; he is likely slowly but surely to lose it all; he must have scraped together every reserve he could lay his hands on for this job, and he has not achieved a great deal.

One must admit that he has dealt us a sharp blow and he sent us reeling back; but we recovered; he has been unable to gain any great advantage from his final success . . . Another reason for his failure is that his air force, although still capable of pulling a fast one, cannot protect his army; for that army *our* Tactical Air Forces are the greatest terror.

7. But when all is said and done I shall always feel that Rundstedt was really beaten by the good fighting qualities of the American soldier and by the teamwork of the Allies.

I would like to say a word about these two points.

8. . . . I have spent my military career with the British soldier and I have come to love him with a great love; and I have now formed a very great affection and admiration for the American soldier. I salute the brave fighting men of America; I never want to fight alongside better soldiers. Just now I am seeing a great deal of the American soldiers . . .

9. . . . It is teamwork that pulls you through dangerous times; it is teamwork that wins battles; it is victories in battle that win wars. I want to put in a strong plea for Allied solidarity at this vital stage of the war; and you can all help in this greatly.

Nothing must be done by anyone that tends to break down the team spirit of our Allied team . . .

10. Let me tell you that the captain of our team is Eisenhower. I am absolutely devoted to Ike; we are the greatest of friends. It grieves me when I see uncomplimentary articles about him in the British press; he bears a great burden, he needs our fullest support, he has a right to expect it, and it is up to all of us to see that he gets it.

Hotton on the N. front of the Ardennes salient . . . as well as gains to the S. of Rochefort against strong opposition.

HOUFFALIZE IN ALLIED HANDS
16 January 1945

Allied advance in the S. sector.
The first German prisoners on the Sauer.

U.S. sponsored "News for the Troops" reporting fresh pressure on Houffalize.

Nr. 269, Mittwoch, 10. Januar 1945

NACHRICHTEN FÜR DIE TRUPPE

Neuer Druck auf Houffalize

Budapest-Besatzung sendet Notrufe aus

Die letzten Meldungen von der grossen Doppelschlacht im Donauraum berichten, dass die Befreiung der in Budapest eingeschlossenen deutschen Besatzung in den nächsten 24 Stunden erreicht werden muss, falls überhaupt ein nennenswerter Bruchteil der 60 000 Mann Besatzung gerettet werden soll.

Beide Seiten haben jetzt alle verfügbaren Truppen in den Kampf geworfen: Generaloberst Friessner, um den sowjetischen Sperriegel vor Budapest zu durchbrechen und die eingeschlossenen Verbände zu befreien, die Sowjets, um den Ansturm solange aufzuhalten, bis sie die Besatzung vor Budapest überwältigt haben.

kämpfen mit russischen T 34 und starken Paksperren, und auch die einbrechende Nacht setzte dem Ringen kein Ende.

Funksprüche aus dem belagerten Budapest ermahnen alle Einheiten zur grössten Eile. Die Kampfbedingungen in den rauchenden Trümmern der ungarischen Hauptstadt sind jetzt derart geworden, dass die Besatzung nur noch kurze Zeit aushalten kann.

Viele Stützpunkte mussten bereits den Kampf einstellen, weil kein Brot, kein Wasser

Der Kampfraum in den Ardennen.

Der Frontverlauf im Elsass

Die letzte Nachschubstrasse Rundstedts schwer bedroht

Die Schlüsselstellung Houffalize in den Ardennen, das

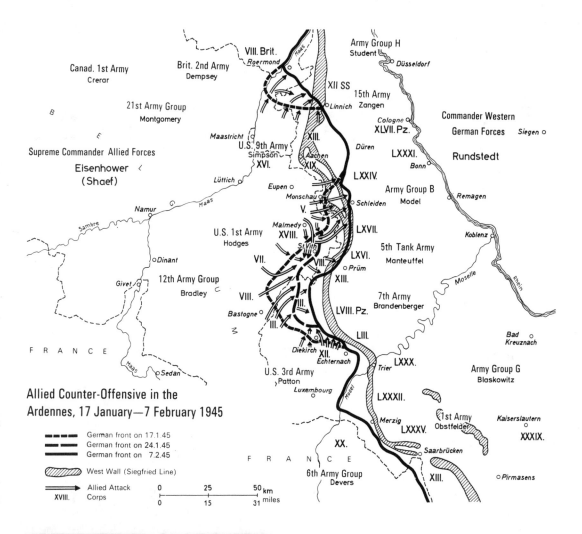

Allied Counter-Offensive in the Ardennes, 17 January—7 February 1945

- - - - German front on 17.1.45
— — — German front on 24.1.45
——— German front on 7.2.45

West Wall (Siegfried Line)

→ Allied Attack
XVIII. Corps

0	25	50 km
0	15	31 miles

"SACRIFICE" FOR THE TROOPS

January 1945

Fuehrer's order of the day of 10 January 1945:

The donation of clothing and equipment is just another sacrifice asked of the German nation for its soldiers. I therefore decree that anyone misappropriating goods donated or intended for collection or in any way preventing such goods from reaching their destination will be sentenced to death. This decree takes effect from this broadcast. It applies to the Greater German Reich, to the Government-General (Poland) and to the territories occupied by German troops.

Adolf Hitler.

Extract from Hitler's speech on 1 January 1945:

What our enemies are fighting for, only the Jews among them can tell: what we are fighting for is quite plain. It is the preservation of German man, of our homeland, of our two thousand-year-old culture, of our nation's children and grandchildren . . .

◄ "The world should realize that this country will never capitulate . . ." Hitler, seen here with Martin Bormann, on New Year's Day, 1945.

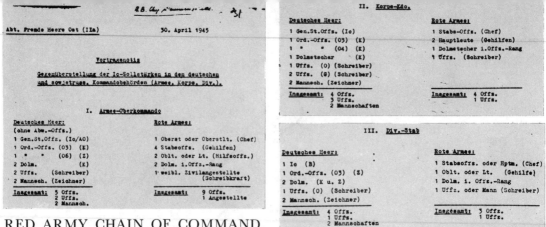

RED ARMY CHAIN OF COMMAND, 1945

Original Sketch based on memorandum by German Intelligence.

From a memorandum prepared by General Gehlen on the structure of German and Soviet intelligence.

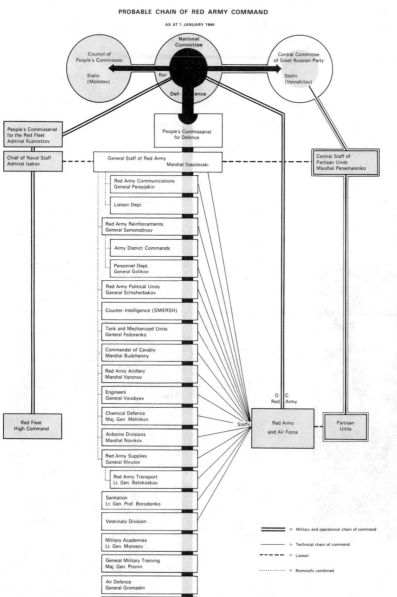

PROBABLE CHAIN OF RED ARMY COMMAND

AS AT 1 JANUARY 1944

THE EASTERN FRONT IN JANUARY 1945

"The Eastern Front is like a House of Cards."

by General Guderian

The vague hope that reports about the impending Russian offensive might turn out to be a gigantic bluff dominated the mood of the Supreme Command . . . To console me, Hitler said at the end of his address: "We have never before had so many reserves at the Eastern Front. This is your achievement. I am grateful to you." I replied: "The Eastern Front is like a house of cards. If it is breached at any point, it must collapse—twelve and a half reserve divisions are not nearly enough for so wide a front."

The position was as follows: the 17th Tank Division near Pinczow, the 16th Tank Division south of Kielce, the 20th Guards Tank Division near Wierzonik and Ostrowicz, the 10th Guards Tank Division near Kamienna, the 19th Tank Division near Radom, the 25th Tank Division near Mogielnica, the 7th Tank Division near Zichenau, the Guards Tank Division "Greater Germany" near Chorzele, the 18th Guards Tank Division east of Johannisburg, the 10th Infantry Division near Nikolaiken, the 10th Cycle Brigade near Sensburg, parts of the Guards Tank Division "Brandenburg" south of Drengfurt, the Armoured Infantry Division "Hermann Goering" west of Gumbinnen, the 2nd Armoured Guards Division "Hermann Goering" on the East Prussian Front southeast of Gumbinnen, the 5th Tank Division near Breitenstein, the 24th Tank Division on the way from Hungary to Rastenburg.

from Guderian: *Erinnerungen eines Soldaten.*

THE RED ARMY GUARDS DIVISIONS

From a briefing by German Intelligence, on 11 February 1945:

In autumn 1941, during the great crisis in the Soviet Army, several Red Army Infantry divisions were re-named Guards Infantry Divisions in accordance with Tsarist custom. At present, there are altogether 119 Guards Infantry Divisions, accounting for about a quarter of the total number of Infantry Divisions. To qualify for the new title, an infantry division must have rendered distinguished service in the field, generally at a high cost in lives. However, a number of newly-formed divisions also qualify for the title of Guards, for instance those composed of former airborne troops. Moreover, all infantry divisions formed out of Guards Rifle Brigades are called Guards Infantry Divisions. The title of Guards is conferred by the Praesidium of the Supreme Soviet of the USSR, as is the special Guards standard bearing the picture of Lenin on one side, and the number of the unit together with the inscription "For our Soviet Homeland" on the other. All Guards wear a special badge, and are entitled to call themselves "Guards Rifleman", "Guards Sergeant", "Guards Lieutenant", etc. When they return to active service after convalescence, they rejoin their own units, whereas all other troops returning to the Front are allocated to new units at random. NCO's and privates in Guards units receive twice the pay, and officers 1½ times the pay of normal Red Army men.

They also differ from ordinary infantry divisions in internal organization. According to KStN 04/500–513, a Guards Infantry Division consists of 10,585 men whereas a normal Infantry Division consists of only 9,354 men. Hence the Guards Infantry Division is 315 men stronger than the normal one. The equipment of a Guards Division is correspondingly greater. Moreover, Guards Infantry Divisions have a greater number of young and strong men allocated to them. Prisoners report that, during recruitment in the re-occupied territories, special stress is laid on this factor. Up to the spring of 1943, the title of Guards used to be the chief means of distinguishing units, but no elevation of Infantry Divisions into Guards Infantry Divisions has occurred since October 1943. Nowadays, distinction is bestowed upon divisions by giving them the names of particular battlefields and by conferring orders on them. In other branches of the service, e.g. in the armoured and artillery units, the Guards title continues to be conferred to this day.

(signed) Gehlen, Maj.-Gen. and Dept. Chief

"Blood for Blood! Death for Death!" Slogans in Soviet sub-machine gun factory.

THE SOVIET OFFENSIVE FROM THE BARANOV BRIDGEHEAD
12 January 1945

German Army Group A report of Soviet operations against the 4th Tank Army.

Objective Berlin

The Soviet objective is Berlin. To reach it, the Soviet flanks had to be protected—in the north by the capture of East Prussia and in the south by an advance into Silesia. The Soviet offensive between the Baltic and the Carpathians began with an artillery attack that pulverized all the German defences. The offensive developed at a breathtaking rate: in East Prussia, Deutsch-Eylau and Allenstein were reached within ten days, and by 26 January the 2nd White Russian Front (Marshal Rokossovsky) had reached the Gulf of Danzig, thus cutting off East Prussia from the rest of the Reich. The German defence collapsed within four days under attacks from the 1st White Russian Front (Marshal Zhukov) and the 1st Ukrainian Front (Marshal Konev). The Red Army covered 190 miles in 12 days. Warsaw fell on 17 January, and on the same day the 1st Ukrainian Front reached the Oder above Breslau. Russian superiority in infantry was 11:1, in armour 7:1, in artillery 20:1.

◄

Engineers laying mines at the front line.

"There will be heavy fighting."

Extract from a talk by General Jodl to the military attachés of Germany's allies, assembled in Berlin on 13 January 1945.

Oddly enough, it has taken the Red Army a very long time to resume its major offensive in the East. So far, the Russians have only attacked Army Group North, fighting several major battles, in all of which they have been held back. These battles can be chalked up as major defensive successes with heavy losses to the enemy. The enemy then switched his attack against Hungary and Budapest. But though the enemy's plans must have been drawn up long ago, he has failed to launch an offensive in the centre, i.e. in the general direction of Crakow, Warsaw and East Prussia. I do not believe that he has been swayed by purely military considerations, and think that his reasoning must have been the following: now that Germany has gone over to the offensive in the West and is fighting the Anglo-Saxons, now that the entire Allied air force—the Americans by day and the British by night—is doing my preparatory work for me, bombing German cities, smashing the German armament industry, pounding the railway network, I have got time on my side, I can afford to wait. Neither the British nor the Americans will get to Berlin, so I am in no hurry: I can quietly see to my equipment; every day is another day gained and brings me an indirect advantage. I shall not strike until I think the time is ripe.

And because of the weather, that would seem to be the case right now. Now, after the frost, the attack, which is probably their big offensive, has been launched against Army Group A, in the general direction of Crakow, and as I heard only this morning, in East Prussia as well. During the last few weeks, much work has been done by both sides, and large forces have been thrown in, though our task in the West (the German Ardennes offensive in December 1944) has necessarily depleted our strength on the Eastern Front. However, the country is covered with a host of defensive positions, and we must wait and see how these major battles develop. The first Tank Divisions have gone into battle last night or this morning.

29 | January

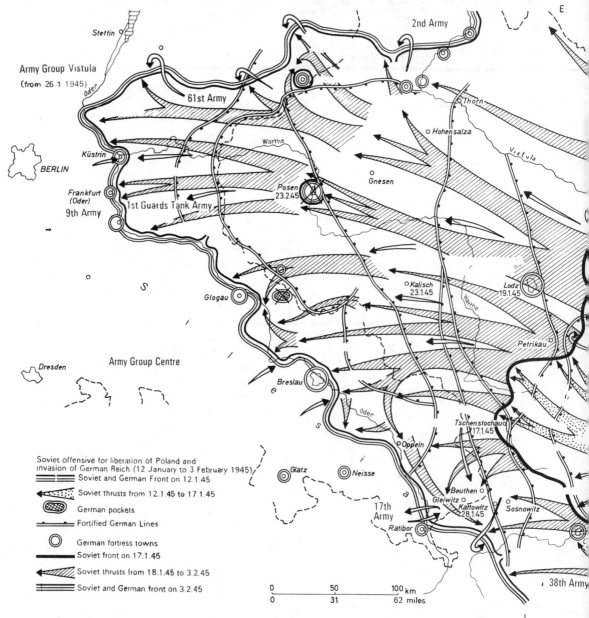

Stettin

Army Group Vistula
(from 26.1 1945)

Oder

BERLIN

Küstrin

Frankfurt
(Oder)

9th Army

61st Army

1st Guards Tank Army

Warthe

Glogau

Dresden

Army Group Centre

Breslau

Oder

2nd Army

E.

Thorn

Hohensalza

Vistula

Gnesen

Posen
23.2.45

Kalisch
23.1.45

Lodz
19.1.45

Warthe

Petrikau

Tschenstochau
17.1.45

Oppeln

Glatz

Neisse

Beuthen

Gleiwitz

Kattowitz
28.1.45

Sosnowitz

17th
Army

Ratibor

38th Army

Soviet offensive for liberation of Poland and
invasion of German Reich (12 January to 3 February 1945)

═══════ Soviet and German Front on 12.1.45

◄▓▓▓ Soviet thrusts from 12.1.45 to 17.1.45

▓▓▓ German pockets

═══════ Fortified German Lines

◯ German fortress towns

━━━━━ Soviet front on 17.1.45

◄▨▨▨ Soviet thrusts from 18.1.45 to 3.2.45

═══════ Soviet and German front on 3.2.45

0   50   100 km
0   31   62 miles

GERMAN AND SOVIET FIELD COMMANDERS ON THE EASTERN FRONT

January 1945

From left to right: General Reinhardt, Commander of Army Group Centre (from 26 January: Army Group North); General Harpe, Commander of Army Group A (from 26 January: Army Group Centre); General Graeser, Commander of the 4th Tank Army.

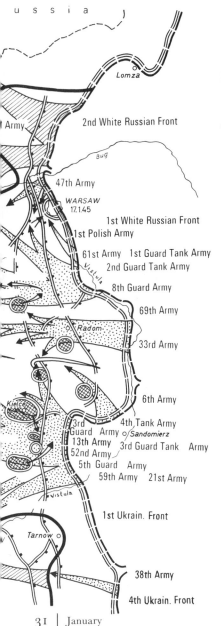

German troops in the snow. "Soviet troops are attacking on all fronts." — *Voelkischer Beobachter* 18 January.

Marshal Zhukov, Commander of the 1st White Russian Front.

Marshal Rokossovsky, Commander of the 2nd White Russian Front.

GUDERIAN'S TELEGRAM TO HITLER, 15 JANUARY 1945

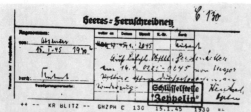

++ KR BLITZ -- GHZPH C 130 15.1.45 1930 =.
AN DEN FUEHRER UND OBERSTEN BEFEHLSHABER DER WEHRMACHT
-- FUEHRERHAUPTQUARTIER --

-- GEHEIME KOMMANDOSACHE CHEFSACHE NUR DURCH OFFIZIER --
-- MEIN FUEHRER AUSRUFEZEICHEN .-

ICH MELDE IHNEN, DASZ SICH DIE LAGE BEI H.GR. A VERSCHAERFT
HAT. DIE AUS DEM BRUECKENKOPF BARANOW NACH WESTEN
DURCHGEBROCHENEN FEINDKRAEFTE(5PZ. KORPS, 2 SELBST. PZ.
VERBAENDE, 14 SCHTZ. DIV.) HABEN NACH DEN BISHER VORLIE-
GENDEN MELDUNGEN DIE A- 2 STELLUNG IN DER ALLGEMEINEN LINIE
SLOMNIKI- SZCZEKOCIN- WESTL. WLOSZCZOWA ERREICHT UND WERDEN
DIESE GEGENUEBER DEN NUR SCHWACHEN DORT STEHENDEN EIGENEN
SICHERUNGEN VORAUSSICHTLICH NOCH HEUTE IN RICHTUNG KRAKAU
UND IN RICHTUNG AUF DIE ALLGEMEINE LINIE KATTOWITZ-
TSCHENSTOCHAU DURCHBRECHEN. DIE AB 16.1. FRUEH IM RAUM
WOLBROM- WARTHENAU MIT ANFAENGEN EINTREFFENDEN BEIDEN
.DIVISIONEN (97.JG.DIV. UND 712.I.D.) WERDEN DEN FEINDL.
STOSZ RICHTUNG OBERSCHLESIEN ZWISCHEN KRAKAU UND TSCHENSTO-
CHAU ZWAR VERZOEGERN, ABER AUF KEINEN FALL FUER LAENGERE
ZEIT AUFHALTEN KOENNEN. DIE GEFAHR FUER DAS OBERSCHLESISCHE
INDUSTRIEGEBIET IST DAHER BRENNEND. .
DAS ROEM. 24.PZ. KORPS- IN SEINER KAMPFKRAFT SEHR STARK
ABGESUNKEN- STEHT GEGENUEBER EINEM MIT 3PZ.KORPS, 3 SELBST
PZ.VERBAENDEN UND 18 SCHTZ. DIV. ANGREIFENDEN FEIND IM
HAERTESTEN KAMPF UM KIELCE. ES IST ZU HOFFEN, DASZ DAS KORPS

EINEN SCHNELLEN VORSTOSZ DES GEGNERS UEBER KIELCE NACH
NORDWESTEN VERHINDERN UND DIE Z.ZT. ABGERISSENE VERBINDUNG
MIT DER OSTW. VON IHM EBENFALLS IN HARTEN KAMPF STEHENDEN
GRUPPE HOHN WIEDERHERSTELLEN KANN. .-
DER SICH BEREITS GESTERN ABZEICHNENDE DURCHBRUCH DES GEGNERS
MIT 1PZ.KORPS UND 19SCHTZ.DIV. AUS DEM BRUECKENKOPF PULAWY
NACH WESTEN IST ZUR GEWISZHEIT GEWORDEN. STARKE FEINDL.
PANZERKRAEFTE HABEN DEN RAUM RADOM ERREICHT. DAS
GEGENUEBER DEM BRUECKENKOPF PULAWY EINGESETZTE ROEM. 56.PZ.
KORPS IST IN SEINER KAMPFKRAFT ERHEBLICH ABGESUNKEN.
MIT WEITEREM VORSTOSZ DER FEINDL. PANZERVERBAENDE NACH WESTEN
IST ZU RECHNEN. .-
AUCH GEGENUEBER DEM ROEM.40.PZ. KORPS HAT DER FEIND AUS DEM
BRUECKENKOPF MAGNUSZEW HERAUS MIT DER NACH SUEDWESTEN ANGESETZTEN
STOSZGRUPPE (16SCHTZ.DIV., VORAUSSICHTLICH 1PZ. KORPS UND 1
SELBST. PZ. VERBAND) DEN DURCHBRUCH ERZWUNGEN. WENN AUCH HIER
DIE GESCHWAECHTEN 19. UND 25.PZ. DIV. ZUSAMMEN MIT DER NOCH
EINIGERMASZEN KAMPFKRAEFTIGEN 45. VOLKS- GREN. DIV. DAS
VORDRINGEN DES FEINDES IN GEWISSEM UMFANGE VERZOEGERN. IN DIESEM
KAMPFRAUM HAT DER GEGNER AM HEUTIGEN TAGE MIT ETWA 15 SCHTZ.
DIV. UND VORAUSSICHTLICH 1 PZ. KORPS AUCH NACH NORDWESTEN
UEBER DIE PILICA ANGEGRIFFEN UND WESTLICH WARKA MIT BISHER
2 DIV. EINEN BRUECKENKOPF UEBER DEN FLUSZ GEBILDET.
DER FEIND IST FERNER AM HEUTIGEN TAGE BEI DER 17.ARMEE IM RAUM
OSTW. JASLO UND AM LINKEN FLUEGEL DER 9. ARMEE IM WEICHSEL
NAREW- DREIECK ZUM ANGRIFF ANGETRETEN UND HAT AN BEIDEN STELLEN
DIE EIGENEN KRAEFTE ERHEBLICH ANGESCHLAGEN.
NEBEN DER BEREITS ERWAEHNTEN BEDROHUNG DES OBERSCHLESISCHEN
INDUSTRIEGEBIETES BIRGT DIE ENTWICKLUNG DER LAGE AM HEUTIGEN
TAGE ZWEI GEFAHRENPUNKTE IN SICH :
1.) DER DURCHBRUCH BEI RADOM DROHT IN VERBINDUNG MIT DEM AUS
DEM BRUECKENKOPF MAGNUSZEW IN ALLGEMEIN SUEDWESTL. RICHTUNG
ZIELENDEN FEINDVORSTOSZ DEN ZUSAMMENHANG ZWISCHEN 4.PZ. ARMEE

UND 9.ARMEE ZU ZERREISZEN. .-
2.) EINE ETWAIGE AUSWEITUNG DES FEINDANGRIFFS UEBER DIE
PILICA NACH NORDWESTEN STELLT DIE WEITERE VERTEIDIGUNG DER
WEICHSELFRONT BEI UND SUEDLICH WARSCHAU IN FRAGE UND KANN
DIE SCHWERWIEGENDSTEN FOLGEN FUER DIE GESAMTE FRONT DER
H.GR. MITTE NACH SICH ZIEHEN.-
DAS HALTEN DER PILICA- FRONT UND DIE WAHRUNG DES ZUSAMMEN
HALTS ZWISCHEN 4. PZ. ARMEE UND 9. ARMEE IST UMSOMEHR
NOTWENDIG, ALS NUR SO DIE VORAUSSETZUNGEN FUER EIGENE
GEGENMASZNAHMEN GEGEN DIE IN GROSZEN WEICHSELBOGEN
OPERIERENDEN FEINDKRAEFTE AUFRECHTERHALTEN WERDEN KOENNEN ..
  ICH HABE MICH DAHER ENTSCHLOSSEN, DAS IM ABTRANSPORT VON
H.GR. MITTE BEFINDLICHE PZ. KORPS''G.D.'' (PZ. GREN.DIV.
''BRANDENBURG'' UND 1. FSCH. PZ. DIV. ''H.G.'') ZUNAECHST
ZUR BEREINIGUNG DES FEINDEINBRUCHS AUF DEM NORDUFER DER
PILICA- ANSCHLIESZEND ZUM ANGRIFF UEBER DIE PILICA NACH
SUEDEN ANZUSETZEN. INWIEWEIT SICH DIESE ABSICHT ANGESICHTS
DER ERST AM 19.1. BEENDETEN VERSAMMLUNG DES KORPS IM RAUM
OSTW. TOMASCOW UND BEI DER MOEGLICHKEIT EINER SCHNELLEN
UNGUENSTIGEN ENTWICKLUNG DER LAGE IM ABSCHNITT DER 9. ARMEE
WIRD DURCHFUEHREN LASSEN, KANN HEUTE NOCH NICHT UEBERSEHEN
WERDEN . ICH BITTE SIE, MEIN FUEHRER, MEINEN ENTSCHLUSZ
HINSICHTLICH DES EINSATZES DES PZ. KORPS''G.D.''
ZU GENEHMIGEN . .-
DIE GESAMTSITUATION IN DER MITTE DER OSTFRONT WIRD WEDER
DURCH DEN GEMELDETEN EINSATZ DES PZ. KORPS'' G. D.''
NOCH DURCH DIE ZUM SCHUTZ DES OBERSCHLESISCHEN INDUSTRIE-
GEBIETES EINTREFFENDEN INF. DIV. ENTSCHEIDEND VERBESSERT.
DIE DIE ENTSCHEIDUNG SUCHENDE RUSS. GROSZOFFENSIVE AUS DEM
GROSZEN WEICHSELBOGEN HERAUS KANN NUR ZUM ERLIEGEN
GEBRACHT WERDEN, WENN DER H.GR. A UNVERZUEGLICH WEITERE
STARKE PANZER- UND INF. VERBAENDE ZUGEFUEHRT WERDEN.

GEZ. GUDERIAN   OKH/ GEN ST D H / OP. ABT. (ROEM. 1 A)
NR. 450 011/45 GKDOS. CHEFS. 15.1.45   ++

BSL : GEZ. GUDERIAN OKH/ GEN ST D H / OP. ABT.
(ROEM. 1▾A) NR. 450011/45 GKDOS. CHEFS. 15.1.45
ERHALTEN KLOSE HPTM HOKW 15.1.45 2045 .+

BT   NOCH UM -- OWD -- AUSHAENDIGUNGSBESTAETIGUNG)

QSL R ERH TEICHERT, HPTM. GHZPH ++

Guderian warns Hitler: "The position of Army Group A has become acute ... The threat to the Upper Silesian industrial region is imminent ... Army Group A needs strong tank and infantry support ...

President Roosevelt's personal message to Marshal Stalin.

Thank you for your encouraging message dated January 15 in regard to Air Marshal Tedder's conference with you, and in regard to the offensive of your Armies on the Soviet–German front.

The past performances of your heroic soldiers and their already demonstrated efficiency in this offensive, give high promise of an early success to our armies on both fronts.

By a skillful coordination of our combined efforts, the time required to force a surrender upon our barbarian enemies will be radically reduced.

As you know, America is putting forth a great effort in the Pacific at a distance of 7,000 miles, and it is my hope that an early collapse of Germany will permit the movement of sufficient forces to the Pacific Area to quickly destroy the Japanese menace to all of our Allied Nations.

17 January 1945.

Soviet tank on the attack.

RADOM AND CRACOW FALL

16 and 19 January 1945

The German line is breached by Soviet troops. Hitler, who arrived in Berlin on 16 January and established his headquarters in the Reich Chancellery, blames the setback on General Harpe (Army Group A) and has him replaced by General Schoerner. The picture shows a German sniper. ▶

Soviet troops entering Cracow

A British soldier advancing under heavy German artillery fire. On 16 January 1945, British troops attacked east of the Maas, on the Dutch–German frontier.

MOPPING UP IN THE ARDENNES AND ALLIED ADVANCE TOWARDS THE ROER 19–26 January 1945.

From Churchill's address to the House of Commons on 18 January, 1945:

"I have seen it suggested that the terrific battle that has been proceeding since December 16 on the American front is an Anglo–American battle. In fact, however, the United States troops have done almost all the fighting and have suffered almost all the losses . . . Only one British army corps has been engaged in this action. All the rest of the thirty or more divisions which have been fighting continuously for the last month, are United States troops. The Americans have engaged thirty or forty men for every one we have engaged, and they have lost sixty to eighty men for every one of ours . . . (This) is undoubtedly the greatest American battle of the war and will, I believe, be regarded as an ever-famous American victory."

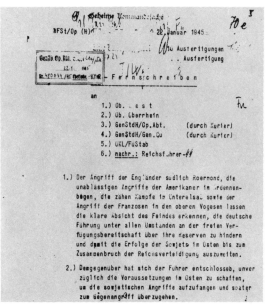

The Supreme Command of the Wehrmacht announced on 19 January 1945:

No major battles have taken place in any sector of the Western Front. Our units continue to offer strong resistance to the British S.E. of Maaseyck. Fighting continues to the S.E. of Malmedy, with minor enemy gains. The Kiekirch garrison has been withdrawn to a new position north of the Sauer. Near Reipertsweiler, American attempts to break out have been frustrated . . .

Teleprinter message from the Supreme Command of the Wehrmacht to the German Supreme Commander, West.

The Fuehrer has decided to create conditions that will facilitate the relief of the hard-pressed German forces in the East . . .

U.S. 1st and 3rd Armies make contact after the fall of Houffalize; in the Ardennes salient, German troops, here shown mounting a local counter-attack, are wiped out.

Some of the four thousand refugees in the Insterburg sector (East Prussia).

RED ARMY ADVANCES ON KOENIGSBERG

13 January 1945

"Help us! Help us!"

Report by Corporal Rehfeld

Suddenly figures loom up in front of us. Are they Russians?—I cannot tell for sure. I push my sub-machine gun forward, release the safety catch and, in the snowstorm, peer at the snow-covered column. Now they are only ten yards away. I recognize women and children among them. I jump up and shout "This way!"—Weeping girls with pale, timid faces fall round my neck. "Help us, please help us." Children whimper "Mummy, Mummy." All the men and women stand round silently, their faces white with cold, their clothes sodden with snow. I am aghast and hold up a young girl who is about to collapse. From their expression I can see the misery, the hardships and the terrible suffering of these dispossessed and uprooted East Prussians. Slowly I walk on ahead of them. There are about thirty people. Many have no coats, and some of the men walk barefoot. The Russians had taken their boots off them . . .

Marshal Vassilevsky, Commander of the Third White Russian Front (left), and Marshal Bagramyan, Commander of the Second Baltic Front.

In East Prussia, three German armies (40 divisions) were annihilated in three major pockets.

The German garrison of Allenstein surrendering on 22 January 1945.

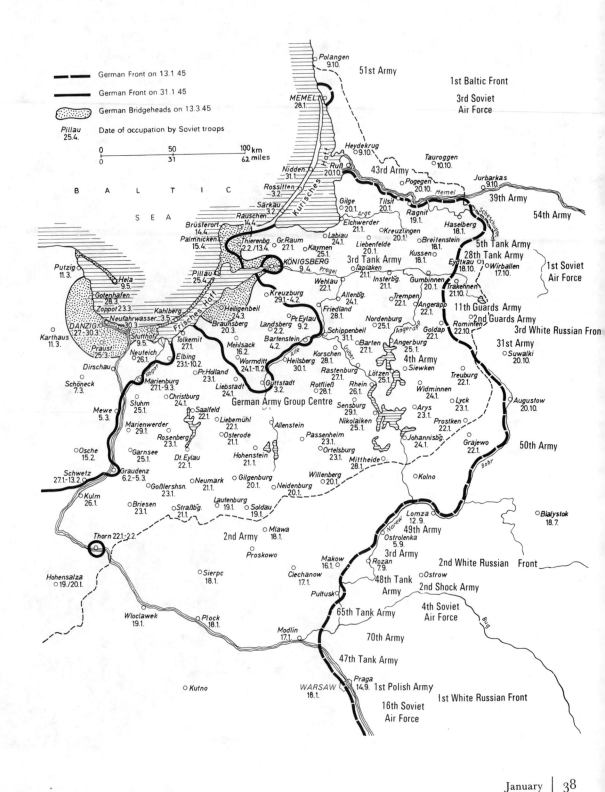

Red Army occupation of East Prussia

German Front on 13.1.45

German Front on 31.1.45

German Bridgeheads on 13.3.45

Pillau
25.4.   Date of occupation by Soviet troops

| 0 | 50 | 100 km |
| 0 | 31 | 62 miles |

Polangen
9.10.   51st Army

1st Baltic Front

3rd Soviet
Air Force

MEMEL
28.1.

Heydekrug
9.10.

Tauroggen
10.10.

43rd Army

Nidden
-31.1.   *Ruß*
20.10.

Pogegen
20.10.   *Jurbarkas*
9.10.

39th Army

Rossitten
-3.2.

Tilsit
20.1.   *Memel*

54th Army

B A L T I C   *Särkau*
-3.2.

Gilge
20.1.   *Ragnit*
19.1.

Rauschen
14.4.   *Elchwerder*
21.1.   *Haselberg*
18.1.

S E A   *Brüsterort*
14.4.   *Labiau*
24.1.   *Kreuzlingen*
20.1.   *Breitenstein*
18.1.

5th Tank Army

Palmnicken
15.4.   *Thierenbg.*
-2.2./13.4.   *Gr.Raum*
27.1.   *Liebenfelde*
20.1.   *Kussen*
18.1.   28th Tank Army

Kaymen
25.1.

1st Soviet
Air Force

KÖNIGSBERG
9.4.   3rd Tank Army

Eydtkau
18.10.   *Wirballen*
17.10.

Putzig
11.3.   *Pillau*
25.4.   *Taplaken*
21.1.

Wehlau
22.1.   *Insterbg.*
21.1.   *Gumbinnen*
20.1.

Hela
9.5.   *Kreuzburg*
29.1.-4.2.   *Allenbg.*
24.1.   *Trempen*
22.1.   *Trakehnen*
21.10.

11th Guards Army

Gotenhafen
28.3.   *Friedland*
28.1.   *Angerapp*
22.1.   2nd Guards Army

Zoppot 23.3.   *Kahlberg*
24.3.   *Heiligenbeil*
24.3.   *Pr.Eylau*
9.2.   *Nordenburg*
25.1.   *Goldap*
22.10.   *Rominten*
22.10.   3rd White Russian Fron

DANZIG
-27.-30.3.   *Braunsberg*
20.3.   *Landsberg*
2.2.   *Schippenbeil*
31.1.   *Barten*
27.1.   *Angerburg*
25.1.   31st Army

Karthaus
11.3.   *Stutthof*   *Tolkemit*
27.1.   *Bartenstein*
4.2.   *Suwalki*
20.10.

Neufahrwasser -3.5.   *Mehlsack*
16.2.   *Korschen*
28.1.   4th Army

Praust
-25.3.   *Neuteich*
26.1.   *Wormditt*
24.1.-11.2.   *Heilsberg*
30.1.   *Rastenburg*
27.1.   *Lötzen*
25.1.   *Siewken*   *Treuburg*
22.1.

Dirschau   *Elbing*
23.1.-10.2.   *Pr.Holland*
23.1.   *Rhein*
26.1.   *Widminnen*
24.1.

Schöneck
7.3.   *Marienburg*
27.1.-9.3.   *Guttstadt*
3.2.   *Rotfließ*
28.1.   *Lyck*
23.1.   *Augustow*
20.10.

Liebstadt
24.1.

Christburg
24.1.   German Army Group Centre   *Sensburg*
29.1.   *Arys*
23.1.   50th Army

Mewe
5.3.   *Stuhm*
25.1.   *Saalfeld*
22.1.   *Nikolaiken*
25.1.   *Prostken*
23.1.

Marienwerder
29.1.   *Liebemühl*
22.1.   *Allenstein*   *Johannisbg.*
24.1.   *Grajewo*
22.1.

Rosenberg
23.1.   *Osterode*
21.1.   *Passenheim*
23.1.   *Mittheide*
28.1.

Osche
15.2.   *Garnsee*
25.1.   *Dt.Eylau*
22.1.   *Hohenstein*
21.1.   *Ortelsburg*
23.1.   *Kolno*

Schwetz
27.1.-13.2.   *Graudenz*
6.2.-5.3.   *Neumark*
21.1.   *Gilgenburg*
20.1.   *Neidenburg*
20.1.   *Willenberg*
20.1.   *Bobr*

Goßlershsn.
23.1.

Kulm
26.1.   *Briesen*
23.1.   *Straßbg.*
21.1.   *Lautenburg*
19.1.   *Soldau*
19.1.

Lomza
12.9.   *Bialystok*
18.7.

Mlawa
18.1.   49th Army

Thorn 22.1.-2.2.   2nd Army   *Ostrolenka*
5.9.

Proskowo   3rd Army

Makow
16.1.   *Rozan*
7.9.   2nd White Russian Front

Hohensalza
19./20.1.   *Sierpc*
18.1.   *Ciechanow*
17.1.   *Ostrow*   48th Tank
Army   2nd Shock Army

Pultusk   65th Tank Army   4th Soviet
Air Force

Wloclawek
19.1.   *Plock*
18.1.   *Modlin*
17.1.   70th Army   *Bug*

47th Tank Army

Kutno   WARSAW
18.1.   *Praga*
14.9. 1st Polish Army   1st White Russian Front

16th Soviet
Air Force

The fourth battle for the Courland in late January 1945.

FALL OF TOLKEMIT; EAST PRUSSIA CUT OFF

26 January 1945

A light field gun on Mint Square, Koenigsberg.

General Gollnik evacuating Memel on 29 January.

To the Commander of Army Group North, respectively Courland.

With effect from 26 January 1945, the following Commanders are transferred: General Reinhardt, Commander of Army Group North, to the Reserve of Army Chief Command; Major-General Heidkaemper, Chief of the General Staff of Army Group North, to the Reserve of the Army Chief Command.

The following appointments come into effect on the same day: General Rendulic, Commander of Army Group North; Major General von Natzmer, Chief of the General Staff of Army Group North; Major General Foersch, Chief of the General Staff of Army Group Courland.

      Chief Command of the Army
      Chief of Army Personnel
      (signed) Burgdorf, Infantry General.

Fall of Gleiwitz (Gliwice) on 24 January, six days after 1st Ukrainian Front had crossed the Silesian frontier.

Marshal Koniev, 1st Ukrainian Front.

SOVIET ADVANCE INTO SILESIA

13 January 1945

Fortress Breslau *from the diary of Emil Heinze*

On Saturday, 20 January 1945, the authorities took hurried measures for the defence of the city. Everywhere members of the Volkssturm could be seen manning the anti-tank guns, and there were rumours that the east bank of the Oder was about to be evacuated. For days, miserable columns of refugees had been marching through the town. With cart and horse, handcarts and prams, they and their families trudged in the icy cold . . . Bartheln had become the new front line. We were told that it and Bischofs-walde had to be evacuated, and that at 9.30 on Monday, all those not doing essential work would have to be at the tram depot. I decided to ignore the official order, and made up my mind to stay behind. Every night, as we went to bed, we knew that our house might collapse about us . . .

Memorandum to German Commanders, Western and Eastern Front, issued on 30/1/45 (No. 0850/45/secret).

Recapitulation and consolidation of instructions as to fortresses, island fortresses, defence regions, fortified localities, local support points, etc.

Fortresses are areas or localities of military importance with permanent fortifications for all-round defence. Fortresses will ensure that the enemy is kept out of the region they dominate. They must tie the enemy down, and thus create conditions for successful counterattacks.

Areas and localities that are comparable to fortresses in military importance, but lack permanent fortifications are called Defence Regions. As such, they have basically the same tasks as Fortresses. The following instructions for Fortresses and their commanders apply equally and without exception to Defence Regions.

Local support points are strongly defended positions in the depth of the battle area. They form the backbone of our defence, and, in the case of enemy breakthroughs, the cornerstones of the entire front and centres of local counterattacks.

Red Army operations in Silesia 12 January to 8 May 1945

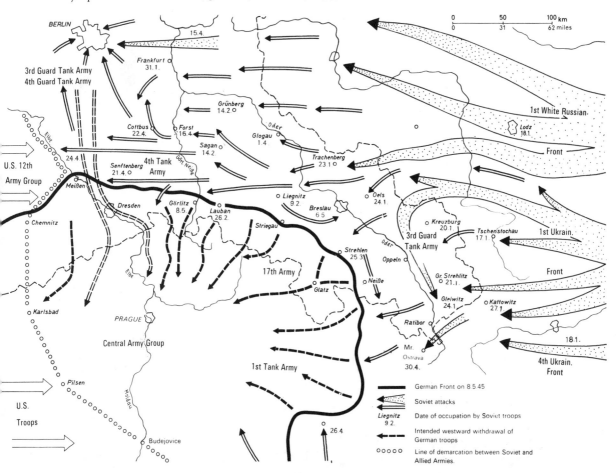

BERLIN

0 — 50 — 100 km
0 — 31 — 62 miles

3rd Guard Tank Army
4th Guard Tank Army

Frankfurt 31.1.

15.4.

U.S. 12th Army Group

Cottbus 22.4.

Senftenberg 21.4.

4th Tank Army

Meißen 24.4

Dresden

Görlitz 8.5.

Chemnitz

Lauban 26.2.

Striegau

Grünberg 14.2.

Forst 16.4.

Sagan 14.2.

Glogau 1.4.

Oder

Trachenberg 23.1

Liegnitz 9.2.

Breslau 6.5

1st White Russian.

Lodz 18.1.

Front

Oels 24.1.

Kreuzburg 20.1

Tschenstochau 17.1.

1st Ukrain.

3rd Guard Tank Army

Front

Karlsbad

Elbe

PRAGUE

17th Army

Strehlen 25.3

Oppeln

Gr. Strehlitz 21.1.

Gleiwitz 24.1

Kattowitz 27.1

Central Army Group

Glatz

Neiße

Ratibor

Mr. Ostrava 30.4.

18.1.

4th Ukrain. Front

Pilsen

Moldau

1st Tank Army

U.S. Troops

Budejovice

26.4

German Front on 8.5.45

Soviet attacks

Liegnitz 9.2. — Date of occupation by Soviet troops

Intended westward withdrawal of German troops

Line of demarcation between Soviet and Allied Armies.

In the command post of an armoured reconnaissance detachment in Silesia.

BEUTHEN (BYTOM) AND KATTOWITZ (KATOWICE) CAPTURED BY RED ARMY

27–29 January 1945

Teleprinter message from Hitler on 28 January 1945

Re: Deployment of Volkssturm.

Experience in the East has shown that Volkssturm, Emergency and Replacement units left to their own devices, lack resilience and are quickly crushed. The striking power of these units, which are numerically strong but inadequately equipped for modern war, can be increased considerably if they are incorporated into the regular army.

I therefore decree: Whenever Volkssturm, Emergency and Replacement units are found side by side with units of the regular army, mixed battle groups (brigades) must be established under unified command.

Soviet Propaganda Poster: "Death to the Fascist reptile."

Allied "News for the Troops" reporting the capture of Upper Silesia, and the fall of Memel.

Nr. 288, Montag, 29. Januar 1945

NACHRICHTEN FÜR DIE TRUPPE

Oberschlesien verloren

Sowjets erobern drei Riesen-Sprit-Werke

Synthetische Produktion fällt auf 20 %

Drei Treibstoffwerke in Schlesien sind bereits durch den russischen Vormarsch überrannt worden: Die beiden Treibstoffwerke der Oberschlesischen Hydrierwerke A.G. in Blechhammer und das Treibstoffwerk der Schaffgotsch-Benzin G.m.b.H. in Deschowitz.

Die drei Werke lieferten zusammen monatlich 50 000 Tonnen Treibstoff und waren erst vor kurzem nach den letzten alliierten Luftangriffen unter grossem Materialaufwand neu aufgebaut worden.

Spezialmaschinen verloren

Unersetzliche Spezialmaschinen, die erst in den letzten 6 Wochen aus anderen Treibstoffwerken im Reich abmontiert und nach Oberschlesien gebracht worden waren, sind in Blechhammer und Deschowitz in die Hand der Sowjets gefallen.

Mehr als 1 000 Mann wertvoller Spezialisten, die von der Wehrmacht für die Treibstoffwerke freigegeben wurden, werden vermisst und befinden sich vermutlich in russischer Gefangenschaft.

Um 20 Prozent gesunken

Durch die Bombenoffensive gegen die deutschen Treibstoffwerke und Raffinerien und durch den Verlust der drei oberschlesischen Treibstoffwerke ist die gesamte synthetische Treibstoffproduktion im Reich auf 20 Prozent des Standes vor einem Jahr abgesunken.

Dagegen ist der monatliche Treibstoffbedarf der Wehrmacht von 75 000 Tonnen im Dezember 1943 auf mehr als 400 000 [...]

Die Frontlinie am 14 Januar vor Beginn der Sowjet-Winteroffensive [...]
Die Frontlinie am [...]

Nur noch ein Fünftel des Gaues Ostpreussen in deutscher Hand

Der folgenschwerste Verlust für den gesamten weiteren Kriegsverlauf seit Beginn der neuen Sowjetoffensive wurde gestern aus Oberschlesien gemeldet, wo die Sowjets die wichtigen Industriestädte Kattowitz, Beuthen und Königshütte genommen haben.

Sowjetpanzer, die das oberschlesische Industriegebiet überrannt haben, werden bereits im Anmarsch auf Mährisch-Ostrau, die Einfallspforte für das böhmischmährische Industriegebiet, gemeldet.

Nach der Einnahme von Kattowitz, Beuthen und Königshütte ist jetzt das gesamte oberschlesische Industriegebiet für die deutsche Kriegswirtschaft verloren gegangen, mit all seinen Stahl- und Walzwerken, Kohlengruben, den grössten europäischen Zinkbergwerken und den Treibstoff-Fabriken, die Oberschlesien seit den Bombenzertörungen im Ruhrgebiet zur grössten Waffenschmiede des Reiches gemacht hatten.

Memel gefallen

Zugleich mit Oberschlesien ging gestern die Festung Memel verloren. Die deutsche Kampfgruppe in Memel streckte jetzt die Waffen, nachdem sie seit Oktober vorigen Jahres dort ausgehalten hatte.

Nach den Meldungen von der übrigen Ostfront stehen fast überall weitere schwere Rückschläge bevor.

In Königsberg brennt das ganze Viertel zwischen dem Alten und Neuen Pregel. Es wurde in einem verzweifelten Versuch, den Vorstoss der Sowjets in die Stadt aufzuhalten, von Pionieren in Brand gesteckt. Gardeschützen der Sowjets stürmen bereits die Vorstädte im Norden und Süden um [...]

THE CONQUEST OF GERMANY

The Advance of the Western Allies from the Rhine and of the Red Army from the Vistula

CHRONOLOGICAL TABLE: February

1945

February: German XXVIII Corps counter-attacks in W. Samland and, with remnants of the 3rd Tank Army established a continuous front from Fischhausen to Neukuhren. XXVIII Corps becomes Army Group Samland and takes control of all troops in Samland and in Koenigsberg.

1/2: Soviet tanks reach the Oder N.W. of Kuestrin (43 miles from Berlin). Thorn surrenders.

2/2: American troops draw up along the Siegfried Line (West Wall) in the Aachen–Saar sector. French troops enter Colmar.

Red Cross representatives discuss aid to concentration camp inmates with the SS.

Father Alfred Delp, S.J. and Count Helmuth Moltke hanged for their part in the anti-Hitler plot (20/7/44).

Breslau: Commissioner Hanke presents colours to the newly formed *Volkssturm* militia units.

3/2: The German News Agency reports that the President of the People's Court, Dr. Roland Freisler, died during an air raid in Berlin. He was killed by a collapsing beam, still clutching the file of F. von Schlabrendorff.

4/2: U.S. troops breach the main defences of the Siegfried line. U.S. 9th Army troops attack in the Juelich sector.

Red Army troops consolidate their Oder bridgeheads near Schurgast and Ohlau, and prepare to strike S. and W. via Grottkau.

5/2: U.S. 1st and 3rd Armies penetrate further into the Siegfried line defences.

Marshal Zhukov's troops reach the Oder and establish a bridgehead N.W. of Kuestrin. Marshal Koniev's troops cross the Oder further S., between Breslau and Oppeln.

6/2: Brieg, Ohlau, Grottkau and Steinau fall to the Red Army.

7/2: U.S. 3rd Army crosses the Rhine in several places.

Red Army crosses the Breslau–Berlin Autobahn.

8/2: Canadian troops launch Operation "Veritable", S.E. of Nijmegen. Kranenburg (a village on the Nijmegen–Cleves road) is captured. The battle of the Reichswald (the big forest along the frontier) begins. American troops advance in the S.

Red Army resumes its advance on the Oder estuary.

10/2: Canadian troops capture the Dutch village of Millingen and reach the W. bank of the Rhine.

Marshal Koniev's troops cross the Oder N.W. of Breslau. Elbing and Preussisch–Eylau (E. Prussia) fall to the Red Army.

11/2: Troops of the Canadian 1st Army take Cleves.

Red Army occupies Liegnitz and draws up before Breslau. Fall of Steinau, Lueben, Neumarkt and Kanth. Bunzlau in Soviet hands.

12/2: Women called up for service in *Volkssturm*.

13/2: British troops breach the second belt of Siegfried Line defences.

Breslau completely surrounded. Garrison of 150,000 cut off. Red Army surrounds Glogau.

15/2: Germans set up summary courts on orders of Minister of Justice.

British and Canadian troops extend their hold on the W. bank of the Rhine, along a 10-mile stretch from Millingen to a point near Emmerich.

Troops of the 1st Ukrainian Front capture Gruenberg and advance into Brandenburg Province. Fall of Naumburg and Konitz.

17/2: On the Canadian 1st Army front, British West Country infantry advances up to 2 miles S. of Cleves and comes within 1½ miles both of Goch and Calcar.

Red Army reaches the Lauban sector.

18/2: Canadian troops storm Goch. U.S. 3rd Army expands its bridgehead into Reich territory on a 28-mile front.

Soviet infantry continues to close up the Neisse, N. of Goerlitz. General Chernyakhovsky, Commander of the 3rd White Russian Front is killed in action in East Prussia, and is replaced by Marshal Vassilevsky.

19/2: Himmler contacts Count Bernadotte through Schellenberg.

Street fighting in Goch. U.S. troops breach the Siegfried Line N. of Echternach. German troops make desperate efforts to break out from Koenigsberg.

20/2: SHAEF (Supreme Headquarters Allied Expeditionary Force) established at Rheims. U.S. 20th Armoured Division lands in Europe. German resistance S. of Goch continues. U.S. 3rd Army makes further progress through the main belt of the Siegfried Line.

Red Army advances on Danzig, and captures Bobersberg.

21/2: Goch captured. Canadians advance on Guelders. Allies enter Saarburg. Street fighting in Forbach.

Red Army takes Czersk. Heavy fighting for Mewe, 40 miles from Danzig.

22/2: U.S. 3rd Army crosses the Saar. Fall of Saarburg and Moyland. 5,000 German troops surrender in the Trier sector.

Red Army captures 3 suburbs of Breslau. Soviet troops cross the Neisse on a broad front. Zinten in E. Prussia is captured.

23/2: U.S. 9th and 1st Armies launch a powerful offensive across the Roer river, E. of Aachen. Capture of Dueren. Fall of Forbach on the Saar front.

Soviet troops capture Poznan (Posen) after a siege lasting one month. Major General Mattern surrenders with 23,000 survivors. German resistance in Arnswalde (Pomerania) collapses. Soviet troops enter the S. precincts of Breslau.

24/2: German attempts to recapture Rurich (in the Roer sector) are frustrated. Fall of Juelich.

Street fighting in Lichtenfeld (E. Prussia).

25/2: U.S. 9th Army crosses the Roer at Linnich and advances N. towards Erkelenz. Dueren falls. Allied forces 20 miles from Cologne along a solid 30-mile front.

Heavy street fighting in Breslau.

26/2: Himmler orders the setting up of emergency courts.

Troops of U.S. 3rd Army shell Bitburg. U.S. 4th Tank Division, advancing 7 miles in 24 hours, crosses the Nims river 12½ miles N.E. of Echternach.

Soviet troops break through to the Baltic in Pomerania.

27/2: Drastic reduction in German rations. There is now less bread than in 1918.

British troops overrun Calcar and Grieth.

28/2: Advancing on Cologne, U.S. 1st Army crosses the Erft river. U.S. 9th Army advances to within 16 miles of Cologne.

Marshal Rokossovsky's troops, advancing on the Baltic, capture Neu-Stettin and Prechlau.

End of February: Von Vietinghoff-Scheel recalled to Italy and General Rendulic detailed to Courland.

WEST WALL (SIEGFRIED LINE) BREACHED BY U.S. 9th, 1st AND 3rd ARMIES

2 to 22 February 1945

General Patton,
Commander U.S.
3rd Army.

Breaching of the West Wall

By General Patton

During the course of these operations, 90 Division alone put out one hundred and twenty pillboxes in about forty-eight hours, with the loss of less than one hundred and twenty men. This feat was accomplished by careful reconnaissance, then smothering the embrasure with machine-gun and rifle fire, and using dynamite charges against the back door, or else by using self-propelled 155 mm. guns at short range. At three hundred yards the 155 shell will remove a pillbox for every round fired . . .

From one point on the road along which 76 Division had successfully advanced, fifteen pillboxes were visible in addition to dragons' teeth and anti-tank ditches. Yet this relatively green division went through them. We visited the command pillbox for the sector. It consisted of a three-storey submerged barracks with toilets, shower baths, a hospital, laundry, kitchen, storerooms, and every conceivable convenience plus an enormous telephone installation. Electricity and heat were produced by a pair of identical diesel engines with generators. Yet the whole offensive capacity of this installation consisted of two machine-guns and a 60 mm. mortar operating from steel cupolas which worked up and down by means of hydraulic lifts. The 60 mm. mortar was peculiar in that it was operated by remote control. As in all cases, this particular pillbox was taken by a dynamite charge against the back door. We found marks on the cupolas, which were ten inches thick, where our 90 mm. shells, fired at a range of two hundred yards, had simply bounced.

Eisenhower inspecting Juelich, captured after a battle lasting from 4 to 24 February.

Like Juelich, many towns and villages . . .

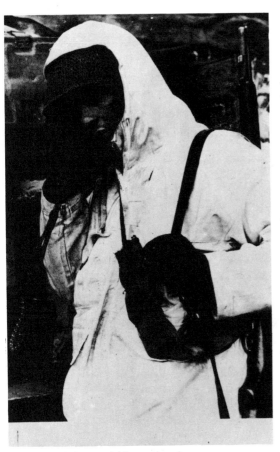

A scout reporting on the latest situation.

On 3 February, SHAEF announced that all Belgium had been cleared of German troops. Our photograph shows field guns in action before the evacuation.

. . . were destroyed by heavy bombardment.

THE RED ARMY NEAR KUESTRIN ON THE ODER

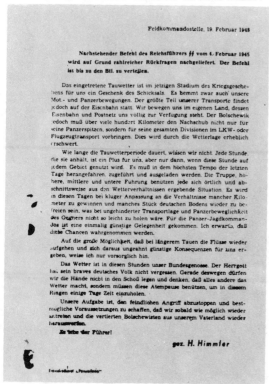

Himmler's Proclamation on his appointment as C.-in-C. Army Group Vistula. "The weather is our ally—let us seize the opportunity and eject the bestial Bolsheviks from our Fatherland . . ."

"News for the Troops" reporting the shelling of German towns on the W. bank of the Oder.

GENERAL LASCH APPOINTED FORTRESS COMMANDER OF KOENIGSBERG

5 February 1945

Comrades!

In this grave hour, I have been charged to take command of Fortress Koenigsberg.

I shall do everything I can to do my duty.

I ask you, comrades, to show the same determination.

The Fatherland needs our unconditional and unflinching devotion. Only by answering its call resolutely, by standing shoulder to shoulder, can we ensure any kind of future for our people. Resourcelessness is tantamount to complete and dishonourable collapse.

Show your true German comradeship, support the weak!

We shall fight for the Fatherland, preserving our honour, if not our lives. I call upon everyone who has worn his tunic in honour, to be faithful to the immortal spirit of the German soldier!

signed Lasch
Infantry General.

Volkssturm-man guarding Party Offices in Koenigsberg.

A Prussian family takes to the road.

The Battles round Breslau

By General Sachsenheimer

During the night of 10 February, the advance of Russian tank concentrations along the Kanth–Breslau Autobahn could no longer be stemmed, and our side was thrown into increasing confusion . . . Near Leuthen and Radaxdorf, my troops were repeatedly attacked from the south. In several places, we had to withdraw several hundred yards, for instance near Leuthen, where I shall never forget the dear old lady who refused to leave her family home, and kept giving me news of enemy movements over the public telephone system. Nothing would persuade her to leave her birthplace.

Our movements were dictated by the fact that the enemy, advancing remorselessly along the Autobahn, had thrown a ring round Breslau. At the same time, he had succeeded in surrounding Battle Group Sachs on the Breslau perimeter.

On 13 February, I received a signal ordering the Battle Group to hold on to the N.W. perimeter. But even while I was making the necessary arrangements, I was dumbfounded to receive a further radio message ordering the Battle Group to break out and to join forces with the main unit south of the Autobahn. After handing over all our guns and vehicles to the Fortress, some 1,400 men, divided into three columns, started for the Autobahn after nightfall. There were numerous clashes with the enemy, followed by hand-to-hand fighting at daybreak, particularly on the Autobahn-bridge near Kostenblut, near Pohlsdorf and at Hochvorwerk Farm. Some 800 men succeeded in breaking out; one column dug in at Breslau, its leaders having decided that no breakout could be effected before dawn.

The German News Agency announced on 7 February 1945:

SS Reichsfuehrer Heinrich Himmler has ordered the summary trial of several unprincipled and corrupt officials who have proved unworthy of the confidence placed in them during this arduous period. The court has found von Salisch, former SS Standartenfuehrer and Police President of Bromberg guilty of cowardice and dereliction of duty, and accordingly has sentenced him to death. He has since been executed by a firing squad. Former Governor Kuehn (Bromberg) and former mayor Ernst, have been deprived of their civic rights and offices, and sent to a punishment battalion. The District Leader of Bromberg, Rampf has been dealt with similarly.

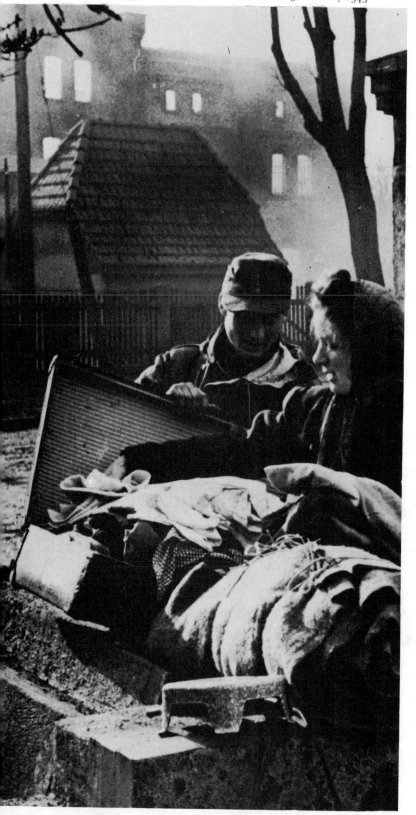

In early February, Lueben and Steinau were recaptured by the Germans. Civilians making ready to flee to the West.

"News for the Troops" reporting that Breslau is about to be cut off.

Commissioner Hanke swearing in new Volkssturm units in Breslau.

British Typhoons taking off in support of the Canadian offensive.

CANADIANS OPEN ALLIED OFFENSIVE SOUTH-EAST OF NIJMEGEN

8 February 1945

The Opening Phase of Operation "Veritable"

By R. W. Thompson

Between six o'clock and nine o'clock, there was scarcely a sound in all the region of the Maas from Nijmegen to below the village of Cuijk. Men lay or squatted or stood about in barns, schools, vehicles, heads propped on hands, waiting, seeming thoughtful, some sleeping. The darkness came like a benison, and shortly before nine o'clock a muffled roar grew out of the western sky, rose to a crescendo overhead, and within seconds exploded in the opening deluge of the air bombardment. Nearly two thousand tons of high explosive thundered down upon the ancient town of Cleves, to heave it out by the roots in eruptions of dreadful violence. Most men knew the meaning of that shuddering impact of sound:

D minus one. Heavy bombers will obliterate Emmerich, Cleves, Goch . . .

Not only Emmerich, Cleves and Goch but also the smaller townships of Weeze, Udem and Calcar, key links in the main enemy defensive line.

Slowly the sky lightened, and at half past seven o'clock the barrage lifted for ten minutes of an eerie silence in which all normal movement seemed deadened and unreal. Tanks, kangaroos and a host of vehicles lumbered forward all lurid with eerie fluorescent panels, giving them a look of fury as though they had come up dripping with blood and fire from hell, or the depths of the Maas.

When the barrage lifted from its opening phases at half past ten o'clock, and the forward troops advanced on its heels through the minefields, it seemed that no man could have lived in the enemy positions, that no tree could still be left standing in all the Reichswald forest. The Glasgow Highlanders, leading the attack in the centre, were within five hundred yards of the enemy, All but one of their flail tanks had bogged down on the start line, and the infantry went on alone. Behind them the one remaining flail cleared a path through the minefield for the tanks, and the tanks of the Coldstreams surged through to engage anti-tank guns and 88's before they, too, bogged down.

German troops with machine guns and "Panzer-fists" on their way to battle.

British engineers clearing German minefields.

British and Canadian troops of the 2nd Army during a rapid advance on 8 February.

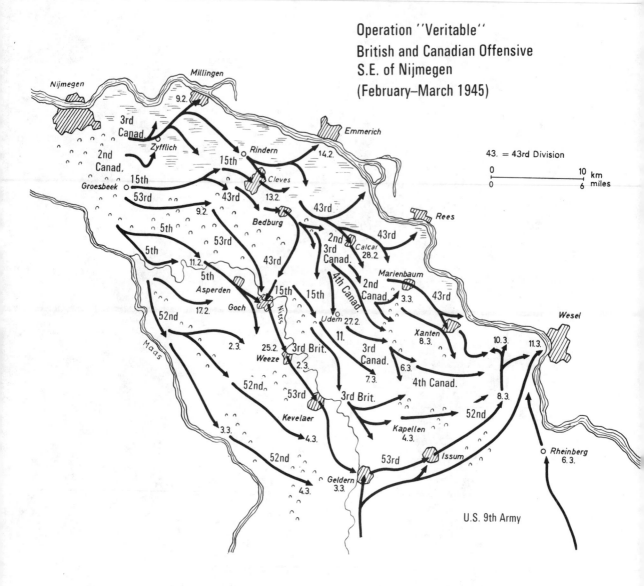

Operation "Veritable"
British and Canadian Offensive
S.E. of Nijmegen
(February–March 1945)

43. = 43rd Division

Nijmegen

Millingen

9.2.

Emmerich

3rd Canad.

Zyfflich

2nd Canad.

Rindern

15th

14.2.

Cleves

13.2.

43rd

Rees

Groesbeek

15th

53rd

9.2.

43rd

Bedburg

43rd

43rd

5th

53rd

43rd

2nd
3rd
Canad.

Calcar
28.2.

43rd

5th

11.2.

Marienbaum

5th

Asperden

15th

15th

4th Canad.

2nd Canad.

3.3.

Wesel

52nd

17.2.

Goch

Niers

Udem 27.2.

11.

43rd

Xanten
8.3.

10.3.

11.3.

2.3.

25.2.

3rd Brit.

3rd Canad.

Weeze

2.3.

7.3.

6.3.

8.3.

52nd

53rd

3rd Brit.

4th Canad.

Maas

3.3.

Kevelaer

Kapellen
4.3.

52nd

Rheinberg
6.3.

52nd

4.3.

53rd

Issum

U.S. 9th Army

4.3.

Geldern
3.3.

FALL OF KRANENBURG
AND CLEVES

9 and 11 February 1945

Canadians mop up Kranenburg on the German border
in preparation for their advance on Cleves.

On 12 February SHAEF announced the crossing of the German border in the Reichswald sector.

The first German prisoners captured during the British and Canadian offensive.

Scottish troops entering Cleves.

Heavy fighting developed in the Reichswald, where the Germans had dug in, on 11 February 1945.

By 15 February, Allied troops had advanced to the Grave–Groesbeek–Cleves–Emmerich line.

British field guns south of Cleves.

Capitulation of Schneidemuehl on 11 February 1945. German soldiers being marched off to prison camps.

RED ARMY ADVANCE IN SILESIA

February 1945.

German troops made repeated attempts to halt the Soviet advance.

Befehl Nr. 2

Oels   den _12 Februar_ 1945

Laut Befehl des Frontoberkommandos wird die gesamte männliche Bevölkerung deutscher Volks- oder Staatsangehörigkeit zum Arbeitsdienst mobilisiert.

Hierzu befehle ich:

1. Die gesamte männliche Bevölkerung — Deutsche und deutsche Staatsangehörige — im Alter von 17 bis 50 Jahren hat sich innerhalb 48 Stunden nach Veröffentlichung dieses Befehls bei der Einberufungs- stelle _In der Stadt Oels Volast Theater Ohrauer Strasse_ zwecks Registrierung und gleichzeitiger Absendung zur Arbeit zu melden.

Russian call-up of male citizens of Oels (Silesia) for labour service.

Soviet troops in house-to-house fighting in Breslau.

DRUMHEAD COURT MARTIALS SET UP BY GERMAN MINISTER OF JUSTICE

15 February 1945

The German News Agency announced that Dr. Thierack, the Minister of Justice, has issued the following order:

The struggle for the survival of the German Reich demands the utmost resolution and devotion of every German. Anyone trying to evade his duty to the community, and especially those guilty of cowardice or selfishness, will immediately be brought to justice with all severity, lest the failure of one individual redound to the discredit of the entire Reich. On the orders of the Fuehrer, and with the full accord of the Ministry of Justice, the Head of the Reichs Chancellery, the Ministry of the Interior and the Party Chancellery, it is therefore decreed that:

I. Summary courts of justice will be set up in all parts of the Reich threatened by the enemy.

II 1. Such courts will consist of a judge as President, and a political leader or official of the NSDAP and an officer of the Wehrmacht, the Waffen SS or the police as assessors. 2. Members of the court and a public prosecutor will be appointed by the Regional Commissar for Defence.

III 1. The summary court will be competent to deal with all acts likely to undermine German resolution or striking power. 2. The procedure will be that laid down in the penal code.

IV 1. The court will be competent to pass death sentences, acquit prisoners, or to refer cases to the common courts of justice. All death sentences must be confirmed by the Commissar for the Defence, who will also determine the place, time, and manner of execution.

2. Whenever the Commissar for Defence is not available, and immediate execution is deemed essential, the public prosecutor will act in his stead.

V. All regulations needed for the amplification, alteration and implementation of the above decree will be passed by the Minister of Justice in conjunction with the Minister of the Interior and the Head of the Party Chancellery.

VI. The decree comes into effect with its publication in the press and its announcement over the German radio network.

German civilians returning to occupied territory.

Execution of prisoners by Summary Court. Spring 1945.

TOTAL WAR ON THE HOME FRONT

In accordance with the total war measures, all able-bodied German women were conscripted for armament production—generally in underground factories.

The German railway network is paralysed by air raids. Tickets being sold at improvised counters. ▶

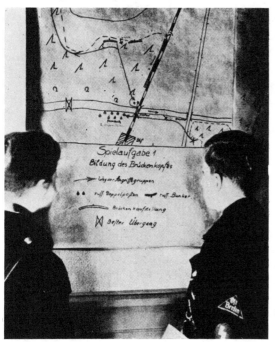

Fourteen and fifteen-year-olds being given pre-military training before their call-up in March.

Soviet gun immobilized at Metgethen.

GERMAN COUNTER-OFFENSIVE HELPS TO RE-OPEN KOENIGSBERG–PILLAU ROAD

19–20 February 1945

From the Logbook of Battle Group Malotka (First Infantry Division):

19 February, 5:15 a.m.: Riflemen drew up in complete darkness. 1st Company, on the right flank, rushed enemy positions.

7:30 a.m.: Mopping up of enemy trench. Main enemy line overrun, running battles with panzer fists and bazookas. *2 p.m.:* Following the surprise night attack on a 1-kilometer front, the battalion captured or destroyed 13 heavy anti-tank guns and 26 machine guns.

20 February: The entire line was held despite heavy losses. At about 11 p.m. the exhausted battle group (Hitler youth who had not slept for two nights, fighting continuously and covering 50 km between engagements) was relieved by a battalion from Koenigsberg. Of the original group of 7 officers, 340 NCO's and men, 2 officers and approximately 45 men were killed and 208 men were wounded.

Father and son being decorated with the Iron Cross (2nd Class) after the battle of Metgethen.

ALLIES CAPTURE GOCH ON THE RHINE

19–21 February 1945

"Germany is quite powerless in the face of so much technical superiority!"

From the diary of Rev. Brimmer:

Monday, 19 February, at 10:15 a.m.: The first British soldiers, their guns at the ready, advanced across the rubble of the two chapels on Church Square and entered the church . . . Just as the British came in, the SS blew up the central aisle . . . A few minutes later, the first of the two Niers bridges went up into the air . . . Yet only two days later, the first British vehicles were able to cross the river by an improvised bridge.

Wednesday, 21 February: The British have occupied the whole town. Column after column now pours into Goch. There is an ever-greater concentration of guns and lorries, so that at times the streets are three-deep in British vehicles. Germany is quite powerless in the face of so much technical superiority!

German gun firing at approaching British armour.

After two days of bitter street-fighting, Canadian troops entered Goch and advanced towards Geldern. At the same time, U.S. troops broke through the West Wall defences (Siegfried Line) N.W. of Echternach.

German refugees returning to Goch. At about the same time, Himmler approached Count Bernadotte, and Eisenhower transferred his HQ to Rheims.

HIMMLER'S MEETING WITH COUNT FOLKE BERNADOTTE

12 February 1945

Himmler: "We made a mistake . . ."

Count Folke Bernadotte in The Fall of the Curtain:

Every German would fight like a lion before he gave up hope, Himmler declared, when I asked him if he didn't think it meaningless to go on with the war, as Germany could not possibly be victorious. Certainly, the military situation was grave, but not hopeless . . .

I said that the Swedish Red Cross was very anxious to obtain permission to work in the concentration camps, especially in those where Norwegians and Danes were interned.

Himmler: This would probably be very useful, and I see no reason why permission to do this should not be granted.

Bernadotte: And to facilitate the work, the Norwegians and Danes in question should be collected into two camps, one for each group. The total number of Norwegian and Danish prisoners is probably somewhere about thirteen thousand.

Himmler: That figure is greatly exaggerated. I don't know the exact number, but I should not think it can be more than two or three thousand. However, I will look into the matter.

Himmler had accepted my proposal. He also agreed that the aged, the sick, and mothers, should be allowed to return to Norway, after having been assembled in the camps . . .

After this, our conversation became more general, and the Head of the Gestapo led it on to the Bolshevik danger, much on the same lines as Ribbentrop. He predicted that the end of Europe would come if the German Eastern Front were to break down, for the Second World War was a war between Europeans and Asiatics. There would be no future for Europe if the Allies were victorious. Only in the last week more than a hundred thousand German women, varying in age from sixteen to eighty, had been violated by the Russian hordes—he simply could not understand Sweden's blindness in the face of the immense danger from the East.

Bernadotte: But Germany was allied to Russia during part of this war. How does that fit in with what you have just said?

Himmler: I thought you would say that. We made a mistake, but we soon realized that the Russian armed might was so great that it was only a matter of time before it would be turned against us.

Himmler at the height of his power attending a Nazi rally.

American troops entering Dueren on 23 February.

The American offensive was preceded by 45-minute bombardment of enemy defences with 1,000 guns.

German troops counter-attacking in the Roer sector. Meanwhile Hitler proclaimed from Berlin: "This day I prophesy the final victory of the German Reich!"

SS slogan on a house captured by the Allies: "The SS trust in their Fuehrer".

Air power was a decisive factor in moulding Allied strategy.

Family hostages   10/2/1945 3:15 a.m.

The combination of depleted units, and the deployment of youthful and inadequate reinforcements, have had an untoward effect on morale. Moreover, the front is so wide that the influence of officers and Party officials is no longer as effective as it might be. Hence the danger of desertion has increased, and preventive measures are urgently needed. One of our Armies has accordingly asked that the measures regarding the arrest of family-hostages be made known to the troops. It should, however, be remembered that the threat of arresting dependants has lost much of its force, particularly when the families concerned are in enemy-occupied territory.

Signed: HAUSSER
Commander of Army Group G.

On 25 February, the U.S. 9th Army crossed the Roer near Linnich and advanced north towards Erkelenz. Berlin was still the main objective of the Western Allies.

Death and Destruction after the battle for Poznan.

POZNAN (POSEN) CAPITULATES

23 February 1945

"The hour commands us to do our duty . . ."

By General Mattern

The enemy attack on Fortress Posen has begun. On the Fuehrer's orders, and as our duty dictates in any case, we shall defend the fortress to the last man. You know that the enemy onslaught is aimed at the German people and the German Fatherland. Never do German soldiers fight more valiantly than in the defence of their homeland. We, too, comrades, will make the enemy pay dearly in blood for every inch of our soil. The knowledge that the eyes of the entire nation are upon us in these fateful days, will redouble our resolve. The enemy, who saw himself within grasp of his objective, has been brought to a halt. We shall continue to bar his way. His onslaught will and must be broken. The hour commands us to do our duty. It will find us prepared! Destiny helps those who help themselves.

A message to all SS leaders: "Persevere . . . Do your duty . . . Hit back with an iron fist . . ."

VOLKSSTURM SENT TO THE EASTERN FRONT

From a Volkssturm unit near Guben on the Neisse:

On 21 February, just after we had left our quarters in the Hindenburg School, the school building was hit by a shell. As we crossed the town and made for the village of Gross-Besen, we were struck by the change. The evacuation had apparently begun. The town was being shelled from the hills in the East. We reached Gross-Besen, 4 km down the Neisse from Guben, without any losses. Here our company, which had been reduced to 50 men, was ordered to defend the left bank of the river. We dug in, and next day we could see that the Russians had occupied the airfield across the river. Although the Russians did not attack in force, they fired at everyone who showed his head, and we did likewise. In the first few days, several of us were killed or wounded by grenades. On 26/2 we were reinforced by infantrymen, who extended our position. Our company had to fetch the necessary material at night, and was also ordered to build a trench from Gross-Besen to our post. The Russians kept us under constant fire.

Children coming to the rescue of the Fatherland.

Volkssturm men in action.

ALLIED MILITARY GOVERNMENT IN OCCUPIED AREAS

PROCLAMATION TO THE GERMAN PEOPLE

I, General Dwight D. Eisenhower, Supreme Commander, Allied Expeditionary force, do hereby proclaim as follows:

The Allied forces serving under my command have now entered Germany. We come as conquerors, but not as oppressors. In the area of Germany occupied by the forces under my command, we shall obliterate Nazism and German militarism, overthrow Nazi rule, dissolve the Nazi Party, and abolish the cruel, oppressive, and discriminatory laws and institutions which the Party has created. We shall eradicate that German militarism which has so often disrupted the peace of the world. Military and party leaders, the Gestapo, and others suspected of crimes and atrocities will be tried, and, if guilty, punished as they deserve.

Supreme legislative, judicial, and executive authority and powers within the occupied territory are vested in me as Supreme Commander and Military Governor, and the Military Government is established to exercise these powers under my direction. All persons in the occupied territory will obey immediately and without question all enactments and orders of the Military Government. Military Government courts will be established for the punishment of offenders. Resistance to the Allied Forces will be ruthlessly stamped out. Other serious offences will be dealt with severely.

All German courts and educational institutions within the occupied territory are suspended. The *Volksgerichtshof*, the *Sondergerichte* (the so-called "People's Courts" and "Special Courts") are deprived of authority throughout the occupied territory. Reopening of the criminal and civil courts and educational institutions will be authorised when conditions permit.

All officials are charged with the duty of remaining at their posts until further orders, and obeying and enforcing all orders or directions of Military Government or the Allied authorities. This applies also to officials, employees and workers of all public undertakings and utilities and to all other persons engaged in essential work.

U.S. flag being hoisted in a small village on the Luxembourg border (right). (Below): Eisenhower's proclamation to the German people being put up.

PERSEVERE!

Establishment of Flying Courts-Martial in Berlin, 13 February 1945:

With the express permission of the SS Reichsfuehrer, the Commander of Army District III has made the following arrangements on the establishment and competence of Summary Courts in the area under his command:

1. Summary Courts for dealing with crimes committed by members of the Wehrmacht or the Waffen SS will be set up at selected points in the patrol area;

2. Summary Courts will only pass sentences of death or grant acquittals. Cases that do not call for a death sentence, or require further investigation will be referred to normal courts martial.

3. Summary Courts will have a Wehrmacht judge as president and two soldiers as assessors.

4. By virtue of the powers vested in me by SS Reichsfuehrer and Commander of the Replacement Army, all sentences passed by a Summary Court are subject to confirmation by me.

5. Such confirmation must be obtained immediately, if necessary over the telephone, so that death sentences can be carried out without delay.

6. Death sentences will be carried out in the vicinity of the Court, normally by a firing squad, but in the case of particularly base scoundrels by hanging.

*

Let no-one think that the Party is so simple or so self-satisfied as to be insensitive to certain underhand activities following our military setbacks. In the midst of stormy battles, exerting all its strength, ordering and moulding the nation's life, day and night, the Party keeps a watchful eye on all that happens . . .

Though the times scorch the soul of every National Socialist, we are uncowed, knowing as we do that, by exerting all our power, we can and will turn the tide . . .

From: *Volkssturm*, Vol. 4–5, 1945.

Typical scene at a Berlin tram stop (left). (Below): As Allied bombers continued to take their toll, the populace tried to rescue what furniture they could. A lorry in Munich.

Hitler's order contains detailed instructions on how the Koenigsberg–Pillau road, recaptured on 19 February, is to be kept open. Attacks on the Samland peninsula must be intensified. 4th Army is to hold on at all costs. Every available man to be released for front-line service.

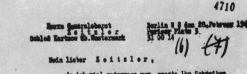

WITHDRAWAL OF WEHRMACHT FIELD HQ IN THE EAST

Supreme Command of the German Army
WFSt/Qu2 No. 002005/45 K

Fuehrer's Headquarters, 26/2/45

Re: Withdrawal from territory threatened by the enemy.

Withdrawals of Wehrmacht command posts in enemy-threatened territory will be subject to the following conditions:

Within the territories under the command of our Army Groups in the East, the transfer of all command posts to the rear requires the express permission of the Supreme Commander of the Army Group as chief territorial officer of the Wehrmacht.

In the West, permission will be given by Supreme Commander Western Army. Outside the territory controlled by the various Army Groups, all withdrawals of military establishments are proscribed on principle.

signed: Keitel.

Albert Speer, Minister of Armaments, expressing his regret that he cannot obtain the reinstatement of General Zeitzler, Chief of the General Staff, whose devotion to the Fuehrer is unquestioned.

Canadian soldier with three German prisoners.

"FAMILY HOSTAGES":

Hitler's order of 8 March 1945: Anyone captured without being wounded or without having fought to the limit of his powers, has forfeited his honour. He is expelled from the fellowship of decent and brave soldiers. His dependants will be held responsible . . .

THE CONQUEST OF GERMANY

The Advance of the Western Allies from the Rhine and of the Red Army from the Vistula.

CHRONOLOGICAL TABLE: March

1945

1–5/3: Germans counter-attack near Lauban.

2/3: Canadian First Army fight their way into Weeze and advance on Geldern. Allies capture Krefeld, Trier, Viesen, Suechteln, Venlo and Roermond. Allied troops reach the Rhine at Osterath and Neuss.

Soviet tanks cut the Stettin–Danzig coastal road and isolate E. Pomerania and W. Prussia from the rest of the Reich. As a result, civilian refugees are forced to make for the north, in the direction of Kolberg, Danzig and Gdynia (Gotenhafen).

3/3: U.S. 9th Army troops advancing N.E. of Venlo make a firm junction with British troops of the Canadian 1st Army striking south from Kevelaer.

4/3: Canadians advance on Xanten. Only three German bridgeheads on the left bank of the Rhine are left. Withdrawal of German troops across the river. Fall of Neuss. Leverkusen, Duesseldorf and Duisburg under fire.

Marshal Zhukov's and Marshal Rokossovski's troops reach the Baltic coast near Koeslin and Kolberg. Other troops of the First White Russian Front advance to the Oder S.W. of Stargard (Starogard) and capture Pyritz.

5/3: The 1929 class called up by the Wehrmacht and sent to the front.

U.S. tanks and infantry enter suburbs of Cologne. Fall of Xanten, Euskirchen and Schleiden.

Red Army captures Stargard.

6/3: U.S. troops take Cologne.

Troops of the Second White Russian Front capture the ancient Polish city of Grudziadz (Graudenz). Surrender by Major-General Fricke and 5,000 survivors.

7/3: U.S. 1st Army under General Hodges crosses the Rhine over the Ludendorff railway bridge at Remagen. U.S. 3rd Army under General Patton reaches the Rhine N.W. of Coblenz. German 7th Army surrounded in the Cologne–Coblenz–Trier sector; 60,000 Germans cut off in the Eifel sector.

Red Army enters Kolberg (population: 80,000, more than half of them refugees). Soviet troops take Gollnow, Mewe (Gniew), Massow and Stepenitz at the mouth of the Oder and reach Altdamm, 4½ miles from Stettin.

Soviet High Command announces the capture of a large German pocket S. of Schievelbein (Major-General Krappe and 8,000 men taken prisoner) and the repulse of German counter-attacks in the Lake Balaton sector in Hungary.

8/3: U.S. 1st Army establishes a strong build-up on the east bank of the Rhine, near Remagen. Fall of Bonn.

Ring round Danzig and Gdynia is tightened. Second White Russian Front captures the town of Koscierzyna in the former Polish Corridor. 30,000 prisoners taken at Wollin (Wolin). Red Army draws up outside Stettin.

10/3: Canadian First Army successfully completes operations "Veritable" and "Blockbuster". U.S. 3rd Army reaches the Moselle near Kochem.

11/3: Hitler visits an Army Corps on the Oder front, on the occasion of "Heroes' Day".

21,000 German soldiers surrender in the Wesel pocket. Soviet troops surround the harbours of Danzig and Gdynia.

12/3: Himmler–Kersten agreement: No concentration camp prisoners will be killed on the approach of the Allies (agreement was not kept).

General Weiss is appointed C.-in-C. Army Group North, General von Saucken C.-in-C. Second Army.

Marshal Zhukov's troops capture Kuestrin on the east bank of the Oder. Germans continue to resist in the Stettin bridgehead.

13/3: Red Army launches attack on Heiligenbein pocket. Soviet forces gain control of the whole 150-mile Pomeranian coastline.

Middle of March: General Rendulic transferred to Vienna. General Hilpert, Commander of the 16th Army in Courland, appointed C.-in-C. Army Group Courland.

15/3: U.S. 3rd Army crosses Moselle S.W. of Coblenz. U.S. 7th Army launches operation "Undertone".

German forces in E. Prussia split into two. Units of the 3rd White Russian Front break through to the Baltic coast, S.W. of Koenigsberg. All remaining women and children evacuated from Kolberg by sea. Soviet forces advance to the centre of the town. Red Army launches offensive in Upper Silesia.

17/3: Eisenhower warns civilian populations of Frankfort-on-Main and Mannheim-Ludwigshafen that their cities are about to become combat areas, and urges them to leave without delay.

18/3: Allied troops capture Coblenz, Bad Kreuznach and Merzig.

Soviet troops take Kolberg on the Baltic, thus eliminating the last German pocket between the Oder estuary and Danzig. Fall of Neustadt.

19/3: British patrols reach Randwijk on the Lower Rhine.

Hitler passes his "Nero Decree" (scorched earth policy), and orders the destruction of all important munition, provision and raw material installations together with railway and road communications.

20/3: Hitler decorates 20 Hitler youths with the Iron Cross for outstanding services at the front. General Heinrici replaces Himmler as C.-in-C. Army Group Vistula. German resistance west of the Rhine collapses. U.S. 3rd and 7th Armies link up.

21/3: U.S. 3rd Army enters Mainz and Ludwigshafen. Homberg surrenders.

22/3: Field-Marshal Kesselring replaces Field-Marshal von Rundstedt as C.-in-C. Western front.

U.S. 3rd Army crosses Rhine at Mainz. U.S. tanks draw up before Speyer.

23/3: 300,000 Allied troops, including Montgomery's 21st Army Group cross the Rhine north of Xanten and establish bridgeheads. 6,000 Allied planes participate in the biggest airborne operation of the war, landing 40,000 troops east of the Rhine.

25/3: Allies cross the Rhine at various new points. U.S. 3rd Army, under General Patton breaks out from their bridgehead between Mainz and Worms and, in a spectacular 27-mile advance, brushes aside all resistance. Crossing of the Main. Occupation of Darmstadt.

Soviet troops take Heiligenbeil in E. Prussia. Troops of 2nd White Russian Front overrun the Oliva suburb of Danzig.

26/3: U.S. 3rd Army reaches Frankfort and enters the town across the Niederrad bridge in the south. Allies capture Offenbach.

27/3: General Eisenhower declares in a press interview that the Germans in the West were "a whipped army incapable of throwing in sufficient strength to stop the Allies . . . The crossing of the Rhine marks the end of one phase of the campaign and the beginning of another". British troops reach Mechelen. Wiesbaden in Allied hands.

28/3: General Eisenhower decides to change the plan and direction of the Allied advance: the final aim is no longer Berlin but Leipzig. The main burden of the battle will now be borne by the 12th Army Group together with the 1st, 3rd and 15th U.S. Armies, and no longer by Montgomery's 21st Army Group.

Soviet troops take Gdynia.

General Krebs replaces General Guderian as Chief of the German General Staff.

29/3: Canadian troops clear Emmerich despite heavy German resistance. Allied troops capture Mannheim, Duisburg and Marburg. U.S. 1st Army occupies Wetzlar and Giessen. Battles for Frankfort-on-Main cease.

French troops cross the Rhine near Germersheim.

30/3: Americans capture Heidelberg.

Soviet troops take Danzig. First Ukrainian Front overruns Ratibor in Upper Silesia.

30–31/3: U.S. troops draw up at the N. border of Wurtemberg Province.

31/3: Seventh U.S. Army advances into the Wuerzburg–Schweinfurt–Kitzingen sector. French troops invade Baden.

Heavy artillery fire to the north, south and west of Breslau. The city in flames.

Volkssturm men securing a street-crossing.

Goebbels in recaptured Lauban.

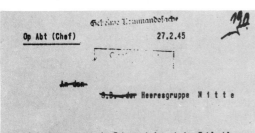

Op Abt (Chef)   27.2.45

_____
_____\

an den

O.B. der Heeresgruppe M i t t e

1.) Die sowjetische Führung hat nach dem Fehlschlagen
des raschen Durchstoßes über Oder und Lausitzer
Neiße nach Westen sich unter starkem Umgruppieren
offenbar entschlossen, durch Angriff in südlicher
und südwestlicher Richtung die deutschen Kräfte
in Schlesien in die schlesisch-böhmischen Rand-
gebirge zurückzuwerfen, um damit jede Bedrohung
der tiefen Südflanke auszuschalten. Die schnelle
Inbesitznahme der Industriegebiete um Mähr.Ostrau
und Waldenburg wird dabei gleichzeitig verfolgt.

2.) Es ist Aufgabe der Heeresgruppe Mitte, unter
wendigem Einsatz der zugeführten Panzerverbände
in begrenzten Offensivstößen die planmäßige Be-
reitstellung des Feindes zum Großangriff immer
wieder zu zerschlagen. Hierzu stimme ich das für
die ersten März-Tage beabsichtigten Angriff der
Heeresgruppe beiderseits Lauban zu.

3.) Nach dem Freikämpfen der über Lauban auf Hirschberg führenden Bahn ist der Kampf der Heeresgruppe Mitte so zu führen, daß ohne jeden Zeit-
verlust mit starken Kräften zum Entsatz der

- 2 -

- 2 -

Festung Breslau angegriffen werden kann, um
dabei sich baldigst in den Besitz der Oder-Linie
Oppeln - Breslau zu setzen.

4.) Die Abwehr an der Lausitzer Neiße ist durch
Einsatz starker Flak-Verbände und durch Aus-
schöpfen aller nur denkbaren Aushilfen so zu
festigen, daß auch nach Wegzug der Eingreif-
verbände die erfolgreiche Verteidigung dieses
Abschnittes gewährleistet bleibt.

Teleprinter message from Operational Division to German Army Group Centre. The enemy counter-offensive must be stopped and Breslau must be relieved. All available forces to be thrown into the operation.

GERMAN COUNTER-OFFENSIVE
AT LAUBAN IN SILESIA 1–5 March 1945

Canadian troops preparing to attack Weeze. (Weeze and Crefeld fell on 2 March.)

Allied troops advancing in the wake of a flame-thrower attack.

German Volkssturm prisoners.

U.S. 9TH AND CANADIAN 1ST ARMIES LINK UP BETWEEN THE RIVERS MAAS AND RHINE

3 March 1945

General Eisenhower's non-fraternization order

By Ernest Leiser, Stars and Stripes *Staff Writer*

On 5 March, at the beginning of a three-week lull before what was to be the final death blow at the Wehrmacht, a *Stars and Stripes* dispatch from the Rhineland said that Gen. Eisenhower's orders forbidding fraternization were getting their first real test.

"Today, in the 25-mile wide Roer–Rhine strip," the dispatch read, "the minor problems of Aachen have suddenly become big ones. In many towns civilians cluster round U.S. soldiers, just as they did in liberated countries. Most of them seem determined to make friends . . . Soldiers react quickly when they meet friendly people, especially if the people are pretty young girls. Some soldiers though objectively agreeing that fraternization is wrong, subjectively long for non-GI companionship. Some others don't care. To them non-fraternization is just a brass-imposed problem, they say, and they'll fraternize so long as they think there is a good chance they won't get caught. There are a great many Germans around. At the moment they are friendly and the soldiers are lonely. The enforcement of the rule, for a while at least, will be lax." The article concluded: "Thus non-fraternization will be, in considerable measure, an individual problem. How the GIs work out the problem for themselves may prove to be the acid test for the non-fraternization order."

U.S. troops in Blatzheim, on the road leading to Cologne.

Germans resisting in an isolated pocket.

Ninth Army officers discussing the next attack.

ADVANCE ON XANTEN 4 March 1945

Canadian troops north of Sonsbeck.
Neuss fell on 4 March, Euskirchen and Xanten on 5 March

GENERAL DE GAULLE CALLS FOR RHINE CROSSING
4 March 1945

General de Gaulle's views on the strategic and tactical factors influencing a Rhine crossing by the French First Army

On March 4 I received General de Lattre in Paris and explained that for reasons of national interest his army must cross the Rhine. De Lattre asked nothing better but observed—and rightly—that his sector, lying opposite the mountainous Black Forest region for its entire length along the right bank, was poorly equipped to effect a crossing by force. The operation would be a hazardous one against an enemy occupying the fortifications of the Siegfried Line in the valley and entrenched in dominating positions further to the rear; particularly since the Allied command was going to allocate the French forces only a minimum of munitions.

Furthermore, even if our men succeeded in surmounting this first obstacle, they would then have to penetrate a most difficult region, rising in successive ramparts of peaks and forests and ill-suited for manoeuvring and strategy.

"On the other hand," de Lattre pointed out, "once the French front is enlarged towards the north to include both Lauterbourg and Speyer along the Rhine, we shall have better prospects. Actually, my army would find an advantageous base in this area, the right bank would be relatively easy to reach, and once the river was crossed, my left wing would be able to drive through the Pforzheim gap towards Stuttgart and bypass the natural fortress of the Black Forest on the north and east." Preparing in advance arguments which he drew from comradeship as well as from tactics in order to convince the Allied command, de Lattre assured me that in the next few days he would extend his sector as far as Speyer.

Furthermore, as frequently happens in arguments among allies, the enemy himself was to make matters easier for us. On March 7, General Bradley's troops had seized the bridge at Remagen, between Coblenz and Bonn, astonishingly enough still intact, and had immediately assured a bridgehead on the right bank. Consequently the Germans now opposed us on the left bank below Coblenz with only scattered resistance, and by the twelfth the Allies had reached the Rhine everywhere north of the Moselle. But south of this river the situation was not the same. The vast Saar salient remained in German hands. The enemy, covered on his right by the course of the Moselle, held the Siegfried Line along the Treves–Saarbruecken–Lauterbourg front, which was deeper and better fortified in this sector than in any other. Before he could bring his new army groups to the right bank, General Eisenhower would first have to liquidate this pocket. The battle was to be a hard one; although the French First Army was not asked to do so, since the engagement occurred outside its normal zone, it nevertheless found means of participating, operating along the Rhine on the Americans' right and also seizing, on the river's Palatine bank, the desired base of operations from which to invade Baden and Wurtemberg.

German prisoners in captured Dormagen on 5 March.

General Jean de Lattre de Tassigny, Commander of the French 1st Army.

Volkssturm man lying in wait for Soviet tanks.

ROKOSSOVSKI AND ZHUKOV REACH THE BALTIC COAST

4 March 1945

Whoever refuses to fight will be rubbed out

Fight like Red Indians, attack like lions! Be cunning! Fire until you have spent your last cartridge, until the last blow! Every trick to hold your position and to beat the Bolshevik is good and fair. There is no turning back. Whoever refuses to fight and runs away will be rubbed out! Kill all cowards, wise-acres and pessimists!

The District Leader of Koenigsberg
on 2 March 1945.

◀ Graudenz capitulates on 6 March.

Soviet troops advance on Koeslin. ▼

The Baltic is cut off from the West. A straggler fleeing to the north along the frozen *Haff*.

Official Nazi paper reporting "successes" in E. Prussia on 11 March 1945, shortly before the encirclement of Danzig.

German soldiers in the Pyritz sector. The town was taken by the Red Army on 4 March.

Bormann calling for 6,000 boys of the 1929 class and for the setting up of a woman's battalion—with the Fuehrer's permission.

One of the last postage stamps issued by the "Greater German Reich". "A nation rises up in arms".—The food supply goes from bad to worse. Ration cards are no longer honoured in many places.

THE CLASS OF 1929 CALLED UP

5 March 1945

"Hundreds of thousands of lads like him . . ."

From a speech by Secretary of State Werner Naumann on 23 March 1945 in Munich:

A 12-year-old German boy approached a Canadian soldier and begged him for chocolate in broken English. I can just imagine the soldier replying: "Hallo boy, here, chocolate, chocolate". And according to Reuter, the foolish Canadian began to rummage in his pockets. At this moment, the boy drew a pistol and shot the Canadian in the stomach. That, they claimed, was all you can expect of Germany's youth. Demoralized and wild. All I can say is: give us hundreds of thousands of lads like him, and we shall win the war!

Playing fast and loose with the "Flower of the Nation".

On 9 March 1945, Erich Kaestner made the following entry in his diary (Notabene 45).

Today's leading article in the *Voelkischer Beobachter* has been perpetrated by one Lt. Karl Heinz Stockhausen. Yet he is not the real criminal. He is only a bloody puppet. He can neither write nor think, but that is not his fault. Perhaps he is a young hero. In any case he is quite green. The real wire-pullers, who have long since taken to their heels or put an end to their miserable lives, have told him that all is fair so long as it helps to postpone the end.

"Our young soldiers", the article is headed. Karl Heinz—strains of ye good old student corps days—writes: "Young soldiers, remember you have nothing to lose! Or do any of you really believe that life under a hail of enemy bombs, in panic fear of the enemy's barbarities is worth preserving? The enemy wages war remorselessly! He, too, has thrown boys into battle. But these boys, who have had their wits dulled by Bolshevism from an early age and who have grown up as a herd of sheep, cannot hold a candle to you, who have proved your fine mettle in the Hitler Youth!"

And so, although they know it all is to no avail, the Nazis get one adolescent to incite the rest. Could anyone beat them at their game of playing fast and loose with the "flower of the nation"? They remind 17-year-old boys of their days in the Hitler Youth. But they keep discreetly silent about the Hitler Youth Division, because it is no more. It was armed with anti-tank mines, meant to stick to Russian armour. The mines were a fiasco. They refused to stick to anything. And so the children had to run beside the steel juggernauts and press the explosives against the wall until they and the tanks were both blown sky-high . . .

Fifteen-year-old German "soldiers" in captivity. Youngsters found the collapse of a world built on lies particularly hard to bear. ▶

SHAEF reported on 6 March that Allied troops had entered Cologne.

Film still of street-fighting in Cologne. The cathedral can be seen in the background.

THE FALL OF COLOGNE

6 March 1945

The Remagen Bridge

By Milton Shulman

7 March had seen a splendid *coup de main* by a few enterprising men of the U.S. 1st Army, who, seizing the chance of a moment, rushed the bridge at Remagen and unexpectedly provided the Allies with their first bridgehead across the Rhine. This stroke disorganised the Germans and drew off forces waiting to oppose the massive blow impending to the north. A small armoured spearhead of the 9th U.S. Armour Division, reaching the crest of a hill overlooking Remagen, was astonished to see below it, still standing and apparently undamaged, the Ludendorff railway bridge spanning the Rhine. With the dash and courage of men who make history, an American platoon charged into the town and made its way to the bridge. Hardly had they reached it when two of the demolition charges exploded, damaging the easternmost span of the bridge but leaving the roadway intact. Despite these warnings the American infantry continued on over the bridge, while engineers quickly cut the wires controlling the remaining charges. At four o'clock that afternoon 1st U.S. Army had crossed the Rhine! . . .

Under pain of death, a special (German) engineer regiment had been made responsible for seeing that the bridge was blown up before the Americans threatened it. But, as in the case of General Schlemm in the Reichswald, no bridge was to be demolished too soon, since fleeing German units would otherwise be cut off from their final escape route. At Cologne a bridge prepared for demolition had been prematurely blown up by bombs falling in the neighbourhood, and as a result a large German force had been trapped and captured west of the river. It had therefore been ordered that no charge was to be placed on a bridge until the very last moment . . . Surprised and dumbfounded, the Germans watched the Americans pouring across the Rhine, too helpless to do anything but gape.

(Flower 981)

The intact Ludendorff Bridge near Remagen. The German officers who failed to blow it up were executed. ▶

First U.S. ARMY CROSS THE RHINE NEAR REMAGEN

7 March 1945

"Brad, we've gotten a bridge!"

By General O. Bradley

Suddenly my phone rang. It was Hodges calling from Spa.

"Brad," he called, with more composure than the good news warranted, "Brad, we've gotten a bridge."

"A bridge? You mean you've got one intact on the Rhine?"

"Yep," Hodges replied, "Leonard nabbed the one at Remagen before they blew it up—"

"Hot dog, Courtney," I said, "this will bust him wide open. Are you getting your stuff across?"

"Just as fast as we can push it over," he said. "Tubby's got the Navy moving in now with a ferry service and I'm having the engineers throw a couple of spare pontoon bridges across to the bridgehead."

I pulled the long lead wire from my phone over towards the map-board. "Shove everything you can across it, Courtney," I said, "and button the bridgehead up tightly. It'll probably take the other fellow a couple of days to pull enough stuff together to hit you."

Before the Germans could counter-attack, the American bridgehead was extended and further troops were rushed across the river.

AMERICANS IN BONN
8 March 1945

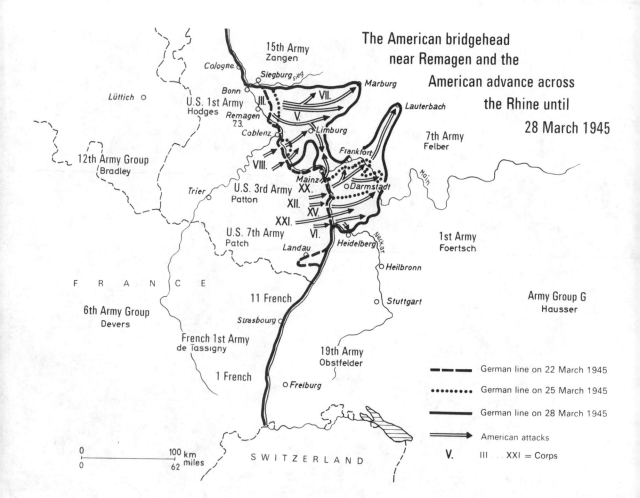

The American bridgehead
near Remagen and the
American advance across
the Rhine until
28 March 1945

15th Army
Zangen

Cologne

Siegburg Sieg

Marburg

Lüttich O

Bonn

VII.

Lauterbach

U.S. 1st Army
Hodges

III.

Remagen
7.3.

V.

7th Army
Felber

Coblenz

Limburg

12th Army Group
Bradley

VIII.

Frankfort

Mainz

Trier

U.S. 3rd Army
Patton

XX.

O Darmstadt

XII.

XV.

XXI.

U.S. 7th Army
Patch

VI.

1st Army
Foertsch

Landau

Heidelberg

Neckar

F R A N C E

O Heilbronn

6th Army Group
Devers

11 French

O Stuttgart

Army Group G
Hausser

Strasbourg O

French 1st Army
de Tassigny

19th Army
Obstfelder

1 French

O Freiburg

German line on 22 March 1945

German line on 25 March 1945

German line on 28 March 1945

American attacks

S W I T Z E R L A N D

V.   III . . . XXI = Corps

0   100 km
0   62 miles

Nr. 327, Freitag,
9. März 1945

NACHRICHTEN FÜR DIE TRUPPE

Eisenhower geht über den Rhein

Starke USA-Kräfte fassen auf dem rechten Ufer Fuss

DER schwerste Schlag gegen die Verteidigung des Reiches im Westen seit der Landung der Alliierten in der Normandie ist jetzt am Rhein

"News for the Troops" reporting U.S. Rhine crossing.

Bonn and Bad Godesberg in U.S. hands (8 March).

American soldiers streaming through Remagen on their way across the Rhine.

HEROES' DAY. HITLER VISITS THE EASTERN FRONT

Goering representing Hitler at the celebrations in Berlin, at about the same time that 21,000 German soldiers were being marched off into captivity at the Rhine. In Hitler's order on the occasion of "Heroes' Day", we can read: "In history, only those fall by the wayside who have been judged and found wanting . . ."

The Himmler–Kersten Agreement on Concentration Camp Prisoners

On 12 March 1945 Himmler, in a darkened room of the SS Sanatorium at Hohenlychen, signed the following agreement in the presence of Kersten and Brandt. Himmler himself added the heading:

Agreement in the name of humanity

It was decided:

1. That concentration camps will not be blown up.
2. On the approach of Allied troops, a white flag will be hoisted.
3. No more Jews will be killed, and Jews will be treated like other prisoners.
4. Sweden is allowed to send food parcels to individual Jewish prisoners.

Signed Himmler

Kersten (Himmler's physician)

On "Heroes' Day", Hitler saw fit to neglect his onerous duties as Supreme Commander and visited his troops in the Oder sector.

GENERAL WEISS BECOMES
C.-IN-C. ARMY GROUP NORTH

12 March 1945

General Weiss, the new Commander of East Prussia.

Fighting has again flared up outside Stettin. Soviet attempts to break through the defence belt in the S. sector have been frustrated, after minor advances by the enemy. 59 Soviet tanks have been destroyed.

The Kolberg garrison, effectively supported by the Navy, is holding out against overwhelming enemy forces.

In W. Prussia, our troops have been able to resist strong enemy pressure S.E. of Braunsberg and S.W. of Koenigsberg in continuous heavy battles. Our troops have breached the enemy front in several places, thus repulsing the Soviet offensive. 146 of the 200 Soviet tanks thrown into the attack have been destroyed. German fighters have shot down 30 enemy planes in heavy air battles.

On 12 March, Soviet troops captured Kuestrin, while heavy battles continued round the German Oder-bridgehead near Stettin. The photograph shows German anti-aircraft guns arriving at the Oder.

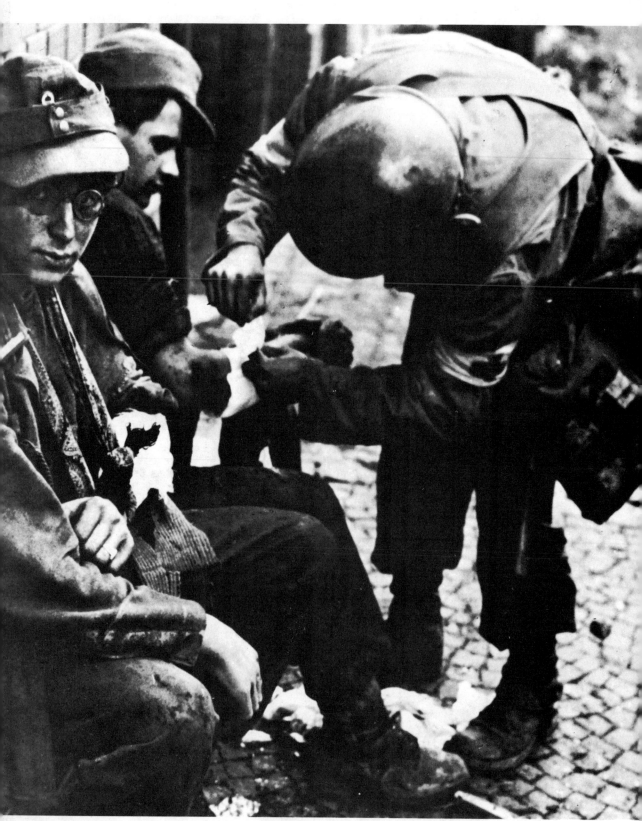

U.S. medical orderly rendering first-aid to German prisoners captured by U.S. 7th Army.

Troops of U.S. 3rd Army crossing the Moselle S.W. of Coblenz, while U.S. 7th Army launches Operation "Overtone" against the Siegfried defences.

Constant Allied air-attacks undermined the morale of the retreating German army.

U.S. 3RD ARMY CROSSES THE MOSELLE NEAR COBLENZ

15 March 1945

From the Wehrmacht bulletin of 16 March 1945:

The battle between the rivers Moselle, Saar and Rhine continues. South of Bad Muenster-am-Stein, enemy armour has been stopped by our reserves. In the Bad Kreuznach sector, the enemy tried to tighten his hold to the E. and S.W. but was opposed by German reinforcements brought into the area. In S. Hunsrueck, on the lower and middle Saar, the battle continues against enemy forces advancing from the N.W., particularly in the Birkenfeld sector. Near Saarbruecken and on either side of Hagenau, enemy pressure has abated, but N.E. of Saargemuend our defences are under heavy attack.

Extensive attacks by American terror-planes have caused widespread damage to Reich territory, and especially to villages in Thuringia and Saxony. British planes have dropped bombs on several towns in Rhenish Westphalia during daylight attacks. At night, Berlin and Nuremberg were raided by strong British formations.

After an air raid on a Palatine village. ▶

Preparing for their last great offensive, Soviet troops throw a pontoon bridge across the Oder.

Frankfurt-on-Oder is turned into a fortified town. The garrison commander supervising the erection of a tank barrier.

German soldiers and foreign auxiliaries advancing under the protection of the town walls.

GERMAN DEFENCE ON THE ODER AND SOVIET OFFENSIVE IN SILESIA

15 March 1945

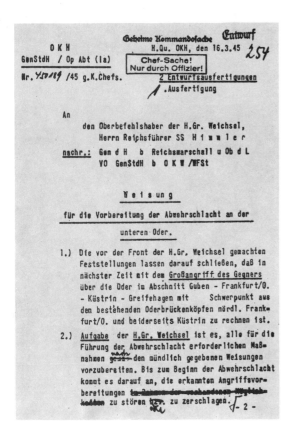

General Staff Memo to Himmler: Army Group Vistula, under Himmler's command, must prepare to meet a major Soviet thrust across the Oder.

Foreign auxiliaries in house-to-house fights. Soviet spearheads meet in Neustadt on 18 March 1945.

COBLENZ, WORMS, KAISER-LAUTERN AND SAAR-BRUECKEN FALL TO THE AMERICANS

18–20 March 1945

General Patch, Commander of U.S. 7th Army.

German defenders in Lueben.

U.S. soldiers storming a village.

Spearheads of the U.S. 3rd and 7th Armies effecting a junction. The Frankfurt–Cologne Autobahn is cut.

VÖLKISCHER ❋ BEOBACHTER

Münchener Ausgabe
33. Ausgabe / 58. Jahrgang / Einzelpreis 15 Rpf.

"Freiheit und Brot!"

Münchener Ausgabe
München, Spezialnummer März 1945

Kampfblatt der nationalsozialistischen Bewegung
Großdeutschlands

«Auf nach Sibirien!»?

Die Urheber des Unglücks der Welt

"Morsche Knochen..."

Soll das deutsche Volk ausgerottet werden? Ja!

Copy of Allied pamphlet dropped in the guise of a special edition of the *Voelkischer Beobachter*, the official Nazi paper. The pamphlet suggests that the German "offensive" against the Soviet Union will end in Siberia, that the Nazis are the sole cause of the world's misfortunes: that the German set-backs in the East are no more than Hitler's just desserts; and that the Nazis are determined to let the whole German nation perish.

German soldiers surrender in ever-increasing numbers. Photograph taken in the Trier sector.

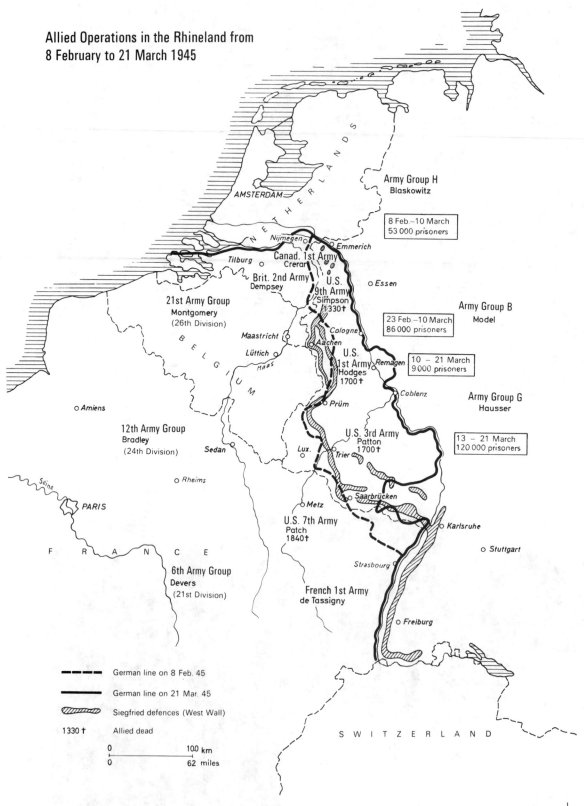

Allied Operations in the Rhineland from
8 February to 21 March 1945

Army Group H
Blaskowitz

8 Feb.–10 March
53 000 prisoners

AMSTERDAM

N E T H E R L A N D S

Nijmegen

Emmerich

Canad. 1st Army
Crerar

Tilburg

Brit. 2nd Army
Dempsey

U.S.
9th Army
Simpson
1330†

Essen

Army Group B
Model

23 Feb.–10 March
86 000 prisoners

21st Army Group
Montgomery
(26th Division)

B E L G I U M

Maastricht

Lüttich

Cologne

Aachen

U.S.
1st Army
Hodges
1700†

Remagen

10 – 21 March
9 000 prisoners

Maas

Amiens

Coblenz

Army Group G
Hausser

Prüm

12th Army Group
Bradley
(24th Division)

Sedan

Lux.

U.S. 3rd Army
Patton
1700†

Trier

13 – 21 March
120 000 prisoners

Rheims

Seine

PARIS

Metz

Saarbrücken

Karlsruhe

U.S. 7th Army
Patch
1840†

Stuttgart

F   R   A   N   C   E

6th Army Group
Devers
(21st Division)

Strasbourg

French 1st Army
de Tassigny

Freiburg

German line on 8 Feb. 45

German line on 21 Mar. 45

Siegfried defences (West Wall)

1330†   Allied dead

0 ————— 100 km
0 ————— 62 miles

S W I T Z E R L A N D

Hitler ventures from his bunker to decorate children who have rendered distinguished service at the front. Secretary of State Naumann had this to say on the subject: "It was one of the most moving situations I every witnessed. The youngest, a 12-year-old Hitler cub . . . had arrested a spy, and when Hitler asked him how he had discovered the man, he replied: 'He wore his corporal's stripe on the wrong arm, my Fuehrer' . . ."

HITLER'S LAST APPEARANCE
IN PUBLIC 20 March 1945

HITLER'S "NERO DECREE"

19 and 30 March 1945

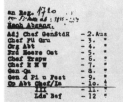

Hitler's detailed instructions on the implementation of his scorched earth policy. The instructions lay down conditions for the blowing up of industrial plant, bridges, roadworks and railway lines. Speer protested against the decree on 29 March.

KESSELRING APPOINTED C.-IN-C. WESTERN FORCES 22 March 1945

Field-Marshal Kesselring, who replaced Rundstedt, told his staff: "Gentlemen, I am Germany's new secret weapon."

U.S. troops crossing the Rhine south of Mainz on 22 March.

AMERICANS CROSS THE RHINE AT MAINZ 22 March 1945

The German High Command announced on 24 March:

The Mainz garrison has succeeded in fighting its way back to the right bank of the Rhine after heavy attacks. Using shock tank formations, the Americans have crossed the Rhine at Oppenheim and have established a small bridgehead.

Over the Rhine, then, let us go!

Montgomery's message to the Armies on 25 March 1945:

1. On the 7th February I told you we were going into the ring for the final and last round; there would be no time limit; we would continue fighting until our opponent was knocked out. The last round is going very well on both sides of the ring—and overhead.

2. In the West, the enemy has lost the Rhineland, and with it the flower of at least four armies—the Parachute Army, Fifth Panzer Army, Fifteenth Army, and Seventh Army; the First Army, further to the south, is now being added to the list.

In the Rhineland battles, the enemy has lost about 150,000 prisoners, and there are many more to come; his total casualties amount to about 250,000 since 8th February.

3. In the East, the enemy has lost all Pomerania east of the Oder, an area as large as the Rhineland; and three more German armies have been routed. The Russian armies are within about 35 miles of Berlin.

4. Overhead, the Allied Air Forces are pounding Germany day and night. It will be interesting to see how much longer the Germans can stand it.

5. The enemy has in fact been driven into a corner, and he cannot escape.

Events are moving rapidly.

The complete and decisive defeat of the Germans is certain; there is no possibility of doubt on this matter.

6. 21 ARMY GROUP WILL NOW CROSS THE RHINE.

The enemy possibly thinks he is safe behind this great river obstacle. We all agree that it is a great obstacle; but we will show the enemy that he is far from safe behind it. This great Allied fighting machine, composed of integrated land and air forces, will deal with the problem in no uncertain manner.

7. And having crossed the Rhine, we will crack about in the plains of Northern Germany, chasing the enemy from pillar to post. The swifter and the more energetic our action, the sooner the war will be over, and that is what we all desire; to get on with the job and finish off the German war as soon as possible.

8. Over the Rhine, then, let us go. And good hunting to you all on the other side.

9. May "the Lord mighty in battle" give us the victory in this our latest undertaking, as He has done in all our battles since we landed in Normandy on D-Day.

Allied airborne troops on their way to the East (top).
Right: Grave of a German airman shot down near the
Rhine on 21 March.

MONTGOMERY'S 21ST ARMY GROUP CROSSES THE RHINE NEAR WESEL

24 March 1945

Three Commanders of the 21st Army Group, from left to
right: Field-Marshal Montgomery, C.-in-C.; Major-
General John B. Andersen (U.S. 16th Army Corps) and
(extreme right) General W. H. Simpson (U.S. 9th Army). ▼

The British 6th and U.S. 17th Airborne Divisions, in the biggest airborne operation of the war, succeeded in landing great numbers of men and masses of supplies across the Rhine, at about 10 a.m. on 24 March 1945.

"Several Gliders were burning briskly . . ."

by Lieutenant-Colonel J. C. Watts, R.A.M.C.

A few parachutes failed to open, and one such landed a few feet away, the container, about four feet long and eighteen inches across, burying half its length in the ground with a squelchy thud. The landing zone looked rather like a fairground in process of closing down, the discarded parachutes resembling strung tents, and all the litter of war lying around. Only the still figures of the dead gave an air of grim reality to the scene. Several gliders were burning briskly, having been caught in a burst of machine-gun fire on landing, which had ignited the petrol in the jeep inside. The British glider was a better proposition than the American Waco, which was of fabric over a steel framework. If it crashed the occupants were trapped in a case, whereas the British Horsa, being of wood, could be quickly chopped through, although this was usually unnecessary, as it tended to fall apart.

I saw one burnt-out Waco with the charred bodies of the occupants, the whole looking for all the world as if some monster had set a birdcage on a bonfire.

Allied airborne troops suffered many casualties . . . ▶

◀ A wounded soldier of the U.S. 17th Airborne Division.

British troops crossing the Rhine at dawn on 24 March.

From the German High Command communiqué of 25 March 1945

On the Rhine front, between Rees and Dinslaken, our troops are fighting a heavy defensive battle against the attacking British 2nd Army and parts of the U.S. 9th Army. In several sectors, the enemy, who has suffered heavy casualties, was able to cross the Rhine and to break our main line. On either side of Wesel, where heavy street fighting is taking place, our troops were successful in throwing the enemy back to the banks of the Rhine.

Yesterday morning, British airborne troops landed to the rear of our positions in the Lower Rhine sector. Our units were able to shoot down 50 of the 121 transport gliders before they could land, and then launched an attack on the troops that had landed. Yesterday at noon, the Americans also landed strong airborne contingents between the Lower Lippe and the Lower Roer and these, too, were attacked from several quarters.

German alert. The last great battle in the West is about to begin.

Scottish troops disembarking near Wesel, on the east bank of the Rhine.

CHURCHILL ON THE RHINE 24 March 1945

German soldiers killed during an air attack.

Churchill, Lord Alanbrooke and Montgomery on the Rhine.

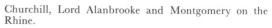

German paratroopers, Hitler's shock troops, being thrown in against the Allies.

WESEL FALLS TO THE ALLIES
24 March 1945

Wesel was almost totally destroyed during the battles.

Lt.-Colonel Ross, Commander of Wesel, in a P.O.W. camp.

After crossing the Rhine in the south, the U.S. 3rd and 7th Armies launched a general offensive east of the river.

Ludwigshafen was cleared of Germans on 24 March after heavy street-fighting lasting two days.

Despite strong resistance, U.S. tanks broke through to the Main.

U.S. 3RD AND 7TH ARMIES MAKE FURTHER RHINE CROSSINGS IN THE SOUTH

25–26 March 1945

Eisenhower's double envelopment theory.

From the diary of Field Marshal Viscount Alanbrooke

I had a talk with Ike on the question of the surrender of Kesselring and all the other purely military surrenders. He also wanted to know whether I agreed with his present plans of pushing in the south for Frankfurt and Kassel. I told him that, with the Germans crumbling as they are, the whole situation is now altered. Evidently the Boche is cracking and what we want now is to push him relentlessly, wherever we can, until he crumbles. In his present condition we certainly have the necessary strength for a double envelopment strategy, which I did not consider applicable when he was still in a position to resist seriously.

Refugees in the path of Soviet troops in E. Prussia. Kolberg has fallen.

RED ARMY CAPTURES GULF OF DANZIG AND HEILIGENBEIL 23–25 March 1945

Doenitz inspecting naval units serving with the infantry in the Oder sector (March 1945)

Foreign Minister von Ribbentrop venturing into a trench on the Oder front (March 1945)

On 25 March Heiligenbeil fell. The campaign ended with 80,000 Germans dead and 50,000 missing.

U.S. THIRD ARMY IN
FRANKFURT-ON-MAIN

26 March 1945

On 26 March American troops entered Frankfurt across the Niederrad bridge in the South.

In the North, British and Canadian troops advanced along the Lower Rhine. For one German soldier, here being led off in the village of Brunen, the war was over.

On 24 March German paratroops put up a stubborn resistance round Rees (shown in the picture).

GERMAN COLLAPSE IN THE WEST

27 March 1945

Eisenhower: "Unconditional surrender but only by force"

On 27 March, General Eisenhower declared in a Press interview at SHAEF, Paris, that the Germans in the West were a "whipped army". He emphasised, however, that it was not yet time to "ring the bells" and that the enemy could form a defensive line in Central Germany at a point where Allied supply lines were stretched out, though he did not believe that the German resistance could be prolonged. He added that unconditional surrender would not be achieved by negotiation but only by forces.

"We can't shoot everybody . . ."

From the diary of Major-General Stemmermann

Late on 24 March, Gauleiter Sprenger gave orders to evacuate the entire population of Frankfurt-on-Main. Along roads threatened by artillery fire, low-flying aircraft and American armour! And it was with this masterpiece of improvisation, so beloved of the Party, that the provincial governor decided to terminate his work for the good of his capital . . . Soon afterwards, came reports that the majority of the population had no intention of heeding his orders. "They'll just have to stay then," the Party officer said. "After all, we can't shoot everybody who disobeys the order." And so the leaders decamped, leaving their offices in a state of utter chaos and confusion.

"News for the Troops" reporting German collapse in the West. The map shows areas subject to "merciless bombardment" by the Allies, together with the seven safety zones for which civilians were urged to leave without delay by General Eisenhower.

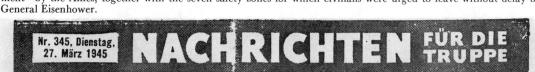

Auflösung im Westen

Front bricht von Emmerich bis Karlsruhe

AN der gesamten Rheinfront von Emmerich bis hinunter nach Karlsruhe ist seit gestern abend nach den letzten Meldungen die deutsche Abwehr im gleichen Stadium der Auflösung wie unmittelbar vor dem völligen Zusammenbruch in Frankreich.

Während im Norden massierte Panzer- und Infanteriekräfte der Alliierten die deutsche Verteidigung unter Einsatz einer noch nie dagewesenen Materialüberlegenheit zertrümmern und bereits mehr als 30 km ostwärts des Rheins stehen, rasen im Süden Panzerspitzen der Alliierten bereits auf bayrischem Gebiet nach allen Richtungen vor, ohne auf geordneten Widerstand zu stossen.

Aschaffenburg wurde überrannt, kaum 12 Stunden nach dem Fall von Darmstadt. Die Mainbrücke in Aschaffenburg fiel den Amerikanern unzerstört in die Hand und USA-Panzerspitzen schwärmen ostwärts des Mains in Richtung Würzburg vor. Auch die Mainbrücken von Hanau und Seligenstadt sind in alliierter Hand.

Lebensmittel-

THE DEFENCE OF BRESLAU, MARCH 1945

General Hermann
Niehoff, the last
Commander of
Breslau garrison

Tank Army Supreme Command 1	Army H.Q.
1st Adjutant	2 March 1945; 12:15 a.m.

To Major-General Niehoff

I am ordered to inform you that General Schoerner proposes to entrust you with an exceedingly difficult task. The scope of the new command far exceeds that of a Commanding Officer. The decision will be made this evening and, moreover, by the highest power in the land . . .

A Volkssturm man in Breslau

From the diary of Emil Heinze

13–14 March: Carried sandbags in the Railway Administration Building. The whole place is being transformed into a strong point. The sanctified halls, which few ordinary mortals were formerly allowed to enter, have been cleared of all their contents, in case they go up in flames. All the furniture, records, etc. have been thrown into the ponds in the marshes. The allotments near the marshes have been levelled, so as to give our riflemen a clear field. Whole suburbs have been razed, in an attempt to rob the enemy of cover. A guard has been posted on a nearby hill, to sound a piercing whistle on the approach of enemy aircraft. We had to come and go through the defunct railway station. The main entrance was full of corpses.

16th March: R. got me leave today. When I returned in the evening the sergeant reproached me, saying that my substitute had been killed in my absence. I offered sincere apologies for remaining alive, and was able to console him.

26–27 March: Transferred to the sanitary company. Chief task: clearing rubble and digging out corpses.

Early April: Easter brought the heaviest air-raids yet. Entire suburbs destroyed. On 9 April we saw an 8 mm. film in the sick bay. It was called Holiday from Yourself.

Until the surrender in May . . .

. . . every house in Breslau had to be taken by force

A transport ship being unloaded in Libau, Courland.

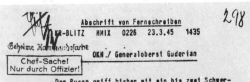

THE BATTLE FOR COURLAND

March 1945

General Rendulic,
Commander of Army
Group Courland
from 12 March 1945

The Sixth Courland Battle

On 18 March, Soviet forces launched a new attack on Frauenburg. The sixth Courland battle had begun. After prolonged hand-to-hand fighting, the German line gave way. The Germans then decided to make a last-ditch stand. The 12th Infantry Division went over to a counter-attack, and on 23 March broke the striking power of the Soviets. Early in April, the battle fizzled out, with the Soviets having gained slight ground but failing to reach their objective. Soviet losses: 533 prisoners, 263 tanks, 249 machine guns, 185 guns, 29 mortars and 27 aircraft. No further attack was launched in April, the Red Army awaiting further developments in the Reich itself.

General Rendulic warning General Guderian of the dangers to the German forces in Courland: extended lines, lack of reserves and shortage of ammunition all favour the enemy.

View from look-out across the Oder

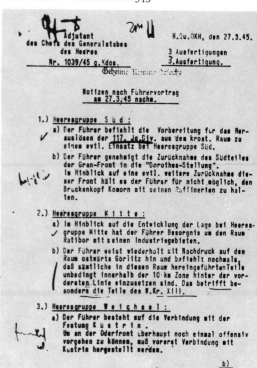

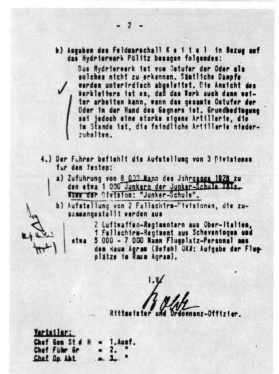

German bridgehead being reinforced across a bridge in Stettin.

Memorandum prepared by Capt. Gerhard Boldt (acting adjutant to the Chief of the German General Staff) after Hitler's address of 27 March. Army Group South may withdraw to prepared positions; Army Group Centre must hold the Ratibor sector; Army Group Vistula must keep the road to Duestrin open; 3 new divisions must be formed for service at the Western Front.

German troops withdrawing near Jaegendorf in Silesia.

THE SOVIET ADVANCE IN SILESIA

The Red Army in Neisse, Upper Silesia

From the report of a priest

Early on Saturday, before Palm Sunday (24 March) the Russians entered Neisse, a town in Upper Silesia with a population of 40,000. Some 20 priests and lay-brothers together with some 200 nuns stayed behind to care for the old and infirm. 2,000 civilians also elected to stay on. Despite an eight-day siege and constant bombardment, Neisse was still relatively intact . . . Like a flood, the Red Army poured into the town. They also broke into our house, where they immediately took all our watches and other valuables. They demanded the sacramental wine and then broke up all the furniture. They did not even spare the altar in the cellar, on which we had just celebrated Holy Mass, and snatched up all our chalices and monstrances. Girls and women, including nuns, were raped continuously, with the Red Army men, led by their officers, queueing up before their victims. During the first night alone, many nuns and other women were raped no less than 50 times. The nuns, who resisted with all their strength, were either shot down, or else beaten until they were too exhausted to continue the struggle.

That was the night when they drove us all out. After a long march, we arrived at a small village and were herded into a tiny room, where we could neither sit nor lie down. Next day, the priests were interrogated, one by one, by a Secret Police (GPU) Officer. He was a lecturer on Leninism at Leningrad University. He tried to win us over for propaganda work, and promised us large churches and influential positions if only we would collaborate. His standard of education may be gathered from his question whether the Pope was a Catholic or a Protestant. After checking up on our activities during the last ten years, he had all of us sent further back from the front.

From Kaps: *Die Trägodie Schlesiens 1945/46* (The Tragedy of Silesia 1945–46), Munich, 1962.

". . . How our soldiers deal with the German women."

From the letter of a Russian soldier

I am sitting here writing a letter to you, my Hanka. I offer you, dear Hanka, my right hand, and kiss you on your sweet mouth . . .

As to the front, you know what is happening there just as well as I do. I am near Koenigsberg right now . . .

Now I should like to tell you how our soldiers deal with the German women. These women are having a terrible time. The men are not so badly off, but the women have it very hard. That's because of the soldiers. One holds them down, while another has his will with them. Some of the women could not stand it and died, so that leading personalities had to calm their menfolk down, for the whole thing was indescribable.

People are well off here. Although the soil is sandy, they live better than we do at home. When you come into a house, you simply don't know where to look first. There are so many good things. Almost every house has a piano. Something to make music on. About as big as a table. Pity I don't understand the German language. When they talk to me, I open my eyes wide and just stand there gawping like a sheep. Still, there is a lot of misery about. They put poison into their food and drink, and many of them have died. When they drink poisoned schnapps, they live for about 20 hours before they die.

From Zenter: *Illustr. Geschichte des Zweiten Weltkrieges* (Illustr. History of the Second World War)

EISENHOWER'S FATEFUL DECISION: LEIPZIG INSTEAD OF BERLIN

28 March 1945

Churchill (left) was disconcerted to learn that Eisenhower (right) was prepared to leave Berlin to the Russians and told him: "I deem it highly important that we should shake hands with the Russians as far to the east as possible . . ."

Montgomery: "I think we are making a terrible mistake . . ."

Eisenhower's decision and its consequences

Yet on that very day, without reference to the Combined Chiefs of Staff or a word to the Commander-in-Chief British forces which still constituted nearly a third of his army, Eisenhower despatched a telegram to Stalin informing him that he proposed, after encircling the Ruhr, to concentrate in Central Germany for an advance, on an Erfurt-Leipzig axis, towards the Upper Elbe, there to await the arrival of the Russians. His object, he explained, was to cut Germany in half, separate the northern defenders from the southern and thereafter concentrate his main forces against the supposed "National Redoubt" in the Austrian Alps, in which, it was rumoured, Hitler and the Nazi fanatics intended to hold out until new secret weapons or a split in the Grand Alliance came to their aid . . .

Montgomery who was all set to go on to Berlin and now had to abandon his plan, wrote in his Memoirs: "I had always put Berlin as a priority objective; it was a political centre and if we could beat the Russians to it things would be much easier for us in the post-war years. It will be remembered that in his letter to me dated the 15th September 1944, Eisenhower had agreed with me about the great importance of the German capital, and had said: 'Clearly, Berlin is the main prize' . . .

But now he did not agree. His latest view was expressed in a message he sent me on 31st March 1945 which ended with the following sentence: 'You will note that in none of this do I mention Berlin. That place has become, so far as I am concerned, nothing but a geographical location, and I have never been interested in these. My purpose is to destroy the enemy's forces and his powers to resist.' It was useless for me to pursue the matter further. We had had so much argument on great issues already . . ."

Personal Message to Marshal Stalin from General Eisenhower on 28 March 1945:

1. My immediate operations are designed to encircle and destroy the enemy forces defending the Ruhr, and to isolate that area from the rest of Germany. This will be accomplished by developing around north of the Ruhr and from Frankfurt through Kassel line until I close the ring. The enemy thus enclosed will then be mopped up.

2. I estimate that this phase of operations will end late in April or even earlier, and my next task will be to divide the remaining enemy forces by joining hands with your forces.

3. For my forces the best axis on which to effect this junction would be Erfurt-Leipzig-Dresden. I believe, moreover, that this is the area to which main German governmental departments are being moved. It is along this axis that I propose to make my main effort. In addition, as soon as the situation allows, a secondary advance will be made to effect a junction with your forces in the area Regensburg-Linz, thereby preventing the consolidation of German resistance in Redoubt in Southern Germany.

4. Before deciding firmly on my plans, it is, I think, most important they should be co-ordinated as closely as possible with yours both as to direction and timing. Could you, therefore, tell me your intentions and let me know how far the proposals outlined in this message conform tó your probable action.

5. If we are to complete the destruction of German armies without delay, I regard it as essential that we co-ordinate our action and make every effort to perfect the liaison between our advancing forces. I am prepared to send officers to you for this purpose.

At the same time that Eisenhower made his fateful decision, the U.S. 7th Army entered Heidelberg.

HITLER DISMISSES GUDERIAN FROM HIS POST AS CHIEF OF THE ARMY GENERAL STAFF 28 March 1945

Hitler and his General Staff

The events leading to Guderian's dismissal

On 28 March, Guderian and Busse were summoned to the Reichs Chancellery. After an icy greeting, Busse was ordered to make his report on the impending offensive in Kuestrin. Busse had hardly begun, when Hitler let fly a string of irrelevant abuse. His irate remarks were directed not only at Busse but at the attacking troops as well. — Then Guderian raised his powerful and loud voice and cut Hitler short. Controlling his emotion, he presented his prepared report, flinging every word at Hitler with clear deliberation. He rejected all Hitler's insinuations as to the campaign, the officers and the men. Hitler could not get a word in edgeways . . .

Then Hitler jerked out of his chair, with an agility that no one present would have credited. His face was purple. His left arm, and indeed the entire left half of his body, shook more violently than ever before, and it seemed as if he were about to hurl himself at Guderian. The General froze, and so did everyone else. For seconds, there was a deadly hush, broken only by the heavy breathing of the two men. Then words gushed out of Hitler's mouth. Recriminations and insults followed in quick succession. Kuestrin and the Oder were completely forgotten. The stream of abuse took in the entire General Staff, the entire Officers' Corps. Every setback during the past few months was laid at their door. Once again, the unbridgeable gulf between Hitler and the General Staff, between the old Officers' Corps and the Party was made manifest. The two were worlds apart. Guderian, too, became more and more incensed, repeating his old complaints against Hitler's military leadership, and quite particularly against the refusal to call off the Ardennes offensive until it was too late; the abandonment of the Courland Front and the withdrawal of 23 divisions; the unforgivable weakening of the Western Front in favour of the Eastern; the deployment of troops in the Lake Balaton offensive, and Hitler's unwarranted desertion of the population of E. Germany.

At this point, the assembled company awoke from the trance into which this unique, macabre scene had transported tham all. Major von Freytag-Loringhoven, Guderian's adjutant, expected the immediate arrest of his chief. He hastened to the telephone in the anteroom, rang up General Krebs, and implored him to summon Guderian to the telephone and keep him there discussing some news from the front or other . . .

At the end of the meeting, Hitler asked Keitel and Guderian to stay behind. Guderian was relieved of his post and granted leave of absence. Two days later, on 30 March, after handing over to his successor, General Krebs, Guderian finally left the German H.Q. at Zossen.

From Boldt: *Die letzten Tage der Reichskanzlei*
(The last days of the Reich Chancellery)

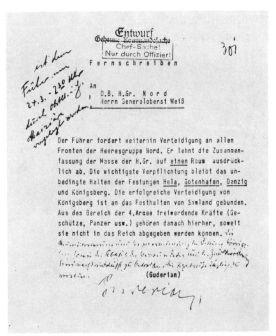

Draft of a teleprinter message by Guderian to General Weiss, questioning Hitler's decision to refuse the concentration of Army Group G into a single sector.

General Guderian, who succeeded Zeitzler as Chief of the General Staff, was himself dismissed by Hitler, and succeeded by General Krebs on 28 March.

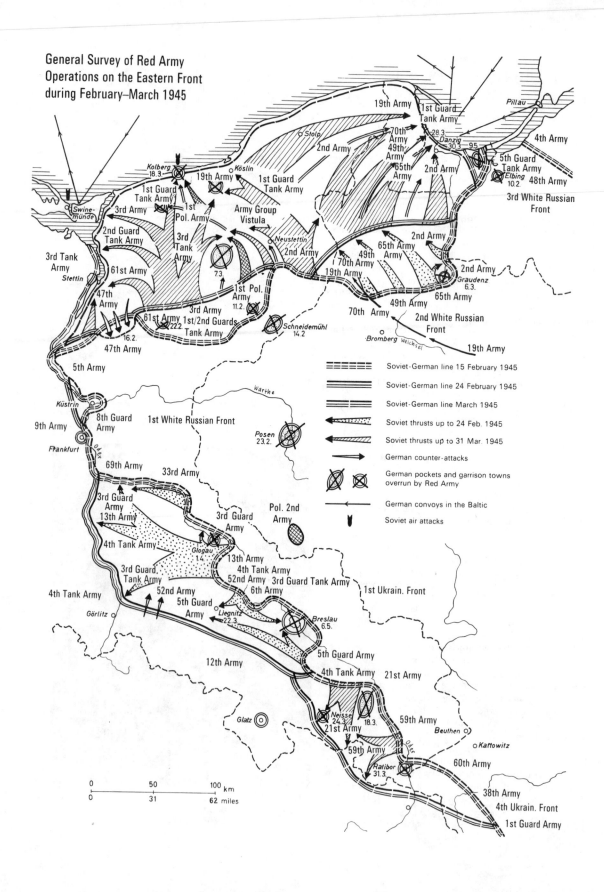

General Survey of Red Army
Operations on the Eastern Front
during February–March 1945

19th Army   1st Guard
             Tank Army   Pillau
70th   4th Army
Army   28.3.
49th   Danzig
2nd Army Army 30.3. 9.5.
65th   5th Guard
Army 2nd Army   Tank Army
                      Elbing 48th Army
                      10.2.
                      3rd White Russian
                      Front

Stolp
Köslin
Kolberg 19th Army   1st Guard
18.3.   Tank Army
1st Guard
Tank Army   1st   Army Group
3rd Army 1st   Vistula
          Pol. Army
Swine-   3rd   Neustettin   2nd Army
münde   Tank   2nd Army   65th Army
          Army   49th   2nd Army
2nd Guard 7.3.   Army
Tank Army   70th Army Graudenz
3rd Tank   1st Pol.   19th Army 6.3.
Army   Army   65th Army
Stettin 61st Army 11.2.   49th Army
                                  70th Army 2nd White Russian
47th   Front
Army   3rd Army
         61st Army 1st/2nd Guards Schneidemühl
         22.2.   Tank Army   14.2.   Bromberg Weichsel
16.2.   19th Army
47th Army

5th Army   Warthe

Küstrin
         8th Guard   1st White Russian Front
9th Army Army
Frankfurt   Posen
                             23.2.
69th Army   33rd Army

3rd Guard
Army
13th Army   3rd Guard   Pol. 2nd
             Army   Army
4th Tank Army
          Glogau
          1.4.   13th Army
3rd Guard   4th Tank Army
Tank Army   52nd Army 3rd Guard Tank Army
                  6th Army   1st Ukrain. Front
4th Tank Army 52nd Army
               5th Guard
Görlitz   Army   Liegnitz   Breslau
               22.3.   6.5.
                             5th Guard Army
          12th Army
                      4th Tank Army 21st Army
Glatz   Neisse   59th Army
          21st Army 24.3. 18.3. Beuthen
                  59th Army   Kattowitz
                      Ratibor   60th Army
                      31.3.
                                   38th Army
                                   4th Ukrain. Front
                                   1st Guard Army

Legend

≡≡≡ Soviet-German line 15 February 1945
=== Soviet-German line 24 February 1945
=== Soviet-German line March 1945
◄▦▦ Soviet thrusts up to 24 Feb. 1945
◄▦▦ Soviet thrusts up to 31 Mar. 1945
←   German counter-attacks
⊗   German pockets and garrison towns
     overrun by Red Army
←   German convoys in the Baltic
▼   Soviet air attacks

0   50   100
0   31   62 miles km

After street battles lasting many days, Soviet tanks put down German resistance in Danzig.

DANZIG TAKEN BY MARSHAL ROKOSSOVSKY'S TROOPS 30 March 1945

Marshal Rokossovsky's proclamation to the garrisons of Danzig and Gdynia

Generals, officers and men of the German Second Army!

Yesterday, 23 March 1945, my troops captured Zoppot, thus cutting your surrounded forces in two. The garrisons of Danzig and Gdynia are now separated. Our guns are shelling the harbours of Danzig and Gdynia and the entrances to them. The iron ring round your troops is tightening all the time.

In these circumstances, all resistance is senseless and can only lead to your own destruction and that of hundreds of thousands of women, children and old people.

I therefore call upon you

1. To lay down your arms at once and to surrender under a white flag, individually, by groups, sections, companies, batallions and regiments.

2. I guarantee the lives and possessions of all those who surrender. All officers and soldiers who fail to surrender will be destroyed in the impending attack.

You bear full responsibility for the fate of the civilian population.

24 March 1945

The Commander of the Second White Russian Front,
Marshal of the Soviet Union, Rokossovsky.

An order by the Feuhrer issued on 31 March 1945, illustrating the gulf between Hitler's ideas and the reality at the front. The 2nd Army will hold the peninsula and prevent the enemy from making use of the harbours of Gdynia and Danzig; Koenigsberg must be held; supply routes to Danzig must be protected; HQ personnel in Army Group North must be reduced to a minimum.

THE CONQUEST OF GERMANY

The Advance of the Western Allies from the Rhine and of the Red Army from the Vistula

CHRONOLOGICAL TABLE:

1945

1/4: Some 100,000 German troops (Army Group B) surrounded in Ruhr pocket. Isolated attacks by U.S. 7th Army on both sides of the Neckar river. First contacts with French units on left flank.

Glogau falls to the Red Army.

2/4: Formation of Werwolf (a specially trained German guerilla force). Goebbels and Bormann call for a last ditch stand.

Staff of Army Group North dissolved; 4th Army takes over in Samland.

3/4: German supply lines in Holland threatened by advance of Canadian 1st Army. Aschaffenburg taken by U.S. 7th Army.

3–4/4: Oxhoeft, across from Hela (Gulf of Danzig) and north of Gdynia evacuated by German troops.

4/4: British tanks enter Osnabrueck. 10th Armoured Division (U.S. 7th Army) attacks Heilbronn.

4–5/4: French troops capture Karlsruhe and cross the west border of Wurtemberg.

5/4: U.S. 3rd Army enters Eisenach.

6/4: German papers admit that defeat is unavoidable.

Last hospital train leaves Koenigsberg for Pillau.

7/4: Allied airborne troops land east of Zuider Zee. Canadian 1st Army strikes north. Capture of Hamm and Soest. U.S. troops take Goettingen and occupy Hannoversch–Muenden, Schweinfurt, Bad Mergentheim and Crailsheim.

8/4: British parachute troops cut last railway link between Holland and Germany, at a point between Groningen and Zwolle. Castrop–Rauxel occupied. Units of U.S. 3rd Army continue to mop up German forces in the Thuringian Forest. Hildesheim falls to the Allies.

Koenigsberg once again cut off from Pillau. Attempt to break out at night frustrated by Red Army. Troops of the 3rd White Russian Front enter Koenigsberg. Heavy Soviet artillery attack on Breslau.

9/4: British tanks advance on Bremen. U.S. 9th Army begins attack on Hanover. Americans take Mischede and Georgenthal.

Koenigsberg surrenders to the 3rd White Russian Front. Remnants of German units withdraw to Samland peninsula.

10/4: U.S. 9th Army takes Hanover and crosses the new Hanover–Hamburg Autobahn. Gelsenkirchen falls. Essen occupied.

General Lasch (Koenigsberg) is taken prisoner by the Red Army. General von Saucken takes command of German 2nd and 4th Armies, and becomes C.-in-C. East Prussia.

10–12/4: Soviet troops unleash terror in Koenigsberg. Red Army advances on Pillau.

11/4: Troops of the U.S. 3rd Army liberate Buchenwald Concentration Camp near Weimar and POW camp in the Bad Sulza area. American troops reach the Elbe south of Magdeburg.

12/4: Allies take Braunschweig (Brunswick), Neustadt, Weimar, Heilbronn, Celle and a number of smaller towns. U.S. 1st Army draws up before Leipzig.

13/4: British troops enter Arnhem. Hitler's order of the day: "Berlin remains German; Vienna will be German again . . ."

14/4: Canadian 1st Army assumes military control of the Netherlands. British 2nd Army advances to the outskirts of Bremen. In the Ruhr pocket, with the bulk of Army Group B under General Model, the U.S. 1st and 9th Armies link up, cutting the pocket into two. American troops reach the Elbe at Dessau. Units of U.S. 3rd Army capture Gera in Thuringia. U.S. troops capture Bayreuth. Franz von Papen is taken prisoner.

15/4: British troops discover some 40,000 survivors and 13,000 bodies in Belsen (chiefly Jews). Canadians reach the North Sea near the mouth of the river Ems. American troops take Merseburg and Leuna. Units of French 1st Army cross the Rhine north of Kehl, capture Kehl, overrun Offenburg and advance to the precincts of Lahr.

16/4: Canadians occupy Leeuwarden and Groningen in their advance on W. Holland. British infantry reaches the edge of Bremen. Elberfeld and Wuppertal overrun by U.S. troops. German resistance in the Bayreuth–Hof sector collapses.

3rd White Russian Front makes further progress in Samland. Red Army launches general offensive along the Oder front opposite Berlin, engaging the German 9th Army at 6:30 a.m. and the 4th Tank Army at 7:30 a.m.

17/4: A total of 755,573 German prisoners has been taken on the W. Front, during the period 1–16 April. The 20th Infantry Division of the U.S. 9th Army launches attack on Magdeburg. U.S. 3rd Army captures Solingen, Duesseldorf and Braulage. Brettheim destroyed and Rothenburg occupied. French troops overrun Freudenstadt and split the German 19th Army into two. Fall of Nagold and Horb.

18/4: Canadians cut off Germans in W. Holland. British troops take Soltau, Uelzen and Lueneburg. In the Ruhr pocket, German troops under General Model (suicide on 21 April) cease all organized resistance. A total of 325,000 German prisoners taken during the battle for the pocket. American troops occupy Magdeburg, Brinkum, and a number of small towns. U.S. 3rd Army swings left and prepares to advance on Austria and Czechoslovakia.

19/4: Goebbels starts his last propaganda campaign. The order of the day is "Persevere!"

British tanks of the 11th Armoured Division reach the Elbe at Lauenburg. The 2nd and 69th Divisions of the U.S. 1st Army take Leipzig. Units of U.S. 7th Army enter Nuremberg.

20/4: 114th Infantry Division of U.S. 7th Army occupies Schwaebisch Gmuend. Other units of the 7th Army overrun Sulzbach and Backnang. Americans in Schorndorf. French troops enter Stuttgart from the south and occupy the city. Sigmaringen and Freiburg captured.

Soviet spearheads reach the river Spree and the precincts of Berlin. General Niehoff, Commander of Breslau, distributes chocolate on the occasion of Hitler's birthday.

21/4: Himmler meets Masur, Representative of the World Jewish Congress at Gut Harzwalde near Berlin; he agrees to release 100 Jewish women from Ravensbrueck Concentration Camp.

22/4: Red Army takes Kottbus and draws up before the inner defences of Berlin.

23–24/4: Himmler asks Count Bernadotte to negotiate a separate peace with the Western Allies.

23/4: Fourteen political prisoners (20/3/44 uprising) including Albrecht Haushofer, are shot in the neck by SS men.

British troops enter Bremen and Harburg. U.S. 1st Army occupies Dessau.

Soviet troops enter Berlin from the east and south. Red Army takes Potsdam and Frankfurt-on-Oder.

24/4: Units of the U.S. 7th Army cross the Danube at Dillingen. Fall of Urach, Muensingen and Ulm.

Berlin is almost completely surrounded; Soviet spearheads link up near Nauen. Red Army reaches Belgern on the Elbe.

25/4: Himmler's armistice offer reaches London.

Bremen is cleared by British troops.

Fall of Pillau.

Berlin is cut off.

Street fighting in the Ruhr. The German High Command announced on 2 April that heavy fighting had broken out round Recklinghausen, in the north of the industrial region. On 3 April came the announcement that the Americans had successfully breached the German defences south of Bielefeld.

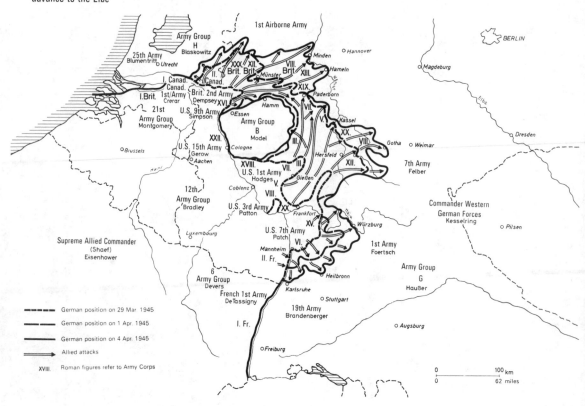

The Ruhr pocket and the Allied
advance to the Elbe

1st Airborne Army

BERLIN

Army Group
H
Blaskowitz

25th Army
Blumentritt

Utrecht

Hannover

Magdeburg

Minden

XXX XII.   VIII.
Brit. Brit.   Brit.   *Münster* XIII. *Hamelin*

Elbe

I. Canad.
Canad. II.
I.Brit. Canad.
Brit. 2nd Army
1st/Army Dempsey
Crerar XVI.
U.S. 9th Army
Simpson *Essen*
Hamm

XIX

Paderborn

VII.

Dresden

XXII.
Cologne Army Group
B
Model

XVIII.
U.S. 15th Army *Aachen*
Gerow

III.   XX.
V. *Kassel*
Gotha *Weimar*

VIII.

XII.

7th Army
Felber

VII.
XVIII.
U.S. 1st Army
Hodges *Hersfeld*

12th.
Army Group *Coblenz*
Bradley V. *Gießen*
U.S. 3rd Army VIII.
Patton XX. *Frankfurt*

Commander Western
German Forces
Kesselring

Pilsen

XV.
U.S. 7th Army *Würzburg*
Patch VI.
Mannheim
II. Fr.

1st Army
Foertsch

Supreme Allied Commander
(Shaef)
Eisenhower

Luxembourg

Heilbronn

Army Group
G
Haußer

6
Army Group *Karlsruhe*
Devers
French 1st Army
DeTassigny

19th Army
Brandenberger

Stuttgart

Augsburg

I. Fr.

Freiburg

German position on 29 Mar. 1945
German position on 1 Apr. 1945
German position on 4 Apr. 1945
Allied attacks

XVIII.   Roman figures refer to Army Corps

0 ———— 100 km
0 ———— 62 miles

American gunners during alert in the battle for the Ruhr.

Allied leaflet instructing civilians on method of surrender in the surrounded Ruhr sector.

ARMY GROUP B
SURROUNDED IN THE RUHR

1 April 1945

A stricken B-26 Marauder bomber.

Troops of the U.S. 9th Army entering Duisburg.

German prisoners captured in Muenster.

Armed Hitler youths and a Volkssturm man in a village in Hesse (April 1945)

"WERWOLF" APPEAL AND "FLAG DECREE"

2–3 April 1945

On 2 April, the German News Agency announced the following proclamation by Martin Bormann:

National-Socialists, Party Comrades! After the collapse of 1918, we gave ourselves body and soul to the struggle for our national preservation. The hour of greatest danger has now struck. The threat of renewed enslavement calls for our every and final effort. From now on, let us resolve to oppose the invader with a remorseless will. Provincial and district leaders and other Party officials will carry on the good fight in their own territory, will vanquish or die. Only scoundrels will leave their post without the Fuehrer's express orders, will refuse to fight to the last breath. Lift up your courage and stamp out every trace of weakness! The hour admits of only one slogan: Victory or death . . .

"Flag Decree"	Prov. Council of Ratenau
Radio Proclamation	Received on 7 April 1945
To CO Wurzburg, Regensburg, Ansbach	Urgent

The SS Reichs-Fuehrer has decreed:

1. At the present stage of the war, all that matters is perseverance and a remorseless will to achieve victory.

2. Severe measures must be taken against anyone hanging out white sheets, opening tank barriers, refusing to do Volkssturm service or committing similar offences.

3. All male inhabitants of a house displaying a white flag will be shot. This measure must be implemented without a moment's delay.

The Commander of Civil Police
to the Provincial Governor
No. 49/45 KdO-VS

A pamphlet distributed by the "Werwolf" in Upper Bavaria on 25 April. "We shall punish every traitor and his entire family . . . Our revenge is deadly!"

```
»Der Werwolf"                                    An allen Orten, den 25.4.45
   Oberbayern

                        W a r n u n g

             an alle Verräter und Liebediener des Feindes.

   Der oberbayerische Werwolf warnt vorsorglich alle diejenigen, di
   dem Feind Vorschub leisten wollen oder Deutsche und deren Angehöri-
   ge bedrohen oder schikanieren, die Adolf Hitler die Treue hielten.

   Wir warnen! Verräter und Verbrecher am Volk büßen mit ihrem Leben
   und dem Leben ihrer ganzen Sippe.

   Dorfgemeinschaften, die sich versündigen am Leben der Unseren,
   oder die weiße Fahne zeigen, werden ein vernichtendes Haberfeld-
   treiben früher oder später erleben.

                   Unsere Rache ist tödlich!
             ===============================

                                              »Der Werwolf"
                                                 Oberbayern
```

German girls caught sniping at Allied soldiers.

Secretary of State Naumann declared in Munich on 23 March:

The enemy fully realizes that the occupation of Germany is an impossibility—after more than 20 years of National Socialist education, 20 or 30 million Germans simply will not allow themselves to be thrown out of their homeland. If the enemy should try, he will unleash a partisan war under the banner of the Werwolf, such as the world has never witnessed before. We shall give them a reception beyond anything they can imagine . . .

From Captain Boldt's diary:

It quickly appeared that the "Werwolf" campaign was completely futile. Not even Hitler's élite corps obeyed the summons. When the Sixth SS Mountain Division, which had been specially brought in from Norway, was surrounded in the Taunus hills, Hitler ordered all 15,000 of them to split up into small groups and to join the Werwolf organization. But it all came to nothing . . .

ALLIIERTES OBERKOMMANDO

(Supreme Headquarters Allied Expeditionary Force)

BEFEHL

AN DIE VERSPRENGTEN DEUTSCHEN TRUPPENTEILE

Das schnelle Vordringen der Alliierten hat es mit sich gebracht, dass zahlreiche deutsche Einheiten versprengt und aufgelöst worden sind und daher von zuständiger deutscher Seite keine Befehle mehr erhalten können.

Um nutzlose Opfer an Menschenleben zu vermeiden, ergeht daher folgender Befehl:

1.) Deutsche Soldaten, die abgeschnitten oder versprengt wurden, sowie Einheiten, die vom deutschen Kommando keine Befehle mehr erhalten, haben sich beim nächstliegenden alliierten Truppenteil zu melden.

2.) Bis dahin ist der Einheitsführer bezw. rangälteste Unteroffizier für die Disziplin seiner Mannschaft verantwortlich. Die umstehenden Verhaltungsmassregeln für versprengte Einheiten treten mit sofortiger Wirksamkeit in Kraft.

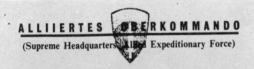

DWIGHT D. EISENHOWER
Oberbefehlshaber der Alliierten Streitkräfte

Allied pamphlet calling on German soldiers cut off from their units to surrender, and to avoid unnecessary loss of life.

Laßt Euch nicht evakuieren!

verlangt der Feind in seinen Flugblättern.

Warum plötzlich diese „Fürsorge"?

Warum diese Anteilnahme?

Er hat Deine Wohnungen zerstört, seit Jahren mordet er mit seinen Bomben — und jede Nacht kommt er noch und sät weitere Vernichtung.

Nun ist er auf einmal „besorgt" um Dich?

WARUM?

Hier seine Gründe:

Er braucht

Arbeiter für Hütten und Gruben,

Helfer für die Kriegsindustrie,

Männer, die Minen räumen,

Männer und Frauen zum Schanzen,

Frauen und Mädchen für seine Bordelle.

Er will

schon jetzt größere Teile des deutschen Volkes in seine Befehlsgewalt bringen,

unsere Widerstandskraft schwächen,

seine oft proklamierten Vernichtungspläne zur Ausrottung des deutschen Volkes verwirklichen.

German counter-pamphlet explaining that the Allies are not so much concerned with saving life as with finding workers for industry, for minesweeping and for building trenches, and women for their brothels.

Canadian advance in Holland cuts off German supply routes.

CANADIANS AND BRITISH ADVANCE IN EAST HOLLAND

3 April 1945

Hitler on the situation in Holland:

All these lousy countries only exist because a few leading European powers cannot agree on how to swallow them up. If Germany's power were destroyed, all of them would be wiped off the map of Europe . . . I get absolutely wild when people keep telling me: "For goodness' sake don't do anything to hurt them, to sully their honour!" None of them have any honour to sully . . .

Dutch Resistance fighters after the liberation of Winterswijk.

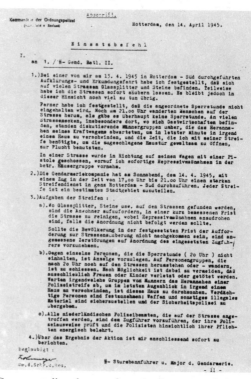

German police decree of 14 April 1945, ordering the Dutch gendarmerie to clear the streets of Rotterdam of all glass splinters, to make sure that the curfew is not broken, and to check the papers of all Dutch policemen they meet in the street.

THE GERMANS IN HOLLAND

1945

Rauter, Commander of the German Security Police in Holland.

WARNUNG!

Geräumtes Gebiet!

Holländische Zivilpersonen, die in diesem Gebiet OHNE gültigen Ausweis angetroffen werden, werden als Spione oder Terroristen angesehen und erschossen

Der Kommandant

Placard warning all unauthorised Dutch civilians not to enter restricted area on pain of death.

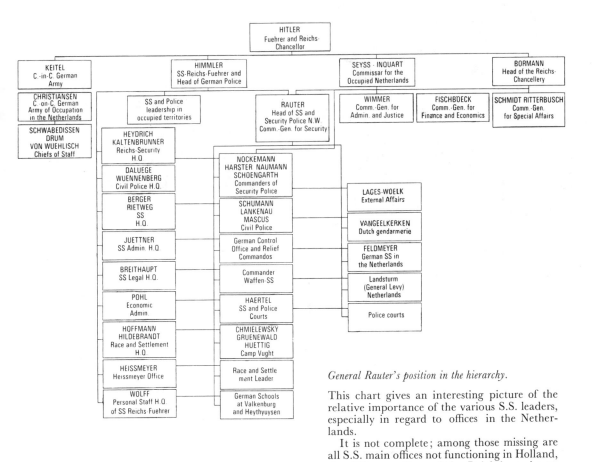

General Rauter's position in the hierarchy.

This chart gives an interesting picture of the relative importance of the various S.S. leaders, especially in regard to offices in the Netherlands.

It is not complete; among those missing are all S.S. main offices not functioning in Holland, the different offices of the Reichskommissars, as well as those controlled by the Security Police and Disciplinary Police.

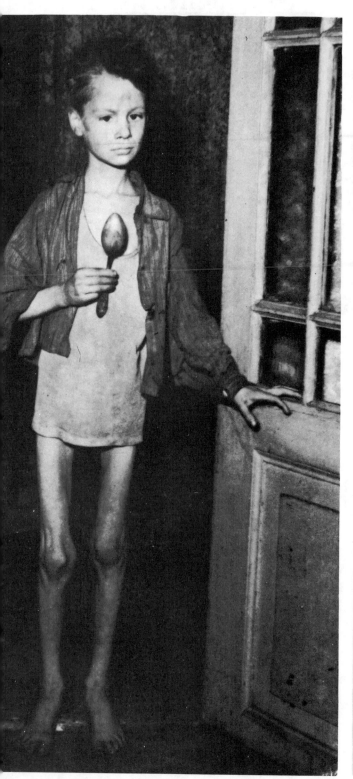

During the hunger winter of 1944 some 15,000 Dutch people died of starvation.

By opening locks and destroying dykes, the Germans flooded some 100,000 acres of Dutch soil.

ALLIIERTES KOMMANDO
(Supreme Headquarters Expeditionary Force)

BEKANNTMACHUNG
an die deutsche Garnison
der Festung Holland

Ihr wisst genau: Vier-einhalb Millionen holländische Zivilpersonen verhungern hinter Euren Linien.

Ihr wisst genau: Die Reichsregierung ist nicht mehr Träger der tatsächlichen Regierungsgewalt. Ihre Autorität beschränkt sich auf einige wenige Widerstandstaschen in Deutschland.

Ihr wisst genau: Das deutsche Heer besteht nicht mehr als geschlossene, einsatzfähige Waffe.

Und doch befolgt Ihr noch immer den verbrecherischen Befehl, bis zum Äussersten Widerstand zu leisten. Euer Widerstand bedeutet für Tausende holländischer Zivilpersonen den Hungertod und für Holland noch grössere Verwüstung.

Um in dieser Endphase der Kämpfe die Leiden der holländischen Bevölkerung zu lindern, hat der Alliierte Oberbefehlshaber angeordnet, dass die holländische Zivilbevölkerung durch Abwurf mit Lebensmitteln versorgt werden soll. Für diese Lebensmittel-Transporte wird eine grosse Anzahl von Flugzeugen aller Muster bei Tag und bei Nacht eingesetzt werden. Diese Flugzeuge dienen nicht den Zwecken des Krieges. Sie dienen der Hilfe für eine notleidende Bevölkerung. Sie werden in niedriger Flughöhe einfliegen und sich aller Aktionen enthalten, die in irgendeiner Weise die militärischen Operationen beeinflussen könnten. Es wird keine Bombenabwürfe geben, keinen Bordwaffenbeschuss und keine Angriffshandlung. Auf Anordnung des Alliierten Oberbefehlshabers ergehen daher an Euch folgende Weisungen:

1. Wer den alliierten Flugzeugen, die Lebensmittel für die holländische Zivilbevölkerung befördern, Abwehr entgegensetzt oder sie an der Durchführung ihrer Hilfsmission zu hindern versucht, begeht ein Verbrechen gegen die Gebote der Menschlichkeit. Wer ein solches Verbrechen begeht, entweder indem er den Befehl gibt, Feuer auf unsere Flugzeuge zu eröffnen, oder indem er einen Befehl dieser Art ausführt, muss gewärtigen, dass er am Tage der Abrechnung für seine Tat zur vollen Verantwortung gezogen wird.

2. Wer den Versuch unternimmt, die von den Alliierten abgeworfenen Lebensmittel der holländischen Bevölkerung zu entziehen, begeht gleichfalls ein Verbrechen gegen die Gebote der Menschlichkeit und wird gleichfalls zur vollen Verantwortung gezogen werden.

3. Es ist Euer eigenes Interesse, bei der Verteilung der Lebensmittel an die holländische Zivilbevölkerung nach besten Kräften mitzuwirken.

Allied pamphlet asking German soldiers, in the name of humanity, not to interfere with the distribution of food parcels dropped by Allied planes over Holland.

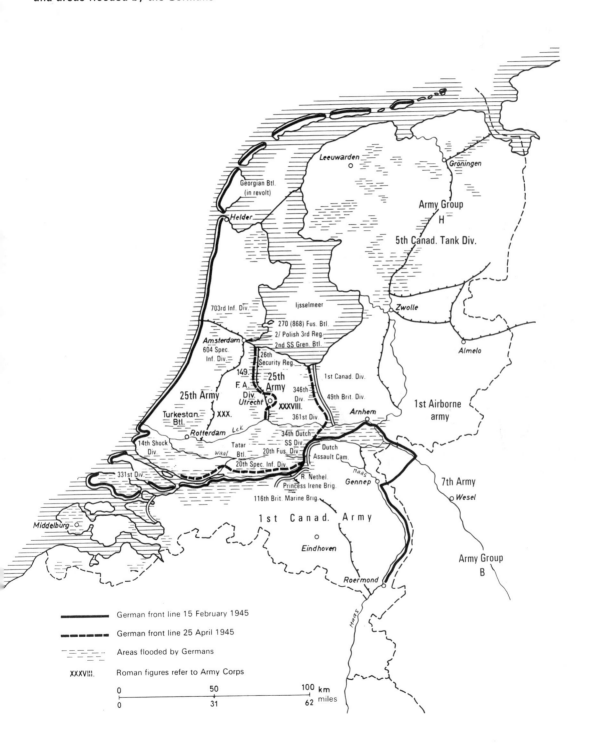

Holland in February–April 1945.
Position of German troops,
British and Canadian operations,
and areas flooded by the Germans

Leeuwarden

Groningen

Georgian Btl.
(in revolt)

Army Group
H

5th Canad. Tank Div.

Helder

703rd Inf. Div.

Ijsselmeer

Zwolle

270 (868) Fus. Btl.

2/ Polish 3rd Reg.

2nd SS Gren. Btl.

Almelo

Amsterdam
604 Spec.
Inf. Div.

26th
Security Reg.

149.
F. A.
Div.
Utrecht

25th
Army

1st Canad. Div.

346th
Div.

49th Brit. Div.

25th Army

XXXVIII.

Arnhem

1st Airborne
army

Turkestan.
Btl.

XXX.

361st Div.

Rotterdam

Lek

14th Shock
Div.

Tatar
Btl.

Waal

34th Dutch
SS Div.

20th Fus. Div.

Dutch
Assault Cam.

20th Spec. Inf. Div.

Maas

7th Army

331st Div.

R. Nethel.

Princess Irene Brig.

Gennep

Wesel

116th Brit. Marine Brig.

1st   Canad.   Army

Middelburg

Eindhoven

Army Group
B

Roermond

Maas

German front line 15 February 1945

German front line 25 April 1945

Areas flooded by Germans

XXXVIII.   Roman figures refer to Army Corps

0	50	100	km
0	31	62	miles

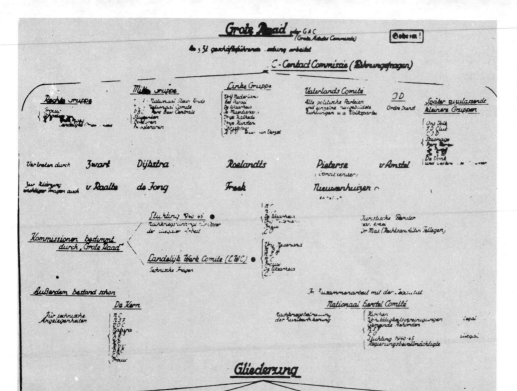

A survey by the German Secret Service of the organization of the various resistance groups in Holland, showing the link-up between military resistance groups, civil resistance groups, the illegal press and technical branches. The strength of the Dutch Resistance may be gathered from the fact that the Germans were estimated to have killed 2,000–3,000 resistance members during the war.

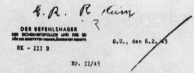

Headings of illegal Dutch newspapers with various political tendencies.

Dutch Resistance pamphlet: The new Germany needs men not corpses. Capitulate!

DER BEFEHLSHABER
DER SICHERHEITSPOLIZEI UND DES SD
FÜR DIE BESETZTEN NIEDERLÄNDISCHEN GEBIETE

SK - III B

O.U., den 6.2.'45

Nr. II/45

Betrifft: Politische Auswertung der illegalen Presse.

Fast die gesamte illegale Presse befasst sich mit dem Arbeitseinsatz und den durch die Wehrmacht durchgeführten Razzien. Die Artikel bringen alle die bekannten kritischen Argumente und gipfeln übereinstimmend in der Aufforderung, die deutschen Massnahmen soweit nur irgend möglich zu durchkreuzen. Neues wird dabei nicht gesagt.

Auch der "Offene Brief der Ärzte an Seyss-Inquart" wird von fast allen illegalen Presseerzeugnissen in mehr oder weniger grossen Auszügen gebracht. In dem Brief werden besonders folgende Punkte hervorgehoben.
1.) Protest gegen die "Gleichschaltung des "Roten Kreuzes""
2.) Die Hungersnot. Die durch die Deutschen ausgegebenen Rationen für Erwachsene haben nur einen Nährwert von 600 - 800 Kalorien, das ist weniger als die Hälfte dessen, was ein ruhender Mensch nötig hat um am Leben zu bleiben und weniger als ein Drittel dessen, was ein arbeitender Mensch braucht.
3.) "Tuberculose, Dysentherie, Typhus und Kinderlähmung nehmen schnell zu". Dyphterie- und Scharlach-Epedemien hätten grösseres Ausmass angenommen, die Gefahr des Flecktyphus sei nicht zu übersehen. "An diesem Zustand ist der Besetzer schuld."
4.) Der Abtransport von Gütern und Vorräten.
5.) "Grausamer als dies alles ist wohl die in immer grösseres Unfang und in immer roher Weise durchgeführte Wegführung und die gezwungene Arbeitseinsatz niederländischer Männer in der feindlichen Kriegsorganisation."

Der Brief endet "...Sie weisen zum Schluss darauf hin, dass die deutsche besetzende Macht durch das Fortsetzen dieser Misshandlungen des niederländischen Volkes jeden Anspruch auf Achtung durch die Menschheit Preis gibt".

Im Einzelnen wird folgende zusammenfassende Übersicht gegeben:

1.) HET PAROOL
Nr. 66 (Den Haag) vom 17.1.'45

"Der britische Minister Richard Law hat mit seinen amerikanischen Kollegen Stettinius Unterhandlungen geführt, zufolge deren beschlossen wurde, regelmässig Güter in das befreite Europa zu transportieren, während zugleich den nationalen Importprogramme der Regierungen der befreiten Gebiete mehr Aufmerksamkeit geschenkt werden soll".

-3-

Nr. 95 (Utrecht) vom 25.1.'45.

"Eisenbahner! Wisst ihr was Euer Streik jetzt auch bedeutet!"

Das "Nationale Dagblad" habe eine neue Möglichkeit entdeckt, den Deutschen bei ihren Deportationsplänen zu helfen. Der Eisenbahnerstreik müsse gebrochen werden, denn dann sei wenigstens die Möglichkeit, die niederländischen Männer, vor denen die Nazis solche Angst hätten, zu deportieren..... Selbst wenn 2 Züge pro Tag führen, allein für den Transport der Männer, würde es ungefähr 300 Tage dauern, bevor alle in Frage kommenden weg wären und das müssten dann deutsche Züge sein, denn niederländische Züge führen nicht.
Das "Nationale Dagblad" wird dann angegriffen wegen seines Aufrufs an die Eisenbahner im Hinblick auf die hungernde Bevölkerung. ..."Von Sorge über die Ernährung unseres Volkes gesprochen, meine Herren, gehört dazu auch das Verbot für Frauen und Kinder, das Essen, das sie so ganz und gar nötig haben dort zu holen, wo es vorhanden ist, über der IJsol. ...: Unser Eisenbahnerstreik war nötig seinerzeit und ist es auch jetzt noch. Seht, wie unsere Männer noch immer hier laufen, weil es keine Züge gibt".

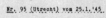

2.) DE WAARHEID
vom 17.1.'45

"Lebensmittel kommen an".

"In Antwerpen werden jetzt Lebensmittel für die befreiten niederländischen Gebiete zur Verteilung zur Verfügung gestellt. Die englische Königin hat ausserdem 4 Kolonnen von je 11 Lastautos, worunter Kantinen-, Wasser- und Küchenwagen, für die Lebensmittelversorgung der befreiten Niederlande geschenkt."

"Lokomotiven".

"Der niederländische Gesandte in Schweden hat die ersten von 50 Lokomotiven, die durch die niederländische Regierung bei einer schwedischen Firma bestellt waren, in Empfang genommen."

vom 24.1.'45

"Unter den Panier von Lenin - nach Berlin!!!"

Der 21.Todestag von Lenin stand in der ganzen Sowjet-Union im Zeichen der mächtigen Offensive. Es ist nicht nur ein Symbol, dass die donnernden Salutschüsse zur Ehre der grossen Siege vor dem Lenin-Mausoleum auf dem Roten Platz in Moskau gelöst wurden. "Unter Lenins Panier- und Stalins Führung" schrieb die Prawda letzten Sonntag, "Marschieren die roten Armeen". Den beiden ist es zu danken, dass die Sowjet-Union jetzt in der vordersten Linie der Völker steht, die die Freiheit erkämpfen werden. Woher entlohnen die Sowjet-Völker diese wunderbare Kraft, so fragt General-Major Galadjanov in der "Krasnaja Swesda"? Aus dem durch Lenin begründeten gesellschaftlichen Grundbegriff, aus seiner Ideologie und aus der durch Stalin begründeten brüderlichen Zusammenarbeit der in der Sowjet-Union

-4-

Two pages from a German Secret Service report on the activities of the illegal Dutch press. The report states that, during the period under review, the illegal press concentrated mainly on attacks against the conscription of workers and the German raids on the big cities, and offered advice on how to resist or evade the latest German orders.

Russian women workers were locked in a cellar by German police in Osnabrueck and poisoned by smoke, shortly before the arrival of British tanks. The photograph shows one of the few survivors being given artificial respiration.

BRITISH TANKS IN OSNABRUECK 4 April 1945

British soldiers in Osnabrueck. Patton's tanks entered Kassel two days earlier.

Deutsche Zivilisten!

Amerikanische Truppen sind im Anmarsch auf Eure Ortschaft!

In kurzer Zeit werden sie Euer Städtchen erreicht haben. Für die Bevölkerung besteht kein Anlass zur Befürchtung, denn die amerikanische Armee führt nicht gegen Zivilisten Krieg.

Um Euch und Eure Ortschaft vor Kriegsschäden zu bewahren, müsst Ihr die folgenden Vorschriften genau beobachten:

1. *Wenn sich Soldaten in Eurem Städtchen befinden, versucht Euer Aeussersтes, sie zur Aufgabe des Widerstandes zu bewegen. Wenn Eure Ortschaft sich nicht friedlich ergibt, wird sie durch Kampfhandlung genommen. Und Kampfhandlung bedeutet Zerstörung.*

2. *Verbergt Euch in Euren Kellern, die Euch Schutz bieten. Bleibt in den Kellern, auch nachdem die ersten amerikanischen Truppen in Eure Ortschaft eingezogen sind. Sendet eine kleine Gruppe von Bevollmächtigten aus (nicht mehr als 3), die dem amerikanischen Kommandanten die Ortschaft übergeben. Alle anderen Bürger bleiben in ihren Kellern, bis sie von den Behörden anderweitig angewiesen werden.*

3. *Gewährt Mitgliedern der deutschen Wehrmacht, die den Kampf einstellen wollen und sich aller Waffen entledigt haben, Zuflucht in Euren Verstecken! Nach Einnahme Eurer Ortschaft müsst Ihr die Behörden sofort von der Anwesenheit deutscher Soldaten verständigen und die Soldaten der Militärbehörde zuführen.*

Der Befehlshaber
der amerikanischen Truppen

Allied pamphlet calling upon German civilians to persuade the troops to surrender, and to offer assistance to all those who lay down their arms.

A group of German soldiers in N. Wurtemberg.

THE STRUGGLE FOR HEILBRONN AND THE FRENCH ADVANCE ON SOUTH GERMANY

4–12 April 1945

The Fall of Heilbronn

Condensed from U.S. Divisional History.

On 12 April, German resistance collapsed after a 9-day battle. At 15:30 hours the town was finally cleared of Germans. While the 2nd Batallion (399th Reg.) occupied the barracks on the edge of the town, the 397th Regiment took the hills to the N.E. . . . The capture of Heilbronn meant that the road to Stuttgart was open . . .

The French Advance

From the War Memoirs of General de Gaulle.

I was eager to see our men on the other side too, not only in a spirit of national emulation, but also because reasons of high policy made it essential that de Lattre have time to drive as far as Stuttgart before his neighbour Patch reached the city himself. A personal telegram which I sent on the twentyninth to the commander of our First Army urged him to make all possible haste. "My dear General," I wrote, "you must cross the Rhine, even if the Americans do not help you and you are obliged to use boats. The matter is one of the highest national interest. Karlsruhe and Stuttgart expect, even if they do not desire you . . ."

. . . In fact, on the evening of 30 March, elements of the II Army Corps began to effect the crossing—the 2nd Moroccan Division at Germersheim, which it had reached only the night before. At Leimersheim, on 1 April—Easter Sunday—the 9th Colonial Division undertook the crossing in its turn. The air support provided for all our units was meagre, and they had at their disposal only an extremely reduced amount of special apparatus for the crossing. But by ingenious planning, several boats proved to be enough to move the advance guards across. As for bridges, General Dromard, in command of the Army Engineers, had prepared them far in advance. Foreseeing that he would have to construct them eventually and that when the occasion arose he could count only on himself, Dromard had collected the necessary material beforehand on our own territory. At Speyer, a French ten-ton bridge was opened. On the fourth, 130,000 French troops and 20,000 vehicles were already on the right bank. Karlsruhe was taken the same day. On 7 April, accompanied by Diethelm, de Lattre, Juin and Dromard, I had the proud duty of crossing the Rhine . . .

Allied Jeeps and tanks became familiar sights in south Germany. ▶

Troops of the 3rd U.S. Army entering Eisenach on 5 April. Minden, Bielefeld, and Detmold were occupied on the same day; Goetingen fell on 7 April.

Civilians removing tank barriers so as to avoid an artillery attack.

Fraternization despite official disapproval.

U.S. troops liberating Allied prisoners from a German camp near Hammelburg

ADVANCE OF THIRD U.S. ARMY INTO CENTRAL GERMANY

5 April 1945

"I am tired of war, of human beings . . ."

By an American Soldier

The countryside grew extremely hilly and wooded; small towns, flying surrender flags, lay hidden in hollows. In the swiftness of pursuit, one company by mistake often seized another company's town and had to double back to take its own objective. The convoy of trucks rushed into the towns; the infantrymen hopped down, cleared out the snipers, rounded up the prisoners, jumped into the trucks again and set out for the next town. Some days, in this fashion, as many as thirty miles were covered.

. . . The entire convoy pulled up in a higgledy-piggledy village with small, low cottages and a few round, turreted, medieval buildings that seemed to have no windows. The place looked like a page from a Mother Goose painting book. It was full noon; the dusty road and white cottages, the bed sheets and tablecloths gave back a white glare. When the trucks stopped, the men jumped down, and then there were khaki uniforms swarming everywhere over the bleached whiteness of the little street, opening gates, going into back yards searching for eggs, forcing open front doors to loot and hunt for liquor.

Not knowing how long we were to stay, we sat in the kitchen of one of the little houses, having our lunch. The old woman who lived there had just been dispossessed . . . The kitchen was crowded with men walking about, eating and talking; Silly Willie was frying a can of C-ration hash and causing a stench.

. . . At that moment, two line-company boys smashed down the flimsy back door of the house with their rifles and came in, asking, "This place been looted yet?" The old woman who lived in the house had returned and there was a commotion behind me in the room. Either someone had burned the bottom out of her only good pot or she had seen someone going out of the house with her only good pot. At any rate, she set up a loud keening about it and taxed Phil, who had promised her that nothing would be disturbed. "Hey, get her the hell outta here," someone was saying. "What's she bitchin' about, anyway? Go on,

ya old bastard, git out! Git outta here!" She took herself off on her sore feet, whimpering and crying, followed by a few oaths and careless laughter. Sipping my tea, looking out of the window at the sunlit back yard, the thought suddenly came to me, I'm tired of this, tired of war, of human beings, of everything.

. . . And yet, only a few days before, on Good Friday, during the attack a half mile ahead on the town of Eisenach, I had seen the high wire gates of a slave-labour camp being swung open by men of our battalion, and the inmates, with a rush and a tremendous roar, had come pouring out on to the street. For me, it was one of the most thrilling moments of the war. They surrounded the handful of us who were there—I had come down the street with Phil to watch—and they crowded about to shake our hands, to thank us individually, laughing and crying and in their jubilation addressing us in their native tongues. There were no interpreters; we could only smile and smile and continue shaking hands. I offered my cigarettes around until they were gone and kept asking, "Polsky? Russki?" In time I could feel my smile growing stretched but there was nothing to do but go on smiling and smiling and shaking hands. A few of the slave labourers, their meagre possessions slung over their shoulders, giving us a wave and a cheer as they came out, pointed to a direction —to the east, probably—and struck off without a backward glance. Then two slave labourers ran up the street, each with a bottle of liquor, and at that they all scattered and began to burst into the nearby houses in search of liquor to celebrate their freedom. The American troops were a half-step ahead of them in the search and a fast-paced looting contest started up.

Later in the afternoon, when large numbers of German soldiers were captured and marched up the street in their long muddy overcoats, hands over their heads, some of the slave labourers ran alongside, catcalling and shouting and pointing out the SS troops to the American guards. Other slave labourers, by then happily drunk, were roaming up and down the street, five and six abreast, arms linked, careless of shellfire, singing their national songs. Still others, looking dazed and without plans, leaned against the wire enclosure that had been their homes. A few went wearily inside. Within a few hours, all of them seemed to grow as accustomed to the sight of us as we grew of them.

Lester Atwell.

FRENCH ARMY ADVANCES IN BADEN AND WURTEMBERG

5 April 1945

While the First French Army—the photograph shows a medical orderly rendering First Aid—advanced into S. Germany, de Gaulle ordered an attack on the German Atlantic defences. The Germans in the Gironde estuary, in La Rochelle and in Bordeaux were defeated before the month was out.

Entwurf

5.April 1945

Der Oberbürgermeister
der Stadt der Auslandsdeutschen

An den   Streng vertraulich!
Herrn ... und Höheren Polizeiführer
General der Waffen-SS H o f m a n n
(14) S t u t t g a r t O
Gänsheidestr.26

Lieber Parteigenosse Hofmann!

Ich habe in diesen Tagen Vorbereitungen für die Weiterführung der
städtischen Verwaltung für den Fall der Feindbesetzung der Stadt in der
Form und in dem Rahmen einer Notverwaltung getroffen. Mein Erlass vom
29.3.1945 ist als Anlage beigefügt. Das Inkrafttreten der Notverwaltung
habe ich mir noch vorbehalten.

Nachdem nun die Freiheitsbewegung (Wehrwolf) aufgerufen worden ist, besteht die Notwendigkeit, klare Verhältnisse hinsichtlich der Notverwaltungen der Gemeinden zu schaffen. Diese Notverwaltungen beruhen auf
Erlässen des Reichsinnenministers Reichsführers-SS Himmler. Sie sind
notwendig, um, soweit dies unter den gegebenen Verhältnissen irgendwie
möglich sein wird, unserer Bevölkerung auch im Falle der Feindbesetzung
die Lebensmöglichkeiten zu erhalten. Es ist deshalb auch vom Reichsinnen-
minister ausdrücklich angeordnet worden:

    "Die Durchführung der Verwaltungs- und Versorgungsaufgaben und die
    Wahrnehmung des Ordnungsdienstes sind nicht als Dienstleistungen für
    den Feind anzusehen, auch dann nicht, wenn u.a. hierfür Verhandlun-
    gen mit den feindlichen Besatzungskräften erforderlich werden."

Die Besetzung der Notverwaltung mit brauchbaren Kräften und vor allem
auch das Funktionieren der Notverwaltung hängt nun natürlich entscheidend davon ab, dass diese Gefolgschaftsangehörigen nicht Gefahr laufen,
bei pflichtgemässer Ausübung ihres zweifellos überaus schwierigen Amtes
auch noch von unseren eigenen Leuten, von der Freiheitsbewegung, erschossen zu werden. Diese Männer stehen ohnedies in grösster Gefahr, vom Feind
drangsaliert zu werden, wenn sie die Auflagen, die ihnen von der Besat-
zungsmacht gestellt werden, nicht erfüllen können oder, weil es sich um
Arbeiten für den Feind handeln würde, nicht erfüllen dürfen. Vielleicht
noch grösser ist die Gefahr, dass die Kräfte der Notverwaltung, vor allem
die leitenden Kräfte, als Repressalien gegen die Aktion der Freiheitsbewegung hingerichtet werden. Um so wichtiger ist es, dass diese Gefolgschaftsangehörigen der Notverwaltung von der Freiheitsbewegung Unterstützung und nicht etwa Anfeindung erfahren.

Ich wäre Ihnen besonders dankbar, wenn Sie dafür besorgt wären, dass die
Männer der Freiheitsbewegung auf diese Gesichtspunkte nachdrücklich auf-
merksam gemacht werden.

                                         Heil Hitler!
                                            Ihr

                                         (gez.) Strölin

Confidential letter by the mayor of Stuttgart explaining
what arrangements he is making for running the town in
case of Allied occupation, and asking that Werwolf
members be instructed not to look upon his arrangements
as a betrayal of the Fuehrer.

Crailsheim in N. Wurtemberg changed hands several
times in about the middle of April.

Retreating German soldiers.

AMERICANS BEFORE CRAILSHEIM AND IN N. WURTEMBERG

Early April 1945

"Crailsheim back in our hands"

Condensed from U.S. Divisional History

On 7 April Hankin's armoured group was able to improve its
position in Crailsheim by occupying Ingersheim, Altenmuenster and
the airfield nearby. On 8 April, it became clear that the Germans had
recovered from the shock of our sudden tank advance on Crailsheim.
At daybreak, they launched the first of many severe attacks. After
preliminary mortar fire, 600 SS engineers attacked from the N.E., E.
and S.E. The N.E. column was quickly beaten back. The two other
attacks were more successful; they overran our perimeter and advanced
to the edge of the town. It was only toward noon that the attackers
could be beaten back after suffering heavy losses. Some of our heavy
tanks went in pursuit and occupied Altenmuenster for the second time,
but returned to Crailsheim during the night. Another contingent
combed Ingersheim for enemy soldiers; a third occupied the airfield.
By noon, Crailsheim was back in our hands.

SHAEF announced on 10 April 1945 that the S. Crailsheim
spearhead had been extended despite heavy enemy pressure.
Further west, Allied troops threw the enemy back to the
Kocher. There was heavy street-fighting in Heilbronn. South
of Karlsruhe, the Germans were holding out in the Siegfried
defences. In the Ruhr pocket, Allied troops entered the N.W.
precincts of Essen, reached Hirschberg and captured Mes-
chede.

Volkssturm men reporting for duty in N. Wurtemberg. ▶

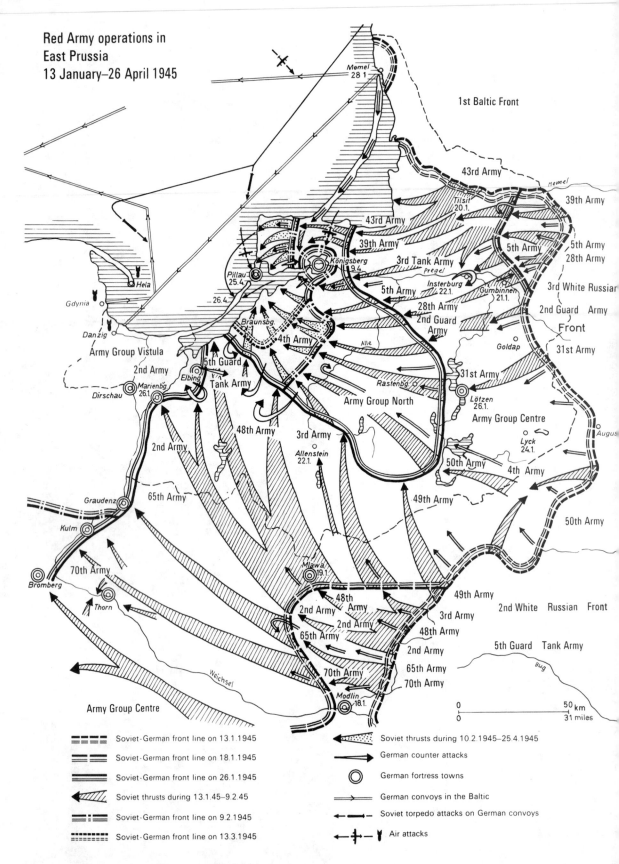

Red Army operations in East Prussia 13 January–26 April 1945

1st Baltic Front

Memel 28.1

43rd Army

39th Army

Memel

Tilsit 20.1

43rd Army

39th Army

5th Army
28th Army

3rd Tank Army

Königsberg 9.4

Pillau 25.4 —26.4

Insterburg 22.1

Gumbinnen 21.1

3rd White Russian

Pregel

5th Army

28th Army

2nd Guard Army

2nd Guard Army

Front

Hela

Gdynia

Danzig

Braunsbg. 1

4th Army

Goldap

31st Army

Army Group Vistula

2nd Army

5th Guard Tank Army

Elbing

Alle

Army Group North

Rastenbg.

31st Army

Lötzen 26.1

Army Group Centre

Marienbg. 26.1

Dirschau

48th Army

3rd Army

Allenstein 22.1

Lyck 24.1

Augus

50th Army

4th Army

Graudenz

65th Army

49th Army

50th Army

Kulm

Bromberg

70th Army

Thorn

Mlawa 19.1

48th Army

49th Army

2nd White Russian Front

2nd Army

3rd Army

2nd Army

48th Army

5th Guard Tank Army

65th Army

2nd Army

Bug

70th Army

65th Army

70th Army

Weichsel

Modlin 18.1

0   50 km
0   31 miles

Army Group Centre

▬▬▬▬ Soviet-German front line on 13.1.1945	Soviet thrusts during 10.2.1945–25.4.1945
▬ ▬ ▬ Soviet-German front line on 18.1.1945	→ German counter attacks
▬▬▬ Soviet-German front line on 26.1.1945	◎ German fortress towns
◀▨ Soviet thrusts during 13.1.45–9.2.45	German convoys in the Baltic
▬ ▬ Soviet-German front line on 9.2.1945	Soviet torpedo attacks on German convoys
▬▬▬▬ Soviet-German front line on 13.3.1945	Air attacks

German anti-tank gun in Koenigsberg.

THE FINAL BATTLE FOR KOENIGSBERG

6 April 1945

Gun fire from all sides

Major Lewinski, 192nd Grenadier Regiment, reporting on an attempt to break out of Koenigsberg during 8–10 April 1945.

At about 2 a.m. we drew up with the reinforced 192nd on our right and the remnants of the 171st on our left. Before us lay a railway cutting—the line from Central to North Station. We quickly overran the Russian outposts, and advanced into the cemetery. Here we ran into our first bit of trouble. Fire from all sides, together with salvoes from "Stalin-organs" rained down on us. What with barbed wire fences and so many paths, we found it extremely difficult to make our way across this difficult terrain. Our only guide was a Russian loud-speaker van to our right, which kept pouring a stream of propaganda into the night . . . After clearing the fence at the edge of the cemetery, we kept to the left. Here we separated from Major Harmann, who took his gunners straight on. After some time, however, he realized that there was no escaping in that direction, and he returned to Koenigsberg.

Suddenly we found ourselves on Holsteiner Dam, on the banks of the Pregel. It had grown damnably light, but we had no choice, and so on we went along the Dam in a westerly direction. There were still some 40–50 of us. Many had been lost in the cemetery. We went past Russian-occupied houses unnoticed, but then our scouts were spotted near the granaries. All hell was let loose in no time at all. They fired at us from every window and from the opposite bank of the river, as well. Firing back in all directions, we withdrew to the edge of the granaries, and then turned off to the right. We dared not continue along the Dam, for meanwhile the whole area had been alerted and we could not possibly get by. It was 5 a.m. now, and visibility was fairly good despite the morning mists.

Crossing the flooded marsh area between Moditten and Gross–Holstein, we managed to break through during the night of 9 April, after hiding in the marshes throughout the day. Nearby, there was another group of some 20 men with a few officers of the 171st Regiment, together with several men from the 548th Volks-Grenadiers who had gone into action just before we did. Their attempt to break out had failed; only a few isolated groups and light guns had got through. Major-General Sudau had fallen soon after the attack near the Luisen Kirche.

During the day, we could see a dying city, veiled in smoke and fire, into which the fiery trails of the heavy guns tore fresh wounds time and again. From isolated spots we could still hear the clacking of odd machine guns, until finally the last sounds of battle were stilled. At dusk, there were only the black clouds and the uncanny red glow of the smoke rising over the dead city . . .

Guards of the 3rd White Russian Front entering Koenigsberg on 8 April.

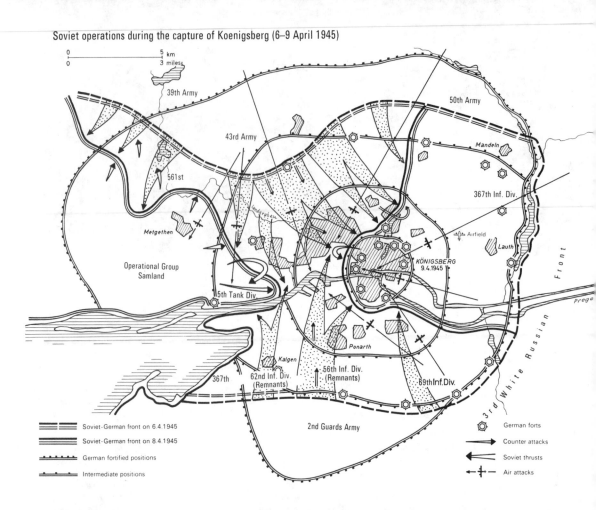

Soviet operations during the capture of Koenigsberg (6–9 April 1945)

0 ___ 5 km
0 ___ 3 miles

39th Army

50th Army

43rd Army

561st

Mandeln

367th Inf. Div.

Metgethen

Airfield

Lauth

Operational Group
Samland

KÖNIGSBERG
9.4.1945

5th Tank Div.

Prege

Kalgen

Ponarth

367th

62nd Inf. Div.
(Remnants)

56th Inf. Div.
(Remnants)

69th Inf.Div.

2nd Guards Army

3rd White Russian Front

Soviet-German front on 6.4.1945	German forts
Soviet-German front on 8.4.1945	Counter attacks
German fortified positions	Soviet thrusts
Intermediate positions	Air attacks

Soviet soldiers during street battles in Koenigsberg.

KOENIGSBERG CAPITULATES

9 April 1945

General Lasch, the last Commander of Koenigsberg. Hitler sentenced him to death *in absentia* and had his family arrested.

5:20 p.m.: "Ammunition gone, stores destroyed . . ."

Under concentrated artillery fire, our breakout attempt failed despite initial successes, and we suffered heavy casualties . . .

This failure decided the fortress commandant to avoid further senseless losses and to capitulate in the morning of 9 April, by which time it had become clear that there was no prospect of relief from outside. Some of the units had become completely demoralized, and one Regiment of 367th Infantry Division had gone over to the enemy.

Nevertheless the fighting continued throughout the day. At 5:20 p.m. the Commander broadcast his last message: "Ammunition gone, stores destroyed." In the evening, General Lasch succeeded in re-establishing contact with the Russian command. Shortly after midnight, he signed the capitulation of the fortress, and was marched off to a prison camp. The rest of the 61st Infantry Division did not lay down arms until 6:30 a.m. on 10 April. During the honourable surrender, the Russians at first allowed all officers to retain their arms. According to Russian estimates, more than 27,000 German soldiers were captured in Koenigsberg.

From: *Beiträge zur Militär und Kriegsgeschichte* (Contributions to Military and War History) *Vol. V.*

Koenigsberg after the battle.

Koenigsberg: German soldiers being led into captivity.

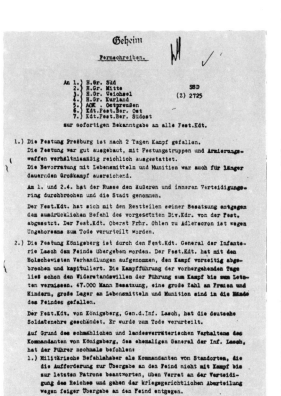

Hitler's order to all fortress commanders to fight to the last cartridge.

U.S. 3rd Army reaching the Elbe, south of Magdeburg, on 11 April

"News for the Troops" reporting American advance on Magdeburg from the Elbe. One day earlier, Admiral Doenitz had declared: "Within a year at the latest, but probably still in 1945, Europe will come to realize that Adolf Hitler is the only great European statesman . . ."

Nr. 361, Donnerstag, 12. April 1945

NACHRICHTEN FÜR DIE TRUPPE

Amerikaner an der Elbe
130 km vor Berlin

An Braunschweig vorbei—Panzer rollen auf Magdeburg

ALLIIERTE Panzer erreichten gestern abend die Elbe bei Magdeburg.

Die Alliierten stehen hier nur etwa 130 km von Berlin und nur 185 von den Sowjets an der Oder. Der Panzerverband, der an der Elbe auftauchte, war von Hannover aus an Braunschweig vorbeigerollt und ohne Widerstand zu finden bis an die Elbe vorgedrungen.

THE AMERICANS AT THE ELBE, NEAR MAGDEBURG

11 April 1945

Allied planes preparing for low-level attacks in support of the advancing armies.

Waffen-SS officer being captured.

LIBERATION OF BUCHENWALD CONCENTRATION CAMP

11 April 1945

For hundreds of prisoners, liberation came too late.

Generals Eisenhower, Bradley and Patton standing aghast before a heap of charred Russian and Polish corpses.

The liberation of Buchenwald

On Wednesday, 11 April at noon, there were only some 21,000 prisoners left in the camp. It looked as if all of them were about to be killed. But the SS did nothing. At 10:30 a.m., the First Camp Leader informed LA I that the camp would be surrendered. This news was reassuring, though it was known that the SS had requested planes from nearby Nora airport to blow up the camp. Hence everyone remained on the alert. One-and-a-half hours later, when a message came over the loudspeaker ordering all SS men to report at once to H.Q. outside, hopes rose higher still. Soon afterwards the SS began to withdraw.

The delight of the 21,000 was indescribable. The skeleton organization which the Communist Party had drawn up for the camp was immediately brought into being, with an International Committee and Individual Committees for the various nationalities: 5,000 Frenchmen, 3,500 Poles and Polish Jews, 2,200 Germans, 2,000 Russians, 2,000 Czechs, 2,000 Ukrainians, 600 Yugoslavs, 400 Dutchmen, 500 Austrians, 200 Italians, 200 Spaniards, and some 3,000 prisoners of other nationalities.

But even while the camp was resounding with cries of jubilation, some of the 26,000 prisoners, sent out of Buchenwald during the last week, were choking and starving to death in railway trucks on the edge of Dachau Concentration Camp.

From E. Kogon: Der SS-Staat (The SS State)

Naked, Crisscrossed like Matches, and about as Substantial . . .

By Colonel Charles Codman

Inside the gate is a spacious yard of rough flagstones. By prearrangement, our Military Government officer and a number of French prisoners were waiting for us— Colonel Marhes, formerly head of the Resistance movement in northern France, and Marcel Paul, member of the Paris Municipal Council; General Audebert of the Cavalry, and General Challe, Aviation. All of them in for "resistance activities" . . .

"You might as well see the end-product first," the Military Government officer said, "and then work backwards."

While not large, the crematory is, as I remember it, the only solidly constructed building in the camp. In a smaller yard, enclosed by a wooden fence, a large wagon like a farmer's cart had just been brought in. Over it the flies buzzed busily. The contents, the Military Government officer explained, were part of the day's toll—thirty or forty bodies, naked, crisscrossed like matches, and about as substantial. The crematory itself is not unlike the standard variety, with certain additional features. It seems that the routine was as follows: Prisoners who died from "natural causes" were simply carted into the ground floor of the crematory proper and tossed into six coke ovens, in which are still to be seen the charred remains of the last over-hasty and incomplete job that the arrival of our troops interrupted.

The unusual feature is the basement. Here, according to eye-witnesses whom I have no reason to disbelieve, were brought prisoners condemned of capital crimes— for example, attempting to escape, insubordination, stealing a potato, smiling in ranks—usually in groups of twenty or so at a time. They were lined up against the walls, each one under a hook fixed at a height of about eight feet from the floor. (The hooks are no longer there. They were hastily removed the day we came in, but the emplacements are clearly visible.) A short slip-noose was placed about the neck of the condemned, who was then raised by the guards the distance necessary to affix the end of the noose to the hook.

If the ensuing strangulation took too long a time to suit the mood of the guards, they beat out the brains of the condemned with a long-handled club resembling a potato masher . . .

Externally, Barrack 61 is like the other barracks, roughly a hundred and fifty feet long by thirty feet wide. Inside, four tiers of wooden shelves incline slightly towards the central corridor. In the rush season this single barrack housed twenty-three hundred "non-workers" that tuberculosis, dysentery, pneumonia and plain starvation had rendered incapable of the daily twelve-hour stretch at the armament factory or nearby quarries . . .

On one shelf barer than the rest, three shadowy figures huddled together for warmth. Cold comfort for the outside two, since the middle one had been dead for several hours . . .

Barrack 47 was like it, but frankly, I hadn't the stomach.

Nameless victim on the edge of the road: one of the thousands butchered by the SS during the so-called "evacuations"—the death marches of concentration camp inmates to the West.

DEATH MARCHES OF CONCENTRATION CAMP PRISONERS FROM SACHSENHAUSEN, ORANIENBURG AND RAVENSBRUECK

April 1945

Drawn by six female skeletons

Now they ordered those three completely senseless marches of starving men and women towards the last outpost of the shrinking Reich, where the guards might feel safe from the Russians . . . The story of Suhren's car ride with Odette Churchill, his hostage, has become known throughout the world. Less known is his remark to a Red Cross representative, who had reproached Kaindl, Commandant of Sachsenhausen Concentration Camp, with leaving a host of corpses lying about. "No such thing ever happened under my command," said Suhren.

It would appear that, on 24 April, shortly before the gates were closed for the last time, Hoess (the Commandant of Auschwitz) gave orders that all women who decided to remain behind must be spared. The temptation to shoot them must have been great. One of the guards, in the Sachsenhausen column, believed he was doing the sick a service by killing them. Another could barely be stopped from doing away with nine men huddled under a single blanket. "I simply can't leave them in that state," he said. When Red Cross men picked up the stragglers, the poor wretches begged them not to shoot. Custom dies slowly in an SS-State . . . But perhaps the most memorable scene in this German panorama was played out on 28 April, when the wife of a Ravensbrueck SS officer disported herself in a carriage drawn by six female skeletons. She was suffering from indigestion, after having stuffed herself with raisins.

From G. Reitlinger: *Die Endloesung*
(The Final Solution)

The Bolshevik–Jewish enemy stands before the gates . . . If everyone of you does his duty, the Asian attack will collapse . . . Berlin will stay German, Vienna will be German again, and Europe will never become Russian.

Millions like him had begun to ask themselves what they were fighting for.

The Allied advance on Central and Southern Germany continues: Braunschweig (Brunswick), Neustadt, Weimar, Celle, Heilbronn, Kulmbach, Gera and Bayreuth all fell during 12–14 April.

BRAUNSCHWEIG, WEIMAR AND GERA OCCUPIED 12–14 April 1945

A captured Nazi Party boss.

"They were forced into it all . . ."

Southern Germany, 13 April

Somewhere in Bavaria. Germans step out of the wood fully armed and you make your peace with the world because a Jeep and a Luger aren't much good against a platoon of Krauts. But the Germans stop you only to surrender . . .

German civilians come with blacklists of Nazis, and Nazis who get picked up give you a sad tale of woe of how they were forced into it all. But they can't lie their way out because there are too many people around who denounced them and the evidence is easy to collect if you go after it.

Peter Furst in *Stars and Stripes*

British advance in Holland. Arnhem is captured after two days of bitter street fighting.

BRITISH TROOPS TAKE ARNHEM AND ADVANCE ON BREMEN
13 April 1945

An R.A.F. Liberator on its way to Germany.

British troops entering the precincts of Bremen on 23 April.

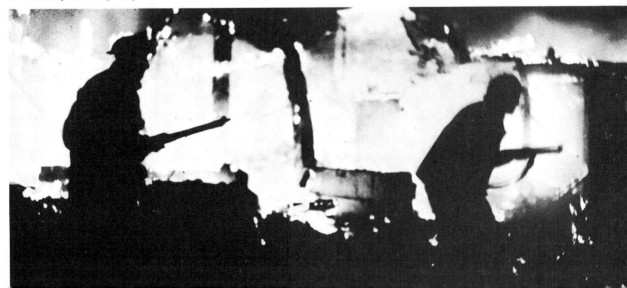

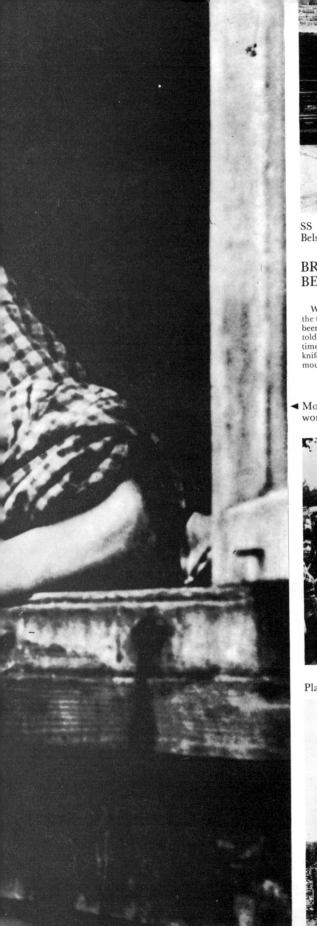

SS Hauptsturmfuehrer Josef Kramer, Commandant of Belsen Concentration Camp.

BRITISH TROOPS LIBERATE
BERGEN–BELSEN 15 April 1945

While I was moving the corpses, I often noticed strange wounds on the thighs of many of them. At first, I thought these wounds must have been caused by gunshots at close range, but when I asked a friend, he told me that many prisoners cut off pieces of flesh and ate them. Next time I went into the mortuary I did, in fact, see a prisoner draw a knife, cut a piece out of the leg of a body, and quickly put it into his mouth, shaking for fear that anyone should catch him at it.

H. O. Le Druillenec, a concentration camp inmate from Jersey.

◄ More than 40,000 starving prisoners, including this woman, were found at Belsen.

Plaque erected in Belsen.

THIS IS THE SITE OF
THE INFAMOUS BELSEN CONCENTRATION CAMP
Liberated by the British on 15 April 1945.

10,000 UNBURIED DEAD WERE FOUND HERE.
ANOTHER 13,000 HAVE SINCE DIED.
ALL OF THEM VICTIMS OF THE
GERMAN NEW ORDER IN EUROPE,
AND AN EXAMPLE OF NAZI KULTUR.

MARSHAL ZHUKOV'S TROOPS
LAUNCH ATTACK ON BERLIN

16 April 1945

Extract from the records of Army Group Centre on 16 April 1945:

After a gunfire barrage lasting two hours and with maximum air support, the enemy launched his attack across the Neisse from the expected strongpoints between Penzig and Rothenburg and between Muskau and Forst. After heavy fighting and severe losses on both sides, the enemy finally succeeded in crossing the Neisse near both points and advanced westwards. In addition to 4 Infantry Armies, the enemy also threw the 4th Tank Army and the 3rd Guards Tank Army into the attack. No detailed information on the deployment of the Tank Armies is available. The enemy attack was brought to a halt along a line running from Gross–Krauschau through Mueckenhain, Wehrkirch to Rothenburg in the Rothenburg sector, and along a line running from Tschenitz through Doebern, Gross–Koelzig and Simmersdorf to Forst in the Muskau sector . . .

The 4th Tank Army has orders to hold the front against enemy attacks expected on 17 April. The 10th SS Tank Division has been diverted to the east of Spreefurt, whence it can be thrown into either the Rothenburg or the Muskau sector, as the situation demands. 31 enemy tanks have been destroyed. Three enemy Corps have breached the right flank of the 4th Tank Army and have advanced to within 8 km N.W. of Auspitz. Our defences N.W. of Auspitz, into which we have thrown our last reserves, have been breached in several places. A counter-attack by the 8th Tank Division has proved abortive. The position on this flank of the Army Group is perilous in the extreme. We have taken every conceivable counter-measure . . .

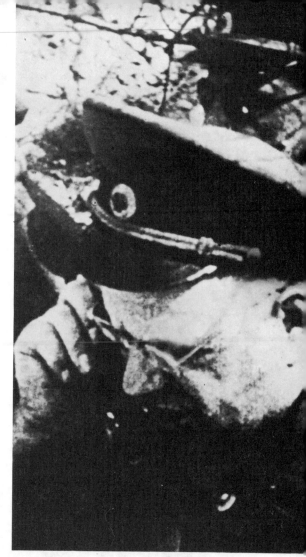

General Zhukov in his command post. ▶

Soviet advance into country held by the German 4th Tank and 9th Armies.

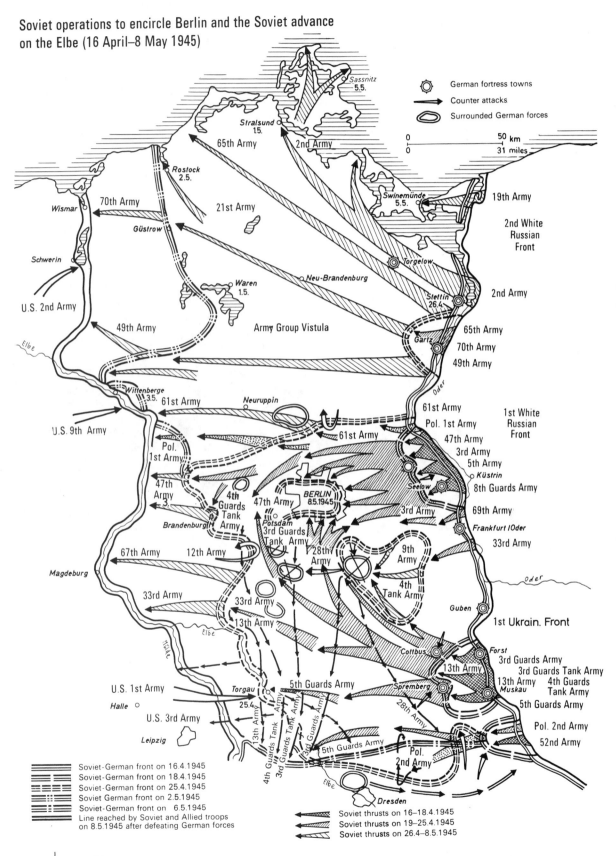

Soviet operations to encircle Berlin and the Soviet advance on the Elbe (16 April–8 May 1945)

German fortress towns
Counter attacks
Surrounded German forces

| 0 | | 50 km |
| 0 | | 31 miles |

Sassnitz 5.5.

Stralsund 15.

65th Army

2nd Army

Rostock 2.5.

19th Army

70th Army

21st Army

Swinemünde 5.5.

2nd White Russian Front

Wismar

Güstrow

Schwerin

Neu-Brandenburg

Torgelow

2nd Army

Waren 1.5.

Stettin 26.4.

U.S. 2nd Army

49th Army

Army Group Vistula

Gartz

65th Army
70th Army
49th Army

Elbe

Wittenberge 3.5.

61st Army

Neuruppin

61st Army

61st Army
Pol. 1st Army

1st White Russian Front

U.S. 9th Army

Pol. 1st Army

47th Army
3rd Army
5th Army

Küstrin

47th Army

4th Guards Tank Army

Brandenburg

BERLIN 8.5.1945

47th Army

Potsdam
3rd Guards Tank Army

Seelow

8th Guards Army

3rd Army

69th Army

Frankfurt /Oder

33rd Army

Magdeburg

67th Army

12th Army

28th Army

9th Army

4th Tank Army

Oder

33rd Army

33rd Army

13th Army

Guben

1st Ukrain. Front

Halle

Elbe

Cottbus

Forst

3rd Guards Army

U.S. 1st Army

Torgau 25.4.

5th Guards Army

Spremberg

13th Army

13th Army
Muskau

3rd Guards Tank Army
4th Guards Tank Army
5th Guards Army

Halle

U.S. 3rd Army

Leipzig

13th Army

4th Guards Tank Army
3rd Guards Tank Army

5th Guards Army

28th Army

Pol. 2nd Army
52nd Army

5th Guards Army

Pol. 2nd Army

Elbe

Dresden

Soviet-German front on 16.4.1945
Soviet-German front on 18.4.1945
Soviet-German front on 25.4.1945
Soviet German front on 2.5.1945
Soviet-German front on 6.5.1945
Line reached by Soviet and Allied troops on 8.5.1945 after defeating German forces

Soviet thrusts on 16–18.4.1945
Soviet thrusts on 19–25.4.1945
Soviet thrusts on 26.4–8.5.1945

Soviet bombers attacking Berlin.

Volkssturm men building tank barriers in Berlin.

Air force auxiliaries and Hitler Youth being thrown into the defence of the German capital.

The split-up of the Ruhr pocket and the U.S. advance
to the Elbe (5–18 April 1945)

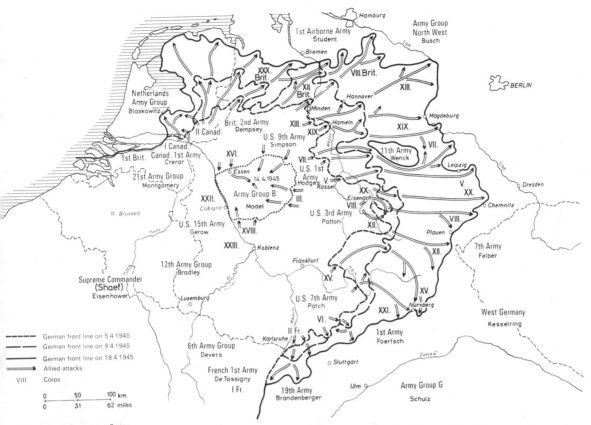

German prisoners of war.

The mopping up of the Ruhr pocket began on 12 April. Essen, Gelsenkirchen, Bochum, Dortmund and Luedenscheid were occupied on 15 April. On 19 April SHAEF announced that all organized German resistance in the Ruhr pocket had ceased.

ARMY GROUP B CAPITULATES IN THE RUHR BASIN 18 April 1945

"For the Sake of your Nation's Future, Lay Down your arms at Once . . ."

By General Ridgway

I decided to make one more try. I sat down and composed a personal letter to General Model, and think that part of the text of it might be of interest here. The date was 15 April 1945:

Neither history nor the military profession records any nobler character, any more brilliant master of warfare, any more dutiful subordinate, than the American General, Robert E. Lee. Eighty years ago this month, his loyal command reduced in numbers, stripped of its means of effective fighting and completely surrounded by overwhelming forces, he chose an honourable capitulation.

This same choice is now yours. In the light of a soldier's honour, for the reputation of the German Officer Corps, for the sake of your nation's future, lay down your arms at once. The German lives you will save are sorely needed to restore your people to their proper place in society. The German cities you will preserve are irreplaceable necessities for your people's welfare.

Branstetter delivered this letter. He came back with Model's Chief of Staff. It was no use, they said, Model would not consider any plea whatever. That was that. I could do no more. From now on the blood was upon Model's head.

Advance in the South

From General de Gaulle's War Memoirs

While General Bradley's army group encircled Marshal Model's German forces in the Ruhr Basin and brought them to capitulation, then crossed the Weser in the central Reich, that of General Devers advanced southward from the Main. But Devers, instead of marching east as well, tended to bear towards the south. If the French let him continue, this movement would press Patch's army against de Lattre's, block the latter close to the Rhine, and limit the German territory we occupied to a few shreds of Baden. Here, operations also had a direct bearing on the political realm. Therefore I informed de Lattre, even before his troops began to cross the Rhine, to what extent his army's action would be serving the national interest. We had agreed that in any case the First Army should seize Stuttgart. The capital of Wurtemberg would be, in fact, the open door to the Danube, Bavaria and Austria for our troops. Its possession would assure us, furthermore, an important pledge to support our intentions as to the French zone of occupation.

Field-Marshal Model, Commander of the surrounded German Army Group. (Model committed suicide on 21 April 1945.)

NACHRICHTEN FÜR DIE TRUPPE

USA-Panzer stürmen Nürnberg

VS räumt Strassensperren

Der Endkampf um Berlin beginnt—Leipzig fast eingeschlossen—Halle fällt

NÜRNBERG, die Stadt der Reichsparteitage, ist gestern abend durch einen überraschenden Vorstoss der Amerikaner überrumpelt worden und bereits zur Hälfte in amerikanischer Hand.

Nach den letzten Meldungen dringen die Amerikaner mit Flammenwerfer-Panzern und Sturmgeschützen in den Stadtkern von Nürnberg vor, wo nur noch vereinzelt Widerstand geleistet wird.

Das Tempo des Vorstosses ist so schnell, dass der Stadt voraussichtlich die totale Zerstörung erspart bleiben wird, die in anderen Städten jedesmal durch schwere Strassenkämpfe verursacht wurde.

Der Volkssturm hat die meisten Strassensperren und Panzergräben geräumt, um Nürnberg eine sinnlose Verwüstung zu ersparen.

Der Einmarsch der USA-Panzer kam zuerst von Nordosten und dann, nachdem sie bereits von allen Seiten eingeschlossen war.

Die Nachricht, dass die Amerikaner in Nürnberg eingebrochen sind, folgt auf einen Tag, an dem Schlag auf Schlag Berichte über neue tiefe Einbrüche der Alliierten in Richtung Berlin, Dresden und Hamburg eintrafen.

Generalfeldmarschall
ERNST BUSCH.
Seine Aufgabe : Berlin zu halten.

Gross-Offensive an Oder- und Neisse-Front bricht los

Mit einem Trommelfeuer, das alle Bewohner bis nach Berlin kurz nach drei Uhr morgens aus dem Schlaf in die Luftschutzkeller scheuchte, begannen die Sowjets gestern die Grossoffensive, mit der sie das noch unbesetzte Rest-Reich zwischen Oder und Elbe überrennen und die Reichshauptstadt in Hand bringen wollen.

Tausende von Panzern, riesige Artilleriezusammenballungen und zahllose Flugzeugverbände wurden eingesetzt, denen von deutscher Seite auch nicht annähernd gleichstarkes Material entgegengestellt werden kann. Allein am Neisseabschnitt werden die russischen Sturmdivisionen auf über eine Million Mann geschätzt.

Über den Kampfverlauf wurden bisher nur spärliche Mitteilungen durchgegeben. Bekannt wurde nur, dass die Sowjets an den unteren Oder im ersten Ansturm die Abwehr am Westufer bezwungen und bei Schwedt einen neuen Brückenkopf errichtet haben, aus dem heraus sie die Autobahn Stettin-Berlin zu gewinnen suchen.

Den direkten Stoss auf Berlin führen aber Verbände, die aus den Brückenköpfen zwischen Fürstenberg und dem Oderbruch nördlich Küstrin vordringen.

Die gepanzerten Angriffskeilen der Sowjets bahnen Schlachtgeschwader den Weg, die mit Raketen und Bomben die Bunker zerschmettern, während die Munitionslager sprengen und die Reserven ausseinandergehen, so dass sie die Kampffront kommen.

Deutsche werden Deutsche.

Russische Fallschirmjäger werden rings um Berlin abgesetzt und unterbinden die Befehlsübermittlung. Deutsche Offiziere in Wehrmachtuniform, die sich auf Raketen der Kriegsgefangenschaft in Russland dem Moskauer Offizierskomitee angeschlossen haben, fordern mit Lautsprechern die deutschen Truppen auf, den sinnlosen Widerstand einzustellen und die letzten noch unversehrten Städte im Reich vor der Vernichtung durch Weiterkämpfen zu bewahren.

Vor der Grossoffensive der Sowjets, die sich bereits von Stettin bis weit nach Ratibor in Oberschlesien ausdehnt, verblassten gestern die Kämpfe am Südabschnitt der Ostfront, wo die Russen nur noch 80 Kilometer von Linz und knapp 200 Kilometer von dem Führerhauptquartier am Obersalzberg entfernt sind.

Die Sowjets dringen nach der Einnahme von St. Pölten auf beiden Donauufern weiter vor. Sie haben bereits den halben Weg von Wien nach Linz zurückgelegt.

(Fortsetzung Seite 3)

Stützpunkt Gironde-Nord vor dem Fall

Nur Stunden haben das Grossangriffs auf die abgeschriebenen Atlantikstützpunkte Gironde-Nord und Gironde-Süd nach Berichten aus Zürich, den Kernstück von Gironde-Nord, den Kopf ein Artillerie eingestellt und sich gefangen gegeben.

Viele deutsche Truppen sind dem vorgestrigen Brandangriff amerikanischer Bomber zum Opfer gefallen.

fallen, bei dem neuartige Brandkanister geworfen wurden, die ihre Brandflüssigkeit in einem weiten Gebiet verspritzen.

Nach letzten Meldungen ist der grösste Teil von Gironde-Nord bereits in alliierter Hand. Nur vereinzelte Widerstandsnester setzen den Kampf fort.

Südlich der Gironde-Mündung greifen etwa 500 schwere viermotorige Bomber gestern wieder die deutschen Geschützstellungen im Gebiet über Pointe de Grave mit verheerender Wirkung an. Auch die Bombardement durch französische Kriegsschiffe dauert an. Nur zwei der deutschen schweren Küstenbatterien feuern noch.

Brillanten für Mauss

Das Eichenlaub mit Schwertern und Brillanten zum Ritterkreuz des Eisernen Kreuzes erhielt Generalleutnant Karl Mauss, Kommandeur der Thüringischen 7. Panzer-Division, als 26. Soldat der deutschen Wehrmacht.

100 RM sind nur noch 25 Schweiz. Rappen wert

Den bisher tiefsten Stand seit der Inflation im Sommer 1923 erreichte gestern am Reichsmark im freien Devisenhandel in der Schweiz, wo nach Berichten aus Zürich, die Papiermark nur noch den zehntausendsten Teil ihres amtlichen Tauschwertes hat.

Während der amtliche Kurs eines Hundertmarkscheins 172,50 Schweizer Franken ist, erhielt man im freien Devisenhandel in diesem Fall 25 Rappen für 100 Mark.

Der katastrophale Kurssturz der Reichsmark im neutralen Ausland wird verursacht:

1. Durch den Zusammenbruch der nationalsozialistischen Reichsregierung, deren Währungsgarantie jetzt völlig wertlos geworden ist.

2. Durch die steigende Ausgabe von Notgeld im Reich, wobei niemand weiss, wieviel Notgeld schon ausgegeben wurde.

Weitere Städte, die jetzt Notgeld ausgeben, weil sie infolge des Transportchaos keine Reichsbanknoten beschaffen können, sind Civitas, Waldenburg, Freiburg im Breisgau, Marburg, Grünstadt und Klagenfurt.

Über Chemnitz hinaus

Am schnellsten geht der Vormarsch in Sachsen vor sich weiter. Nach den letzten Meldungen sind amerikanische Panzerspitzen über Chemnitz hinaus auf die Autobahn Dresden weiter vorgestossen.

In Chemnitz selbst geht der Widerstand rasch zuende. Der Westteil der Stadt ist bereits von den Alliierten besetzt.

In Halle hat die Besatzung den Kampf eingestellt.

Kurz nachdem Batterien das Feuer auf Halle eröffneten, liess der Kampfkommandant der neue Fahne aufziehen, um die Stadt vor der totalen Vernichtung zu retten.

Dagegen sind in Leipzig mehr als 1 Million Einwohner weiterhin dem Vernichtungsfeuer zahlreicher Batterien ausgesetzt.

Die Stadt ist jetzt fast völlig eingeschlossen, nachdem die amerikaner rückwärts Leipzig bis Wurzen vorgestossen sind.

Von den jüngsten Abschnitten liegen noch folgende Meldungen vor:

20 km vor Hamburg

Im Vorstoss auf Hamburg sind die Alliierten bis auf 20 km an die Hafenstadt herangekommen.

Einheiten der 2. Marine-Infanteriedivision wurden gestern zwischen Winzendorf und Lüneburg nach verlustreichem Kampf geworfen. Sie wurden auf dem Rückzug nach Hamburg von der alliierten Luftwaffe zusammengeschossen und zusammengebombt.

In Bremen dringen flammenverfende Panzer und Sturmgeschütze in die Neustadt vor. Der Vorort Brinkum musste geräumt werden.

Altenburg rettet sich: Leipzig muss sterben

Zwei Städte haben gestern durch verschiedene Entscheidungen ihrer Bürgermeister ein verschiedenes Schicksal erlebt.

Der Bürgermeister von Altenburg in Thüringen erklärte seine Stadt zur offenen Stadt, sodass die Amerikaner sie kampflos besetzten.

In Leipzig wollte der Kampfkommandant gleichfalls die Stadt zur offenen Stadt erklären und sie kampflos übergeben. Aber der Oberbürgermeister von Leipzig, SS-Gruppenführer Freyberg, der auf der Kriegsverbrecherliste steht, und das umzingelten Stadt nicht weg kann, widersetzte sich dem Beschluss.

Letzter Führer-Appell an die Ost-Divisionen

Der Führer hat gestern einen letzten Durchhaltebefehl an die Soldaten der Ostfront erlassen, in dem er sie auffordert: "Der Vernichtungsoffensive der Sowjets Stand zu halten und den bolschewistischen Ansturm vor der Reichshauptstadt in einem Blutbad zu ersticken.

"Wer sich ihren eigenen Knien voraussprechen," so heisst es in den letzten Tagesbefehl des Führers, "und es ist seit dem Januar dieses Jahres alles geschehen, um eine starke Front aufzubauen. Eine gewaltige Artillerie empfängt den Feind. Die Ausfälle unserer Infanterie sind durch zahlreiche neue Einheiten ergänzt. Alarmeinheiten, Neuaufstellungen und Volkssturm verstärken unsere Front. Der Bolschewist wird diesmal das alte Schicksal Asiens erleben, das heisst, er muss und wird vor der Hauptstadt des Deutschen Reichs verbluten."

In alter Siegeszuversicht

Der Führer gibt dann in seinem Tagesbefehl bekannt, dass zahlreiche deutsche Offiziere und Soldaten in deutscher Uniform gemeinsam mit den Sowjets gegen die Verteidiger Berlins kämpfen und fordert die Truppe auf, überall, auch in den eigenen Reihen, nach Verrätern Ausschau zu halten.

"Wer Befehl zum Rückzug gibt," so befiehlt der Führer, "ist sofort festzunehmen und nötigenfalls augenblicklich umzulegen, ganz gleich, welchen Rang er besitzt."

Der Führer gibt dann seiner unerschütterlichen Zuversicht in den deutschen Endsieg Ausdruck und erklärt:

"Der letzte Ansturm Asiens wird genau so zerbrechen, wie schon oft der Einbruch unserer Gegner im Westen trotz allem scheitern wird. Berlin bleibt deutsch, Wien wird wieder deutsch und Europa wird niemals russisch."

Zwei Fronten treffen sich

Bologna wird von Süden und Osten bedroht

Die ganze italienische von Küste zu Küste ist in Bewegung, nachdem die Alliierten gestern früh auch an der ganzen Front zwischen der Ligurischen Küste und Bologna zum Grossangriff übergegangen sind.

Nach dem am Sonntag gemeldeten Fall von Imola war die grosse Stützpunkt Bologna jetzt von Süden und Osten bedroht. Alliierte Verbände wurden zuletzt nur 25 km südostwärts Bologna und etwa 30 km vor den Eisenbahnknotenpunkt Ferrara gemeldet.

Dem neuen Vorstoss ginge Luftangriffe voran, bei denen die Alliierten alls übertrafen, was die Wehrmacht in Italien bisher erlebt hatte. Fast 4 000 Bomber deckten die Abwehrstellungen südlich Bologna mit Bomben ein.

Dönitz besucht Dönitzdivision

Grossadmiral Dönitz besuchte gestern am Nordabschnitt der Oderfront Einheiten der Marine-Infanterie-Division "Grossadmiral Dönitz", einer Kustenbatterieeinheiten am Stettiner Haff.

Der Oberbefehlshaber der Kriegsmarine war kaatern im Sonderflugzeug am seinen Hauptquartier auf Schloss Kiel eingetroffen, das durch Tiefenbangriffe gestern in der letzten Zufluchtsstätte der Partei in den Salzburger Bergen liegt.

Title-page of *News for the Troops* (published by the Americans) reporting the storming of Nuremberg by U.S. troops, the beginning of a major offensive on the Oder and Neisse, the meeting of Soviet and Allied forces, and the devaluation of the mark. On 21 April 1945, Churchill declared in Bristol: "I do not think the period when official festivities and and rejoicings shall be embarked on need be long delayed."

MAGDEBURG AND LEIPZIG CAPTURED 18–19 April 1945

U.S. Soldiers on the outskirts of Magdeburg.

U.S. 7th Army troops during the four-day battle for Nuremberg.

Patrols of the U.S. 90th Infantry Division crossing the Czechoslovak border on 18 April.

NUREMBERG FALLS 21 April 1945

HITLER'S 56TH BIRTHDAY

20 April 1945

From Goebbels' broadcast on the eve of Hitler's birthday:

"German people! Today, millions of people throughout the world are looking to this man, full of hope that he may yet discover a way out of the great evil that now plagues mankind. He will surely save all the nations, but we Germans, in particular, owe him a great debt of gratitude; proudly and ready for battle we follow him as one man."

*

On 20 April the last round of congratulations was being proffered in the bunker of the Reichs-Chancellery. Once again, the Heads of State and of the Wehrmacht—Goering, Ribbentrop, Bormann, Keitel, Doenitz, Jodl, Himmler, Goebbels, Speer, Krebs, Koller *et al.* —were assembled to pay their birthday tribute to their Fuehrer and Supreme Commander. A telegram was also received from Mussolini.

*

Hitler thanks Mussolini on 21 April 1945:

My thanks to you, Duce, for your birthday wishes. The struggle for our survival is at its height. With unlimited resources, Bolshevism and the armies of Jewry are straining to join their malignant forces in Europe so as to cause chaos in our Continent. Utterly unafraid of death, the German people and all those who are of like mind, will see to it that this onslaught is thwarted, at whatever cost, and thus alter the course of this war by their unique heroism. At this historic moment, in which the fate of Europe is being decided for centuries to come, I send you my most cordial greetings. Adolf Hitler.

*

It was the last relatively normal day in the Reichs-Chancellery. Hitler, too, felt that, despite the catastrophic threat to the Reich, his birthday was a joyous occasion, and thought seriously of going up into the mountains. After all, it was April—and in April he had always taken Eva Braun to Obersalzberg . . . On 21 April, Hitler was rudely awakened from these reveries: the first Russian grenades had begun to fall on the centre of Berlin . . .

From Domarus: *Hitler Reden und Proklamationen*
(Hitler's speeches and proclamations) Vol. II, 1963

Hitler's most obedient soldier, Field Marshal Schoerner, offering his congratulations in the Fuehrer's bunker.

The MURDER OF ALBRECHT HAUSHOFER AND 13 OTHER POLITICAL PRISONERS

23 April 1945

During the last night of Nazi rule, fourteen inmates of Lehrter St. Prison in Berlin were fetched from their cells and told that they were being released, subject to confirmation by Prinz Albrecht Strasse (Gestapo H.Q.). When the fourteen passed the prison gate they were joined by an equal number of guards in black uniform. The prisoners had barely taken a few steps into the spring night—hearing the liberators' gunfire at close quarters—before they were all felled by shots in the neck. When the dead were discovered, one of them was still clasping a bundle of poems in his hand. He was Albrecht Haushofer. The man who lifted him up was his own brother, just released from prison himself. The verses he took from the dead man's hand bore the title *Moabiter Sonette* (Sonnets from Moabit Prison).

From R. Hildebrandt's epilogue to the sonnets,
Berlin 1946.

XXII COMRADES

By Albrecht Haushofer

When into reveries I dully sank,
I saw the heroes' host file in,
Yorck, Moltke, Schulenberg, Schwerin,
'side Hassel, Popitz, Helfferich and Planck—

Not one who quivered like a reed,
not one who, ruling in his tower,
with glorious strength, did in the fatal hour,
forget his people or their need.

Those borne away nourish our hope,
all men of noble rank and fame,
who paced these cells, yet felt no shame—

And so they waited for the rope.
Times are when madness rules the land.
Then noblest heads roll in the sand.

"Times are when madness rules the land": One of millions of German women in a burning city.

Luftwaffe Commando report on final dispositions for the
defence of Stuttgart.

STUTTGART OCCUPIED

22 April 1945

*General de Lattre de Tassigny to General de Gaulle on 21 April
1945:*

"Complete success of operations engaged the last fifteen days in
Wurtemberg, in the Black Forest and in Baden. The Danube has been
crossed along a line of over 60 kilometres below Donaueschingen. We
have entered Stuttgart from the south, completing the encirclement
of important enemy forces. In the plain of Baden, Alt Breisach and
Freiburg are in our hands. The Black Forest is completely surrounded."

*

Mayor Stroelin of Stuttgart:

Accompanied by French officers, we were taken to French H.Q. at
the *Gasthof zum Ritter* in Degerloch. It was a glorious sunny day. For
Stuttgart, the war was over. Tanks and lorries blocked the road.
Captured German soldiers and Volkssturm men filed past. I had to
wait for a short time before being led to the Commanding General.
When I was face to face with him, I said: "I am the Mayor of Stuttgart
I surrender the town." It was 11 a.m. on 22 April 1945.

Volkssturm men checking civilian passes one day before
the French entered Stuttgart.

A street in Stuttgart in April 1945.

HIMMLER'S PEACE OFFER TO THE WESTERN POWERS THROUGH COUNT BERNADOTTE

23–24 April 1945

"My Fuehrer, it is five seconds to midnight!"

During the night of 20 April, as I was about to leave the Fuehrer's bunker, and just after Hitler had spoken to me about the treachery of the 4th Army, Hewel from the Foreign Office stuck his head through the door and asked: "My Fuehrer, do you have any further orders for me tonight?" When Hitler said no, Hewel added: "My Fuehrer, it is five seconds to midnight. If there is anything you can still do by political means, now is the time to try." In a low, almost monotonous, voice, Hitler replied, as he left the room with tired and faltering steps: "Politics? I am no longer interested; the whole thing revolts me. When I am dead you will get a bellyful of politics." His voice told us he knew the game was up . . .

General Dethleffsen in *KTB*
(German Supreme Command War Diary)

Count Bernadotte.

Heinrich Himmler.

Himmler—a bourgeois with all the habits of a good *paterfamilias*.

Hannah Arendt in Jewish Frontier

There is more to be learned from the characteristic personality of the man who can boast that he was the organizing spirit of the murder. Heinrich Himmler is not one of those intellectuals stemming from the dim No-Man's Land between the Bohemian and the Pimp, whose significance in the composition of the Nazi élite has been repeatedly stressed of late. He is neither a Bohemian like Goebbels, nor a sex criminal like Streicher, nor a perverted fanatic like Hitler, nor an adventurer like Goering. He is a "bourgeois" with all the outer aspect of respectability, all the habits of a good *paterfamilias* who does not betray his wife and anxiously seeks to secure a decent future for his children; and he has consciously built up his newest terror organization, covering the whole country, on the assumption that most people are not bohemians nor fanatics, nor adventurers, nor sex maniacs, nor sadists, but first and foremost job-holders and good family men . . .

We have been so accustomed to admire or gently ridicule the family man's kind concern and earnest concentration on the welfare of his family, his solemn determination to make life easy for his wife and children, that we hardly noticed how the devoted *paterfamilias*, worried about nothing so much as his security, was transformed under the pressure of the chaotic economic conditions of our time into an involuntary adventurer, who for all his industry and care could never be certain what the next day would bring. The docility of this type was already manifest in the very early period of Nazi "gleichschaltung". It became clear that for the sake of his pension, his life insurance, the security of his wife and children, such a man was ready to sacrifice his beliefs, his honour, and his human dignity. It needed only the Satanic genius of Himmler to discover that after such degradation he was entirely prepared to do literally anything when the ante was raised and the bare existence of his family was threatened. The only condition he put was that he should be fully exempted from responsibility for his acts . . .

When his occupation forces him to murder people he does not regard himself as a murderer because he has not done it out of inclination but in his professional capacity. Out of sheer passion he would never do harm to a fly.

Himmler: "I admit that Germany is beaten."

By Count Bernadotte

At 3 a.m. the following morning I was awakened by the telephone. It was the Chief of the Flensburg Gestapo, who informed me that Brigadefuehrer Schellenberg wished to speak to me about a most urgent matter. As I had promised to visit another camp in Jutland which had been prepared for Scandinavian prisoners of war arriving from Germany, I was only able to go to Flensburg later in the day, and met Schellenberg there at 3 p.m.

That was on 23 April. Schellenberg lost no time in letting off his bombshell. Hitler was finished. It was thought that he could not live more than a couple of days at the outside.

That same day, Doctor Goebbels had announced that the Fuehrer had arrived in Berlin where he would in person lead the defence.

Schellenberg continued his report of the situation.

Schellenberg: Himmler has decided to bring about a meeting with General Eisenhower to inform him that he is willing to give orders to the German forces in the West to capitulate. Would you be prepared to take this message to General Eisenhower?

Bernadotte: It would be better if Himmler's wishes were transmitted to the Swedish Government, who could then, if they were willing, transmit them to the representatives of the Western Powers. But in no circumstances will I forward such a communiqué to the Swedish Minister of Foreign Affairs, Gunther, unless Himmler promises that the German forces in Norway and Denmark shall capitulate too . . .

Schellenberg declared that he quite understood my points of view and said that he would endeavour to make them clear to Himmler before the latter and I met again. He got on to Himmler on the telephone, and it was arranged that we should meet in Lubeck that night, the night of April 23–24th.

*

"I admit that Germany is beaten." The Head of the Gestapo uttered these words with a resigned gesture. What was going to happen?

Himmler: In the situation which has now arisen, I consider my hands free. In order to save as great a part of Germany as possible from Russian invasion I am willing to capitulate on the Western front to enable the Western Allies to advance rapidly towards the East. But I am not prepared to capitulate on the Eastern front. I have always been, and shall always remain, a sworn enemy of Bolshevism. In the beginning of the World War I fought tooth and nail against the Russo–German pact. Are you willing to forward a communiqué on these lines to the Swedish Minister for Foreign Affairs, so that he can inform the Western Powers of my proposal?

On April 23rd 1945 Heinrich Himmler came to this place, where a branch of the Royal Swedish Legation was established, to ask me to inform the Supreme Commander of the Allied Forces that he was prepared to surrender with the German armed forces to British, American or Swedish troops

This was the first time during several talks I had with him that Himmler admitted that Germany was beaten

The Swedish Government informed the Governments in London and Washington accordingly. A few days later, the complete and unconditional surrender of Germany followed.

F Bernadotte

Am 23 April 1945 kam Heinrich Himmler in dieses Haus, in dem eine Abordnung der Königlich Schwedischen Gesandschaft untergebracht war, und bat mich, dem Oberkommandierenden der alliierten Streitkräfte mitzuteilen, daß er bereit sei sich mit der gesamten deutschen Wehrmacht den britischen, amerikanischen oder schwedischen Truppen zu ergeben

Hier gab Himmler zum ersten Male zu, daß Deutschland geschlagen sei. Die schwedische Regierung benachrichtigte hierüber die Regierung in London und Washington. Einige Tage später folgte die vollständige und bedingungslose Kapitulation.

F Bernadotte

The house in Hohen-Luechen near Luebeck, in which Himmler met Bernadotte.

Bernadotte: In my view it is quite impossible to persuade the allies to accept capitulation on the Western front while hostilities continue on the Eastern front. Britain and America will certainly not agree to any special truce of this kind with Germany.

Himmler: I can see how difficult it is; but in any event I must try to save millions of Germans from Russian occupation.

Bernadotte: I am only prepared to transmit your plea to the Swedish Foreign Minister if you promise that Denmark and Norway will be included in the capitulation.

Himmler, without hesitation, replied that he was prepared to do that, and had no objection to the occupation of Denmark and Norway by British, American or Swedish troops. He made only one condition; that Denmark and Norway must not be occupied by Russian troops. I asked him what he intended to do if his plea was rejected or ignored. "In that case," he replied, "I shall take command of a battalion on the Eastern front and get myself killed in action." It is generally known that Himmler did not put this plan into effect.

*

The Allies sent the following telegram in reply:

"A German capitulation can be accepted only if it embraces all fronts. . . . Wherever resistance continues the Allies will press their attacks until they have achieved complete victory."

Hitler fell into a furious rage

by Gerhard Boldt

The news of Himmler's peace offer affected Hitler far more adversely than that of the alleged desertion or treachery of Hermann Goering. Goering had at least asked permission to take over by telegram, thus showing that he still recognized Hitler's authority. Himmler, on the other hand, had completely ignored "his Fuehrer" and had taken matters into his own hand without so much as by your leave. To make things worse, Hitler had always considered Himmler one of his most faithful and devoted followers. What little trust he still had in the loyalty and comradeship of his men collapsed at that moment. Hitler fell into a furious rage, and his hatred and disdain had to be seen to be believed. He called Himmler's negotiations behind his back one of the most shameless acts of treachery in German history.

From: *Die letzten Tage der Reichskanzlei*
(The last days of the Reichs-Chancellery)

WITHDRAWAL OF GERMAN TROOPS FROM SAMLAND

Late April 1945

Marshal Vassilevsky, Commander of the 3rd White Russian Front made the following appeal to German soldiers in Samland on 11 April 1945:

Our forces are greatly superior, and your continued resistance is senseless. It can only lead to your own destruction and that of countless civilians in the Pillau sector. To avoid unnecessary bloodshed, I therefore call upon you to lay down your arms within 24 hours . . .

German troops withdrawing to Pillau, which was taken by the Red Army on 25 April.

The "History of the 21st Division" on the withdrawal of the last German soldiers from Samland:

On Peyse peninsula much the same was happening as in Follendorf. The last units in this sector, detachments of the 5th Tank Division, destroyed all their guns, once their plan to break through the Russian lines in the east and to reach the Oder had been frustrated. The collapse was clear for all to see: white flags on all the bunkers crammed with wounded soldiers. As the Stalin organs began to blast the forest, even the last vestiges of resistance collapsed. Countless men were taken prisoner that night. Only a very few had adequate physical or mental strength to escape across the sea. At Neplecken, only a single sailing boat had made fast, and when it became obvious that no further boats could be expected, a small group started on a forced march south along the beach, where large numbers of men from other divisions were waiting for transport or preparing for surrender. At dawn, the tiny remnant was able to board a small anti-aircraft vessel.

Two wounded German soldiers on the Samland front in April 1945.

Soviet planes on their way to Berlin.

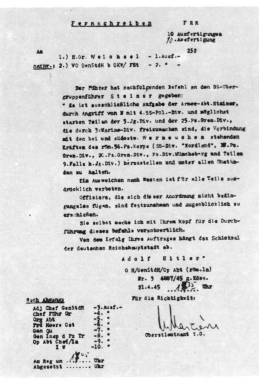

An die Bevölkerung von Berlin

Berlin ist eingekesselt!

Die Rote Armee hat einen festen Ring um die Stadt gelegt. Dieser Ring wird unter den Schlägen der Roten Armee immer enger. Bei der katastrophalen Lage der deutschen Truppen an den anderen Frontabschnitten wäre es geradezu töricht an eine Hilfe für das eingeschlossene Berlin zu glauben

Die Reste der im Raum von Frankfurt a. O. zerschlagenen deutschen Divisionen sind im Raum südlich Beeskow eingeschlossen und strecken zu Tausenden die Waffen. Die untere Oder wurde auf breiter Front überschritten. Stettin ist besetzt. Hier sind die Russen 30 km über

Soviet pamphlet telling the people of Berlin that their city is surrounded.

BERLIN IS SURROUNDED

25 April 1945

The opportunity Eisenhower failed to take

On the day that the Americans reached the river (Elbe), Roosevelt died at Warm Springs. His last message to Churchill, sent that morning, contained the words—the very epitome of the hopes he had nursed for a united world—"I would minimize the general Soviet problem as much as possible." Two days later, on 16 April, seizing for the second time the opportunity Eisenhower had failed to take, the Russians resumed their attack on the eastern defences of Germany. By the 21st—three days after Field-Marshal Model surrendered the Ruhr—the Red Army reached the outskirts of Berlin. By the 25th the city was surrounded with Hitler inside it . . .

From Bryant: *Triumph in the West.*

Soviet guns during the attack on Berlin.

Hitler's order to SS-Obergruppenfuehrer Steiner to stand fast. "The fate of the German capital depends on you!"

THE DIVISION OF GERMANY

The political background and the last war conferences of the Allies.

CHRONOLOGICAL TABLE: January–April 1945

1945

1/1: The Communist Lublin Committee becomes the Provisional Government of Poland, despite protests by the Polish Government in London.

6/1: British forward their operational plan for N.W. Europe to Americans.

18/1: Provisional Government of Poland transferred from Lublin to Warsaw.

30/1: Czechoslovak Government-in-exile severs diplomatic relations with Polish Government-in-exile and recognizes the Lublin Provisional Government.

30/1–2/2: Roosevelt and Churchill hold preliminary discussions on Yalta Conference in Malta.

4–11/2: Yalta Conference between Stalin, Roosevelt and Churchill.

6/2: Yalta: Soviet Union agrees with Western allies on the division of Germany into zones of occupation.

10/2: Yalta: France invited to take a zone of occupation.

20/2: The Provisional Government of Hungary signs armistice agreement in Moscow. Hungary undertakes to pay reparations and to repeal all legislation incorporating Czechoslovak, Rumanian and Yugoslav territories.

27/2: The King of Rumania is forced by Vishinsky, the Soviet Foreign Minister, to appoint a Communist government.

February: Poland takes over civil administration of German territory east of the Oder–Neisse line.

March: Creation of five new Polish provinces: Mazuria, Upper Silesia, Lower Silesia, Pomerania and Danzig. Some 9·3 million German inhabitants are expelled from these provinces.

12/4: Sudden death of President Roosevelt at Warm Springs, Georgia. Harry S. Truman becomes the new President of the United States.

16–18/4: British discuss future military plans with General Eisenhower.

21/4: Poland signs 30-year pact of mutual friendship and assistance with the Soviet Union.

23/4: Molotov in Washington: State Department and President Truman appeal for compromise on Polish question.

25/4–26/6: San Francisco Conference on the organization of the United Nations. Foundation of UNO.

THE POLITICAL TUG OF WAR BETWEEN THE WESTERN ALLIES AND THE SOVIET UNION IN 1945

On 3 January 1945, M. Osubka-Morawski, the Premier of the Polish Government in Lublin, addressed the Polish National Council and, according to AFP, told them:

I speak in the name of the Provisional Government of the Polish Republic, which has been set up in the liberated parts of Poland in accordance with the 1921 Constitution. In our view, the ultimate Polish Government will be appointed by the Sejm (Parliament), which in turn is to be elected by universal suffrage. Once the ultimate government is formed, we shall immediately hand over to it . . .

In London, at the beginning of the war: General Sikorski (left), Premier of the Polish Government-in-exile, with Churchill and General de Gaulle.

Churchill's Views on the Polish discussions at Yalta.

Poland was discussed at no fewer than seven out of the eight plenary meetings of the Yalta Conference, and the British record contains an interchange on this topic of nearly eighteen thousand words between Stalin, Roosevelt and myself. Aided by our Foreign Ministers and their subordinates, who also held tense and detailed debate at separate meetings among themselves, we finally produced a declaration . . .

*

The Joint Allied Declaration on Poland at Yalta

The three heads of Governments consider that the Eastern frontier of Poland should follow the Curzon Line, with digressions from it in some regions of five to eight kilometres in favour of Poland. They recognize that Poland must receive substantial accessions of territory in the north and west. They feel that the opinion of the new Polish Provisional Government of National Unity should be sought in due course on the extent of these accessions, and that the final delimitation of the western frontier of Poland should thereafter await the Peace Conference.

*

Churchill's Comment on the Yalta meeting of 7 February

"How soon," asked the President, "will it be possible to hold elections?"

"Within a month," Stalin replied, "unless there is some catastrophe on the front, which is improbable."

I said that this would of course set our minds at rest, and we could wholeheartedly support a freely elected Government which would supersede everything else, but we must not ask for anything which would in any way hamper the military operations.

*

On 23 April 1945, Osobka-Morawski, the Premier of the Lublin Government, announced at a press conference (Reuter):

We need people who agree with our foreign policy and with our social reforms. Only such a government can do its work properly. We need the collaboration of men who accept the Yalta decisions, not only formally, but in fact. We are making every effort to contact such people. What we do not want are Fascists . . .

On 5 January 1945, TASS announced the recognition of the Provisional Government of Poland in Lublin by the Soviet Union. In the photograph, S. Moczelewski (centre) is shown presenting his credentials as Ambassador of the Provisional Government in Moscow. On the extreme left: M. I. Kalinin, Chairman of the Presidium of the Supreme Soviet.

ROOSEVELT AND CHURCHILL MEET IN MALTA

3 February 1945

Roosevelt and Churchill, accompanied by daughters Anne and Sarah, meet in Malta for preliminary discussions on the Yalta Conference.

Arrival in Yalta: Roosevelt and Churchill inspect a Soviet guard of honour. On the extreme left: V. Molotov, the Soviet Foreign Minister.

THE YALTA CONFERENCE 4–11 February 1945

From the Diaries of Field Marshal Viscount Alanbrooke.

4 February, Yalta: At 5 p.m. we met at the American Headquarters. They are living in the old Yalta Tsar's palace. We had a round table conference consisting of Stalin with Maisky interpreting for him, Molotov, Antonov, Admiral Kuznetsov and Marshal of Aviation Khudyakov, President, Leahy, Marshall, King, Stettinius, Harriman and Deane, P.M., three Chiefs of Staff, Eden, "Pug", Alex and Clark Kerr. Meetings started with the usual compliments, followed by an opening statement by Stalin calling on Antonov to give an account of the war. He gave an excellent and very clear talk, but not much we did not know. Marshall then described the situation on the Western Front. Tomorrow at 12 noon we are to discuss the co-ordination of our military actions and offensives, as Stalin considered the war might well go on till the summer and it was very desirable that our offensive actions should coincide . . .

5 February: At 11:30 we drove to Antonov's H.Q., half-way to Yalta . . . At dinner Winston came up to me and asked me . . . to give him results of our meetings. I gave him a full account and asked him how he had been getting on. The highlight of his remarks was that the President had said that the Americans would only remain in Germany for two years after the end of the war. France could assist in the Army of Occupation but was not to be represented on the Inter-Allied Commission in Berlin . . .

6 February: At 12 noon we went to Antonov's H.Q. and had a three hours' conference . . . While we were at work the Foreign Secretaries also met, and the high ones again at 4 p.m.

8 February: Our dinner was, as I expected, a lengthy affair. We left here at 8:45 p.m. and returned shortly after 1 a.m. The dinner, as usual, consisted of a series of toasts which went on continuously with the result that most of the courses were cold before they reached one or before one could settle down to try and eat them. Stalin was in the very best of form, and was full of fun and good humour, apparently thoroughly enjoying himself. The standard of the speeches was remarkably low and mostly consisted of insincere, slimy sort of slush! . . .

9 February: At 12 noon we had our Plenary meeting with the P.M. and President and had our Final Report approved, and received our usual reward of compliments on our good work! . . .

*

Declaration on Liberated Europe:

The Premier of the U.S.S.R., the Prime Minister of the United Kingdom, and the President of the United States of America have consulted with each other in the common interests of the peoples of their countries and those of Liberated Europe. They jointly declare their mutual agreement to concert during the temporary period of instability in Liberated Europe the policies of their three Governments in assisting the peoples of Europe liberated from the domination of Nazi Germany, and the people of the former Axis satellite States to solve by democratic means their pressing political and economic problems. The establishment of order in Europe and the rebuilding of national economic life must be achieved by processes which will enable the liberated peoples to destroy the last vestiges of Nazism and Fascism and to create democratic institutions of their own choice. This is a principle of the Atlantic Charter—the right of all peoples to choose the form of government under which they will live—the restoration of sovereign rights and self-government to those peoples who have been forcibly deprived of them by the aggressor nations. To foster the conditions in which the liberated peoples may exercise these rights, the three Governments will jointly assist the people in any liberated European State or former Axis satellite State in Europe where, in their judgment, conditions require: (a) to establish conditions of peace; (b) to carry out emergency measures for the relief of distressed people; (c) to form interim Governmental authorities broadly representative of all democratic elements and pledged to the earliest possible establishment through free elections of Governments responsive to the will of the people; and (d) to facilitate where necessary the holding of such elections.

The British Prime Minister and Chiefs of Staff. From left to right: Sir Charles Portal, Marshal of the Royal Air Force; Field Marshal The Viscount Alanbrooke, General Sir L. C. Hollis (standing), General Sir Hastings Ismay (standing) and Admiral of the Fleet Sir Andrew Cunningham.

The three Governments will consult the other United Nations and provisional authority or other Governments in Europe when matters of direct interest to themselves are under consideration. When, in the opinion of the three Governments, conditions in any liberated European State or any former Axis satellite State in Europe make such action necessary, they will immediately consult together on the measure necessary to discharge the joint responsibilities set forth in this Declaration.

By this Declaration we re-affirm our faith in the principles of the Atlantic Charter, our pledge in the Declaration by the United Nations, and our determination to build in co-operation with other peace-loving nations a world under law, dedicated to peace, security, freedom and the general well-being of all mankind. In issuing this Declaration the three powers express the hope that the French Provisional Government may be associated with themselves in the procedure suggested.

Stalin given all he asks for

From the War Memoirs of General de Gaulle

While the "Big Three" were conferring at Yalta, I felt I must publicly call France to their attention, if indeed they had forgotten her. On 5 February, speaking on the wireless, I gave this warning: "As for the future peace settlement, we have informed our allies that France will of course be committed to absolutely nothing she has not been in a position to discuss and approve in the same way as the others. I specify that the presence of French forces from one end of the Rhine to the other, the separation of the territories on the left bank of the Rhine and of the Ruhr Basin from what will be the German State, the independence of the Polish, Czech, Austrian and Balkan nations are conditions which France judges to be essential . . . We are not distressed, moreover, by the likelihood that it will be up to us to bring some of them to realization, for we are 106 million men, united under the French flag, in immediate proximity to what concerns us most directly . . ."

Lastly the "Big Three" announced that they had "come to an agreement" regarding the Polish question. They decided that Poland would be bounded, on the east, by the Curzon line and would receive, in the north and west, "a substantial increase of territory". As for the political regime, no allusion was made to free elections. A Government, referred to as one of "national unity", was to be formed "starting with the provisional Government already functioning in the country", that is, the Polish Committee of Liberation, known as the "Lublin Committee". No doubt, it was indicated, the latter would be enlarged "to include democratic leaders residing in Poland and abroad". But since there was no reference to the London Government-in-exile, since the composition of the new Government remained quite unspecified, since no control on the part of the western powers was provided for, there could be no doubts as to the kind of Government Poland would receive. Nor as to the authority that would be established in Yugoslavia. Although in regard to this country the Yalta communiqué referred to the ratification by a future "National Assembly", as a matter of fact Tito's dictatorship was recognized unconditionally. Thus Stalin was given all he asked for in Warsaw and Belgrade. To this, and this only, France was not—and for good reasons—invited to accede.

Soviet guard outside the Livadia Palace, where the Yalta conference was held.

The Soviet (upper left), American (upper right) and British (in the foreground) delegations with their advisers.

From the decisions taken at Yalta on 12 February 1945:

The following statement is made by the Prime Minister of Great Britain, the President of the United States, and the Chairman of the Council of People's Commissars of the Union of Soviet Socialist Republics on the result of the Crimea Conference:

II. *Occupation and Control of Germany:* We have agreed on common policies and plans for enforcing the unconditional surrender terms which we shall impose together on Nazi Germany after German armed resistance has been finally crushed. These terms will not be made known until the final defeat of Germany is accomplished. Under the agreed plans, the forces of the three Powers will each occupy a separate zone of Germany. Co-ordinated administration and control has been provided for through a central Control Commission consisting of the Supreme Commanders of the three Powers with headquarters in Berlin. It has been agreed that France should be invited by the three Powers, if she should so desire, to take a zone of occupation, and to participate as fourth member of the Control Commission. The limits of the French zone will be agreed by the four Governments concerned through their representatives on the European Advisory Commission.

It is our inflexible purpose to destroy German militarism and Nazism and to ensure that Germany will never again be able to disturb the peace of the world. We are determined to disarm and disband all German armed forces; break up for all time the German General Staff that has repeatedly contrived the resurgence of German militarism; remove or destroy all German military equipment; eliminate or control all German industry that could be used for military production; bring all War criminals to justice and swift punishment; exact reparation in kind for the destruction wrought by Germans; wipe out the Nazi Party, Nazi laws, organizations, and institutions; remove all Nazi and militaristic influences from public offices and from the cultural and economic life of the German people; and take in harmony such other measures as may be necessary to the future peace and safety of the world. It is not our purpose to destroy the people of Germany, but only when Nazism and militarism have been extirpated will there be hope for a decent life for Germans and a place for them in the comity of nations.

IV. *United Nations' Conference:* We are resolved upon the earliest possible establishment with our Allies of a general international organization to maintain peace and security. We believe that this is essential both to prevent aggression and to remove the political, economic and social causes of war through the close and continuing collaboration of all peace-loving people. The foundations were laid at Dunbarton Oaks. On the important question of voting procedure, however, agreement was not there reached. The present conference has been able to resolve the difficulty. We have agreed that a Conference of United Nations should be called to meet at San Francisco, on 25 April 1945, to prepare the Charter of such an organization along the lines proposed at Dunbarton Oaks. The Government of China and Provisional Government of France will be immediately consulted and invited to sponsor invitations to the Conference jointly with the Governments of the United States, Great Britain and the U.S.S.R. As soon as consultation with China and France has been completed, the text of the proposals on voting procedure will be made public.

On 20 February, the White House issued the following statement:

General de Gaulle, President of the French Provisional Government, was invited by President Roosevelt to meet him in Algiers. The invitation was given to him in Paris by the U.S. Ambassador, Mr. Jefferson Caffery, and was sent from Yalta 6 days in advance of the President's arrival in Algiers . . . The President was most disappointed when advised that official business did not permit the General to come to Algiers. Questions of mutual interest and importance to France and the United States are pending.

SOVIET MOVES IN EUROPE

We are faced with a barbarian invasion

by Harry S. Truman

The Soviet Union, Ambassador Harriman told me, had two policies which they thought they could successfully pursue at the same time. One was the policy of co-operation with the United States and Great Britain, and the second was the extension of Soviet control over neighbouring states by independent action. He said that certain elements around Stalin misinterpreted our generosity and our desire to co-operate as an indication of softness so that the Soviet Government could do as it pleased without risking challenge from the United States . . .

Ambassador Harriman continued that, in his judgment, we were faced with "a barbarian invasion of Europe". He was convinced that Soviet control over any foreign country meant not only that their

Stalin, the political victor of Yalta, in conversation with Churchill during a break in the conference.

influence would be paramount in that country's foreign relations but also that the Soviet system with its secret police and its extinction of freedom of speech would prevail. In his opinion, we had to decide what our attitude would be in the face of these unpleasant facts . . .

Before leaving, Harriman took me aside and said, "Frankly, one of the reasons that made me rush back to Washington was the fear that you did not understand, as I had seen Roosevelt understand, that Stalin is breaking his agreements. My fear was inspired by the fact that you could not have had time to catch up with all the recent cables (on the Polish question and the San Francisco Conference) . . ."

Thousands of German prisoners of war being marched through Moscow in celebration of the Soviet victory.

Franklin D. Roosevelt. President of the United States from 1933 to 1945.

The news of Roosevelt's death shocked the American nation.

THE DEATH OF FRANKLIN D. ROOSEVELT

12 April 1945

"Army-Navy Dead: ROOSEVELT, Franklin D., Commander-in-Chief."

In the third month of his fourth term as President, Roosevelt had gone to his second home, the Little White House on top of Pine Mountain, in Warm Springs, Georgia for a badly needed rest. Shortly after noon on April 12, 1945, the President sat quietly before the fireplace of his cottage while an artist near by sketched his portrait.

Suddenly he spoke: "I have a terrific headache." Those were his last words. In a few minutes he lost consciousness and died two hours later from the effects of a massive cerebral haemorrhage.

The news of the President's death soon was spread by flashes and bulletins to every corner of the world. Millions of people were plunged into grief by the tidings. At first they refused to believe it, but then had to accept it. Everywhere there were choked whispers: "Roosevelt is dead! Roosevelt is dead!" Men and women gave way to frank, unashamed tears . . .

Most people were inclined to agree with the verdict of Winston Churchill: "I conceived an admiration for him as a statesman, a man of affairs, and a war leader. I felt the utmost confidence in his upright, inspiring character and outlook, and a personal regard—affection I must say—for him beyond my power to express today . . . It is indeed a loss, a bitter loss to humanity, that those heartbeats are stilled forever."

The press announcement was unique and a real tribute:

ARMY-NAVY

CASUALTY LIST

Washington, April 13—Following are the latest casualties in the military services, including next-of-kin.

Army-Navy Dead

ROOSEVELT, Franklin D., Commander-in-Chief, wife, Mrs. Anna Eleanor Roosevelt, the White House.

HARRY S. TRUMAN BECOMES PRESIDENT OF THE UNITED STATES

Stalin's Telegram to President Truman

13 April 1945

"In the name of the Soviet Government and in my own, I wish to convey to the Government of the United States of America our sincere condolences on the premature death of President Roosevelt. The American people and the United Nations have lost in Franklin Roosevelt a great statesman of world significance and a pioneer in the organization of peace and security after the war. The Soviet Government expresses its sincere sympathy to the American people and its conviction that the friendship between the great Powers who have shouldered the main burden of the war against the common enemy will continue to develop in future." J. STALIN

In a brief 20-minute speech President Truman outlined his course of action. The Axis could expect no more favourable terms than "unconditional surrender" as proclaimed by President Roosevelt at Casablanca in 1943. War criminals would be punished. Allied military action would continue under the same admirals and generals chosen by Roosevelt. A world organization to prevent future wars must become an accomplished fact. The great nations of the world must demonstrate that they would "serve" and not "dominate" in the scheme of things.

From the inaugural address of H. S. Truman to a joint session of Congress on 16 April 1945 (United Press):

So that there can be no possible misunderstanding, both Germany and Japan can be certain, beyond any shadow of doubt, that America will continue the fight for freedom until no vestige of resistance remains. We are deeply conscious of the fact that much hard fighting is still ahead of us. Having to pay such a heavy price to make complete victory certain, America will never become a party to any plan for partial victory. To settle for merely another temporary respite would surely jeopardize the future security of the world. Our demand has been, and remains, unconditional surrender. We will not traffic with the breakers of the peace on the terms of the peace.

Show of solidarity: American G.I.'s and Red Army men after their meeting at Torgau on the Elbe.

THE MEETING ON THE ELBE AND THE DIVISION OF GERMANY

The last operations of the W. Allies and the Red Army on both sides of the Elbe and in S. Germany to the surrender of the Wehrmacht.

CHRONOLOGICAL TABLE:

1945

25/4: Soviet and American troops link up at Torgau on the Elbe. Eisenhower halts his armies on the Mulde and Elbe.

26/4: Bremen completely in British hands. U.S. troops cross the Danube near Ingolstadt. Black forest completely encircled by French 1st Army.

Stettin falls to the 2nd White Russian Front. 3rd Russian Front begins to mop up the *Frische Nehrung* in East Prussia.

27/4: U.S. troops occupy Straubing and Kempten. U.S. 1st Army advances further into Austria.

R.A.F. bombers drop food parcels for the starving population of Holland.

Red Army captures Prenzlau and Angermuende in Pomerania.

28/4: Canadians capture Wilhelmshaven and Emden. U.S. troops occupy Augsberg and Landsberg on the river Lech. French units clear the Upper Swabian sector and turn south towards Vorarlberg, Austria.

28–29/4: British troops cross the Lower Elbe at 2 a.m. and establish a bridgehead on the east bank.

General Heinrici, Commander of Army Group Vistula, is replaced by General Tippelskirch.

28–30/4: The Bavarian Freedom Movement, broadcasting on the Munich wave length (after occupying the radio station) calls for an end to the senseless resistance in Bavaria.

29/4: The German Supreme Command moves from Fuerstenberg to Dobbin in S. Mecklenburg.

British troops advance into Mecklenburg. U.S. troops liberate some 110,000 Allied prisoners-of-war in Moosburg. Troops of the U.S. 7th Army liberate Dachau concentration camp; other units are reported S.W. of Munich. Americans advance east from the Tirschenreuth-Schoensee sector. Troops of the French 1st Army capture Friedrichshafen on Lake Constance.

Troops of the 2nd White Russian Front occupy Anklam, on the road to Stralsund, and advance into Mecklenburg.

30/4: U.S. 7th Army occupies Munich. U.S. troops in the Murnau sector prepare to advance on Innsbruck.

Churchill suggests the capture of Prague to Eisenhower.

Moravska-Ostrova falls to the Red Army.

April–May: Civilian refugees from the East are held up by German troops crossing the Elbe. Most are captured by the advancing Red Army.

1/5: British troops advance into Mecklenburg across the Elbe. Field-Marshal von Rundstedt captured in Bad Toelz. American troops reach Seefeld in the Tyrol, while French clear Bregenz and Vorarlberg. Field Marshals List and von Leeb and Admiral Horthy captured by U.S. 7th Army.

Second White Russian Front captures Stralsund.

2/5: British troops take Luebeck, Schwerin and Wismark thus cutting off Schleswig-Holstein and Denmark. Major General von Tippelskirch, Commander of the German 21st Army capitulates to British troops in the Ludwigslust-Eldena-Doemitz sector. In the south, negotiations are started for the surrender of Innsbruck.

Schoerner calls on his troops (Army Group Centre in Bohemia) to rally round Doenitz and to continue the fight.

Soviet troops occupy Rostock and Warnemuende. The Soviet News Agency announces that troops of the 3rd White Russian Front are engaged on mopping-up operations in the *Frische-Nehrung* sector, S.W. of the Baltic port of Pillau.

3/5: Hamburg capitulates to British 2nd Army. Kiel and Flensburg declared open cities. The entire German defence north of the British front line collapses: 500,000 Germans taken prisoner. Americans occupy Passau. French reach Feldkirch in Vorarlberg.

Troops of the 2nd White Russian Front link up with units of the British 2nd Army on the Wismar–Wittenberg road. Troops of the 1st White Russian Army meet U.S. troops S.E. of Wittemberg.

Early May: Danish island of Bornholm occupied by Soviet troops. Some 20,000 German soldiers and refugees on the island are sent back by the Russians via Kolbert.

4/5: U.S. 7th Army reaches Salzburg, Bad Reichenhall and advances on Berchtesgaden. Further advances in Austria.

Soviet troops extend their sector south of Olmuetz.

5/5: U.S. 9th Army gives up its bridgehead on the Elbe. In the S.E., Americans advance on Karlsbad and Pilsen.

6/5: Swinemuende occupied by Soviet troops.

THE FIRST MEETING BETWEEN U.S. AND SOVIET TROOPS AT TORGAU

25 April 1945

Truman's telegram to Stalin of 25 April

President to Marshal Stalin

Personal and top secret

I gratefully acknowledge receipt of your message of 23 April. The following is the draft of the declaration which I propose to issue at a date and time to be decided by General Eisenhower:

"The Anglo–American armies under the command of General Eisenhower have met the Soviet forces where they intended to meet in the heart of Nazi Germany. The enemy has been cut in two.

"This is not the hour of final victory in Europe, but the hour draws near, the hour for which all the American people, all the British people and all the Soviet people have toiled and prayed so long.

"The union of our arms in the heart of Germany has a meaning for the world which the world will not miss. It means, *first,* that the last faint, desperate hope of Hitler and his gangster government has been extinguished. The common front and the common cause of the powers allied in this war against tyranny and inhumanity have been demonstrated in fact as they have long been demonstrated in determination. Nothing can divide or weaken the common purpose of our veteran armies to pursue their victorious purpose to its final allied triumph in Germany.

"*Second,* the junction of our forces at this moment signalizes to ourselves and to the world that the collaboration of our nations in the cause of peace and freedom is an effective collaboration which can surmount the greatest difficulties of the most extensive campaign in military history and succeed. Nations which can plan and fight together shoulder to shoulder in the face of such obstacles of distance and of language and of communications as we have overcome, can live together and can work together in the common labour of the organization of the world for peace.

"*Finally,* this great triumph of Allied arms and Allied strategy is such a tribute to the courage and determination of Franklin Roosevelt as no words could ever speak, and that could be accomplished only by the persistence and the courage of the fighting soldiers and sailors of the Allied nations.

"But, until our enemies are finally subdued in Europe and in the Pacific, there must be no relaxation of effort on the home front in support of our heroic soldiers and sailors, as we all know there will be no pause on the battle fronts."

The Last Operations in April and May 1945

At the end of April, Bradley reached the Elbe and established contact, around Torgau, with Zhukov's troops, which had just taken Berlin. To the north, Montgomery had seized Hamburg and early in May took Kiel and Luebeck, within reach of Rokossovsky, who had succeeded Marshal Chernyakhovsky, killed in February, in the East Prussian theatre. Thus the German occupation forces in Denmark were cut off from the Reich, as were those who had remained in Holland under Blaskowitz. To the south, three Allied armies were marching on the redoubt in the Bavarian and Austrian Alps where the enemy might have hoped to hold fast. Patton penetrated into Czechoslovakia, where he seized Plzon, and, in Austria, reached Linz, close by Tolbukhin's Russians, who had taken and passed Vienna; Patch seized Munich and drove as far as Innsbruck; de Lattre launched his armoured units and his Moroccan divisions into the Tyrol, one column driving up the Iller, another bordering Lake Constance. In the Vorarlberg, the French advance guards engaged the German Twenty-fifth Army, new in the order of battle but formed from a host of fragments and whose leader, General Schmidt, immediately offered to surrender. On 6 May the French flag was floating over the Arlberg pass. Meanwhile, Leclerc's division, hurriedly returning west and put at the head of Patch's army, had reached Berchtesgaden.

The hand-shakes of ordinary soldiers are more sincere than the message of the politicians, for to them the link-up means that the war will soon be over. ▶

The Commander of U.S. 69th Division, Major-General Reinhard, and Major-General Russakov, Commander of of the Soviet 58th Guards Division, shaking hands in Torgau.

These Cossack guards have come a long way: from the Volga, over the Dnieper, Vistula, Oder and Spree right up to the Elbe.

SHAEF announced on 26 April 1945, that Allied troops were attacking Bremen from the south and east.

BREMEN CAPTURED BY BRITISH TROOPS

26 April 1945

Allied leaflet. "Further fighting means the destruction of German industry, chaos to family life, and useless personal sacrifice." ▶

View of Bremen in April 1945.

WEITERMACHEN
bedeutet :

FÜR DEUTSCHLAND-

Ständig wachsende Verheerung durch Material-
schlachten auf deutschem Boden im Osten und
Westen. Vernichtung der letzten Voraussetzungen
für den Wiederaufbau nach dem Kriege.

FÜR DEINE FAMILIE-

Ständig wachsende Gefahren durch den ein-
rollenden Krieg. Selbstmörderische Volkssturm-
Einsätze, Bombardierungen, immer mehr
Nahrungsknappheit, Parteiterror und schliesslich
Chaos.

FÜR DICH-

Ständig wachsende Material-Unterle-
genheit, in der Deine Opferbereitschaft
allein nichts ausrichten kann. Ein Selbst-
opfer in letzter Stunde, das seinen
Zweck verloren hat.

ZG 119

Scattered German troops in full retreat in S. Wurtemberg. German remnants in the Schwarzwald completely surrounded by French 1st Army.

FRENCH DRIVE TO LAKE CONSTANCE. AMERICANS CROSS THE DANUBE AT INGOLSTADT

23–26 April 1945

SHAEF announced on 23 and 24 April that the bridgehead on the south bank of the Danube, S.E. of Donaueschingen had been extended by 40 miles as far as Sigmaringen . . . On the S.W. edge of the Schwarzwald pocket, Waldkirch, Freiburg and Gretzhausen were reached after advances of up to 10 miles . . . Allied units advancing east through Sigmaringen were drawn up before Ehingen . . .

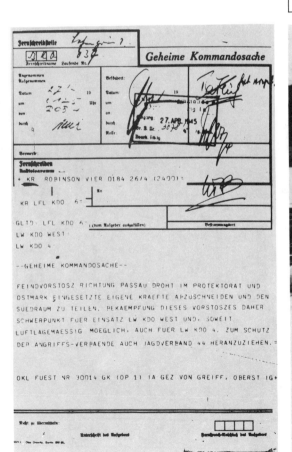

Teletype message of 27 April to Luftwaffe Commands West and 4: Enemy advance on Passau threatens Austria and must be thrown back at all costs.

Tanks of the U.S. 3rd Army crossing the Danube.

Troops of the British 1st Commando Brigade and the 15th (Scottish) Division crossing the Lower Elbe in Buffaloes at Lauenburg.

BRITISH TROOPS REACH THE ELBE AT LAUENBURG

28 April 1945

At the same time that British troops reached the Elbe, troops of the 2nd White Russian Front under Marshal Rokossovsky entered Mecklenburg. On 29 April, the Red Army occupied Anklam on the road to Stralsund, and on 1 May took Stralsund itself. Rostock and Warnemuende fell on 2 May.

German POW's; 13–16 year-old boys with their Major.

After his clash with Field-Marshal Keitel, General Heinrici, Himmler's successor as Commander of Army Group Vistula was replaced by General von Tippelskirch.

KEITEL CLASHES WITH HEINRICI

28 April 1945

"Marshal Keitel, if you want these men to be shot . . ."

As Keitel, filled with the "historical and moral importance of his mission, was riding along the roads north of Berlin, he noticed to his amazement that troops of the 7th Tank Division and 25th Armoured Infantry Division were marching north. These troops were part of Heinrici's Third Tank Army, and were supposed to be on their way to Berlin. Instead, they were being moved northward in an attempt to halt the Russian break-through at Neubrandenburg.

At first Keitel did not want to believe his eyes—but there could be no doubt. Heinrici had defied Keitel's and Jodl's strictest orders. Trembling with fury, Keitel went in search of Heinrici. He found him on a road near Neubrandenburg, close to the front, accompanied by General von Manteuffel. Processions of wounded and disarmed soldiers and endless treks of refugees were moving past.

Keitel, his face purple, called Heinrici to account. He spoke of insubordination, treason, cowardice and sabotage, accused Heinrici of weakness, and shouted that if Heinrici had only taken Rendulic in Vienna as an example and shot a few thousand deserters or strung them up on the nearest tree, his armies would not now be on the retreat.

Von Manteuffel, shaking with indignation, sought the eye of Heinrici. He was a front line soldier like Heinrici, and had never had too much confidence in Jodl or in Keitel. During the last few days he had almost learned to feel contempt for them. This scene was the end.

But short, grey-haired Heinrici looked up at Keitel with perfect self-control. He knew he had done right. His movements were intended to bring his Army Group, and as many civilians as possible, to the west, into the area between the northern reaches of the Elbe River and the Baltic Sea.

Heinrici waited quietly until Keitel's shouting stopped. Then he pointed at the column marching along the road —the refugees, and soldiers without rifles, without guns, without ammunition, without vehicles, without armour, exhausted and hopeless and pursued by forces outnumbering them fifteen times.

"Marshal Keitel," Heinrici said, "if you want these men to be shot, will you please begin!"

To that day, Keitel had not seen the front. He had never seen a firing squad at work. He looked about him in confusion, repeated his orders to move on to Berlin, added severe threats in case of another instance of disobedience, and drove off.

From J. Thorwald: *Flight in the Winter*.

Five German soldiers surrendering to an American GI of the 36th Infantry Division on the Elbe front.

GERMAN SOLDIERS AND CIVILIANS FLEEING TO THE ELBE April 1945

While many refugees succeeded in reaching the Elbe, many more were overtaken by the Red Army.

FIXING THE DEMARCATION LINE ON THE ELBE Late April 1945

Capt. McMahon of the U.S. 9th Army carrying a German child across a half-destroyed Elbe bridge.

Soviet and American officers studying the map in Wittenberg on 28 April.

OPERATION "PHEASANT SHOOT" BY BAVARIAN FREEDOM FIGHTERS

27/28 April 1945

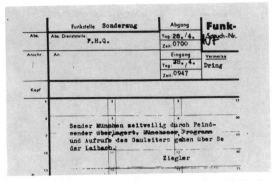

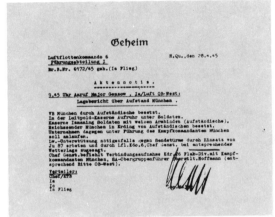

Top: Radio signal that Radio Munich will "temporarily" broadcast from Laibach (Ljubljana). Below: Secret memorandum by German 6th Air Commando on Munich revolt: Rebellion among soldiers in Luitpold and Ismening Barracks; Radio Munich occupied by rebels; air-force support may be needed.

Capt. Gerngross's "Pheasant Shoot"

During the past few weeks it had become clear that only decisive action could save Munich from total destruction. Capt. Gerngross got hold of a number of prisoners from Moosburg Camp and, with the help of Major Braun in Freising, sent them together with U.S. Lt. McNamara, the French officer Miremont, and two German officers, through the German lines to make contact with the Americans.

Shortly before midnight on Friday, 27 April 1945, Capt. Gerngross sounded the alert in the Saar Barracks. When the whole company had lined up in the corridor, the Captain told them: "The moment for which all of us have toiled, has arrived at last. We must put an end to this pointless war and save the rest of our country from senseless destruction. That means action. It also means risking our lives. I know I shall not be alone, when I call upon you to follow me on the road to freedom. You can choose for me or against me, but whoever joins me now, must stay to the end. I hereby absolve you all from your oath of loyalty to Hitler!" . . .

A few minutes past midnight—it was now Saturday, 28 April, Capt. Gerngross's Mercedes left the Barracks with two German officers, Leiling and Spoetzl, and the American Lt. Leigh, while fellow conspirators in Munich and Upper Bavaria were informed by radio and courier that the "Pheasant Shoot" was on. The captain's car raced along the dark road towards Sternberg. It was making for the Schornerhof, the headquarters of Governor von Epp and his Staff . . . When von Epp wavered he was taken prisoner. He and Major von Caracciola, his adjutant, who was in league with the rebels, were driven to the English Garden, whence, after a short stay, they were taken to Freising by Lt. Leiling and put in charge of Major Braun. Negotiations with von Epp then dragged on endlessly . . .

Meanwhile Sgt. Niedermayer of the Interpreters' Corps and a squad of riflemen raided and seized Freimann Radio Station. However, the actual transmitter was in Erding, and had still to be taken by a company of Panzer Grenadiers from Freising under Lt. Reiter. At 3 a.m., the transmitter was ready to go on the air, and Capt. Gerngross broadcast the first proclamation of the Bavarian Freedom Fighters: "Stop fighting—lay down your arms —destroy the Nazis wherever you meet them—Hoist white flags! Allied troops are approaching Munich . . ." This message was repeated over and over again by Radio Erding . . . Major Braun had meanwhile realized that von Epp was quite incapable of taking any decisive steps and let him go. Major Caracciola, who still hoped to use his influence on von Epp or the Army leaders, refused to remain in safety in Freising. He drove with von Epp to Munich and then, by a roundabout route, to the High Command in Kempfenhausen. This brought him into the clutches of *Gauleiter* Giesler, who had suddenly been galvanized into hysterical activity. Soon afterwards, a Gestapo convoy drew up and carried von Epp and Caracciola off to Munich . . . Caracciola was immediately declared a "defeatist", sentenced to death, and shot in the Ministry courtyard . . .

All points in Munich held by the Bavarian Freedom Fighters were now attacked by SS men; the rebels had to withdraw from the town and re-assembled near the Erding transmitter. At 11.30 a.m. the current was cut off, and the voice of Free Bavaria was silenced . . . Everything seemed lost and yet it was not so. The voice of Munich had been heard throughout the land and had not fallen on deaf ears. More than 40,000 battle-worn troops on the Glonn and Ammer fronts laid down their arms, the ranks dissolved, and soldiers began to stream along roads and pathways leading to the Isar line . . .

From Otto Zierer: *Die Abenteuer der vielgeliebten Stadt Muenchen* (The adventurous history of the dearly beloved city of Munich) Vol. III.

MUNICH OCCUPIED BY TROOPS OF THE U.S. 7TH ARMY

30 April 1945

Villagers in S. Wurtemberg taking their possessions to safety. On 30 April, Allied tanks advanced on Lake Constance through Wangen.

SHAEF announced on 30 April that Allied tanks had entered the suburbs of Munich.

The destroyed Sternecker Brauhaus where Hitler founded his Nazi party (left).

German prisoners-of-war being shunted through the streets of Munich.

GERMAN FORCES ON 30 APRIL 1945

Relative strength of Allied and German troops in mid-January and mid-April 1945

	Western Front		Italian Front	
	mid-Jan.	mid-April	mid-Jan.	mid-April
Armoured Divisions				
Allies	20	23	4	4
Germans	15	16	4	4
Other Divisions				
Allies	52	68	19	20
Germans	67	74	23	23
All Divisions				
Allies	72	91	23	24
Germans	82	90	27	27

The withdrawal of the German Army High Command (OKW) from Zossen to Flensburg–Muerwik on 20 April–3 May 1945. ▶

Two German orders of 29 April 1945

Recent developments have given rise to a host of idle rumours and misconceptions, particularly in outlying positions (Atlantic fortifications, Crete, Rhodes). Here reassurance in the form of constant and close contacts with the High Command by means of continuous directives and clear instructions is essential. Our soldiers must be told that all that matters is obedience and the implementation of High Command orders in every way, irrespective of the outcome of the struggle for Berlin.

signed: Jodl

*

Stories about the formation of a Bavarian Liberation Committee and about surrender offers by Reichsfuehrer Himmler or of an armistice on the Western Front are so much enemy propaganda. The Fuehrer himself is leading the battle for Berlin. Now, more than ever before, orders must be obeyed and the instructions of the High Command observed in every detail.

C.-in-C. German Naval Forces.

Numerical survey of divisions	Army Groups	Armies	Corps	Divisions
	E		LXIX (Special)	Stm.-Brig. S.E.
Tk. divs. –			XV Coss. Cav.	1st Cos.
Pz. Gr. divs. –				2nd Cos.
In. divs. 7				11th Lw.-Fd. Div.
+½	**S.E.**		XXI Alpine	22nd Vk.-Gr. Div.
Rifle divs. 1	XXXIV			369th Croat
Alpine divs. 2	(withdrawing)			7th SS Alpine
				181st
10½				41st
All. divs. 3			XV Alpine	373rd Croat
				639 Security Reg.
			LXXXXI (Special)	104th Rifle
				20th Rifle Reg.
			LXXXXVII (Special)	237th
				188th Alpine
				392nd Ct. (Remn.)

Numerical survey of divisions	Army Groups	Armies	Corps	Division
Tk. divs. 11	**South**		LXVIII	71st
Tk. Gr. divs. 1	9th SS Tk.			13th SS Alpin
Inf. divs. 12	9th Alpine			118th Rifle
Rifle divs. 3	(in formation)		XXII Mountain	297th
Alpine divs. 2		**2nd Tank**		Szentlaszlo D
29			I Cav.	23rd Tank
Allied divs. 1				4th Cav.
Arriving 1				3rd Cav. Pan
				16th SS Gr.
			IV SS Tk.	3rd Tk. Shoc
				5th SS Tk. Sh
				14th SS-Waff
		6th		Gr. (Ukrai
				1st)
			III Tk.	1st Volks-Alp
				1st Tk.

Numerical survey of divisions	Army Groups	Armies	Corps	Divisions
		6th Tk. 117th Rifle (arriving)	I SS Tk.	1st SS Tk., 356th Assault, 12th SS Tk., 710th
			II SS Tk.	3rd SS Tk., Fuehrer-Gr. Div.
		8th	XXXXIII	96th, 48th Volks-Gr., 101st Rifle Assault
			"F.H." Tk.	2nd "F.M." Tk. Shock, 211th Assault, 357th Volks-Gr., 25th Tk., 44th "H & D" Shock
		1st Tk.	XXIV Tk. 304th	6th Tk., 8th Tk., 1st Tk. "F.H." +711th Shock +182nd Shock, 46th Volks-Gr., 10th Parachute (arriving)
			XXIX	8th Rifle, 19th Tk.+Spec. Unit "Olmuetz", 271st
			LXXII	76th Shock, 15th Shock, 601st Special Unit, 153rd Shock
			XXXXIX Alpine	520th Volks-Gr., 253rd+16th Hung., 3rd Alpine+ 97th Rifle
			LIX	715th, 544th Volks-Gr., 371st, 75th, 78th Volkssturm, 154th
Tk. divs. 11 Tk. Gr. divs. 4 In. divs. 39 Rifle divs. 4 Alpine divs. 2 — 60 — Allied divs. 1	**Centre** 600th Russian 2nd "R" SS Tk.		XI	4th Alpine, 10th Pz. Gr., 16th Tk., 254th, 17th Tk.
		17th 18th SS Tk.	XXXX Tk.	68th, 1st Ski-Rifle, 168th Shock, 168th Shock, 45th Shock
			XVII	31st Shock, 359th, 208th
			Fortress Breslau	
			VIII	100th Rifle, 20th SS Shock
		4th Tk. 269th Assault	LVII Tank	6th Volks-Gr., 72nd, 17th
			Kohlsdorfen Group	615th Special Staff, 464th, 545th Shock
			"G.D." Tk.	1st Pz. Para. "Brandenburh" Pz. Gr., 20th Tk., 193rd
			General Moser Gr.	404th
			Pz.-Para. Corps. "H.G."	2nd Para. Gr. "H.G.", Shock Gp. "Frundsberg" (Remnants of 10th SS Tank)

Numerical survey of divisions	Army Groups	Armies	Corps	Divisions
			LXXXX	464th, 469th, 404th
			Iv (repl.)	Dresden Comd.
	West G	24th		405th
		19th (present position unknown)	XVIII SS	352nd Volks Gr., 106th, 719th, 89th
			LXXX	559th Volks Gr., 47th Volks Gr., 246th Volks Gr., 716th
			LXIV	16th Volks Gr., 189th
Tk. divs. 2 Tk. Gr. divs. 1 In. divs. 21 +1 Alpine divs. 1 — 25½		**1st** (Present position unknown)	LXIV	16th Volks Gr., 189th
			XIII	198th, 19th Volks Gr., 553rd Volks Gr.
			XIII SS	38th SS, 212th Volks Gr., 2nd Alpine, 17th SS Pz. Gr., Graf von Hobe Div., 350th Special
			LXXXII	36th, 416th
		North-Western Command		MO-West Shock, IV Labour Service, XV Pioneer
		North-Eastern Command		Berchtesgaden Defence Area
Tk. divs. 1 Tk. Gr. divs. 2 In. divs. 14 +½ Rifle divs. 2 Alpine divs. 2 — 21½ All. divs. 4		**7th** (2nd Tk. (arriving))	XII	347th Volks Gr., 413th, Benniche Gr. Div.
			LXXXV	11th Tk., Replacement and Training Units, 655th Pioneer Brig.
			IV Flak	508th Flak Brig.
		As at 12/4/45 Present state unknown		
	C	**Liguria** LXXXXVII	LXXV	5th Alpine, 2nd Italian ("Littorio"), 34th
		4th Italian Alpine ("Monte Rosa")	Lombardia	3rd Ital. Mar. ("San Marco"), 134th Brigade, 4th Ital. Alpine ("Monte Rosa")
	South-West 155th (forming) 90th Tk. Gr. 29th Tk. Gr.	**14th**	LI Alpine	148th, 1st Ital. ("Italia"), 232nd, 114th Rifle, 334th Volks Gr.
			XIV Tk.	94th, 8th Alpine, 65th
		10th	I Para.	305th, 1st Para. Rifle, 278th Volks Gr., 4th Para. Rifle, 26th Tk.
			LXXVI Tk.	98th Volks Gr., 362nd, 42nd Rifle, 162nd (Turkestan)
			LXXIII Special	Emergency Units

½ Brigade
  Replacement and Training Divisions
Total: 145 + 3/2 +

From: *Kriegstagebuch des Oberkommandos der Wehrmacht*, Vol . I.

While Eisenhower halts at the Elbe to await the arrival of Soviet troops, Montgomery decides to advance on the Baltic, thus preventing Soviet occupation of Schleswig–Holstein and Denmark.

MONTGOMERY'S 21ST ARMY GROUP ADVANCES INTO MECKLENBURG   1 May 1945

British troops capture Wiemar and Schwerin on 2 May. Right: A German "Red Cross auxiliary" captured at Luebeck. ▶

On 2 May, General Eisenhower issued the following statement:

A meeting took place at Luebeck at 1 a.m. on 24 April between Count Folke Bernadotte of the International Red Cross and Reichs-Fuehrer Heinrich Himmler. At this meeting Himmler admitted that Germany was finished . . . Nothing which either Doenitz or Himmler may say or do will be allowed to drive a wedge between the British and Americans on the one side and the Russians on the other, or can change in any way the agreed operations of the Allied armies.

OCCUPATION OF LUEBECK, SCHWERIN AND WISMAR

2 May 1945

General von Tippelskirch's 21st Army surrendering to British troops on 2 May.

British and Soviet troops link up at Wismar (3 May 1945).

BRITISH 2ND ARMY TAKES HAMBURG 3 May 1945

Hamburg's crippled harbour installations in May 1945. Kiel and Flensburg declared open cities on 3 May. Oldenburg and Travemuende occupied on 4 May.

The German Commander of Hamburg surrendering the city outside the town hall.

Reich-Commissar Seyss-Inquart being placed under arrest in Hamburg (7 May 1945).

American troops entering Pilsen on 5 May.

EISENHOWER CALLS A HALT AT PILSEN. HITLER'S "ALPINE REDOUBT" 30 April–5 May 1945

The Americans for Prague?

On 30 April, Churchill wrote to President Truman that "the liberation of Prague and as much as possible of the territory of Western Czechoslovakia by your forces might make the whole difference to the post-war situation in Czechoslovakia, and might well influence that in nearby countries . . . Of course, such a move by Eisenhower must not interfere with his main operation against the Germans, but should be brought to his attention." A week later, Churchill approached Eisenhower directly, but heard that his plan was "to halt his advance generally on the west bank of the Elbe and along the 1937 boundary of Czechoslovakia. If the situation warranted he would cross it to the general line Karlsbad-Pilsen-Budejovice. The Russians agreed to this and the movement was made. But on 4 May, the Russians reacted strongly to a fresh proposal to continue the advance of the Third U.S. Army to the river Vltava, which flows through Prague. This would not have suited them at all. So the Americans "halted while the Red Army cleared the east and west banks of the Moldau river and occupied Prague". The city fell on 9 May, two days after the general surrender was signed at Rheims.

German generals comment on the setting-up of an "Alpine redoubt"

Field Marshal Kesselring: From the purely military point of view, the Alpine redoubt would only have been useful . . . if it could have served as a base for large-scale operations to surround and smash the enemy. That proved impossible—all the rest was sheer fantasy.

*

General Rendulic: I know that the mountain redoubt was being planned at one time. However, that's just about as far as we got with it. In any case, nothing had been done by the time I arrived in Austria. Our troops had to build what defences we had themselves . . .

*

Air-Force General Koller: The whole thing is confounded nonsense! The Tyrol is crammed with hospitals, administrative departments, state and party officials, all of whom had taken to the mountains. Supplies will run out after three weeks . . .

General Leclerc (French 2nd Armoured Division), the winner of the race for Hitler's mountain fastness in Berchtesgaden. On 4 May, his soldiers tore down the German flag (below).

THE GERMAN COLLAPSE IN HUNGARY, YUGOSLAVIA, ITALY, CZECHOSLOVAKIA AND AUSTRIA

The advance of Soviet, Yugoslav and Allied Armies in the S.E. and east to the capitulation of the German Army.

CHRONOLOGICAL TABLE:

1945

4/1: German attempts to break out of Budapest prove abortive.

6/1: Fighting in the Budapest underground.

8/1: Soviet troops storm the Parliament House, the Stock Exchange and the main Post Office in Budapest; last bridges across the Danube are blown up. Red Army advances on Bratislava. Soviet troops in S. Slovakia drive to Komarno, threatening to outflank powerful German forces.

20/1: Provisional Hungarian (Debrecsen) Government signs armistice in Moscow.

21/1: 4th Ukrainian Front captures Novy Sacz (S. Poland) and Presov, Kosice and Bardejov (Czechoslovakia). Heavy fighting S.W. of Budapest (Szekesfehervar sector) where the Germans are trying to forge a corridor to the Danube.

27/1: Rumanian 4th Army captures Dobsina in Czechoslovakia.

13/2: End of fighting in Budapest.

6/3: Germans launch counter-offensive on Lake Balaton.

8/3: SS-General Wolff begins secret negotiations in Switzerland for the surrender of German Army in Italy.

In Belgrade, formation of coalition government with Tito as Premier and Ivan Subasic as Foreign Minister. King Peter II to await referendum before returning from exile.

19/3: In Hungary, Soviet troops take 24 hours to recapture all the territory lost during a 13-day German offensive.

20/3: Yugoslav Army launches general offensive in the Mostar-Višegrad-Drina sector.

22/3: Germans withdraw to prepared positions in Hungary.

30/3: Troops of the 2nd Ukrainian Front launch offensive along the Czechoslovak–Hungarian border and, forcing the rivers Hron and Nitra, advance on Bratislava, the capital of Slovakia. Units of the 3rd Ukrainian Front cross the Austrian frontier north of Köszeg (Hungary). Soviet and Bulgarian troops advance on the river Drava, south of Lake Balaton.

2/4: Nagy Kanisza, a centre of the Hungarian oil industry in Soviet hands. Vienna Radio denies that the Austrian capital has been declared an open city. Soviet troops overrun Wiener Neustadt, Eisenstadt, Neunkirchen and Gloggnitz.

6/4: Yugoslav troops capture Sarajevo.

7/4: Units of 3rd Ukrainian Front enter Vienna from the south.

8/4: Street-fighting in the S. and W. suburbs of Vienna. Other Soviet troops by-pass Vienna and advance on Linz and on Graz.

9/4: Polish 2nd Corps and British 5th Corps launch final (8th Army) offensive in Italy. The river Senio is crossed, and bridge-and bridgeheads are established in the Cuffiana sector.

U.S. 5th Army advances to the precincts of Massa.

Soviet troops gain the upper hand in Vienna.

12/4: British 8th Army forces the Santerno river. Carrara falls.

19/4: German retreat in Italy. Americans prepare to attack La Spezia.

20/4: Units of U.S. 5th Army advance on the Po. Other units by-pass the retreating German troops and advance eastwards.

21/4: Americans enter Bologna from the south; British troops advancing from the west reach the city centre at 6 a.m.

23/4: Units of the U.S. 5th Army force the Po and set up bridge-heads on the north bank. Units of British 8th Army take Ferrara and reach the Po at Pontelagoscuro.

25/4: Yugoslav troops attack Fiume (Rijeka).

26/4: Allies capture Verona and force the river Adige. Capture of Mantua, Reggio and Parma.

27/4: U.S. 5th Army pursues retreating German troops in N. Italy. Americans reach Genoa.

Yugoslav units capture Brod.

28/4: Italian partisans capture and shoot Mussolini at Dongo (Lake Como).

29/4: General von Vietinghoff-Scheel, the German Commander of Army Group S.W., signs unconditional surrender in the Royal Palace in Caserta. Surrender to take effect on 2 May. Milan falls to Italian partisans. Troops of British 8th Army advance on Trieste, and capture Venice.

30/4: U.S. 5th Army reaches Turin.

Marshal Tito's Yugoslav units enter Trieste.

30/4–1/5: Gauleiter Frank in Prague announces over the radio that he will drown any uprising "in a sea of blood"

1/5: Fighting ends in Italy.

Yugoslav partisans occupy Trieste.

2/5: One million German soldiers lay down their arms in Italy. Units of British 8th Army reach Monfalcone and make contact with Yugoslav troops.

3/5: Greek troops land on Rhodes and the small island of Aliminia to the west.

4/5: U.S. 7th Army advancing from Bavaria links up with U.S. 5th Army from Italy on the Brenner Pass.

5/5: As rumours of an impending Allied approach reach Prague, the people stream into the streets to welcome the victors. Frank orders the streets to be cleared and instructs his men to fire at anyone who disobeys. Armed patriots overwhelm the SS in the radio buildings, and broadcast a call to the nation. Patriot rising begins. Patriots occupy Gestapo and Security Police H.Q.

6/5: Americans occupy Pilsen, Linz and Urfahr on the Danube.

Anti-German excesses in Prague.

Forces of General Vlassov (a former Russian officer fighting under German orders, led by General Bunichenko) enter Prague, are greeted as liberators, and join the patriots.

8/5: Goering surrenders to Brigadier-General Stack, commanding U.S. 36th Division, near Salzburg. General Koller, Commander of the Luftwaffe, taken prisoner in Thumersbach (Zeller See).

Yugoslav troops enter Zagreb.

Bunichenko and his troops flee before the advancing Red Army and seek refuge with the Americans. He and Vlassov are handed back to the Russians. German commander in Prague signs agreement whereby all German troops will be immediately withdrawn from the capital.

9/5: Field-Marshal Schoerner, Commander of Army Group Centre, flees to the S.W., is captured by the Americans, and later handed over to the Russians.

Prague: Retreating German soldiers and civilians are surprised by advancing Red Army and completely routed. Attacks on, and expulsions of, Germans continue until the autumn.

12/5: SS-Obergruppenfuehrer Sepp Dietrich captured by Americans. *Mid-May:* The acting mayor of Prague, Professor Pfitzner, is hanged in public. Hacha, the Czechoslovak Quisling dies in prison. Henlein, the leader of the Sudeten Germans, commits suicide. (*Gauleiter* Frank and SS-*Fuehrer* Daluege were hanged by Czechs in 1946.)

Retreating Germans at the Moravian Gate.

On 12 January, Hitler established a special decoration for the destruction of enemy aircraft by small-arms fire.

FOURTH UKRAINIAN FRONT ADVANCES ACROSS THE CARPATHIAN MOUNTAINS INTO BOHEMIA January 1945

Soviet mountain artillery in the Carpathians.

Soviet rocket guns outside Budapest. The Hungarian capital was under attack for more than a month. German attempts to relieve the city in early January were frustrated by the 3rd Ukrainian Front.

THE FINAL STRUGGLE FOR BUDAPEST

6 January–13 February 1945

(Photograph on pp. 184/185)
For days there was bitter street fighting round the Parliament House, the Stock Exchange, the Post Office and the Danube bridges.   ▶

Budapest fell on 13 February. The photograph shows a crashed German aircraft. Some 110,000 German soldiers were marched into captivity.

Troops of the 3rd Ukrainian Front after the capture of Budapest.

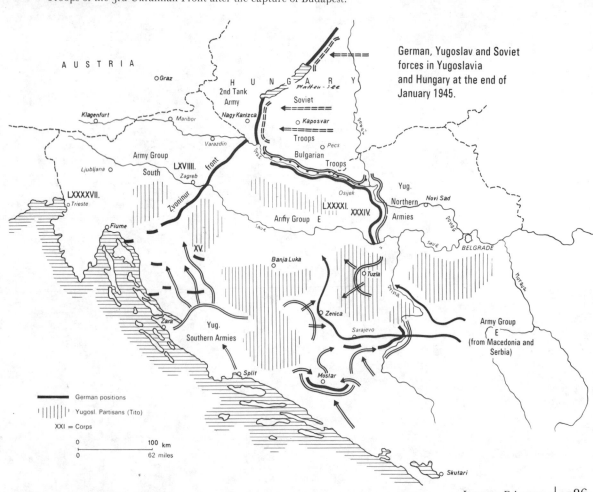

German, Yugoslav and Soviet
forces in Yugoslavia
and Hungary at the end of
January 1945.

AUSTRIA

HUNGARY

Graz

Platten-see

2nd Tank
Army

Soviet

Klagenfurt

Maribor

Nagy Kanizca

Kaposvar

Varazdin

Troops

Pecs

Army Group

Bulgarian

South

LXVIIII.

Troops

Ljubljana

Zagreb

Osijek

Yug.

LXXXVII.

Zvoninur

LXXXI.

XXXIV.

Northern

Trieste

Arfhy Group E

Novi Sad

Fiume

Armies

BELGRADE

XV.

Banja Luka

Tuzla

Zara

Zenica

Yug.
Southern Armies

Sarajevo

Army Group
E
(from Macedonia and
Serbia)

Split

Mostar

German positions

Yugosl. Partisans (Tito)

XXI = Corps

0   100 km
0   62 miles

Skutari

General Woehler's plan in Operation "Fruhlingserwachen" (Spring Awakening) aimed at the destruction of the Red Army in Hungary. The Russians had quite different ideas.

THE LAST GERMAN OFFENSIVE IN HUNGARY

6–22 March 1945.

The German attack was halted on 17 March, when Soviet troops launched a large-scale counter-offensive (right). In 24 hours, they succeeded in recapturing all the territory the Germans had gained during the past 13 days, and advanced on Austria. ►

General Woehler, Commander of Army Group South. After the failure of the Hungarian offensive he was dismissed by Hitler.

GENERAL WOLFF'S NEGOTIATIONS WITH THE ALLIED SECRET SERVICE IN SWITZERLAND
25 February–27 April 1945

SS Obergruppen-fuehrer, General Karl Wolff, head of German police and SS units in Italy.

"A rabid follower of Himmler"

From the Diaries of Field Marshal Viscount Alanbrooke

10 March. Just as I was rushing to make an early start home, a telegram turned up from Alex with certain underground peace proposals. These suggested the surrendering of the whole of Kesselring's army in Italy. However, as Wolff (the SS Commander in Italy) was the main instigator and as he is a rabid SS follower of Himmler, it does not seem very plausible. We are following it up for the present and sending representatives to Switzerland to the selected spot . . .

Chronological account of the most important negotiations between Wolff and the Allies in Switzerland.

On 25 February, exploratory talks were started at Zürich between American OSS agents in Switzerland and Parrilli as General Wolff's representative. A few days later, a delegate of the Strategic Service for Switzerland met SS *Standartenfuehrer* Dollmann, Wolff's colleague, in the Lugano Rotary Club . . .

On 8 March, Allan Dulles saw Wolff in the American Consulate-General in Zurich. It was agreed that Wolff would pave the way for capitulation of the German Southern Army and that, until that time, he would prevent all destructions, reprisals, and searches of partisan-held territory. When Kesselring was recalled from Italy on 9 March, Dulles put three questions to Wolff through Parrilli: (1) Was Wolff able to carry out the plan on his own and what Allied assistance was required; (2) did Wolff think he could win over Kesselring's successor; and (3) could Wolff take suitable action against the new Commander should the latter oppose the plan. Dulles made contact with Allied H.Q. in Caserta and on 14 March, was told that two representatives would be sent to Switzerland to settle details of the capitulation.

On 19 March, Dulles, Wolff and two members of the Allied Chiefs of Staff in Caserta (General Lemnitzer and General Airy) met at Ascona. Wolff declared that, now as before, he could effect the surrender on his own, but recommended that General von Vietinghoff, Kesselring's successor be drawn in, so as to avoid difficulties . . . After his return to Italy, Wolff revealed the entire plan to Vietinghoff and to General Roettinger, the Deputy Commander of the Southern Front, both of whom offered their support.

On 1 April, Allied representatives returned to Ascona to learn through Parrilli what steps Wolff had meanwhile been able to take. It was decided that two German representatives would be taken through the Allied lines to Caserta for the signing of the surrender document . . .

On 27 April, the German representatives were flown to Caserta where they signed the surrender instrument. At Wolff's insistence, Vietinghoff had previously waived all conditions, so as not to jeopardize the final result.

Soviet Suspicions of "Crossword" Operation

By Winston S. Churchill

In February General Karl Wolff, the commander of the SS in Italy, had got into touch through Italian intermediaries with the American Intelligence Service in Switzerland. It was decided to examine the credentials of the persons involved, and the link was given the code-name "Crossword". On 8 March, General Wolff himself appeared at Zürich, and met Mr. Allen Dulles, the head of the American organization. Wolff was bluntly told that there was no question of negotiations, and that if the matter were pursued it could only be on the basis of unconditional surrender. This information was speedily conveyed to Allied Headquarters in Italy and to the American, British and Soviet Governments . . .

*

"Such Distrust, Such Lack of Faith . . ."

From a Telegram by Roosevelt to Stalin on 5 April 1945

(This telegram was sent in reply to a message by Stalin, who had complained about the negotiations in Switzerland and accused the Allies of breach of faith.) I have complete confidence in General Eisenhower, and know that he certainly would inform me before entering into any agreement with the Germans. He is instructed to demand, and will demand, unconditional surrender of enemy troops that may be defeated on his front . . . I am certain that there were no negotiations in Berne at any time, and I feel that your information to that effect must have come from German sources, which have made persistent efforts to create dissension between us . . .

Finally, I would say this: it would be one of the great tragedies of history if at the very moment of the victory now within our grasp such distrust, such lack of faith, should prejudice the entire undertaking after the colossal losses of life, material, and treasure involved.

Frankly, I cannot avoid a feeling of bitter resentment toward your informers, whoever they are, for such vile misrepresentations of my actions or those of my trusted subordinates.

THE SITUATION IN YUGOSLAVIA BEFORE THE EMERGENCE OF TITO'S GOVERNMENT

1 January to 10 March 1945

Belgrade, 16 February 1945 (from right to left): Marshal Tito, Field Marshal Alexander, Dr. Ribar, Maj. General Lemnitzer and General Ivanovic.

Recommendations to Tito Agreed by Roosevelt, Churchill and Stalin at the Yalta Conference.

"(a) That the Tito-Subasié agreement should be enforced immediately, and that a new Government should be formed on the basis of this agreement;

"(b) That upon formation the new Government should declare:
1. That the AVNOJ (Anti-Fascist Council of National Liberation of Yugoslavia) should incorporate members of the last Yugoslav National Assembly who had not compromised themselves by collaboration with the enemy, thus creating a body to be known as the Provisional Assembly, and
2. That the AVNOJ's legislative acts should be subject to subsequent ratification by the Constitutional Assembly."

This decision provoked the deepest indignation among the supporters of the National Liberation Movement in Yugoslavia: people were particularly indignant that the AVNOJ had to incorporate members of the 1938 Assembly, which had been elected during the régime of Milan Stojadinović, an Axis man.

*

Field Marshal Alexander's visit to Tito.

Towards the end of February 1945, Field Marshal Alexander, the Commander of the Mediterranean, arrived in Belgrade on an official visit. He had a number of meetings with Tito, at which a plan of co-ordinating operations between the Yugoslav army and the Allied armies was established. An agreement was reached that the Allied forces in Italy should supply the Yugoslav Fourth Army, operating in western parts of the country.

*

Yugoslav Regency Council sworn in.

Borba announced on 5 March 1945, that a Regency Council had been sworn in, and that the Premier of the Royal Yugoslav Government, Dr. Subasić had dismissed all members of his Cabinet under an agreement made with Marshal Tito. At the same time, the National Liberation Committee had resigned as Provisional Government ... The Regency Council accepted both resignations and, after consulting Dr. Ivan Ribar, President of AVNOJ, called upon Josip Broz-Tito, Marshal of the Yugoslav Army, to form a government of national unity ...

German POW's in Slovenia.

January 1945: A Communist demonstration in support of Tito and his army which became the official Yugoslav Army in March.

*

From the programme of the Tito Government.

On 10 March 1945, *Borba* announced that Marshal Tito had explained the programme of his newly-formed Yugoslav Government in a broadcast address to the nation. The new Government, formed under an agreement with Dr. Subasić would have as its first objective the expulsion of the invader from the rest of Yugoslavia. Every muscle must be strained towards that end. The slogan of the day was "Everything for the Front!" The programme of the Government was based on the principles drawn up during the Second Meeting of AVNOJ on 30 November 1945. The Government would pay special attention to the punishments of war criminals and traitors.

*

The Situation on the Yugoslav front at the beginning of 1945.

By November (1944) the whole of Macedonia had been freed. The German "E" group was unable to retreat along the Vardar and Morava valleys and had to turn towards Kossovo to pass through Bosnia. Shortly afterwards Montenegro was also free. The front stood about one hundred kilometres west of Belgrade in Srem, and extended southward to Sarajevo and westward to the Adriatic Sea. There were no longer any Soviet units in Yugoslavia: only in the north, on the River Drava, were there Bulgarian units.

(from: Gedjer, *Tito speaks*)

Troops of the Yugoslav 2nd Army occupying Bihać in the Una valley on 28 March.

FINAL YUGOSLAV OFFENSIVE

20 March 1945

Generals Peko Dapčević and Kosta Nadj (Yugoslav 1st and 3rd Armies).

General Petar Drapšin (Yugoslav 4th Army).

General Loehr, Commander of German Army Group South.

Yugoslav tanks entering the coastal town of Pula at the end of April

Captured German officers in Ilirska Bistrica.

The Yugoslav General Offensive, 20 March to 15 May 1945

Just before the beginning of the Yugoslav Army's general offensive for the final liberation of the country, there were seven German army corps in Yugoslavia (the 15th Mountain, the 15th Cossack, the 21st, 34th, 69th and 97th) with seventeen divisions (the 1st and 2nd Cossack, the 11th, 41st, 104th, 22nd 181st, 7th SS, 369th, 373rd, 392nd, 237th, 188th, 438th, 138th, 14th SS Ruthenian and the Stefan Division). In addition to these forces the Germans in Yugoslavia had naval forces to defend the coast and strong police forces to secure the rear. Under their command stood armed quisling formations of about twenty divisions.

At that time the Yugoslav army was about eight hundred thousand strong, organized into the First, Second, Third and Fourth Armies, and the 2nd, 3rd, 4th, 5th, 6th, 7th, 9th and 10th Corps outside the army groupings.

The general offensive of the Yugoslav army for the final liberation of the country began on 20 March 1945, and developed broadly on the following lines:

The Fourth Army, under the command of Petar Drapšin, broke through the enemy front of the Lika between 20 March and 16 April, liberated the Lika and the Croatian littoral, including the islands, and reached the old Yugoslav–Italian border . . .

The Third Army, under the command of the Kosta Nadj, forced the Drava on 12 April, fanned out through the Podravina, reached a point north of Zagreb, crossed the Austro–Yugoslav border in the sector of Dravograd, and closed the ring round the enemy forces in Yugoslavia with the motorized detachment of the Fourth Army in Carinthia.

The First Army, under the command of Peko Dapčević, penetrated the enemy fortified front in Srem on 12 April, and on 22 April smashed the enemy defences and continued its advance towards Zagreb.

The Second Army, under the command of Koča Popović, went over to the offensive on 5 April, forced the River Bosua (16–17 April), liberated Doboj and reached the River Una. Continuing its operations for the liberation of Zagreb in co-operation with units of the First Army, it freed Zagreb on 8 May. From 10–15 May, together with the First Army, it took part in capturing and destroying the surrounded enemy forces in Slovenia. It is characteristic that the Germans resisted in Yugoslavia even after the surrender of 9 May. They fought till they were destroyed or captured right up to 15 May . . .

(from Dedjer, *Tito Speaks*)

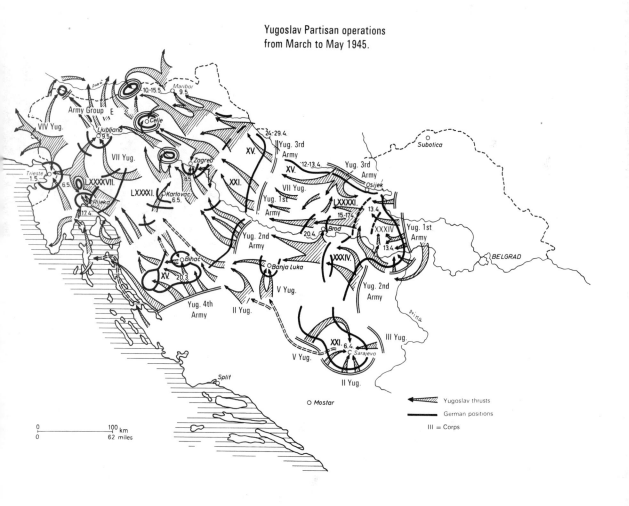

Yugoslav Partisan operations from March to May 1945.

Yugoslav naval party on the way to Istria.

YUGOSLAVIA LIBERATES HERSELF

Troops of Yugoslav 4th Army during street-fighting in Susak, a suburb of Rijeka (Fiume). Late April 1945.

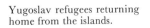

Yugoslav refugees returning home from the islands.

Yugoslav 1st Army entering Zagreb on 8 May. ▼

A group of Czech Partisans.

CZECH PARTISANS HELP THE RED ARMY TO LIBERATE THEIR COUNTRY   January–May 1945

Slovak Partisans clearing a village of German troops.

Czech Partisans manning an armoured train.

BRITISH 8TH ARMY AND U.S. 5TH ARMY LAUNCH FINAL OFFENSIVE IN ITALY   9 April 1945

Field Marshal Sir Harold Alexander, Allied Supreme Commander Mediterranean.

General von Vietinghoff-Scheel, Supreme Commander German Army Group C (S.W.).

Allied Commanders in the Mediterranean

Allied Supreme Commander
Field Marshal Sir Harold Alexander (Br.)

Deputy Supreme Commander
Lt. General J. T. McNarney (U.S.A.)

Allied Naval Commander
Admiral Sir John Cunningham (Br.)

Allied Army Commander
Field Marshal Alexander (Br.)

C.-in-C. 15th Army Group
(U.S. 5th and British 8th Armies)
General Mark Clark (U.S.A.)

Allied Air Commander
Lt. General J. K. Cannon (U.S.A.)

On 9 April, at 1:45 p.m., the Allies launched their last offensive in Italy after bombing German positions between rivers Senio and Santerno.

General Mark Clark, Commander of 15th Army Group, and Lt. General Sir Richard McCreery, Commander of 8th Army, watching Allied air attack.

The Last Allied Offensive in Italy

By Lieutenant-Colonel S. W. Nicholson.

The long hours of suspense dragged slowly by, eyes turning continually to watches. At last at 13:45 hours the distant roar of heavy bombers seemed the signal for the first guns to speak. These were the 3.7s firing a line of air-bursts as markers to guide the heavies on to their target . . . A strange hush fell and the silent minutes and seconds ticked slowly by till at 15:20 hours, with a mighty crash, the gun battle began along the whole front. Shells tore into the stop-banks of the Senio from all angles, some from guns carefully sited to enfilade the reaches of the river, others crashing headlong among the mines and wire and strong-points; others searching deep into the back areas among the guns, dumps, headquarters and supply routes. Suddenly the shelling lifted from the stop-banks, stepping out in a "dragnet" barrage. Then the guns were silent, and for ten minutes Thunderbolts, Spitfires and Kittyhawks took charge of the river, zooming up and down with bombs, rockets and machineguns adding their staccato to the hymn of hate. Back came the guns to pound the banks, play "dragnet" with variations and again give way to the air. In all, five gun attacks and four air attacks – till at 19:20 hours a sudden silence marked H-hour, broken only by the aircraft coming back for a dummy run to keep the enemy heads down and drown the roar of Crocodiles and Wasps clambering up the near bank to sear with flame the already blasted enemy banks. In their tracks the assaulting infantry, with their kapok bridges, struggled forward to the river in the gathering dusk. 19:30 hours; with a roar the protective barrage opened four hundred yards beyond the river line and held there for thirty minutes, a curtain of steel behind which the infantry completed their grisly task. Fresh platoons leapfrogged through, and at H+40 moved forward with the barrage. There was no stopping now . . .

At dawn on the 10th our batteries slipped forward in turn to the prepared positions behind the banks of the Senio and, tired but jubilant gunners were ready to cover the infantry to the Santerno river line.

(From Flower/Rees: *The War 1939–1945*)

Allied H.Q. Mediterranean announced on 10 April that the 8th Army had crossed the river Senio on a broad front.

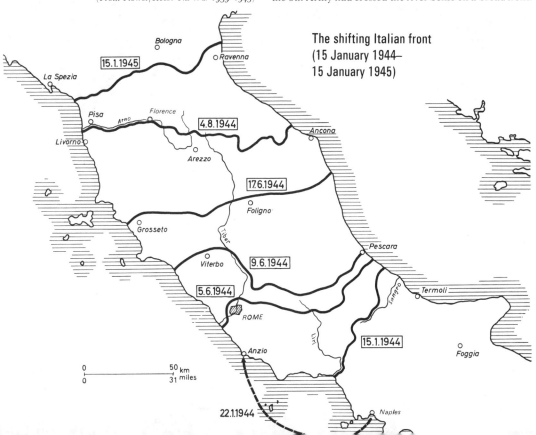

The shifting Italian front
(15 January 1944–
15 January 1945)

Bologna · Ravenna · 15.1.1945 · La Spezia · Pisa · Arno · Florence · 4.8.1944 · Ancona · Livorno · Arezzo · 17.6.1944 · Foligno · Grosseto · Tiber · Pescara · Viterbo · 9.6.1944 · Sangro · Termoli · 5.6.1944 · ROME · Liri · 15.1.1944 · Anzio · Foggia · 22.1.1944 · Naples

0   50 km
0   31 miles

The first German prisoners being brought in.

British 8th Army in Lugo (11 April 1945).

ACROSS THE SENIO AND ON TO THE SANTERNO 9–11 April 1945

Flame-thrower on the bank of the river Senio.

THE 3RD UKRAINIAN FRONT ENTERS VIENNA 2 April 1945

On 7 April, Soviet troops forced the Danube and entered Vienna.

Wiener Ausgabe   81. Ausg. 58 Jahrg. Einzelpreis: **15 Pf.**   „Freiheit und Brot!"   Wien, Donnerstag, 5. April 1945   **Wiener Ausgabe**

VÖLKISCHER BEOBACHTER

Kampfblatt der nationalsozialistischen Bewegung Großdeutschlands

Kurasche!

Versteifter Widerstand im Süden Wiens

Eigene Gegenstöße verlangsamen den feindlichen Vormarsch

Wachsende deutsche Gegenwirkung im Westen

Der Ursprung des sowjetischen Ausrottungswillens

Politischer Bankrott der Anglo-Amerikaner

Vienna edition of *Volkischer Beobachter* speaks of increased German resistance in the south of the city. Baldur von Schirach announced over the radio that Vienna had been declared a battle area.

Marshal Malinovsky, Commander of the 2nd Ukrainian Front.

Marshal Tolbukhin, Commander of the 3rd Ukrainian Front.

SS-*Obergruppenfuehrer* Sepp Dietrich, the "defender" of Vienna.

VIENNA FALLS   13 April 1945

From Marshal Tolbukhin's proclamation to the citizens of Vienna of 6 April 1945 (according to "Soviet Foreign Policy"):

The following proposals are made for the preservation of the Austrian capital and its cultural and artistic monuments. (1) All those who hold their city dear, will not desert their homes, but will welcome the eviction of the Germans as a liberation from the horrors of war. (2) Do not allow the Germans to undermine your city, to destroy bridges, or to transform dwelling houses into strong-points. (3) Organize yourselves against the Germans and prevent the destruction of your city by Hitler's men. (4) Every Vienese citizen must prevent the Germans from making off with industrial equipment, goods and provisions, thus robbing the people of Vienna. Citizens of Vienna! Help the Red Army in the liberation of Vienna, your capital, make your contribution to the great cause of ridding Austria of the German yoke.

The Commander of the 3rd Ukrainian Front
Marshal of the Soviet Union Tolbukhin

Hitler's reaction to the fall of Vienna:

Hitler was informed of the fall of Vienna on 14 April 1945. The Austrian front had been defended by the 6th SS Tank Army, led by SS-*Obergruppenfuehrer* Sepp Dietrich. This National Socialist "veteran fighter" had been leader of the "Adolf Hitler Life-Guards" before 1933. When Hitler was told of the retreat of the 6th SS Tank Army and the capture of Vienna, he fell into a furious rage and had the following radio message sent to Sepp Dietrich: "Fuehrer holds that troops did not fight as situation demanded, and accordingly orders that SS-Divisions "Adolf Hitler", "Das Reich", "Totenkopf", and "Hohenstaufen" be deprived of their stripes. These divisions were among the toughest and most battle-tested that the German Army could still boast. The stripes on the sleeve of their uniform were meant to represent the traditional insignia of the "Old Army".

When Sepp Dietrich received Hitler's message, he telegraphed back that he would rather be shot than carry out this order . . .

From Boldt: *Die letzten Tage der Reichskanzlei* (The last days of the Reich-Chancellery)

The Soviet News Agency announced on 14 April that troops of the 3rd and 2nd Ukrainian Fronts had captured Vienna. The photograph shows Soviet engineers laying cables in a suburb of Vienna.

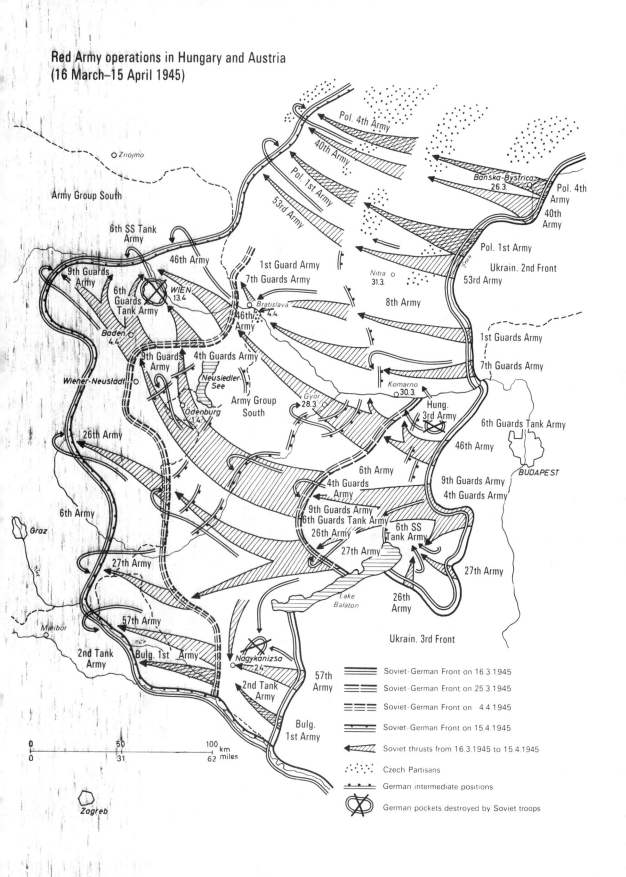

Red Army operations in Hungary and Austria (16 March–15 April 1945)

Znojmo

Army Group South

6th SS Tank Army

9th Guards Army

46th Army

6th Guards Tank Army

WIEN 13.4.

Baden 4.4.

9th Guards Army

Wiener-Neustadt

4th Guards Army

Neusiedler-See

Ödenburg 1.4.

Army Group South

1st Guard Army
7th Guards Army

Bratislava 4.4.

46th Army

Nitra 31.3.

8th Army

Pol. 4th Army

40th Army

Pol. 1st Army

53rd Army

Banska-Bystrica 26.3.

Pol. 4th Army

40th Army

Pol. 1st Army

Ukrain. 2nd Front

53rd Army

1st Guards Army

7th Guards Army

Komarno 30.3.

Gyor 28.3.

Hung. 3rd Army

6th Guards Tank Army

46th Army

BUDAPEST

26th Army

6th Army

6th Army

Graz

27th Army

Maribor

57th Army

2nd Tank Army

Bulg. 1st Army

Nagykanizsa 2.4.

2nd Tank Army

4th Guards Army

9th Guards Army
6th Guards Tank Army
26th Army

27th Army

Lake Balaton

9th Guards Army
4th Guards Army

6th SS Tank Army

27th Army

26th Army

Ukrain. 3rd Front

57th Army

Bulg. 1st Army

Zagreb

▬▬▬▬	Soviet-German Front on 16.3.1945
══════	Soviet-German Front on 25.3.1945
≡≡≡≡	Soviet-German Front on 4.4.1945
▬▬▬▬	Soviet-German Front on 15.4.1945
◄▨▨▨	Soviet thrusts from 16.3.1945 to 15.4.1945
∴∴∴	Czech Partisans
▬•▬•▬	German intermediate positions
⊗	German pockets destroyed by Soviet troops

0   50   100 km
0   31   62 miles

ALLIED ADVANCE ON LA SPEZIA AND FERRARA
11–16 April 1945

Eighth Army men advancing on Carrara.

Interrogation of captured German NCO.

A B-24 Liberator of the 15th USAAF crashing after being hit by anti-aircraft fire. On the west flank of the Italian front, the U.S. 5th Army reached Montese on 14 April and Vergato on 16 April. Meanwhile British troops reached the Sillaro and occupied Medicina.

THE LOWDOWN

Vol. AF LXXIII April 1945, 3rd Edition *** Three Star Final

BATTLE EAST OF BERLIN RAGING

ALLIED TANK LOSSES HUGE

SMALL NATIONS FOR SALE
FAR EAST WAR UNTIL '47?

Harry Truman - the new C-in-C. of the U.S. a'med forces.

Truman - the new man

Unexpectedly Franklin D. Roosevelt passed away. It is probably no! wrong to assume that a gloom was cast over the last days of his life by the knowledge that he had steered the American ship of state on a wrong and fatal course quite against his intentions. Will Harry Truman be the right trustee for the heritage left him by F. D. Roosevelt? *See TRUMAN page 1*

12 out of 18 nations delivered up to Stalin

Anyone who would have said at the time the Atlantic Charter was signed that the U. S. and England

exception of Croatia, Bohemia, Slovakia, Norway, Sweden and Denmark the remaining twelve countries are already being subjected to the terror, cruelty, slavery and wholesale murder of the Bolshevik system.

Roosevelt and Churchill, the big stars of the Atlantic Charter conedy, sold these twelve countries to the Rasputin of nations, Josef Stalin, of whose political theories Churchill said before the war, « Bolshevism is not a policy. It is a disease and a creed. It is a pestilence ». Just the same, for this disease and pestilence, for the betrayal of the small nations, the American soldier has to bleed to death.

G.I.s have no say at Frisco

The one vote conceded to the U. S. for the San Francisco Conference (as contrasted with the three votes of Sovie. Russia) will by no means be represented by a member of the fighting forces.

42 different groups make up this one vote and all the millions of G. I s are represented only by *one* single group. The remaining 41 groups are apportioned to the bankers, manufacturers, women's organizations, churches etc. Thus, the same mistakes will be made again at this confrence as in 1919 at Versailles after World War I. *Soldier!* Look out that after this poor man's fight a rich man's peace will not result in new bread-lines and unemployment for you.

NEWS FLASHES

Between April 1st and April 19th the attacking Bolsheviks lost not less than 2,807 tanks. The battle goes on with utmost force. - Allied tank losses at the Western Front amounted to 1,079 tanks for the same period.

— L o n d o n « Daily Mail» states: The Jap army has not yet suffered any catastrophic losses of men. Its military strength is estimated at four millions, more than half of which are fresh and fully trained. There is no reason to assume that the Jap forces in China would surrender even if the Jap mainland were overcome.

— Owing to floods in the Red River area in central Louisiana, 25,000 people are homeless. More than half a million acres of farmland will be useless for further cultivation.

— The American people this year will probably receive the smallest food rations since the beginning of the war. There will, particularly, be a shortage of meat, butter and sugar.

— The U.S. national debt has reached the sum of about 400 billion dollars. This means a tax burden of ten thousand dollars to be borne by every American family.

The U. S. Navy has transferred to the Red Navy the U. S. cruiser « Milwaukee ».

A German leaflet for Allied soldiers in Italy.   A retreating German Panther tank in Upper Italy.

Maori troops of the 8th Army in Bentivoglio.

German troop concentration being attacked N.E. of Bologna.

ARGENTA IN BRITISH HANDS

18 April 1945

British troops mopping up in Argenta. Allied Mediterranean H.Q. announced . . .

German parachutist killed in the Torrente–Idice sector on 20 April 1945.

. . . that units of the 5th and 8th Armies were less than
10 miles from Bologna.

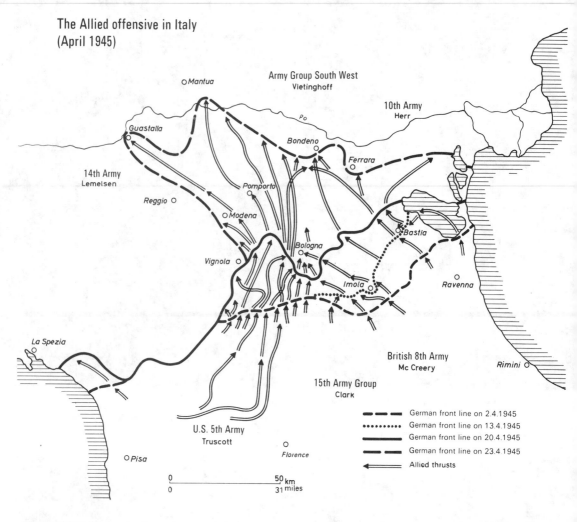

The Allied offensive in Italy
(April 1945)

Army Group South West
Vietinghoff

10th Army
Herr

Mantua

Po

Guastalla

Bondeno

Ferrara

14th Army
Lemelsen

Pomporto

Reggio

Modena

Bastia

Bologna

Vignola

Imola

Ravenna

La Spezia

British 8th Army
Mc Creery

Rimini

15th Army Group
Clark

U.S. 5th Army
Truscott

Florence

Pisa

	German front line on 2.4.1945
	German front line on 13.4.1945
	German front line on 20.4.1945
	German front line on 23.4.1945
	Allied thrusts

0   50 km
0   31 miles

BOLOGNA AND FERRARA OCCUPIED   21 and 23 April 1945

U.S. 5th Army advancing into the Po Valley from the Apennines. Bologna was reached on 21 April.

General Mark Clark, C.-in-C. 15th Army Group, in Bologna. Saluting while the Allied national anthems are being played on 22 April are (from left to right): Generals Clark, Anders, Truscott and Keyes.

British 8th Army reached Ferrara on 23 April. Two German soldiers who tried vainly to hide in civilian clothes.

German resistance collapsed after the capture of Bologna. The photograph shows German prisoners on a U.S. lorry in Bologna.

ALLIES ADVANCE ACROSS THE PO

23 April 1945

The Supreme Command of the Wehrmacht announced on 25 April:

In Italy, the battle centre has shifted from Reggio and Ferrara to the Po, following the advance of strong enemy infantry and tank concentrations.

*

Allied Mediterranean H.Q. announced on 28 April:

With the enemy forces in Northern Italy in complete disintegration, the Allied armies swept forward on all fronts, the 8th Army crossing the Adige in strength near Padua, piercing the so-called "Venetian line" of defences . . . and thrusting towards Padua and Venice. Troops of the 5th Army have captured Verona and are rapidly advancing on Piacenza and Milan. In Liguria, an Allied naval party took over the port of Genoa . . .

Units of the U.S. 5th Army crossing the Po in amphibious vehicles on 23 April.

On 23 April, the U.S. 8th Army reached the Po at Pontelagoscuro and established bridgeheads on the north bank.

GERMAN FRONT IN ITALY COLLAPSES 27 April 1945

On 27 April 1945, the German front in Italy collapsed, and German troops withdrew to the north. Fighting ceased three days later.

Lt.-General Count von Schwerin with Lt.-General Keightley, Commander of the British 5th Corps.

Major-General Pemsel, captured by the Americans near Brescia, in conversation with an interpreter.

MUSSOLINI SHOT BY LT.-COL. VALERIO

28 April 1945

"I shall give you an empire!"

The inglorious end of a sawdust Caesar

Mussolini's nemesis was a Lieutenant-Colonel Valerio, a Communist and former metal worker, who led an expedition "to apply on the spot the decree of the North Italian Committee of National Liberation against those responsible for the catastrophe into which Italy had been led". By accident Valerio and his Partisans on April 28 found Mussolini and his mistress in a farmhouse near the town of Giulano di Mezzegere on Lake Como . . .

Mussolini expressed his resentment at being disturbed. Valerio said calmly: "I have come to free you."

The two prisoners were pushed outside the room. It suddenly dawned upon Mussolini that these were not friends. Then came one of the most unique offers of a bribe in the history of crime: "Let me go," the *Duce* beseeched his captors. "I shall give you an empire!"

Valerio said nothing. The prisoners were pushed into an automobile. On the pretext that he had heard a noise, Valerio stopped the car and stepped out.

"Get out quickly, both of you. Stand at the corner of that wall."

Petacci screamed hysterically, "You can't do that!"

Valerio pumped bullets into Mussolini and his mistress. "I execute the will of the Italian people," he said.

The bodies, plus those of a dozen other Fascists, were brought to Milan for public display in the Piazza Loretto, the huge open square where fifteen Italian patriots had been executed by the Fascists a year before. There, bloody and mudstained, the bodies of Mussolini and the others were dumped like carrion, beaten, kicked, trampled, spat upon . . .

Milton Bracker in *N.Y. Times*

The bodies of Mussolini, Clara Petacci and other Fascists were put on display . . .
. . . in Milan, in the same spot where fifteen anti-Fascists had been executed one year earlier.

Me ne frego—I don't give a damn

By Benito Mussolini

War alone tests human strength to the full, and enables all nations daring to wage it. All other tests are no more than substitutes and fail to confront man with himself in a choice between life and death. Hence all doctrines based on the idea of peace are no more suited to Fascism than any other international schemes—for history has shown that, even if such schemes have to be adopted temporarily for reasons of political expediency, they go by the board as soon as emotion, or national ideals and interests rise up in the heart of the nation. Fascism applies this anti-pacifist spirit even in the life of individuals. The proud motto of our storm troopers: *me ne frego*—a motto that first appeared on the bandage of a wounded fighter—is not merely a Stoic confession of faith, or the expression of a political idea—it also bespeaks a readiness to do battle, to brave danger; it is a new way of Italian life.

From: Mussolini's *Fascism*

A Marauder attacking Venice.

Gurkha troops of the 8th Army in Este.

VENICE AND PADUA OCCUPIED   29 April 1945

German prisoners in the Lido of Venice.

The North Italian Committee of National Liberation achieved its greatest success with the capture of Milan. In the photograph: SS-prisoners in a lorry.

ITALIAN PARTISANS LIBERATE MILAN   25–30 April 1945

An American interpreter calling on captured SS-men to surrender their arms.

American soldiers entering Milan in the wake of the Partisans, on 30 April.

ARMY GROUP C SURRENDERS IN CASERTA
29 April 1945

Draft for the instrument of surrender of all forces under the control of the German C.-in-C. South-West:

1. The German C.-in-C., South-West, agrees to the unconditional surrender of all forces under his command or control on land, sea, or in the air to the Supreme Allied Commander, Mediterranean.

2. The German C.-in-C., South-West, will at once issue orders to all forces under his command to cease active operations on land, sea or in the air at 12:00 hours GMT on May 2, 1945.

3. The German C.-in-C., South-West, agrees to carry out the orders set out in Appendices A, B and C, and any further orders that may be issued by the Supreme Commander, Mediterranean. Disobedience of orders or failure to comply with them will be dealt with in accordance with the accepted laws and usages of war.

4. This instrument comes into effect immediately upon signature, and the orders contained in Appendices A, B and C will take effect at the date and time stipulated under para. 2.

5. This instrument of surrender is written in English and German. The English version is the authentic text. The decision of the Supreme Commander will be final if any doubt or dispute arises as to the meaning or interpretation of the surrender terms.

Secret

6. The instrument of surrender stipulates that it is independent of, without prejudice to, and will be superseded by any general instrument of surrender imposed by or on behalf of the United Nations and applicable to Germany and the German armed forces as a whole.

signed: *Schweinitz*
Lt.-Col. Victor von Schweinitz
Staff of Army Group C
on behalf of
General Von Vietinghoff-Scheel
C.-in-C. South-West

signed: *Wenner*
SS-*Sturmbanfuehrer*
Major Eugen Wenner
on behalf of
SS-*Obergruppenfuehrer*
Colonel Karl Wolff
Supreme SS and Police Commander and
Wehrmacht Pleni-potentiary in Italy

signed: *W. D. Morgan*
Lt.-Gen. W. D. Morgan,
Chief of Staff of Allied Force H.Q.
on behalf of
Field-Marshal H. R. L. G. Alexander,
Supreme Allied Commander,
Mediterranean Theatre of Operations

Place: CASERTA
Date: 29 April 1945
Time: 14:00 hours

Marshal Graziani, Commander of the Italian Army Group, Liguria, being interrogated by Brigadier Howard (U.S.A.).

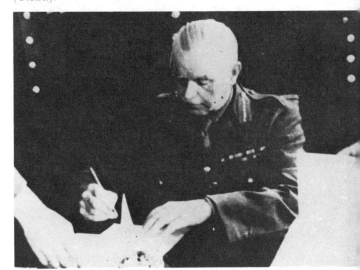

Lt.-General Morgan signing the instrument of surrender.

German representatives signing at Caserta.

Tanks of the 3rd Ukrainian Front in occupied Vienna. Soon afterwards the Red Army advanced as far as Linz in Lower Austria.

The collapse of the German front in Italy and the last operations of Allied forces and the Red Army in S.E. Europe

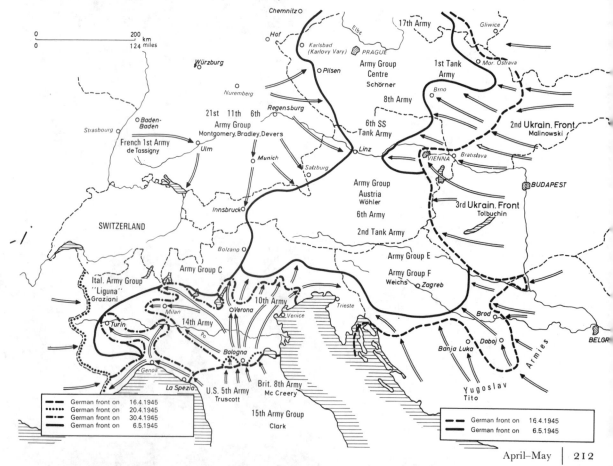

Chemnitz

17th Army

Gliwice

Hof

Elbe

Karlsbad
(Karlovy Vary)

PRAGUE

Würzburg

Pilsen

Army Group
Centre
Schörner

1st Tank
Army

Mor. Ostrava

Nuremberg

8th Army

Brno

21st 11th 6th

Regensburg

Baden-
Baden

Army Group
Montgomery, Bradley, Devers

6th SS
Tank Army

2nd Ukrain. Front
Malinowski

Strasbourg

French 1st Army
de Tassigny

Ulm

Munich

Linz

VIENNA

Bratislava

Salzburg

BUDAPEST

Innsbruck

Army Group
Austria
Wöhler

3rd Ukrain. Front
Tolbuchin

SWITZERLAND

6th Army

Bolzano

2nd Tank Army

Army Group E

Ital. Army Group
"Liguna"
Graziani

Army Group C

Army Group F
Weichs

Zagreb

10th Army

Trieste

Brod

Milan

Verona

Venice

Turin

14th Army

Banja Luka

Doboj

Po

Armies

BELGR

Bologna

Genoa

La Spezia

U.S. 5th Army
Truscott

Brit. 8th Army
Mc Creery

Yugoslav
Tito

15th Army Group
Clark

	German front on	16.4.1945
	German front on	20.4.1945
	German front on	30.4.1945
	German front on	6.5.1945

| | German front on | 16.4.1945 |
| | German front on | 6.5.1945 |

0 — 200 km
0 — 124 miles

Yugoslav troops captured Trieste on 1 May. German troops refuse to surrender to other than British troops and are taken to Monfalcone.

YUGOSLAV AND BRITISH TROOPS IN TRIESTE   4 May 1945

An Order of the Day from Field-Marshal Alexander announced on 3 April that the New Zealand troops under Gen. Freyburg, V.C., had occupied Trieste . . . The New Zealanders, on entering Trieste, found a very confused situation; Marshal Tito's Yugoslav troops, who had been heavily engaged with the enemy, were in the city, while Chetnik bands formerly under Gen. Mihailovitch, and Italian guerrillas were also active . . . It appeared that a delicate position might materialize.

General Freyberg meeting General Borstnar in Monfalcone. Below: A Yugoslav soldier handing his flag to a New Zealander.

THE CZECH UPRISING IN PRAGUE

4–9 May 1945

On 5 May, Prague saw the beginning of an anti-German terror campaign, unleashed by *Gauleiter* Frank's previous order to shoot Czech rebels at sight (see Chronology).

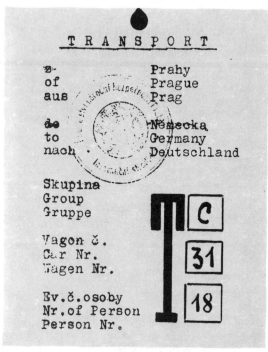

TRANSPORT	
z-	Prahy
of	Prague
aus	Prag
do	Německa
to	Germany
nach	Deutschland
Skupina	
Group	
Gruppe	
Vagon č.	
Car Nr.	
Wagen Nr.	
Ev.č.osoby	
Nr.of Person	
Person Nr.	

T C / 31 / 18

Travel voucher of an expelled German.

First Ukrainian Front occupying Prague on 9 May.

Prague's famous Wenceslaus Square on 9 May 1945, a few hours after the arrival of Marshal Koniev's troops.

Frenchmen fighting in the ranks of the Czech Patriot Army at Vrutky, north of Kremnica.

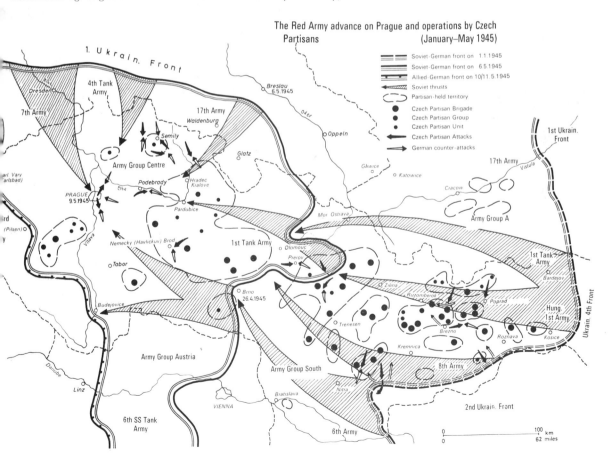

The Red Army advance on Prague and operations by Czech
Partisans   (January–May 1945)

	Soviet-German front on 1.1.1945
	Soviet-German front on 6.5.1945
	Allied-German front on 10/11.5.1945
	Soviet thrusts
	Partisan-held territory
●	Czech Partisan Brigade
	Czech Partisan Group
	Czech Partisan Unit
	Czech Partisan Attacks
	German counter-attacks

1. Ukrain. Front

Dresden
4th Tank Army
7th Army
17th Army
Waldenburg
Breslau
6.5.1945
Oder
Oppeln
Semily
Army Group Centre
Glatz
Gliwice
Katowice
1st Ukrain. Front
17th Army
Vistula
Carl Vary (Carlsbad)
Podebrady
Hradec Kralove
Elbe
PRAGUE
9.5.1945
Pardubice
Mor. Ostrava
Cracow
Army Group A
(Pilsen)
Vltava
Nemecky (Havlickuv) Brod
1st Tank Army
Olomouc
Prerov
1st Tank Army
Bardejov
Tabor
Zilina
Ruzomberok
Poprad
Budejovice
Brno
26.4.1945
Trenesen
Brezno
Hung.
1st Army
Roznava
Kosice
Ukrain. 4th Front
Army Group Austria
Kremnica
Danube
Linz
Army Group South
Nitra
8th Army
6th SS Tank Army
Bratislava
VIENNA
2nd Ukrain. Front
6th Army

0   100 km
0   62 miles

THE GERMAN COLLAPSE
IN THE SOUTH

4–5 May 1945

After the link-up between the U.S. 7th and 5th Armies at the Brenner Pass (4 May), organized German resistance in Austria ceased.

Captured Cossack Divisions and Vlassov units were later handed over to the Russians.

Major-General Gruenther (left foreground, back to camera) discusses the surrender of German troops in Italy with Lt.-Generals Senger and Etterlin (third from left) and Lt.-Colonel von Schweinitz (fourth from left), who signed the Caserta instrument.

Surrender negotiations near the Brenner Pass between U.S. soldiers and German officers.

A Scottish officer discussing surrender terms with SS officers in Austria.

THE CAPTURE OF GOERING AND FIELD-MARSHALS KESSELRING, VON KLEIST, SCHOERNER AND VON RUNDSTEDT Early May 1945

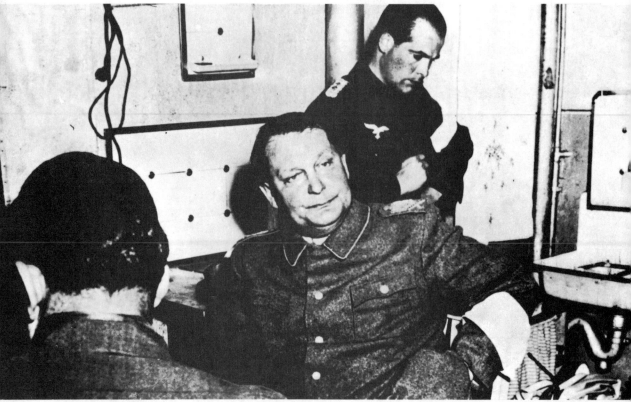

Reichs Marshal Goering, ousted by Hitler on 23 April and confined to Mauterndorf until 5 May, decided to make contact with the Americans through the General Staff of the *Luftwaffe*. Events moved too fast for him, however, and on 8 May he was captured in Fischhorn (Austria).

Field-Marshal von Kleist and General Russwurm (standing) after their capture in Mitterfels (Bavaria). Right: Field-Marshal Schoerner, Commander of Army Group Centre, who deserted and fled to the West in civilian clothes.

Field-Marshal Kesselring with Major-General M. D. Taylor.

Field-Marshal von Rundstedt was taken prisoner in a hospital in Bad Toelz.

GERMAN FRONT COLLAPSES IN YUGOSLAVIA

9–15 May 1945

From Marshal Tito's address over Radio Belgrade on 9 May 1945:

This, the most terrible war in the history of mankind, has robbed Europe of the lives of tens of millions of men. Nazis, Fascists, and their bloodstained henchmen throughout Europe have been wiped out and will no longer be able to disturb the peace . . . Serbs, Croats, Slovenes, Macedonians, Montenegrians and Moslems! The day for which you longed so fervently has arrived. No longer disunited and led into hostile camps, you have all become members of a new and happy Yugoslavia.

*

On 12 May, the Yugoslav General Staff announced the destruction or capture of 6 German divisions, including the Tiger Division, the SS-Prinz-Eugen Divisions, and of 11 Ustasi Divisions (Croat Fascists). Yugoslav forces, the announcement added, had liberated Maribor and Slovenska Bistrica.

Brief Survey of the war in Yugoslavia

The liberation of the whole territory of Yugoslavia was completed during the period from 20 March to 15 May, when the Yugoslav Army inflicted losses of 99,907 dead and 209,639 captured, including many commanders, in particular the Commander of the German front in the south-east, Colonel-General Loehr. It seized 183,622 rifles, 24,454 automatic weapons, 1,520 guns, 3,651 trucks, 40 planes, and much other war material.

Thus ended the war in Yugoslavia. During the final battles alone about 30,000 Yugoslavs were killed and 70,000 wounded. During the whole of the war, Yugoslavia had about 1,700,000 dead, who lost their lives on the battlefield, in concentration camps, or in German captivity. Every ninth Yugoslav gave his life in the war. Material losses were indescribable. More than 820,000 houses were destroyed or burned. Twenty per cent of the railways were made useless. Two-thirds of the livestock was looted. Almost all the big industrial units were damaged.

(from Dedjer, *Tito Speaks*)

THE GERMAN COLLAPSE IN SCANDINAVIA

Occupied Denmark and Norway in 1945; until the German capitulation.

CHRONOLOGICAL TABLE:

1945

January–April: Constant trials of, and death sentences passed on, Danish and Norwegian Resistance fighters (see Table on p. 425).

9/1: Naval battles off the coast of Norway.

13/1: German High Command announces the destruction of 13 enemy aircraft off Norway.

29/1: Naval engagement between German and British forces off the west coast of Norway.

17/2: German High Command announces air battles off the N.W. coast of Norway.

February–March: Germans attack Resistance fighters, brought in from Britain, in the Norwegian fjords.

19/4: German High Command announces the sinking of a British submarine by a patrol boat in Norwegian waters.

2/5: According to unconfirmed reports, Germans have begun to take measures for the evacuation of Denmark and Norway.

The German Commander in Norway, General Boehme, announces that his forces will continue to fight in Norway.

5/5: Danish Resistance Movement takes over in Copenhagen. King of Denmark broadcasts news of his country's liberation.

6/5: Keitel places German units in Denmark under Field-Marshal Busch, C.-in-C., North-West.

7/5: Doenitz orders surrender of German forces in Norway to the Allied Expeditionary Force. All German troops in Norway lay down their arms.

Allied troops occupy Oslo. The Norwegian Parliament calls for calm and order.

8/5: The German High Command announces that Norway had "a quiet day".

9/5: Quisling surrenders to the Oslo police.

13/5: Crown Prince Olaf returns to Norway.

31/5: Norwegian government-in-exile returns home.

7/6: King Haakon returns home.

22/6: Einar Gerhardsen forms new Norwegian government.

24/10: Death sentence on Quisling carried out.

THE GERMANS IN NORWAY, 1945

The German Commanders in Norway (from right to left): General Boehme, Reichs-Commissar Terboven, Admiral Krancke, Air-Force General Roth.

German policeman checking a Norwegian lorry.

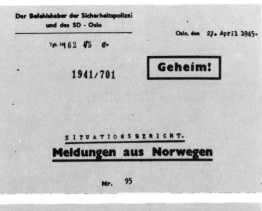

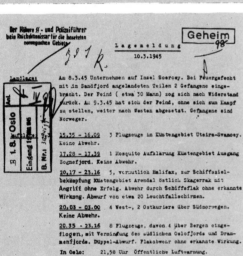

THE DANISH AND NORWEGIAN RESISTANCE MOVEMENTS

From Churchill's New Year Message to the Danish Resistance Group, 1 January 1945:

At the beginning of the New Year, I cannot promise you that the end is near; but I can say that the Nazi beast is cornered and that its destruction is inevitable. The wounds inflicted by the armed might of the Grand Alliance are mortal. And when we in Britain speak of the Grand Alliance, we mean not only the armies, navies and air forces of the United Nations; we mean also the resistance movements throughout Europe, whose members have played so gallant a part in this total war against a brutal and unscrupulous enemy.

To you in the Danish resistance movement, under the brave leadership of the Freedom Council, I say this: We know what price you have paid and are paying for refusing to be tempted by Nazi blandishments or cowed by Nazi threats; we know something of your achievements in harrying and wrecking the German war machine which rolled across your defenceless frontiers nearly five years ago. We admire your steadfastness and your skill. Your resistance is a valuable contribution both to the Allied cause and to the future prosperity of a free Denmark . . .

Gestapo cellars like this one were used for locking up Danish Resistance fighters during their interrogation.

Heading and two pages of German Intelligence report on the situation in Norway. "No matter what uniform we wear, we all pledge our lives to the defence of Fortress Norway."

"I am one of many . . ."

From a letter by Lars Bager Svane to his mother:

Svane was arrested on 4 October 1943, and shot by the Germans on 29 April 1944, in Ryvangen (Copenhagen).

Dearest Mother,

Well, they have come for me. It is now 3 o'clock, and I have another two hours to live. I am still so young, and used to look forward to a long life. But I am not afraid of death—I knew what dangers I was running when I started this work. Though Denmark will soon forget me, I do not regret what I have done for my beloved country . . .

Mother dear, each day you read of many thousands who have died. Try to take my death in the same spirit. Give Father my love. He will soon be home, mark my words, and the two of you will have many more joyful years together. Thank you for a very happy childhood, and for all you have done for me since. Only promise me not to mourn for me; I don't deserve it . . . I thought there was so much more I had to tell you, Mother, but my mind is quite blank; perhaps I have said all there is to be said. Thank you for all the kindness you have shown me in my time.

Farewell, all my dear ones.

Yours Lars.

Factory destroyed by Danish Resistance fighters.

Bekanntmachung

Durch das Kriegsgericht sind am 26. Oktober 1943 wegen Verbrechen gegen die Verordnung zum Schutze der besetzten norwegischen Gebiete vom 12. Oktober 1942 folgende norwegische Staatsangehörige verurteilt worden:

A) Wegen Betätigung für einen Feindstaat und Unterstützung von Agenten:

Johan Jörgensen-Rotvaag	35 Jahre alt, wohnhaft in Rotvaag
Johan Hammer	33 Jahre alt, wohnhaft in Aarviksand
Haakon Kristiansen	27 Jahre alt, wohnhaft in Aarviksand
Edelsten Johansen	22 Jahre alt, wohnhaft in Nordre-Rekvik
Helmer Albrigtsen	24 Jahre alt, wohnhaft in Nordre-Rekvik

zum Tode

B) Wegen Betätigung für einen Feindstaat:

Ottar Jörgensen	19 Jahre alt, wohnhaft in Aarviksand

zum Tode

C) Wegen Unterstützung von Agenten:

Øivind Larsen	47 Jahre alt, wohnhaft in Tromsdalen
Otto Jörgensen	68 Jahre alt, wohnhaft in Rotvaag

zum Tode

Petra Jörgensen	46 Jahre alt, wohnhaft in Aarviksand
Astrid Hansher	23 Jahre alt, wohnhaft in Aarviksand
Dagny Jörgensen	28 Jahre alt, wohnhaft in Rotvaag

zu 15 Jahren Zuchthaus

D) Wegen Nichtanzeige des Aufenthaltsortes von Agenten:

Sigurd Jörgensen	22 Jahre alt, wohnhaft in Aarviksand
Karl Lauritzen	22 Jahre alt, wohnhaft in Nordre-Rekvik
Karl Jörgensen	55 Jahre alt, wohnhaft in Aarviksand
Simon Albrigtsen	50 Jahre alt, wohnhaft in Nordre-Rekvik
Haakon Kristiansen	44 Jahre alt, wohnhaft in Nordre-Rekvik

zu 15 Jahren Zuchthaus

Edvin Jörgensen	64 Jahre alt, wohnhaft in Aarviksand
Freidian Andersen	31 Jahre alt, wohnhaft in Aarviksand
Ingvald Johnsen	24 Jahre alt, wohnhaft in Nordre-Rekvik

zu 12 Jahren Zuchthaus

Einar Jörgensen	30 Jahre alt, wohnhaft in Aarviksand
Bernhard Jörgensen	62 Jahre alt, wohnhaft in Aarviksand

zu 10 Jahren Zuchthaus

Otto Olsen	55 Jahre alt, wohnhaft in Tromsö

zu 6 Jahren Zuchthaus

Das Vermögen aller Verurteilten ist eingezogen. Die Todesstrafen sind vollstreckt.

23 Oktober 1943.

Der Gerichtsherr

List of persons sentenced to death by German court martial in Norway.

Home-made weapons used by Danish patriots.

Oil storage tank in Svelvik blown up by saboteurs. ►

German troops in Denmark and Norway on 12 April 1945
(from Wehrmacht General Staff, Op. Div. III, No. 77802)

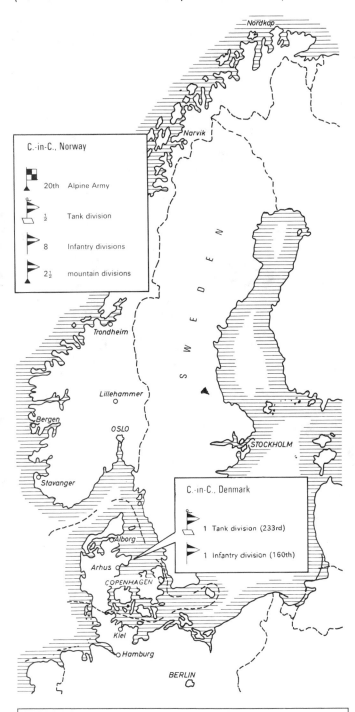

C.-in-C., Norway

⚑	20th	Alpine Army
⚑	½	Tank division
⚑	8	Infantry divisions
⚑	2½	mountain divisions

C.-in-C., Denmark

⚑	1	Tank division (233rd)
⚑	1	Infantry division (160th)

Division of Norway into Resistance districts. ▼

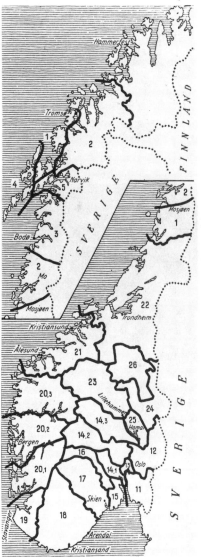

THE GERMAN CAPITULATION IN DENMARK AND NORWAY
4 and 7 May 1945

German troops handing their arms to members of the Danish Resistance Movement. ▶

General Lindemann, Commander of the German Army in Occupied Denmark, 1945.

Order of the Supreme Commander of the German Army to all German troops in Denmark, issued on 6 May 1945:

General Lindemann, and all Army, SS, air-force and other units serving under him are hereby placed under the direct command of Field-Marshal Busch, C.-in-C., North-West, and will be known as the *Lindemann Armee*.

General Lindemann's duties as army commander are hereby vested in Field-Marshal Busch, C.-in-C., North-West. Excluded from this order are all matters affecting the German Navy in Denmark, which will be under the direct control of Supreme Naval Command.

signed: Keitel
Supreme Commander of the Wehrmacht.

Order by the Supreme Commander of the German Army to all German troops in Norway, issued on 7 May 1945:

1. In accordance with the instructions of the Supreme Commander, Allied Expeditionary Forces, the Commander of the 20th Alpine Army will prepare for the surrender of all units of the German Army, Air Force, SS, Police, Administration and other Organizations under his command.

Detailed instructions for the surrender will be given by the G.O.C., Scottish Command, and the Commander of the 13th Group Royal Air Force as delegates of their Supreme Commander. These delegates will leave for Norway by air in the late afternoon of 7 May or in the early morning of 8 May. The British planes will enter at Svennor Light, fly up the Oslo Fjord at an altitude of 1,000 ft, and fire red flares. They will land in Fornebu. Army Command, Norway, will convey the delegates from the airstrip to the appointed meeting place.

2. It must be emphasized once again that the conditions of the capitulation must be observed in full. Hence the evacuation of German forces to Swedish territory cannot be allowed. This, and also independent negotiations with Sweden or any other neutral power would constitute a breach of the surrender terms and, according to Section 2 of the agreement, will have serious consequences for the entire German nation. The crossing of individuals into Sweden before 00.00 hours on 9 May need not be prevented.

signed: Keitel
C.-in-C. Wehrmacht.

The German Commandant of Aarhus surrendering to the Norwegian Resistance Movement on 11 May 1945.

SETTLING ACCOUNTS WITH COLLABORATORS

In July 1945 Prime Minister Gerhardsen described the settling of accounts with the 40,000 Norwegian Quislings as one of the primary tasks of the Norwegian Government, and added: "So far, 18,000 collaborators have been apprehended . . . The guilty will be sentenced and will lose their civic rights."

GERMANS MAKE WAY FOR BRITISH TROOPS

May–June 1945

German airmen leaving Copenhagen with women auxiliaries and wives.

Norwegian policemen—trained in Sweden—entering liberated Oslo by the side of British troops.

KING HAAKON RETURNS HOME

7 June 1945

The King of Norway and his family arriving at Oslo Harbour on 7 June.

THE FIRST POST-WAR GOVERNMENTS OF DENMARK AND NORWAY

The Danish Social-Democrat, V. Buhl (smoking cigar) and his Cabinet.

The Norwegian Social-Democrat, E. Gerhardsen (fourth from left) and his Cabinet.

THE RED FLAG OVER THE REICHS CHANCELLERY

The final struggle for Berlin and the last act in the Fuehrer's bunker   26 April–2 May 1945

CHRONOLOGICAL TABLE:

1945

15/4: Eva Braun arrives from Southern Germany to join Hitler in the Reichs Chancellery.

23/4: Bormann and Goebbels appeal to the people of Berlin to persevere. "Flying" courts-martial tour Berlin.

Goering asks Hitler about his plans for a possible successor and is relieved of office.

23–24/4: Troops of the 1st White Russian Front under Marshal Zhukov capture Frankfurt-on-Oder, Wandlitz, Oranienburg, Birkenwerder, Pankow, Friedrichsfelde, Karlshorst and Koepenick. Troops of the 1st Ukrainian Front under Marshal Koniev take Kottbus, Luebben, Zossen, Luckenwalde, Treuenbrietzen, Belzig, Marienfelde, Trebbin, Rahnsdorf and Teltow.

24/4: General Ritter von Greim is ordered from Munich to report to Hitler at the Reichs Chancellery.

Fighting at Tempelhof airfield. Soviet tanks south of Berlin in Potsdam and S.E. of Brandenburg.

25/4: Berlin is surrounded. Soviet spearheads enter Zehlendorf and Neukoelln. Fighting at the Teltow Canal. The Berlin suburbs of Adlershof, Alt-Glienicke, Tegel, Wittenau, Reinickendorf, Mariendorf and Lankwitz are overrun. German troops withdraw into Central Berlin. New front line: Schoeneberg Town Hall, Halle Gate, Belle-Alliance Square.

26/4: General von Greim seriously wounded by Russian anti-aircraft fire while flying over Berlin. Hanna Reitsch, the crack woman test pilot, lands her machine near the Brandenburg Gate. General Weidling appointed commander of Berlin.

26–27/4: Hitler telephones General Schoerner's H.Q. and calls for the relief of Berlin.

27/4: Hitler orders the flooding of the Berlin underground, thus drowning thousands of soldiers and civilians who had taken refuge in the tunnels. Hitler relieves SS-General Steiner of his post for his failure to lead a counter-attack north of Berlin.

Soviet General Berzarin is appointed Russian Commandant and Military Governor of Berlin. Soviet troops capture Potsdam and Spandau. Soviet spearheads advance to Leipziger Platz and Potsdamer Platz in the heart of Berlin.

28/4: General Krebs makes his last telephone call from the Fuehrer's bunker to Keitel in Fuerstenberg (the new Supreme Command H.Q.). If relief does not come within 48 hours, all is lost. Keitel promises to exert the utmost pressure on Generals Wenck and Busse. Bormann wires to Doenitz: Reichs Chancellery a heap of rubble. Hitler learns of Himmler's contacts with Count Bernadotte in Luebeck.

Soviet troops take 27,000 prisoners in the suburbs of Berlin. Hitler Youth suffer heavy losses in the fighting for bridges across the Havel. Soviet troops take the Halle Gate in the south, and Potsdamer Strasse in the west of Berlin. In the northern sector, German troops continue to offer resistance round the Reichstag and Brandenburg Gate. Fighting in the Wilhelmstrasse in E. Berlin.

28–29/4: Hitler orders Ritter von Greim and Hanna Reitsch to fly to Doenitz's H.Q. at Ploen to arrest the "traitor" Himmler. Himmler denies the whole story. Hitler is married to Eva Braun in the Fuehrer's bunker during the night (with Bormann and Goebbels as witnesses) and dictates his last will and testament. Units of the German 12th Army (General Wenck) are beaten back by Soviet troops in the Beelitz–Ferch–Petzow sector during the night.

29/4: General Weidling reports that Soviet troops have reached Saarlandstrasse in the evening, and that there is fighting between Bismarkstrasse and Kantstrasse in the west. The front line is north of the Grunewald and the Reichs Sports Fields. Hitler Youth Battalion continues to fight at the Havel bridges. Weidling reports that Soviet troops will reach the Fuehrer's bunker on 1 May at the latest. He suggests last breakout attempt, and is supported by Axmann, but Hitler refuses. Hitler orders Krebs to find out from Jodl where Wenck's "spearhead" has got to.

Soviet tanks draw up before Anhalter Bahnhof. Soviet machine guns sweep the Potsdamer Platz and the Hermann Goering Strasse. Soviet shells continue to hit the area round the Reichs Chancellery.

29–30/4: Army H.Q. sends a negative reply to Kreb's enquiry as to the whereabouts of Wenck's Army. Bormann sends an S.O.S. to Doenitz.

29/4–1/5: Soviet guns shell Wilhelmstrasse and the Reichs Chancellery.

30/4: Towards noon, with Soviet troops fighting in the underground tunnels at Friedrichstrasse, Hitler orders his driver Kempka to bring 200 litres of petrol into the garden of the Reichs Chancellery. Hitler lunches with Burgdorf, Krebs, Hewel, Goebbels, Bormann, Naumann, Voss, his secretaries and his cook. At about 3:30 p.m., Hitler shoots himself in his suite. Eva Braun takes poison. Both bodies are carried into the garden by Bormann, Kempka and a few SS officers, soaked in petrol and burned. At the same time, Soviet troops take the Reichstag by storm. At about 5 p.m. Bormann informs Doenitz that he (Doenitz) has been appointed Hitler's successor. No mention of Hitler's death. Bormann proposes direct negotiations with the Soviet Union. Goebbels agrees reluctantly, and General Krebs is given full powers to negotiate. The Commander of Berlin, General Weidling, is informed of Hitler's death and of the proposed negotiations.

1/5: Krebs talks to General Chuikov at about 3 a.m. Krebs returns empty-handed after refusing to agree to an unconditional surrender, for which he lacks Goebbels' authority. At 3:15 p.m. Goebbels and Bormann send a radio message to Doenitz informing him of Hitler's death. In the late afternoon, Goebbels poisons his children and at about 8:30 p.m. orders an SS guard to shoot him and his wife in the garden of the Reichs Chancellery. At his request, the bodies are soaked in petrol and burned. At 9 p.m., Bormann, Naumann, and the remaining guards try to break out from the Chancellery. General Burgdorf commits suicide.

11 p.m.: Those left in the Chancellery and the Fuehrer's bunker try to break out in separate groups. One group includes Bormann, Naumann, Axmann, Dr. Stumpfegger and Hitler's second pilot Beetz. The Bormann group is scattered at Friedrechstrasse Railway Station. Naumann and Axmann succeed in reaching the West separately. Axmann claims that he saw Bormann and Stumfegger killed in Invalidenstrasse.

2/5: Shortly after midnight, General Weidling uses the transmitter of LVII Tank Corps to surrender to the Russians. Weidling calls on Chuikov to sign the instrument of surrender. Russian loudspeakers and leaflets announce Weidling's surrender. Most German units capitulate. Attempts to break out in Halensee, Pankow and W. Berlin lead to fierce hand-to-hand fighting, during which many women and children are killed.

Marshal Stalin announces the fall of Berlin in Order of the Day No. 359.

Berliner Morgenpost of 22 April 1945, announcing Berlin is now in the front line.

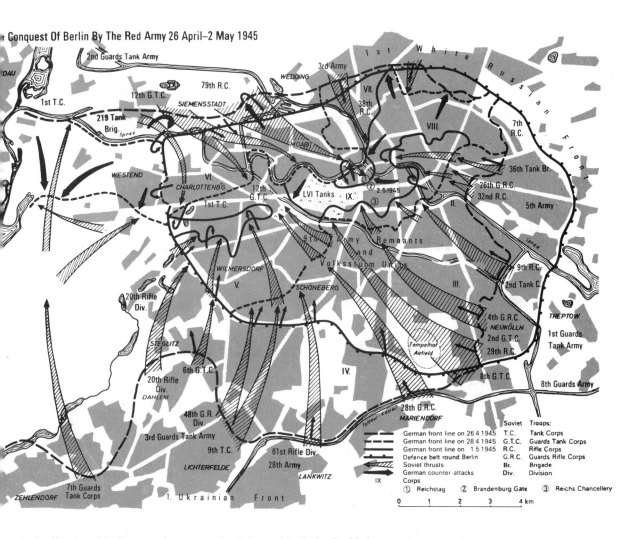

Conquest Of Berlin By The Red Army 26 April–2 May 1945

2nd Guards Tank Army

1st T.C.

79th R.C.

12th G.T.C.   SIEMENSSTADT

219 Tank Brig.   Spree

WEDDING   3rd Army

VII.

38th R.C.

VIII.

WESTEND

VI.   CHARLOTTENB'G.   12th G.T.C.   1st T.C.

MOABIT

LVI Tanks   IX.   ② 2.5.1945   ③

① Reichstag

7th R.C.

36th Tank Br.

26th G.R.C.

32nd R.C.   5th Army

II.

9th Army   Remnants   and   Volkssturm Units

WILMERSDORF   V.   SCHÖNEBERG

III.

9th R.C.

2nd Tank C.

TREPTOW

20th Rifle Div.

STEGLITZ

6th G.T.C.

20th Rifle Div.   DAHLEM

48th G.R. Div.

3rd Guards Tank Army

9th T.C.

LICHTERFELDE

61st Rifle Div.   28th Army

LANKWITZ

Tempelhof Airfield   IV.

Teltow-Kanal

28th G.R.C.   MARIENDORF

4th G.R.C.   NEUKÖLLN

2nd G.T.C.

29th R.C.

8th G.T.C.

1st Guards Tank Army

8th Guards Army

ZEHLENDORF   7th Guards Tank Corps   1. Ukrainian Front

German front line on 26.4.1945		Soviet	Troops:
German front line on 28.4.1945		T.C.	Tank Corps
German front line on 1.5.1945		G.T.C.	Guards Tank Corps
Defence belt round Berlin		R.C.	Rifle Corps
Soviet thrusts		G.R.C.	Guards Rifle Corps
German counter-attacks		Br.	Brigade
IX Corps		Div.	Division

① Reichstag   ② Brandenburg Gate   ③ Reichs Chancellery

0   1   2   3   4 km

Hitler Youth and Volkssturm thrown into the defence of Berlin by Goebbels.

Lesen und weitergeben!

Der Panzerbär

27. April 1945

KAMPFBLATT FÜR DIE VERTEIDIGER GROSS-BERLINS

Bollwerk gegen den Bolschewismus
Berlin: Massengrab für Sowjetpanzer

Rundfunkansprache von Staatssekretär Dr. Naumann
Berlin kämpft für das Reich und Europa

Berlin, 26. April. Der Staatssekretär im Reichsministerium für Volksaufklärung und Propaganda, Stabsleiter Dr. Naumann hielt am Donnerstag folgende Rundfunkansprache:

Deutsche Volksgenossen!

Der Kampf um Berlin tobt nun seit Tagen mit äußerster Härte. Alle Stadtteile tragen schon Spuren dieser großen Schlacht, und unsere weltbekannten Straßen und Plätze sind zu Wahrzeichen eines heroischen Ringens geworden.

Die sowjetischen Befehlshaber, die Stalin die versprochene Morgengabe der eroberten Reichshauptstadt nicht fristgerecht auf den Tisch der Konferenz von San Franzisko legen konnten, treiben zur Stunde ihre Panzerkeile und ihre Schützendivisionen immer rücksichtsloser in verlustreiche Straßenkämpfe. Für sie handelt es sich dabei aber nicht um einen kurzfristigen, außenpolitischen Prestigeerfolg: Der Bolschewismus sieht in der Eroberung Berlins den Schlüssel zur Beherrschung Europas und damit zur Diktatur über die abendländische Welt.

Gegenüber diesem Ansturm der Steppe haben die Verteidiger Berlins einen schweren Stand, aber ihre Haltung entspricht der Größe der Gefahr. Sie sind sich der Bedeutung ihrer Aufgabe bewußt. Sie wissen, daß ihrer Tapferkeit und ihrem Kampfwillen nicht nur das Leben und die Freiheit von Millionen Kindern, Frauen und Männern und die politische Zukunft des Reiches anvertraut ist, sondern auch die zukünftige Gestaltung des Abendlandes. Sie wissen auch, daß der Ansturm des Feindes um so wilder werden wird, je mehr er spürt, daß ein militärischer Einsatz von draußen nicht nähert und im Begriffe ist, ihm den Sieg im letzten Augenblick aus den Händen zu winden.

An der Spitze der Führer

An der Spitze der Verteidigung Berlins steht der Führer. Diese Tatsache allein schon gibt dem Kampf um Berlin sein einmaliges und entscheidendes Gesicht. Wie in der Kampfzeit, wie immer in seinem ganzen Leben, weicht der Führer der letzten Entscheidung nicht aus, sondern stellt sich

Person an die Spitze des Kampfes. Er, der tausend Gründe anführen könnte, die seine Anwesenheit an anderer Stelle als angeblich wichtiger oder nützlicher erscheinen lassen würden, verzichtet auf diese Umwege und gibt damit ein anspornendes Vorbild eines sich selber in jeder Lage treu bleibenden Kämpfers. Niemals ist er im Herzen seiner Soldaten so nahe

ren Stunde. Niemals war er in der Liebe der Männer und Frauen von Berlin fester verankert als jetzt, wo er seine geschichtliche Aufgabe mit der seiner Hauptstadt unlösbar verbunden hat.

Gegenüber den haßerfüllten Verkündigungen der Feindpresse, die es nicht zugeben möchte, daß der Führer des Großdeutschen Reiches in jeder Lage zu seinem Volke steht, wissen die Männer und Frauen von Berlin, daß der Führer bei ihnen

mus für die Reichshauptstadt zu bannen.

Während in diesen bewegten Tagen die Staatsmänner der Westmächte in San Franzisko mit den Sowjets in scheinbarer Freundschaft zusammensitzen und versuchen, durch Kompromisse den bolschewistischen Imperialismus aufzuhalten, der sich noch niemals an Konferenzbeschlüsse gebunden gefühlt hat, tritt der Führer in eigener Person tapfer der bolschewistischen Flut aus dem Osten mit dem letzten Aufgebot seiner besten Kräfte entgegen, fest entschlossen, diesen Ansturm aus der Steppe aufzuhalten und zu brechen. Er kennt die Gefahr des Bolschewismus nicht erst seit heute, wo die unverhohlene Machtgier Moskaus auch in London und Washington mit immer stärkerem Mißtrauen vermerkt wird. Sein Kampf hatte seinen Ursprung in der Notwehr des deutschen Volkes gegen den Bolschewismus. Wenn heute Deutschland und Europa noch nicht sowjetisch sind, so ist dies allein sein Verdienst.

Die großen Probleme des 20. Jahrhunderts, die durch das Maschinenzeitalter hervorgerufenen sozialen Fragen, konnten nur auf dem Wege über den Nationalsozialismus gelöst werden. Nach den Absichten und Plänen des Führers stände heute schon ein unzerstörtes und glückliches Europa als unüberwindbares Bollwerk dem Bolschewismus gegenüber. An der Durchführung dieses Planes, der allen Völkern Europas und der ganzen Kulturwelt nur Segen bringen konnte, wurde der Führer durch Mächte verhindert, die in unglückseliger Verkennung ihrer eigenen Interessen und getäuscht über unser wahres Wollen die Helfer des Bolschewismus wurden. Statt, wie versprochen, den kleinen Völkern Selbständigkeit und Freiheit zu garantieren, wurden diese gerade von ihnen dem Bolschewismus ausgeliefert. Auch ihre Terrorangriffe in Europa waren nicht nur kulturzerstörende Vernichtungsorgien in eigener Sache, sondern vor allem Hilfsdienste zugunsten des Bolschewismus.

Roosevelts Verrat

Für immer wird mit dem Namen Roosevelt die Schuld verbunden sein, daß er mit dem Einsatz seines ganzen Einflusses den Kampf Europas gegen den Bolschewismus in den Rücken gefallen ist.

Jahrelang ist es uns gelungen, aus eigener Kraft dem Ansturm dreier Weltmächte sieg-

Der Panzerbär—Paper for the Defenders of Greater Berlin. Issue of 27 April 1945, reporting that Berlin has become a mass grave for Soviet tanks, and that Berlin is fighting on, not only for Germany, but for the whole of European civilization.

Soviet aircraft in support of ground forces in the battle for Berlin.

GOEBBELS CALLS ON THE PEOPLE OF BERLIN

23 April 1945

"Your *Gauleiter* is amongst you . . ."

From Goebbels' proclamation of 23 April 1945:

I call on you to fight for your city. Fight with everything you have got, for the sake of your wives and your children, your mothers and your parents. Your arms are defending everything we have ever held dear, and all the generations that will come after us. Be proud and courageous! Be inventive and cunning! Your *Gauleiter* is amongst you. He and his colleagues will remain in your midst. His wife and children are here as well. He, who once captured the city with 200 men, will now use every means to galvanize the defense of the capital. The battle for Berlin must become the signal for the whole nation to rise up in battle . . .

*

"It's all up, the war is lost . . ."

The Fuehrer's last conference on 22 April 1945:

Hitler interrupted the report to ask what had happened to General Steiner's offensive . . . There was a long silence and then Hitler was told that the attack had never been launched, and that the withdrawal from Berlin of several units for Steiner's army, on Hitler's orders, had so weakened the front that the Russians had broken through into Berlin.

That was too much for Hitler. He asked everyone except Keitel, Krebs, Jodl, Burgdorf and Bormann to leave the room . . .

Then Hitler started jumping up and down, while he ranted and raved. His face turned white and purple in turns, and he was shaking all over. His voice kept breaking, as he screamed out the words disloyalty, cowardice, treachery and insubordination. There followed accusa-tions against the Wehrmacht and the Waffen-SS, of the kind that previous explosions had brought out in some-what milder form. His outburst culminated in the oath that he would remain in Berlin, with the Berliners, that he would lead the fight personally—let all who wish to desert him and the city do so now. And then something happened that none of those present had ever seen or expected to see: Hitler suddenly returned to his chair and collapsed. Sobbing like a little child, he stammered out: "It's all up . . . the war is lost . . . I shall shoot myself."

Form Boldt: *Die letzten Tage der Reichskanzlei*
(The last days of the Reichs Chancellery)

The people hope for a miracle from the West

Berlin, 22 April:

The situation in Berlin gets worse all the time, as the people keep hoping for a miracle from the West. This Sunday, as on all the preceding days, they stand in long queues outside every food shop, to lay in what supplies they can for the siege ahead.

From the Western precincts, a few scratch units, all of them badly equipped, have been quickly motorized and brought into Berlin. At the same time, streams of fugitives have begun to pour out of the city, using every conceivable means of transport. To the West and N.W. of the city, they merge with the long columns of refugees, concentration camp and POW transports, and Wehrmacht stragglers into a band of aimless rovers who, in panic fear of the Russians and often attacked by low-flying planes, are desperately looking for safety some-where in a westerly direction.

Berlin, 25 April:

Berlin is now defended by LVIII Tank Corps under General Weidling, together with some sorely depleted emer-gency and Volkssturm units. The total number of tanks is in the vicinity of 50 . . .

From Schultz: *Die letzten 30 Tage*
(The last 30 days)

General Chuikov (centre), one of the conquerors of Berlin.

COMMAND POSTS ANHALTER RAILWAY STATION AND POTSDAMER PLATZ

26–27 April 1945

"Heavy losses among wounded and civilians . . ."

From the diary of an officer with the Muencheberg Tank Division:

26 April: Scarlet night. Heavy artillery fire. Uncanny silence. We get shot at from many houses. Foreign workers, no doubt. From the Air Ministry comes news that General Bärenfänger has been relieved of his post of commander of the Berlin garrison. One hour later we hear that General Weidling is the new commander. General Mummert takes charge of the Tank Corps . . . New command post: Anhalter Station. Platforms and control rooms look like an armed camp. Women and children huddle in niches and corners. Others sit about in deckchairs. They all listen for the sounds of battle . . . Suddenly water starts to pour into the station. Screams, sobs, curses. People fighting around the ladders that run through air shafts up to the street. Masses of gurgling water rush over the stairs. Children and wounded are abandoned and trampled to death. The water covers them, rises three feet or more and then slowly goes down. The panic lasts for hours. Many are drowned. Reason: on somebody's orders, engineers have blasted the locks of the canal between Schoeneberg and Mockern Bridges to flood the tunnels against the advancing Russians. Meanwhile heavy fighting has been going on above ground level. Change of position to Potsdamer Platz subway station in the late afternoon. Command post on the first floor, as tunnels still under water. Direct hits on the roof. Heavy losses among wounded and civilians. Smoke pours in through the shell holes. Outside, stacks of Panzerfists go up into the air. Another direct hit, one flight below street level. A horrible sight: men, soldiers, women and children are literally glued to the wall. At nightfall, a short interval in the shooting . . .

27 April: Flying courts-martial unusually prominent today. Most of them very young SS officers. Hardly a decoration among them. Blind and fanatical. The hope of relief and the fear of these courts bring men back to the fighting. General Mummert refuses to allow any further courts-martial in the sector under his command . . . He is determined to shoot down personally any court-martial that appears . . . We cannot hold the Potsdamer Platz, and at about 4 a.m. move through the subway tunnel to Nollendorfplatz. In the tunnel next to ours, the Russians are advancing in the opposite direction . . .

◀
A wounded Hitler Youth who served as courier in the final phase of the battle for Berlin.

Soviet troops crossing the Spree over a damaged bridge on their way to the centre of Berlin.

HITLER ORDERS THE FLOODING OF THE UNDERGROUND RAILWAY

26–27 April 1945

"Then he gave one of the most inhuman orders . . ."

When we arrived for the talk, Hitler rose and we followed him into the conference room. Though no encouraging message from Wenck had been received, Hitler continued to clutch at that straw. Regardless of the fate of the starving, thirsting, and dying population, he was determined to postpone the inevitable end even further. And then he gave one of the most inhuman of all his orders: because the Russians had repeatedly thrown back the German lines by advancing through underground and other railway tunnels to attack the German forces from the rear, he now detailed special units to open the locks of the river Spree, thus flooding the railway tunnels south of the Reichs Chancellery. These tunnels were crammed with civilians and thousands of wounded. They were no longer of interest to him. His insane order cost the lives of very many people.

From Boldt: *Die letzten Tage der Reichskanzlei*
(The last days of the Reichs Chancellery)

*

The Soviet News Agency announced on 27 April 1945:

Troops of the 1st White Russian and 1st Ukrainian Fronts have broken through the strong German defences round Berlin, and approaching from the east and south, have linked up in Berlin and N.W. of Potsdam, thus cutting the last link between Berlin and the outside world. Troops of the 1st White Russian Front have taken Gartenstadt and Siemenstadt and Goerlitzer Railway Station in E. Berlin.

Germans surrendering to Soviet troops in Berlin. ▶

Hitler ten days before his death, with Reichs Youth Leader Axmann and SS-Gruppenfuehrer Fegelein (left) whom Hitler had shot for desertion after hearing of Himmler's "treachery". Right: General Krebs and Hitler's valet Linge.

HITLER'S BUNKER "THE ALTAR OF THE FATHERLAND"

Ritter von Greim and Hanna Reitsch: "We should all kneel down in reverence . . ."

Greim said that Hitler had ordered him and Hanna Reitsch to leave. They only just managed to get away in an Arado (during the night of 28 April). Both kept repeating: "It was our blackest day when we were told that we could not die at our Fuehrer's side." Then they added, while tears kept running down Hanna Reitsch's cheeks: "We should all kneel down in reverence and prayer before the altar of the Fatherland." "What is the altar of the Fatherland?" I asked them, completely taken aback. "Why, the Fuehrer's bunker in Berlin." . . .

From General Koller: *Der letzte monat*
(The last month)

Hitler's leading companions in his bunker at the beginning of the Battle of Berlin:

Eva Braun—Blondi, Hitler's Alsatian bitch and four puppies—Dr. Strumpfegger, Hitler's surgeon—Dr. Joseph Goebbels—Frau Goebbels and four children—Fräulein Manzialy, Hitler's vegetarian cook—Heinz Lorenz of the Ministry of Propaganda—Martin Bormann, Head of the Party Chancellery—*Standartenfuehrer* Zander, Bormann's deputy—SS-*Gruppenfuehrer* Herman Fegelein, Eva Braun's brother-in-law—Col. von Below, Hitler's liaison officer in the Reichs Chancellery—Admiral Voss, Grand-Admiral Doenitz' liaison officer—Ambassador Hewel, Ribbentrop's permanent liaison officer—Major Johanmeier, Hitler's aide-de-camp—Baur, Hitler's first pilot—Beetz, Hitler's second pilot—Dr. Naumann, assistant to Goebbels at the Ministry of Propaganda—*Brigadefuehrer* Albrecht—General Burgdorf—Lt. Col. Weiss, Burgdorf's aide-de-camp—General Krebs, Chief of Staff—Major Bernd von Freytag-Loringhoven, Kreb's aide-de-camp—Capt. Gerhard Boldt, orderly officer.

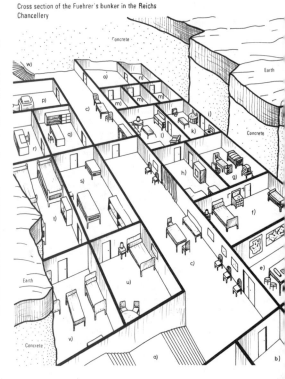

Cross section of the Fuehrer's bunker in the Reichs Chancellery

HITLER YOUTH DEFENDING THE HAVEL BRIDGES

28–29 April 1945

"Most of us were killed . . ."

We asked him how it was that he was fighting when he was only thirteen years old. He pointed to his comrades, many of them from Oranienburg. "The district leader, *Hauptbannfuehrer* Frischefsky, had all of us fetched from our homes by policemen and ordered us to report at SS barracks and on the Castle Square. Then we were divided up into separate squads and attached to various SS and Volkssturm units. We were detailed to fight north and east of the town. Most of us were killed by rifle fire, when we were ordered to attack across an open field. Later the fighting shifted to the centre of the town. For two days. During these two days and nights, Oranienburg changed hands four times. Nearly all of us died. Then the Russians started to hammer us with their Stalin Organs. And when we called it a day and made for home, we were stopped and had to go along to Eden, across the canal. My Youth Group-Leader, who refused, was hanged on the nearest tree by a few SS men and one SA man. He was fifteen. Then the rest of our squad—8 of the original 120—decided to do as we were told. Soon afterwards the bridge across the canal was blown up, and they left us in peace. I met a few schoolmates who told me that the *Hauptbahnfuehrer* himself, his girl friend and Hitler Youth Leader Schiller of the Aerotechnical School had made off to the West two days earlier on bicycles. I then walked to Velten and tried to make for Henningsdorf, where I have an aunt. But just before I got there, I was picked up. Then I had to fight in Reinickendorf, on the Spandau road. Then we pulled out. This morning we were picked up again and ordered to fight right here."

". . . Won't you please give me a cigarette," he begged. I pressed the box into his hand . . .

From H. Altner: *Totentanz Berlin*
(Dance macabre in Berlin)

◀ Explanatory note to cross-section of Fuehrer's bunker:
(a) entrance; (b) anteroom; (c) corridor; (d) dog kennel; (e) conference room; (f) Hitler's bedroom; (g) Hitler's study; (h) antechamber leading to Hitler's private suite; (i) bathroom; (k) Eva Braun's dressing room; (l) Eva Braun's living and dining room; (m) lavatories; (n) washroom; (o) hall; (p) boiler room; (q) servants' lobby; (r) telephone exchange; (s) Goebbels' study; (t) servants' quarters; (u) surgeon's bed-sitting room, later occupied by Goebbels; (v) dispensary and operating theatre; (w) exit.

Hitler Youth defending a Havel bridge with Panzerfists. Most of these boys were killed.

News from Berlin

Reports from the city become more and more harrowing. For a whole week, women, children, old people, the sick, the wounded, soldiers and refugees, have been living in cellars and ruins. Supplies have broken down. Thirst is even worse than hunger—there has been no water for days. Then there are the constant fires, with choking fumes pouring into the cellars and temporary shelters. And over it all a merciless, scorching April sun . . .

From Boldt: *Die letzten Tage der Reichskanzlei*
(The last days of the Reichs Chancellery)

Soviet tanks have won the battle of the Havel bridges. At the same time bitter fighting continues for every house near the Brandenburg Gate and the Wilhelm Strasse.

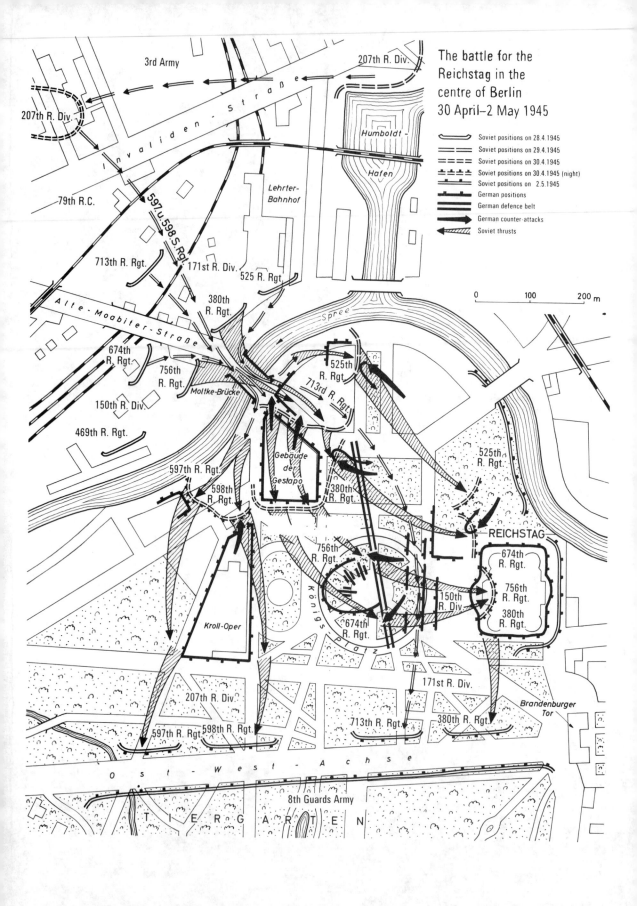

The battle for the
Reichstag in the
centre of Berlin
30 April–2 May 1945

	Soviet positions on 28.4.1945
	Soviet positions on 29.4.1945
	Soviet positions on 30.4.1945
	Soviet positions on 30.4.1945 (night)
	Soviet positions on 2.5.1945
	German positions
	German defence belt
	German counter-attacks
	Soviet thrusts

3rd Army

207th R. Div.

207th R. Div.

Invaliden-Straße

79th R.C.

597.u.598.S.Rgt.

713th R. Rgt.

171st R. Div.

525 R. Rgt.

380th R. Rgt.

Alte-Moabiter-Straße

674th R. Rgt.

756th R. Rgt.

150th R. Div.

469th R. Rgt.

Moltke-Brücke

597th R. Rgt.

598th R. Rgt.

Gebäude der Gestapo

Lehrter-Bahnhof

Humboldt-Hafen

Spree

525th R. Rgt.

713rd R. Rgt.

380th R. Rgt.

0   100   200 m

525th R. Rgt.

REICHSTAG

674th R. Rgt.

756th R. Rgt.

380th R. Rgt.

150th R. Div.

756th R. Rgt.

674th R. Rgt.

Königs-Platz

Kroll-Oper

207th R. Div.

597th R. Rgt.

598th R. Rgt.

171st R. Div.

713th R. Rgt.

380th R. Rgt.

Brandenburger Tor

Ost-West-Achse

8th Guards Army

T I E R G A R T E N

BORMANN SIGNALS: REICHS CHANCELLERY A RUBBLE HEAP

28 April 1945

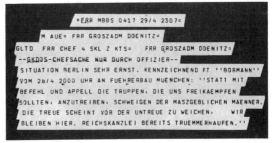

"They went to their death by the hundred thousand . . ."

At about 2 a.m. (28 April), I lay down completely exhausted and tried to catch a few hours' sleep. Noise drifted across from the room next door, where Bormann, Krebs and Burgdorf sat carousing. I must have been asleep for 2½ hours, when Bernd in the bunk beneath me woke me up. "You really are missing something, just listen to that!" he whispered. Burgdorf was shouting at Bormann: "Believe me, I have done my best to smooth things out between Hitler and the Army, so much so that the Wehrmacht has called me a traitor to the German Officers' Corps. Now I realize that they were right all along, that my work was in vain, my idealism misdirected, no, naive and stupid." Breathing heavily, he paused for a moment. Krebs tried to calm him down and begged him to spare Bormann's feelings. But Burgdorf went on regardless: "Just leave me to it, Hans, it has to be said for once. In fortyeight hours it may well be too late. Our young officers went into battle full of faith and idealism. They went to their death by the hundred thousand. But for what? For their Fatherland, for Germany's greatness and future? For a decent life? In their hearts, they did, but nowhere else. They died for you, for your pockets, for your boundless ambitions. Thinking they were fighting for a just cause, our youth allowed themselves to be bled to death on the battle-fields of Europe, sacrificing millions of innocent lives, while you, the Party leaders, waxed richer and richer, living it up like lords, accumulating untold riches, stealing vast estates, building castles, revelling in luxury, deceiving and milking the nation. Our ideals, our morals, our faith, our soul—all these you have ground into dirt; mankind was only a stepping stone for your insatiable greed. You have destroyed our ancient culture, you have broken up our nation. That is your only achievement!"

The general's voice had risen to a roar. Now the bunker was quite still. We could hear his breath come in gasps. Then we heard Bormann's cool, superior and oily voice. All he had to say was this: "My dear fellow, do you really have to be so personal? Even if the others have filled their pockets, I myself am free of all blame. That I swear to you by all I hold dear. Cheers, my friend, and drink up!"

From Boldt: *Die letzten Tage der Reichskanzlei*
(The last days of the Reichs Chancellery)

Bormann's radio message of 28 April on the position of Berlin: "Situation very serious . . . Those ordered to rescue the Fuehrer are keeping silent . . . Disloyalty seems to gain the upper hand everywhere . . . The Reichs Chancellery a rubble heap . . . We are staying on . . ."

◄ General Berzarin, the first Soviet Commandant of Berlin.

By 28 April, Soviet troops had taken some 27,000 ▼ prisoners in Berlin.

Extracts from the first decree by General Berzarin, as Commandant of Berlin.

The "bridal pair" in Obersalzberg, weeks before their wedding.

The marriage document.

HITLER MARRIES EVA BRAUN   29 April 1945

"I say, our Fuehrer got married last night"

Early on 29 April, Bernd woke me up. He was sitting at his desk, busily working. After a while, he looked up and told me, just by the way: "I say, our Fuehrer got married last night." I must have made a very stupid face—but then both of us burst into loud laughter. Then the voice of our Chief, General Krebs, came from behind the dividing curtain: "Have you gone quite mad? How dare you laugh so shamelessly at your Highest Commander? . . ." It was quite incredible, but right in the middle of that night Hitler had seen fit to hold a proper marriage ceremony, registrars, a clear and sonorous Yes, witnesses, a wedding feast, and all. The ceremony was conducted by an official of the Ministry of Propaganda. Goebbels and Bormann were the witnesses. The dinner and celebration were attended by General Krebs, General Burgdorf, Goebbels and wife, Bormann, Hitler's secretaries, and Fräulein Manzialy, his vegetarian cook . . .

From Boldt: *Die letzten Tage der Reichskanzlei*
(The last days of the Reichs Chancellery)

The Soviet Information Bureau announced on 29 April:

Troops of the 1st White Russian Front have continued to clear the streets of Berlin, occupying the N.W. sector of Charlottenburg as far as Bismark Strasse, the west half of Moabit and the east part of Schoeneberg. Troops of the 1st Ukrainian Front have occupied Friedenau and Grunewald in S.W. Berlin . . .

30 April: Troops of the 1st White Russian Front have captured Moabit, Analter Railway Station, Joachimsthal to the north of Berlin, and Neukoelln, Marienwerder, and Liebenwalde. Troops of the 1st Ukrainian Front have occupied the southern part of Wilmersdorf and Hohenzollerndamm and Halensee railway stations . . .

Women and children returning to their homes in the occupied suburbs of Berlin.

On 29 April, General Weidling, the Commander of Berlin, informed Hitler that Soviet troops would reach the Fuehrer's bunker on 1 May at the latest.

GENERAL WENCK'S RELIEF FORCE IS BOGGED DOWN

28–29 April 1945

During the night of 28 April, General Wenck reported to the German Supreme Command in Fuerstenberg that his Army and particularly XX Corps, which had been able to establish temporary contact with the Potsdam garrison, had been forced back along the entire front. No attack on Berlin was now possible, the more so as support from the 9th Army could no longer be expected.

*

Radio message by General Krebs to Supreme Army Command (Jodl) on the evening of 29 April: Request immediate report firstly of the whereabouts of Wenck's spearheads, secondly of time of intended attack, thirdly of the location of 9th Army, fourthly of the precise place in which 9th Army will break through, fifthly of the whereabouts of Holste's spearheads.

The Supreme Command replied at 1 a.m. on 30 April: Firstly, Wenck's spearhead bogged down S. of Schwielow Lake, secondly, 12th Army therefore unable to continue attack on Berlin, thirdly, bulk of 9th Army surrounded, fourthly, Holste's Corps on the defensive.

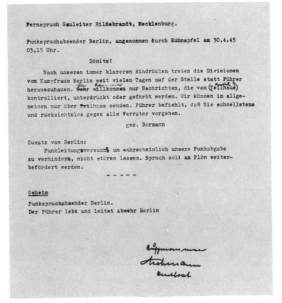

Bormann to Doenitz on 30 April: "Divisions stubbing their toes instead of getting the Fuehrer out . . ."

General Wenck, whose non-existing relief force was Hitler's last hope.

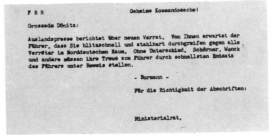

Bormann to Doenitz on 29 April: "Prove your loyalty by immediate relief of Fuehrer . . ."

HITLER'S SUICIDE

30 April 1945, at about 3.30 p.m.

"I hold you responsible for cremating the bodies . . ."

In the morning of 30 April, Hitler summoned Baur, his first pilot, and said: "Baur, I would like to take my leave of you."

With great agitation, the pilot objected: "Surely, you don't intend to end it all?" Hitler replied: "I'm afraid it's come to that. My generals have sold me down the river, my soldiers don't want to go on, and I myself can't carry on like that."

Baur tried to dissuade him, and proposed to fly him to the Argentine, to Japan or to an Arab Sheikh. But Hitler waved him aside: "I have only two alternatives left. I could go into the mountains or join Doenitz in Flensburg. But in a fortnight I would be just where I am now, and I'd have to make the same choice. The war is over now that Berlin is finished, and I stand or fall by the capital. One must have the courage to face things— I am putting an end to it. I know, tomorrow millions of people will curse me—that's fate for you . . ."

Hitler then presented Baur with Lenbach's portrait of Frederick the Great, a portrait in whose magical powers the Fuehrer had trusted throughout these years . . . Hitler continued:

"I have two further orders for you. I hold you responsible for cremating my body and that of my wife. Moreover, I have appointed Doenitz my successor. Bormann has been given several orders, which he must take to Doenitz in person. Make sure you get out of here. It is most important that Bormann gets to Doenitz."

From Domarus: *Hitler—Reden und Proklamationen* (Hitler's speeches and proclamations), Vol. II

The "Fuehrer" at the beginning (left) and at the end of his career. Right: The (alleged) last photograph of Hitler.

Ich selbst und meine Gattin wählen, um der Schande des Absetzens oder der Kapitulation zu entgehen, den Tod. Es ist unser Wille, sofort an der Stelle verbrannt zu werden, an der ich den grössten Teil meiner täglichen Arbeit im Laufe eines zwölfjährigen Dienstes an meinem Volke geleistet habe.

Gegeben zu Berlin, den 29. April 1945, 4.00 Uhr

Conclusion of Hitler's last will and testament: "My wife and I choose death rather than witness the shame of overthrow and capitulation. It is our wish that our bodies be burned immediately in the place where I have done the greater part of my daily work during the twelve years of service to my people."

One day later, on 1 May, at about 8:30 p.m. Goebbels ordered his men to shoot him, after he had poisoned his children.

On 1 May, Goebbels informed Doenitz of Hitler's death (top). Doenitz, who did not suspect suicide, told the nation that Hitler had died a hero's death while defending the Fatherland (below).

HAMBURGER ZEITUNG

Sonder-Ausgabe — *Sonder-Ausgabe*

HAMBURGER ANZEIGER · HAMBURGER FREMDENBLATT · HAMBURGER TAGEBLATT

Der Führer gefallen

Führerhauptquartier, 1. Mai 1945

Der Führer Adolf Hitler ist heute nachmittag auf seinem Befehlsstand in der Reichskanzlei, bis zum letzten Atemzuge gegen den Bolschewismus kämpfend, für Deutschland gefallen.

SOVIET TROOPS STORM THE REICHSTAG
Afternoon of 30 April 1945

At the same time that Hitler put a bullet in his mouth, Soviet troops took the Reichstag by storm.

"In the days to come, examples will be more important than men . . ."

From Goebbels Appendix to the Fuehrer's Political Testament:

The Fuehrer has ordered me to leave Berlin if the defense of the capital should collapse, and to take my place as leading member in the government appointed by him. For the first time in my life, I must categorically refuse to obey the Fuehrer. My wife and children join me in this refusal. In the nightmare of treason that surrounds the Fuehrer in these most critical days of the war, there must be someone at least who will stay with him unconditionally until death . . .

I believe that I am thereby doing the best service to the future of the German people, for in the hard days to come examples will be more important than men. There will always be men to lead the nation to freedom, but reconstruction of national life can only take place on the basis of clear and widely-understood examples. For this reason, together with my wife, and on behalf of my children, who are too young to speak for themselves but who, were they old enough would unreservedly agree with my decision, I express my unalterable resolution not to leave the Reich capital, even if it should fall, but rather at the side of the Fuehrer to end a life that for me personally will have no further value if I cannot spend it in the service of the Fuehrer and at his side.

Berlin, 29 April 1945, 3:30 a.m.   signed: Dr. Goebbels

Bormann's last message to Doenitz: "Testament in force. Will join you as soon as possible. Advise delay publication until then."

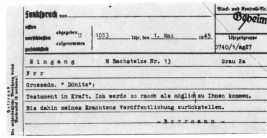

Ghostly scene round the Reichstag at the end of the battle.

GENERAL WEIDLING SURRENDERS   2 May 1945, 8:23 a.m.

General Chuikov: "Write an order regarding complete capitulation . . ."

"You are the commander of the Berlin garrison?" he (Chuikov) asked.

"Yes, I am the commander of the Fiftyseventh Tank Corps."

"Where is Krebs?" Chuikov asked. "What did he say?"

"I saw him yesterday in the Reich Chancellery," Weidling replied. "I thought he would commit suicide. At first he criticized me because unofficial capitulation began yesterday. The order regarding capitulation has been issued to all troops today." . . .

General Sokolovsky entered, with an immediate question: "Where have Hitler and Goebbels gone?"

The question surprised Weidling, but he kept his voice calm. "So far as I know, Goebbels and his family were to commit suicide. The Fuehrer took poison (sic) on April 30. His wife also poisoned herself."

"Did you hear that or see that?" Chuikov asked.

"I was in the Reichs Chancellery on the evening of April 30," Weidling said. "Krebs, Bormann and Goebbels told me about it."

"So the war is over?" Chuikov said, half questioningly.

Weidling sighed. "I think that every unnecessary death is a crime—madness," he said . . .

Sokolovsky cut in again. "Issue an order regarding complete surrender, so that there will be no resistance in individual sectors. Better late than never."

In Berlin, the Red Army took some 70,000 prisoners. In the photograph the last defenders of the Reichs Chancellery being marched into captivity.

General Krebs calling on General Chuikov on 1 May.

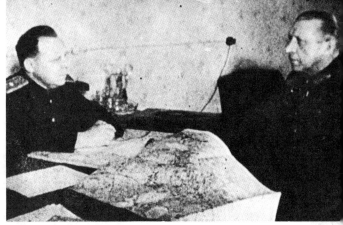

General Weidling (right) surrendering to General Chuikov.

Weidling's sigh was heavy. "We have neither ammunition nor heavy weapons," he said. "Therefore resistance cannot last long. All the Germans have become confused, and they will not believe me that the Fuehrer is dead."

"Write an order regarding complete capitulation," Chuikov told him. "Then your conscience will be clear."

Weidling took off his gloves, pulled his chair closer to the table and set to work with a fountain pen . . .

Weidling shrugged and handed him the draft, and Sokolovsky read it aloud:

On April 30, 1945, the Fuehrer committed suicide, and thus abandoned those who had sworn loyalty to him. According to the Fuehrer's order, you German soldiers would have had to go on fighting for Berlin despite the fact that our ammunition has run out and despite the general situation which makes our further resistance meaningless.

I order the immediate cessation of resistance.

The draft was signed "Weidling, General of Artillery, former District Commandant in the defence of Berlin."

Chuikov spoke. "There is no need to say 'former'. You are still commandant."

"Jawohl," Weidling said in a grunt. "How shall it be headed, as an appeal or an order?"

"An order," Chuikov said . . .

It was twenty-three minutes past eight o'clock on the morning of 2 May 1945.

(from Tully, *Berlin: Story of a Battle*)

"Hope is Fading . . ."

From the Diary of an Officer with the 57th Panzer Division:

1 May: Shell crater after shell crater all around us. The streets are steaming. The smell of the dead is unbearable at times. Last night, on the floor above us, police officers and soldiers celebrated their farewell to life, in spite of the heavy shelling. This morning men and women were lying on the stairs, drunk and in tight embrace . . . Rumour has it that Hitler is dead. Our hopes are fading . . .

2 May: Surrender leaflets in the afternoon. Soviet loudspeakers scream out Weidling's alleged or real call to lay down our arms . . .

3 May: At dawn, attack on the bridge across the Havel at Spandau . . . The bridge is captured. It can only be crossed by jumping. But desperation drives a vast mass of refugees of all ages on to it. They drop off in whole rows. The last serviceable tanks and lorries pave a grisly path through confused heaps of human bodies. The bridge is swimming in blood . . .

4 May: At dawn, isolated columns reach Doeberitz Parade Ground. Here we are met by vastly superior Russian forces. Our ammunition is running out. Bitter fighting for hours. We are completely scattered. We try to get through in tiny groups. We reach Lake Beetz and hide in the reeds, hoping to continue at night.

Soviet troops occupying a suburb of Berlin after the capitulation.

A German eagle at the victors' feet

A German corporal before the ruins of the Reichstag.

From Marshal Stalin's Order of the Day of 2 May 1945: "Troops of the 1st White Russian Front commanded by Marshal Zhukov, with the support of troops of the 1st Ukrainian Front commanded by Marshal Koniev, after stiff street fighting, have today completely captured Berlin, capital of Germany . . ."

*

From the German High Command communique of 4 May: The battle for the Reich capital has come to an end. In a matchless, heroic struggle, troops of all services, loyal to their oath, have resisted to the last breath, as a symbol of the best soldierly bearing."

THE WAR AT SEA IN THE ATLANTIC AND THE BALTIC, 1945

The German Navy during the final phase of the war

CHRONOLOGICAL TABLE

1945

2/1: Admiral Sir Bertram Ramsay, Naval Commander Allied Expeditionary Force, is killed in an aircraft accident.

January–February: Royal Navy loses 15 ships (approximately 36,000 tons) to German mines.

January–March: Admiral Sir Henry Moore's Home Fleet secures convoy routes in the North Sea and prepares for Allied re-entry into Norway and Denmark.

6–8/1: M.T.B.s of the 54th (Norwegian) flotilla sink three large escorted German vessels loaded with iron ore in Norwegian waters.

19/1: Vice-Admiral Sir Harold Burrough, who had been in command at Gibraltar since 1943, is appointed Allied Naval Commander in Admiral Ramsay's place.

22/1: The question of evacuating German refugees by sea is broached at a Fuehrer's Conference.

23/1–8/5: A total of 2,002,602 refugees, soldiers and wounded is evacuated by sea from East Prussia and the Gulf of Danzig. 14,000 men are lost at sea.

30–31/1: Wilhelm Gustloff carrying 5,000 soldiers and refugees sunk by torpedoes. 904 survivors.

3–20/2: British convoy JW/RA 64 of 26 merchantmen and 17 escort vessels attacked by German U-boats and torpedo-bombers stationed in Norway. British losses: 3 merchantmen, 2 frigates and 1 corvette.

9–10/2: The *General von Steuben* carrying 3,000 wounded and refugees, is sunk by a Soviet submarine in the Baltic. 300 survivors are picked up by rescue boats.

February–May: A total of 40 Allied convoys consisting of 811 vessels sail for Murmansk. 720 vessels complete the outward journey to deliver 4 million tons of cargo, 5,000 tanks and more than 7,000 aircraft. Taking the outward and homeward convoys together, Allies lose 89 merchantmen and 18 warships. In the same period, German Fleet loses cruiser *Scharnhorst*, 3 destroyers, and 38 U-boats.

5/3: The German pocket battleship *Admiral Scheer* severely damaged off Pomerania.

9/3: A raiding party from the German garrison in the Channel Islands attacks the port of Granville on the Gulf of St. Malo, doing a good deal of damage and towing out a small British collier.

12/3: German E-boats from Dutch bases attack British ships in the Scheldt, losing 22 "Biber" and "Moltke" boats as well as 16 one-man torpedo boats.

18/3: Some 75,000 men have been evacuated by sea from Kolberg (Pomerania). Last transport on 15 March.

21–22/3: German E-boat attack on British east coast convoy FS. 1734.

25/3: The *Ubena*, carrying 4,000 refugees, is one of the last ships to sail from Danzig.

March: Royal Navy loses 16 merchantmen (42,000 tons) in British coastal waters. German losses in March: 26 ships (nearly 70,000 tons). 463 U-boats in operation. 18 type VII-C-boats operate in the Gulf of Finland and the Gulf of Bothnia (until March).

5–9/4: Last evacuation attempts by German destroyers. Torpedo-boats and E-boats sent to Hela peninsula. A further 43,000 evacuated.

6/4: The *Leipzig*, one of two remaining German cruisers, torpedoed by Soviet submarine.

7–8/4: German E-boat attack on British convoy off the coast of Belgium.

8/4: German pocket battleships withdraw from the Baltic.

9/4: German cruiser *Admiral Scheer* destroyed by bombing in Kiel.

13/4: Last engagement between British frigates and German E-boats at night. Since January, German E-boats have sunk 31 British merchantmen (89,600 tons) during similar engagements, while German midget submarines (*Seehunde*) have sunk 9 British ships (18,000 tons).

16–17/4: The *Goya*, carrying 5,500 soldiers and refugees from Hela to Swinemuende, is hit by 2 Russian torpedoes off Rixhoeft. The ship sinks within 4 minutes. Escort vessels pick up 165 survivors.

16/4: German pocket battleship *Luetzow* sunk by R.A.F.

22/4: British occupy German Naval H.Q. in Buxtehude, capturing a German Admiral and 500 members of the Women's Auxiliary Service.

29/4: Escort groups accompanying British convoy RA. 66 destroy two U-boats in Kola Bay. A British frigate is torpedoed and sunk.

April: 44 German U-boats leave Norway for British coastal waters. All of them are fitted with schnorkel and remain submerged throughout most of the operation. (U-1199 remained under water for 50 days.) During the last five weeks of the war, U-boats off the British coast sink 10 British merchantmen (52,000 tons) and 2 minor warships. German losses: 23 U-boats.

April–May: Because of Red Army threat, U-boat bases transferred from Baltic to Norway. During the last weeks of the war, Beaufighters, Mosquitoes, Typhoons and Liberators operating in this sector destroy 27 German U-boats at sea, and 18 in their bases.

1/5: Evacuation of German troops and civilians by sea continues in every conceivable craft.

4/5: Evacuations from Swinemuende are discontinued. A total of 70,000 people have left from this port. Swinemuende itself is evacuated on 30 April.

6/5: Admiral Doenitz orders all German ships to cease hostilities.

8/5: Numerous minesweepers, fishing boats, E-boats and sailing boats help to evacuate 20,000 (mainly wounded) soldiers from Libau (Kurland) and 7,000 from Windau. The last boat sails from Libau at about 8 p.m. Those left behind are seized by panic. To avoid capture by Soviet troops, thousands of officers and men take to the sea on rafts and small boats. Some succeed in reaching the convoys; others escape to Sweden; many more are drowned.

9/5: U-boats begin to arrive in Loch Eriboll, on the south side of the Pentland Firth to surrender to the Royal Navy. By 15/5, eighteen boats have come in. Altogether, 156 U-boats capitulate, while 221 U-boats are scuttled in German or Norwegian ports by their crews. Two U-boats succeed in reaching the Argentine in late July or early August and are interned. At the close of the war, the cruisers *Prinz Eugen* and *Nuernberg* are the only serviceable major war vessels left to the German Navy. On 24 May, they are escorted by British destroyers from Copenhagen to Wilhelmshaven.

10/5: German U-boats capitulate at various Allied ports.

Depth-charge attack on a U-boat during one of the last naval engagements in the Atlantic off Rhode Island.

The gun-crew of a U-boat during a surface engagement in the Atlantic.

U-BOAT WAR IN THE ATLANTIC 1945

The German Supreme Command reports :

5 February : During concentrated attacks on enemy convoys, our U-boats have sunk 7 merchantmen (54,000 tons) and 2 escort vessels in British waters . . .

5 March : Continuing their operations against enemy convoys, our U-boats sank 10 loaded merchantmen (44,000 tons), 1 destroyer and 1 escort vessel . . .

28 April : Midget submarines have sunk 2 loaded merchantmen (8,000 tons) in heavily guarded convoys plying between the Thames and the Scheldt.

From the monthly statements issued jointly by Prime Minister Churchill and President Roosevelt :

February : The U-boats, making use of their new devices, penetrated further into focal areas of shipping close inshore.

March : During the month of February a moderate number of Allied merchant vessels fell victim to U-boat activity. However, the anti-submarine forces were successful in destroying more enemy submarines this past month . . .

April : Casualties inflicted on U-boats were again severe, and the prolonged and extensive bombing and minelaying policy of the Allies has undoubtedly delayed the introduction of the new type of U-boats . . .

The Commanders of the Allied Naval Forces in the Atlantic (from left to right): Vice-Admiral Burrough, Allied Naval Commander-in-Chief Expeditionary Force (ANCXF); Admiral Horton, C.-in-C. Western Approaches; and Admiral Ingram (left on photograph), C.-in-C. U.S. Naval Forces in the Atlantic.

U-boat activity during the final months

From the Memoirs of Admiral Doenitz:

The reports submitted by U-boat captains returning from operations during February and at the beginning of March furnished ample evidence of the correctness of the January decision to continue to employ our boats as we had been during the weeks recently past.

In March, however, we again became increasingly anxious, since enemy radio traffic contained nothing which gave us any indication of what our U-boats were doing. On 13 March, on the other hand, we received a signal from Lieutenant Becker (U-260) saying that his boat had been badly damaged by a mine while at a depth of 250 feet and some 60 feet off the bottom, that he had managed with great difficulty to reach the surface and that he was about to abandon his sinking boat and land his crew on the Irish coast.

This furnished us with proof that the enemy was laying deep minefields against U-boats. U-boat Command had already anticipated this move and as early as October 1944 had issued instructions on how such mines were to be avoided. The boats were told that, when proceeding through areas presumed to contain minefields of this kind, they should not go deeper than 50 to 100 feet, since it was considered unlikely that the enemy would place mines at a depth where they would be a source of danger to his own shipping . . .

Until after the capitulation, however, we learnt practically nothing with regard to the course of individual engagements or the effectiveness of the counter-measures introduced. It was only after the war had ended that we realized the full extent of the severe defeat we had suffered . . .

When the new types XXI and XXIII were undergoing their trials and their crews were being trained, a series of teething troubles came to light, as was only to be expected with types which had been constructed on a new principle. These defects admittedly delayed both trials and training, but the final results were most satisfactory . . .

The British had watched the development of these new submarines during the past two years with anxiety. At the Yalta Conference in February 1945, the British delegation urged Stalin to capture Danzig as soon as possible, because 30 per cent of the new German U-boats were being built there. "It would be very difficult for the Allied air and surface forces to combat these new types of U-boat, because they have a high underwater speed and are equipped with the latest technical devices."

A Walter-boat, one of the most important U-boats to be produced. The war was over before these boats could be turned out in significant numbers.

A British Mosquito attacking a U-boat. Phase 1: Approach.

Phase 2: Mosquito scores direct hit with rockets and guns.

Phase 3: Oil covers the spot where the U-boat was attacked. A total of 288 U-boats were destroyed during similar attacks.

U-boat Losses in the Second World War

From the Memoirs of Admiral Doenitz

Of the 630 U-boats lost at sea, 603 were destroyed by enemy action, 20 from causes unknown and 7 from accidents.

In port, 81 U-boats were destroyed by air attacks and mines and 42 were lost through other causes.

On evacuation of overseas bases and at the end of the War, 215 U-boats were sunk or blown up by their crews. (Some were later raised by the Allies.) During the War, 38 U-boats were scrapped as a result of irreparable damage or on becoming obsolete; 11 U-boats were handed over to foreign navies or interned in neutral ports after sustaining damage. At the end of the War, 153 U-boats were handed over in British or Allied ports.

A British Liberty ship in a Siberian convoy.

Soviet operations in the North Sea   (January–May 1945)

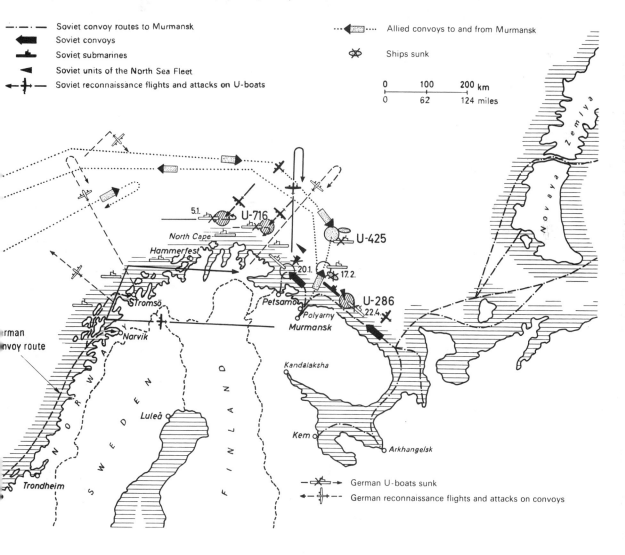

Soviet convoy routes to Murmansk
Soviet convoys
Soviet submarines
Soviet units of the North Sea Fleet
Soviet reconnaissance flights and attacks on U-boats

Allied convoys to and from Murmansk

Ships sunk

| 0 | 100 | 200 km |
| 0 | 62 | 124 miles |

German U-boats sunk
German reconnaissance flights and attacks on convoys

An Allied convoy on the way to Murmansk.

GERMAN ATTACKS ON ARCTIC CONVOYS

January–May 1945

> *Mr. A. V. Alexander, First Lord of the Admiralty, announced in London* that under British naval command, and almost entirely under British naval escort, 739 loaded cargo ships sailed for North Russian ports; that in spite of constant battle against enemy aircraft, U-boats and surface forces, and "frightful" Arctic gales, 677 had arrived safely . . .

From 1941 to 1945, the Allies supplied the Soviet Union with 17,500,900 tons of cargo as part of the Lend-Lease agreement. Bottom left: official handing-over of cargo; bottom right: seeds for desolated Russia ready for loading.

ALLIED ATTACKS ON GERMAN NAVAL BASES IN NORWAY

January–April 1945

British aircraft go in search of German naval bases, transferred from the Baltic to Norway. Left: a Beaufighter attacking Vindspol Fjord on 8 March; right: attack on a German cargo ship.

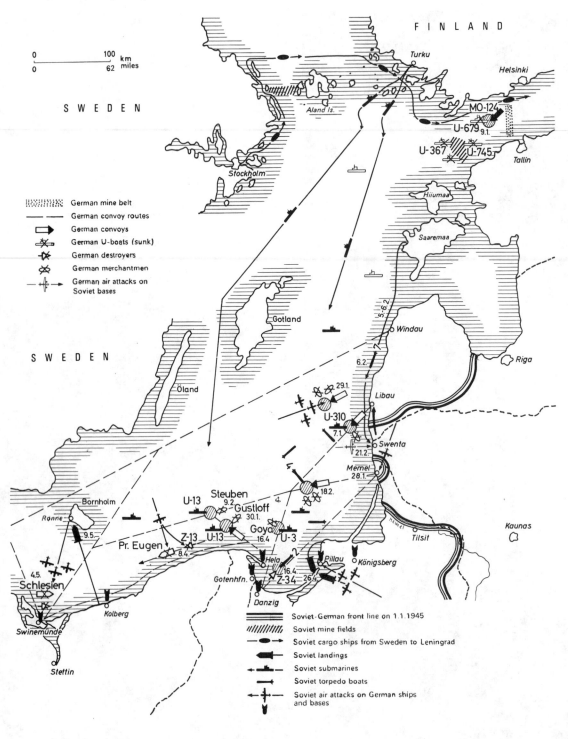

Operations of Soviet Fleet in the Baltic
(January–May 1945)

F I N L A N D

Turku

Helsinki

S W E D E N

Aland Is.

MO-124

U-679 9.1.

U-367

U-745

Tallin

Stockholm

Hiiumaa

Saaremaa

German mine belt

German convoy routes

German convoys

German U-boats (sunk)

German destroyers

German merchantmen

German air attacks on Soviet bases

5.6.2.

Windau

6.2.

Riga

Gotland

7.1.

Libau

S W E D E N

29.1.

U-310

7.1.

Swenta

21.2.

Öland

Memel

28.1.

18.2.

Kaunas

Bornholm

U-13

Steuben
9.2.

Gustloff
30.1.

Goya

U-3

Tilsit

Rönne

9.5.

Z-13

Pr. Eugen

U-13

16.4.

Hela

Pillau

Königsberg

8.4.

16.4.

Z-34

26.4.

4.5.

Schlesien

Gotenhfn.

Danzig

Swinemünde

Kolberg

Stettin

Soviet-German front line on 1.1.1945

Soviet mine fields

Soviet cargo ships from Sweden to Leningrad

Soviet landings

Soviet submarines

Soviet torpedo boats

Soviet air attacks on German ships and bases

0   100 km
0   62 miles

THE GERMAN NAVY HELPS TO EVACUATE GERMAN REFUGEES IN THE BALTIC

January–8 May 1945

Evacuation across the Baltic Sea

From Pillau

25 January–25 April 1945:	451,000 refugees and 141,000 wounded	
		592,000

From Danzig–Gdynia–Hela

In January 1945:	62,000 refugees	
Late January–late April: and at least:	900,000 refugees 300,000 wounded and soldiers	
2 May–8 May 1945 approx.	85,000 persons	
		1,347,000

From Kolberg

Mid-March 1945:	70,000 refugees and 7,500 wounded and soldiers	
		77,500

From Libau–Windau

January–April 1945 approx.	75,000 wounded	
8 May 1945	25,000 soldiers	
		100,000

From Swinemuende

April–May 1945 approx.	70,000 persons	
		70,000

	Total evacuees	2,186,500

Soldiers—most of them wounded—are among those evacuated from isolated E. Prussia.

German ships off Hela in early April. Right: one of the last refugee transports to leave Gdynia.

Refugees boarding a transport vessel near Danzig.

Despite the sinking of the *Wilhelm Gustloff*, the *Steuben* and the *Goya*, most of the evacuees reached their destination safely.

THE SINKING OF THE
WILHELM GUSTLOFF (30–31 January),
THE *STEUBEN* (9–10 February)
AND THE *GOYA* (16–17 April)

"The Abandon Ship signal was still sounding over the decks . . ."

Eye-witness account of the sinking of the Goya

Four minutes before midnight, Brinkmann decided to go up on the bridge for the changing of the watch. The convoy was then some sixty miles off the Pomeranian coast, approximately opposite the port of Stolp, and moving at a speed between nine and ten knots.

Suddenly the ship shook with two blows in rapid succession. She began to sink immediately. She had received two torpedo hits, midship and astern. Within three or four minutes she had disappeared in the water.

But in those few minutes Brinkmann knew horror. The Abandon Ship signal was still sounding over the decks when the holds crashed open and from them burst soldiers, refugees, women, wildly fighting with each other. Black, frantic silhouettes rushed in all directions. Shots cracked, men collapsed or tumbled back into holds.

Brinkmann tried to escape the dance of death on deck

and reach the bridge. But at the foot of the bridge a huge wave caught him and washed him into the sea. Another wave tossed him against one of the life-rafts floating on the water. He saw a sharp jet of fire leap from the waves, and heard the rumble of the boilers exploding below. Then there was silence.

Out of the silence rose the ghostly, gurgling voices of those who had jumped clear or had been washed overboard. To judge by the sound, there must have been several hundreds, among them many women and children. They clung to lifebelts, barrels, and debris. Again there were shots. And then came the last screams of the drowning.

Four soldiers drifted near and caught hold of the ropes on the raft. The other ships of the convoy had disappeared in the night, speeding away under full steam and zig-zagging to avoid torpedoes. For a time there was a strange silence, broken only by the lapping of water over the raft. Then came a scream, the piercing, shrill scream of a woman. It started a shouting and screaming that did not end. He heard blasphemies and curses against the war, Hitler, or Koch, more horrible than he had ever heard before, mingled with invocations to God and the saints that only final agony can press from a human breast. They rose in a chorus so terrible that Brinkmann reached for his pistol to do away with himself—and only after a deep struggle did he drop the weapon into the water, that he might not be tempted again.

Little by little the chorus died down. In its stead, came

Soviet air attack on a German transport ship in the Gulf of Danzig

the awful garglings that break from the mouths of drowning men. Brinkmann in the twilight of approaching death, saw his own past before him. He saw the faults he had committed, all that he had to make up for if he were given another life.

He was aroused by the attack of some desperate swimmers who were trying to throw him from the raft. One of the soldiers who had hung by the ropes was dragged into the deep. Brinkmann and the other soldiers fought fiercely for their lives. The waves put into his hands a drifting piece of wood, and he used it as a club.

An hour later rescue came. The shadow of a large convoy ship passed near them, circling constantly because of the submarine danger. Brinkmann and his fellows tried to shout, but they could only give a weak croak. But they were seen and pulled aboard.

The ship saved ninetyeight people altogether: ninety-four soldiers and four civilians. Ten died on the way to port. Almost all the women had perished before help came. In Copenhagen Brinkmann learned that speed-boats had fished out another eightytwo soldiers and refugees. One hundred and seventy lives had been saved — out of seven thousand.

The last transports from Hela 8–9 May 1945.

In Hela, the destroyers and torpedo-boats were given a rapturous welcome. Never before had ships been packed with so many people so quickly. For thousands the vessels meant heaven-sent salvation at a time when capture by the enemy seemed inevitable. At midnight the war ended in the East as well. At this hour an armada consisting of many hundreds of assorted craft crept westward across the sea. On the morning of 9 May many of them had not even passed Rixhöft, let alone Bornholm. But their desperate determination to evade capture remained undiminished. Again and again the larger ships stopped to assist the smaller vessels. In their bid for freedom, many soldiers had literally pushed a log into the sea, and they now had to be rescued one by one. Some boats broke down and the rest had no alternative but to go to their assistance. The Russians were resolved by any means to drive the motley armada back to its starting places. Although a truce was supposed to operate, Russians continued to attack the German craft with bombs and small arms throughout 9 May. There were many direct hits and severe losses but the frantic westward exodus went on.

From: C. Bekker (*Flucht übers Meer*)

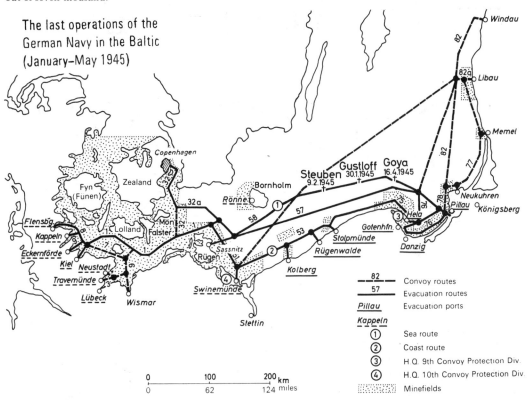

The last operations of the German Navy in the Baltic (January–May 1945)

82 / 57	Convoy routes
	Evacuation routes
Pillau	Evacuation ports
Kappeln	
①	Sea route
②	Coast route
③	H.Q. 9th Convoy Protection Div.
④	H.Q. 10th Convoy Protection Div.
	Minefields

The salvaged wreck of the *Admiral Scheer*, sunk during an air attack on 9 April in Kiel harbour.

One of the German midget submarines operating from Dutch bases until 1945.

THE END OF THE GERMAN NAVY

April–June 1945

Admiral Doenitz's order of 7 May 1945

Radio message to all units.

   In accordance with the unconditional surrender of all German forces, all German ships will refrain from any act of war. The crews are forbidden to scuttle their ships or otherwise to render them unserviceable. Infringements are direct violations of the Grand-Admiral's order, and will have severe repercussions on the German nation.

Naval Command.

Last signal from U-1023
10 May 1945, 3:55 p.m.
To Grand-Admiral:

   In course of 46-day schnorkel assignment, we have sunk 1 merchantman of 8,000 tons and 1 destroyer. Also torpedoed 1 ship of 10,000 tons and 1 ship of 8,000 tons . . . In firm reliance on you, Grand-Admiral, we are about to carry out your hardest order (surrender of U-boats to Allies).

U-1023

The cruisers *Prinz Eugen* (shown in Copenhagen) and *Nuernberg* were the last major surface ships remaining to the German Navy.

Of the 153 U-boats which surrendered, ten each went to the four victors; the rest were scuttled.

THE WAR IN THE AIR OVER GERMANY, 1945

The end of the *Luftwaffe* and the last weeks of the Strategic Air Attack on Germany.

CHRONOLOGICAL TABLE:

1945

1/1: RAF daylight attack on the Dortmund–Ems canal.
1/1–26/4: Allies make a total of 404 bombing raids—267 by day and 137 by night. (During the first three months, 329,000 tons of bombs were dropped.)
2/1: Heavy Allied raids on Nuernberg–Fuerth.
5/1: Two Allied raids on Hanover. Raid on Berlin and 16 railway junctions.
7/1: Night raid on Munich.
8/1: 1,000 U.S. bombers raid Frankfurt. Raids on Linz.
13/1: Raid on railway installations in Saarbruecken.
14/1: Daylight raid on oil refineries in N. Germany (Holstein) and on bridges and steel works.
15/1: Daylight raid by 15th USAAF from Italy on railyards at Augsburg, Reutlingen and Ingolstadt.
16/1: Raid on Magdeburg.
29/1: Daylight attack on railyards at Hamm, Muenster, Coblenz, Niederlahnstein, Kassel and Siegen.
1/2: Heavy raids on Berlin.
3/2: Concentrated daylight raid by U.S. bombers on Berlin.
5/2: Daylight raid on Berlin.
6/2: Concentrated raids on various German railway junctions.
13–14/2: The most severe of all raids on a German city. Dresden raided twice by RAF at night, and again by USAAF in the morning. Some 200,000 persons are presumed killed.
14/2: Two night raids on Chemnitz.
From 18/2: Berlin raided daily and often twice daily.
20–21/2: Raids on Berchtesgaden, Nuremberg and Berlin.
22/2: Some 6,000 Allied aircraft raid 158 railyards inside the Berlin–Leipzig, Kassel, Hamburg and Ludwigslust pentagon. Night raid on Berlin.
23/2: Attack on railway installations in the Leipzig sector.
24/2: Raids on oil refineries and U-boat bases in Hamburg.
25/2: Raids on Munich and strategic objectives in Aschaffenburg and Ulm. Night raids on Berlin and Erfurt.

26/2: Severe raid on Berlin by day.
4/3: For the first time since 1944, German piloted aircraft make a hit and run attack on England.
2,000 Allied bombers raid synthetic oil plants in Hamburg and Gelsenkirchen.
5/3: 12 German aircraft drop bombs in E. Anglia.
1,000 Allied bombers raid Chemnitz and Berlin. Further raids on synthetic oil plants in Hamburg and Gelsenkirchen.
8/3: Raids on Berlin and Dessau.
11/3: RAF drops 5,000 tons of bombs on Dortmund.
12/3: RAF drops, for the first time, a new British "earthquake" bomb weighing 22,000 lbs (nearly 10 tons) during a daylight raid on Bielefeld viaduct.
15/3: Concentrated daylight attack on German General Staff H.Q. at Zossen. Over 6,000 H.E.'s and more than 325,000 incendiaries dropped.
16/3: Air raids on Nuremberg and Wuerzburg.
18/3: Most concentrated raid of war on Berlin.
21/3: Berlin bombed for the 30th night in succession. 1,300 bombers raid German airfields.
22–24/3: 1,500 bombers raid German airfields.
27/3: Last V-2 fired at England. Altogether 1,115 V-2's were dropped on Britain, killing 2,724 and wounding 6,467 people. Total British losses in air raids during the Second World War: approximately 60,000 dead.
3–4/4: Daylight raids on Nordhausen by RAF.
9/4: Concentrated raid on Kiel by RAF. German cruisers *Admiral Scheer* and *Hipper* destroyed.
10/4: Two night raids on Leipzig. Concentrated British night raid on German airfields.
14/4: Raid on Potsdam.
16/4: Severe RAF attack on Swinemuende.
18–19/4: RAF daylight raid on Heligoland.
25/4: Last strategic daylight raid by USAAF on Pilsen and Wangerooge. Last strategic night raid by RAF on Kiel and Munich.

A German airfield in 1945: what few aircraft are left lack fuel. In February 1945, only 1,000 of the planned 235,000 tons of aviation fuel were produced.

THE LUFTWAFFE DURING THE LAST 100 DAYS OF THE WAR

Field-Marshal Ritter von Greim who succeeded Goering as Commander of the German Air Force on 24 April 1945. ▶

General Koller, Chief of Luftwaffe Staff.

Marshal of the Royal Air Force, Sir A. Tedder, Allied Air Supreme Commander.

Hitler: "The entire air force command ought to be hanged on the spot . . ."

21 April: Hitler himself was on the telephone, demanding precise figures about our air support south of Berlin. I told him that such questions could not possibly be answered on the spot, what with the breakdown in communications. "We have to make do with the routine reports that come in automatically in the morning and at night," I said. Hitler was highly incensed.

Later, he rang again and complained that none of our jets had taken off from Prague.

I explained that our airfields were under constant enemy surveillance, and that our planes ran the danger of being destroyed on the ground the moment they emerged from cover. Hitler cursed. "In that case, the jets are no damn good to anybody. The whole Luftwaffe is useless."

"In view of the constant encroachments by the enemy, we are doing all we can. Successes are matters of the past, and in a few days the Luftwaffe will be completely finished," I told him.

In his rage, Hitler mentioned a letter from one Roechling (something I had never even heard of), and yelled: "What he has to say is quite enough for me. The entire air force command ought to be hanged on the spot!"

General Koller: "The end is near . . ."

27 April: I congratulated von Greim (over the telephone) on his promotion to Field-Marshal, but added that as far as his becoming Commander of the Luftwaffe was concerned, all I could offer him was my sincere condolences.

He said: "You are right there."

I asked: "May I know who is to be the new *Luftwaffe* Chief of Staff, so that I may make the necessary arrangements?" "Koller, whatever makes you ask that question?" von Greim said, utterly taken aback.

I replied: "After what has happened during the last few days and after my arrest (in connection with Goering's dismissal) I should have thought that you, Field-Marshal, would appoint a new Chief of Staff, and I, for one, should be most grateful if you did."

"Whatever can you be thinking of, Koller!" Greim exclaimed. "You will, of course, remain at your post. I could not possibly carry on without you. I have told Hitler just that, and I am convinced that we shall get on very well together. You cannot possibly leave me in the lurch now . . ."

"I know where my duty lies," I replied. "But our collaboration will only be of very short duration. There is nothing we can do with the *Luftwaffe*; the end is near."

"Just let's wait and see," von Greim replied. "We must not lose hope, everything is bound to come out all right in the end. I myself have been tremendously encouraged by my meeting with the Fuehrer, and now feel greatly strengthened by his own confidence. It's as if I had drunk from the fountain of youth. The Fuehrer spent a long time by my bedside, discussing everything with me (von Greim had been wounded while trying to land in Berlin). He took back all he said about the *Luftwaffe*; he knows how much we have done: all his accusations were meant for Goering. For us, he had nothing but the highest words of praise. I was overjoyed to hear it."

"Fountain of youth"—indeed, I thought, the whole thing is like a madhouse! What unfathomable flights of fancy will these gentlemen engage in next?

From Koller: *Der letzte Monat* (The last month)

Secret memorandum of German High Command discussion with all Services on deployment of airmen as infantrymen. Luftwaffe to transfer 120,000 men by 10 February.

German Air Force memorandum on transfer of units to strengthen the garrisons of Prague and Innsbruck.

The Me 262, the world's first jet fighter plane. Some 260 were produced before the end of the war. Hitler failed to appreciate the possibilities of this machine, but the Allies were aware of its threat from the moment it first appeared over the front. Other new planes—for instance the HE 162 ("Volksjaeger") or the first rocket-propelled fighter, the Me 163 ("Comet") were never put into service.

ALLIED SUPREMACY IN THE AIR DESPITE THE GERMAN "ME262" AND "V2"

Superiority of 5 to 1.

On 14 January 1945, the C.-in-C. American Air Forces, General Doolittle, wrote to General Spaatz: "We have a superiority of at least five to one now against Germany and yet, in spite of all our hopes, anticipations, dreams and plans, we have as yet not been able to capitalize to the extent which we should . . ."

British Mosquitos taking on bombs.

Introduction of Me 262 Jet Fighters

By General Adolf Galland

In January 1945, we started on the formation of my unit, which Hitler had ordered. The story of what was going on at Brandenburg–Briest, where our 44th Fighter Unit was taking shape, spread quickly to the fighter arm. Our official nomination was J.V.44 . . . Soon after receiving the first planes, we were stationed at Munich–Riem. In the early hours of the morning of 31 March 1945 the J.V.44 took off in close formation, landing in Munich fortytwo minutes later. It had covered the distance of about 300 miles in record time . . .

Operation orders for the Me 262s now changed daily. Conditions in the armament industry were also confused. The period of commissioners, special commissioners, ambassadors of the Fuehrer, commissars and special commissariats had started . . . From February until March

Soviet Air Force achieves supremacy in the East. Their Supreme Commander, Marshal Novikov, described as its primary task "the full support of our land forces". For that reason the Soviet—unlike the Allied—Air Force was made subordinate to the Army Command.

(1945) the jet-fighter command went partly over to the S.A., from whose ranks came the so-called "Commissariats of the Fuehrer for Jet-aircraft" under a general of the Waffen SS appointed by Hitler, although Goering in his turn had appointed a "Special Commissioner for Jet-aircraft" . . .

Operations from Riem started, despite all resistance and difficulties. Naturally, we were able to send up only small units. On landing, the aircraft had to be towed immediately off the field. They were dispersed over the countryside and had to be completely camouflaged. Bringing the aircraft on to the field and the take-off became more and more difficult; eventually it was a matter of luck. One raid followed another.

(from Galland: *The First and the Last*)

V1 and V2 rockets totally destroyed 24,000 houses in the Greater London area, and so damaged a further 760,000 dwellings as to render them uninhabitable. During the winter, some 600,000 less severely damaged houses in the London area were repaired by 143,000 men. A further 500,000 bombed houses were in need of further repair.

Hitler's secret V-weapons were unable to alter the outcome of the war.

THE ALLIED STRATEGIC AIR FORCE IN EUROPE
January–April 1945

U.S. Bombing Survey of September 1945 on the role of air forces in Europe during World War II:

Allied Air Forces at the height of the attack threw 28,000 aircraft and 1,335,000 men into the struggle against Germany. More than 1,440,000 bomber and 2,680,000 fighter sorties were flown. The U.S. lost 79,265 and the U.K. 79,281 men during these sorties. More than 18,000 U.S. and 22,000 British aircraft were lost or damaged beyond repair.

Marshal of the Royal Air Force, Sir A. T. Harris, Commander of the Allied Strategic Air Force in Europe.

Underground H.Q. of Allied Strategic Air Force in S. England. It was here that Sir Arthur Harris and his staff planned the night raids on German targets and discussed the U.S. daylight raids with General Spaatz.

From an interview with Sir Arthur Harris:

"Sir Arthur, how do you justify the bombing?" "I have used my bombers in the same way that an army general uses his guns," said the Air Marshal. "He tries to smooth the way for his troops, and to shorten the battle, by softening the objective. That is precisely what I have been trying to do . . ." "The official *British History of the Strategic Air Offensive against Germany*, which caused such a storm at the time, does not seem to agree with your view of the success of these raids," I interjected.

Sir Arthur adjusted his spectacles while considering the matter. "I should like to make it clear first of all," he said, "that these raids were not my invention. They were ordered by the Staff of the RAF before ever I took over Bomber Command. But I did support the plan because I was convinced of its efficacy . . . Our critics are rather oversimplifying things. By our bombing, we forced the Third Reich to keep millions of able-bodied men at home, serving in the ARP, in the building of shelters, in clearing away rubble, in repairing roads, in toolshops producing new machines for bombed-out factories . . . in all these places, the Germans had to employ men badly needed at the front. In that way, Bomber Command was able to make a decisive contribution to the Allied victory . . ."

"How much of a choice did you have in selecting particular towns for bombardment?" I asked.

"None at all," said the Air Marshal. "I did not bomb a single town on my own initiative, but merely carried out the orders of the General Staff, which, in its turn, took orders from the Cabinet."

"What did these orders consist of?"

"They listed a series of objectives and towns, in order of priority. Each morning, I used this list and the weather situation, to decide what towns were due for attack."

From D. Irving: *Und Deutschlands Städte starben nicht*
(And Germany's cities did not die)

Berlin ARP completely disorganized

Indescribable scenes occurred in Berlin on Saturday, when American bombers launched the heaviest attack of the entire war.

Berlin had not had a major raid for a considerable time. When the attack came—at a time when the Russians were advancing into areas where many Berliners had their week-end cottages before the war—it quickly became apparent that the ARP was seriously disorganized and short of staff. Only a very few fighters went up, and the flak was poor. The undermanned fire brigade had great difficulty in fighting the gigantic fires. From reports published late on Saturday night, we learn that the greatest damage was caused in the areas round the Tempelhof railway stations. The local line was damaged so severely that traffic was partially paralysed. Many Berliners were so shocked by this last visitation that they refused to emerge from their shelters. They stayed where they were, fully expecting further raids during the evening and night.

The refugees from the East found that they had come from the frying pan into the fire. After the first alert, but long before the bombers appeared over the capital, many of them were in a state of panic. They roamed aimlessly through the streets in a vain search for shelter . . .

From *Sydsvanska Dagbladet*, 4 February 1945

During the last phase of the air offensive against Germany (August 1944–26 April 1945), 127 German towns were bombed in 194 daylight and 94 night raids. The population spent most of the time in air-raid shelters and cellars.

Graphic survey of bombs dropped by USAAF and
RAF in Europe during 1941–1945

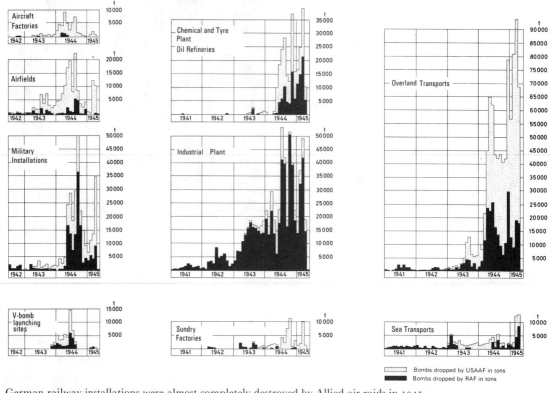

Aircraft Factories
Airfields
Military Installations
Chemical and Tyre Plant
Oil Refineries
Industrial Plant
Overland Transports
V-bomb launching sites
Sundry Factories
Sea Transports

Bombs dropped by USAAF in tons
Bombs dropped by RAF in tons

German railway installations were almost completely destroyed by Allied air raids in 1945.

"TERROR" ATTACK ON NUREMBERG

2 January 1945

On 2 January, 20 February and 16 March 1945, Allied bombers made three concentrated raids on Nuremberg, the city of Hitler's Party Rallies, destroying most of the old quarter.

Der Polizeipräsident
der Städte Nürnberg und Fürth   Nürnberg, den 25. Januar 1945.
als örtlicher Luftschutzleiter
S 1a (3) 55⁵⁰ Nr.04/45 g.

Betrifft: Abschlußmeldung über den schweren Terrorangriff auf den
LS-Ort Nürnberg-Fürth am 2.1.1945.

1) Angriffsdauer: 19.20 Uhr - 20.13 Uhr = 53 Minuten
   ÖLW: 18.33 "
   Fliegeralarm: 18.43 "
   1.Bombenabwurf: 19.20 "
   Entwarnung: 20.24 Uhr.

2) Witterungsverhältnisse:
   Temperatur   - 8°
   Windrichtung   Süd
   Windstärke   1
   Bewölkungsart   ohne Bewölkung
   Niederschläge   -
   Sichtweite   200 m.

3) Stärke des Feindes:
   Etwa 1000 4-mot. Flugzeuge mit Jagdschutz.

4) Angriffstaktik:
   Westeinflug. Anflug im wesentlichen von Süden und Südwesten,
   vereinzelt auch aus anderen Richtungen. Frontbreite von
   Windsheim bis Weißenburg/Bay.

5) Angriffsziel:
   LS-Abschnitte Nord, Mitte und Süd.

6) Angriffshöhe:
   In verschiedenen Höhen zwischen 4000 und 8000 m, teilweise
   jedoch auch 1000 m und darunter.

7) Abwurfmunition:
   Abwurfmittel insgesamt:
   a) Minenbomben   etwa 100
   b) Sprengbomben   "   6000, dav.Blindgänger od.LZZ: 423,-
                                       " entschärft: 415,
                                         selbst detoniert: 2,
   c) Stabbrandbomben in der Masse mit Zerleger oder
      Sprengsatz: etwa 1000 000
      in Leitwerken mit je 1 Bündeln von je 13 Stck.
   d) Leucht- und Markierungsbomben: 110.

                                                    - 2 -

8) Personenschäden:
   a) Bisher an Personenverlusten festgestellt:

	gefallen		verwundet		vermißt	Bemerkungen
	a	b	a	b		
Männer	37	498	1295	434		a) außerhalb LS-Räumen
Frauen	12	869	896	374		b) innerhalb LS-Räumen
Knaben		90	20	10		
Mädchen		83	9	11		
Ordnungspolizei		2	28	1		
H		6	2	2		
T.-N.		15	6			
RAD		4				
Freiw.Feuerwehren			1			
HJ		9				
LS-Polizei	4	25	82	6		
Wehrmacht	3	40	68	11		
Ausländer Kriegsgef.		32				
" Arb.Männer	33	25	51	20		
" Arb.Frauen		6	4	2		
" Kinder						
Gesamtsumme:	89	1705	2462	871	37	
	1794		3333			

   Verschüttete: 2260 an 316 Bergungsstellen
   dav.lebend geborgen: 652
        tot   "   1608 (sind in der Zahl der Gefallenen
                               mit aufgeführt).

   b) Obdachlose: 100 000
      dav.langfristig
      umquartiert: 27 000

9) Gebäude- und Sachschäden: total   schwer   mittel   leicht
   a) Wohngebäude: 4553   2047   2993   7500
                                                                  (geschätzt)

   b) Wirtschaftsgebäude:
      (1) Bank- und Versicherungsgebäude:
                                        total   schwer   mittel   leicht
          im einzelnen: 10   10   1   1
          total: Nürnberger Lebensversicherungsbank A.G., Gothaer
                 Feuerversicherungsbank A.G., Dresdner Bank-Filiale
                 Sulzbacherstr.1, Commersbank, Bayer.Hypotheken-
                 und Wechselbank, Genossenschaftsbank, Städt.Spar-
                 kasse, Städt.Sparkasse Zweigstelle 8, Städt.Spar-
                 kasse Zweigstelle Endterstr.18, Städt.Versicherungs-
                 amt.
          schwer: Witwen- und Waisenkasse, Stuttgarter Allianz,
                  Reichsbank, Bayer.Staatsbank, Vereinsbank, Land-
                  und Forstbank, Bank der Deutschen Arbeit, Brand-
                  versicherungsamt, Sanitätsverein, Dresdner Bank.
          mittel: Versicherung Volksfürsorge.
          leicht: Städt.Sparkasse Zweigstelle Schwabacherstr.14.

The first two pages of a report by the Nuremberg Chief of Police on the raid of 2 January, describing the duration of the raid, the weather conditions, the strength of the attacking force, the tactics used, the objectives hit, the types of bombs dropped, the casualties and the damage.

FEBRUARY 1945: THE DEATH OF DRESDEN 13–14 February 1945

German Air Force report mentioning, *inter alia*, the attack on Dresden by 300 enemy aircraft (Mosquitoes).

Thousands of refugees from the East were resting in Dresden in February, on their way to the West. Most of them were suffocated or burned.

View of burning Dresden from the Technical College.

The Plan of Attack

. . . it would seem more probable that the confirmation of the order to attack Dresden was given in a general spirit of compliance with the memorandum tabled at Yalta by the Soviet Deputy Chief of Staff, General Antonov, on 4th February, in which he suggested that the Western strategic bomber forces might deliver air attacks on communications near the Eastern front . . .

Once the order to bomb Dresden was confirmed Sir Arthur Harris raised no further objections to carrying it out. As he comments in his memoirs *Bomber Offensive*: "The attack on Dresden was at the time considered a military necessity by much more important people than myself."

The First Attack—10: 10 p.m., 13 February

At 10:09 the ticking clock which replaced wireless broadcasts during alerts in Germany was sharply interrupted. The unmistakably Saxon voice of a very agitated announcer broke out of the loudspeakers: "*Achtung, Achtung, Achtung!* The first waves of the large enemy bomber formation have changed course, and are now approaching the city boundaries. There is going to be an attack. The population is instructed to proceed at once to the basements and cellars. The police have instructions to arrest all those who remain in the open . . ."

In his Mosquito three thousand feet above the silent city, the Master Bomber was repeating over and over into his *VHF* transmitter: "Controller to *Plate-rack* Force: Come in and bomb glow of red T.I.s as planned. Bomb . . ."

It was exactly 10:10 p.m.

The Second Attack—1: 30 a.m., 14 February

Zero hour for the second attack on Dresden was 1:30 a.m. At 1:23 a.m. the Blind Illuminator Lancasters released their sticks of flares across the aiming point, and at 1:28 the Master Bomber arrived; to his horror, he found that the whole of the centre of the city was being swept by a violent fire-storm, making it impossible for him to identify the aiming point clearly . . .

(From Irving: *The Destruction of Dresden*)

Richard Pierau barely knew Dresden. All he could have told you was the vague direction of the *Groese Garten*, a large park in the centre of the city. Again and again, impassable craters blocked his path. The soles of his shoes had been scorched away long ago. But he felt no pain. All he knew was that the fiery storm raging round him would soon close into an impassable ring. Shortly after 1 o'clock, he finally reached the park, where thousands were scrambling to safety, weak and exhausted like himself . . . Suddenly he was startled by a scream from thousands of throats. Incredulously he stared at the sky. All four corners of the park were lit up by white "Christmas tree" flares . . . Richard Pierau dropped to the

On the morning of 14 February, some 1,350 U.S. bombers and 900 fighters made a further attack on Dresden.

ground and hid under a park bench. He was gripped by icy fear. Then another load of heavy bombs came screeching down remorselessly and there were more incendiaries . . . Richard Pierau scrabbled in the earth, as hundreds of bombs and mines ploughed up the park. Then suddenly he was blown into the air. He lost consciousness. When he came to next day, he was lying among a heap of dead bodies, about to be taken to a mass grave.

of the powerful blows against Central Germany, promised by the Allied leaders at Yalta. At night, 800 RAF bombers attacked Dresden, capital of Saxony, only some 70 miles from Marshal Koniev's front. The raid was the first major attack on this great industrial centre. A terrific concentration of fires was started in the centre of the city."

(From Irving: *Und Deutschlands stadte starben nicht*)

The third attack — 12 : 12 p.m., 14 February

As the morning of 14 February dawned over Dresden, tens of thousands of people rushed out of the burning city along every road . . . A woman from Cologne, evacuated to Dresden, wrote: "Our ambulances, clearly marked with prominent red crosses were full of badly wounded people. When the low-level attack began, they refused to stay in the vehicles, but scrambled for shelter in the rubble. In front of us stood an open lorry, carrying wounded soldiers. The planes opened up with everything they had. Then the soldiers, too, dropped off the lorry, running, staggering or crawling for dear life. One of them walked straight into the rain of bullets. He died on the spot. Again and again, the planes returned, firing on all the vehicles and killing scores of people . . .

The reaction in London

Churchill presented a minute to his Chiefs of Staff, in which he wrote: "It seems to me that the moment has come when the question of bombing German cities simply for the sake of increasing the terror, should be reviewed . . ." But Air Marshal Portal, Chief of Staff of the RAF, forced Churchill to withdraw this minute.

Similarly, a news item broadcast at 6 p.m. on 14 February 1945, was amended in all further news bulletins. It went as follows: "Last night and again this morning, British and American bombers delivered one

View of centre of Dresden after the hail of bombs.

The number of killed in Dresden—the bodies were burned to prevent epidemics—is now estimated at more than 200,000.

The daily raids on Berlin begun in February were increased during March and April, until they turned into an almost incessant rain of bombs.

BERLIN A SEA OF FIRE

March–April 1945

On 10 April Allied bombers made their last raid on the stricken capital.

Air raids on Southern Germany often came from across the Alps.

GERMAN A.R.P. INCREASINGLY IN THE HANDS OF WOMEN

Telephone operators ("Blitz girls") in the A.R.P. exchange of a German city.

Women air-force auxiliaries plotting the course of an Allied bomber.

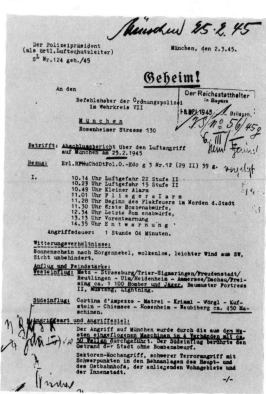

The first two pages of a police report on the Munich raid of 25 February 1945. Duration of raid: 10:14 a.m.–2:35 p.m. Enemy aircraft dropped 5,000–6,000 heavy bombs, 250,000 incendiary bombs and 20,000 leaflets. Casualties: 227 killed and 211 wounded. 209 houses and 8 industrial buildings totally destroyed.

-2-

Abwurfmunition:
```
        5 - 6 000 Sprengbomben zu 500 und 1 000 Lbs
      250 000 Stabbrandbomben (z.T. mit Sprengsätzen)
          300 Brandstiftungsmittelpackungen
ca.    20 000 Flugblätter: "Nachrichten für die Truppe Nr.313
                vom 21., 23. und 24.2.45"
                "Erst im Westen - jetzt im Osten"
       ca. 125 Tages-Zielmarkierungsbomben

          101 Sprengbombenblindgänger
```

II. Personenverluste:

	Gefallene: 227 (ident.211)	Verwundete: 211
Männer	65	111
Frauen	80	65
Kinder	10	8
Wehrmacht	10	11
Schutzpol.	-	2
LS.-Pol.	-	2
Ausl.Männer	14	10
Ausl.Frauen	25	2
Ausl.Kinder	2	-
Kriegsgef.	5	-

```
An 40 Schadenstellen wurden 316 Personen verschüttet
    lebend geborgen    103 Personen
    tot geborgen       197 Personen
an 6 Schadenstellen sind  16 Personen noch verschüttet.

Obdachlose: 20 - 25 000 Personen.
```

III. Gebäude- und Sachschaden:

a) Wohngebäude:

	total	schwer	mittel	leicht
durch Sprengwirkung	103	101	220	162
durch Brand	106	72	133	154

b) Wirtschaftsgebäude:

	total	schwer	mittel	leicht
Bank-u.Versicherungsgebd.	-	1	1	1
Geschäfts-u.Bürohäuser	-	5	-	1
Hotels-u.Großgaststätten	-	2	2	1
Presse, Verlage,Druckerei-en	-	-	-	1
Speicher,Lager,Speditionen	6	13	-	-
Wäschereien,Färbereien, Desinfektionen	2	1	-	-

```
darunter u.a.:
total: Hotel Sächsischer Hof (Spr.), Kohlenlager Rast u.
       Sohn, Sperrholzgrosshandlung,Gressl, Möbellager Trans-
       hand-Transport, Färberei Arnold (Br.)

                                                    -/-
```

Sixteen-year-old auxiliaries with a flak-battery.

A Flying Fortress of the 8th USAAF being hit by flak during an air raid.

A.R.P. auxiliaries being alerted during a geography lesson.

During the entire war, 131 German towns were subjected to major raids, among them Berlin (29 raids), Brunswick (21 raids), Ludwigshafen (21 raids), Mannheim (19 raids), Cologne (18 raids), Hamburg (16 raids), Munich (16 raids) and Hanover (11 raids).

Just one example: The raids on Frankfurt:

4/10/1943	Major day and night raids on the entire town	529 killed
20/12/1943	Night raid. Severe damage in old city and Sachsenhausen	85 ,,
29/ 1/1944	Daylight raid. Major attack on entire town	736 ,,
8/ 2/1944	Daylight raid on town and Bockenheim	320 ,,
18/ 3/1944	Concentrated night raid on entire town	221 ,,
22/ 3/1944	Major night raid on entire town	1,001 ,,
24/ 3/1944	Concentrated daylight raid on entire town	311 ,,
12/ 9/1944	Concentrated night raid on N.W. districts	414 ,,
25/ 9/1944	Daylight raid. Pattern bombing of town	492 ,,
5/11/1944	Daylight raid chiefly on railway centre	273 ,,
29/12/1944	Daylight raid. Pattern bombing of town	64 ,,
9/ 1/1945	Concentrated daylight attack on industrial plant, bombs scattered over town	87 ,,
17/ 2/1945	Daylight raid. Bombs scattered over town	86 ,,
9/ 3/1945	Daylight raid. Concentrated attack on industrial area. Bombing scattered over town	62 ,,
All other raids from 1940 to 1945		878 ,,
	total	5,559 killed

After: *Frankfurter Rundschau*, 19 March 1964.

DEATH ON THE HOME FRONT

Personal messages chalked on the walls of Dresden after the destruction.

Suffocated in Berlin during an air raid. In the entire Reich, 593,000 people were killed in air raids.

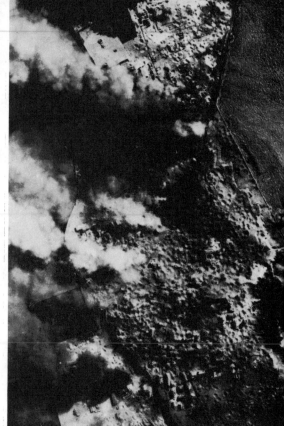

One of the last objectives of Allied bombers: Heligoland before and after the attack by RAF Bomber Command on 18 April 1945.

THE END OF THE STRATEGIC
WAR OVER GERMANY'S SKIES   25 April 1945

Daily Bulletin on enemy aircraft entering German and German occupied territory on 25 April 1945. 1,600 Allied planes entered the Reich on that day.

U.S. leaflet of 30 April 1945, telling German airmen how to land on Allied territory.

DEUTSCHE FLIEGER

Am 29. und 30. April 1945
zwischen Sonnenauf- und Untergang

KÖNNEN

deutsche Flugzeuge
unter Beachtung folgender fünf Punkte

UNGEFÄHRDET

auf dem OSCHERSLEBEN Flugpatz

LANDEN.

1. Überfliegt die Front der amerikanischen Truppen bei Schönebeck längs der Elbe südöstlich von Magdeburg.

2. Flughöhe 1700 Meter, Fahrgestell auslassen.

3. Gerader und horizontaler Kurs bis Oschersleben

4. Zwischen Schönebeck und Oschersleben, von Ost nach West, wird während der angegebenen Zeit ein 15 km breiter Raum frei von FLAK gehalten.

Allied low-level attacks on the Reich became more and more frequent as the war approached its end.

LOW-LEVEL RAIDS BEFORE THE END

April–May 1945

"I have got the machines all right, but not a drop of petrol . . ."

From the memoirs of Count Bernadotte

A few days later in Denmark I had another proof of the paralysis which had seized the Luftwaffe . . . We were just about to take off from a German airfield, when the air raid warning sounded and we saw American fighters attacking some military installations nearby. We threw ourselves into a trench and almost at the same moment nine fighters roared over our heads, their machine guns firing for all they were worth. The attack lasted for several hours, and when it was over, I sought out the German Commander and asked him why he had not ordered some of his own machines to go up, for I had seen them well camouflaged, on the outlying parts of the airfield. He shrugged his shoulders and replied: "Oh, I have got the machines all right, but not a drop of petrol, so they are of no use to me at all."

Many German aircraft were destroyed on the ground just before the end of the war.

THE MILITARY VICTORY OF THE ALLIES

The capitulation of the *Wehrmacht* and the end of the Doenitz Government

CHRONOLOGICAL TABLE:

1945

1/5: Doenitz appoints Field-Marshal Kesselring Supreme Commander of Southern Germany.

2/5: The Red Cross takes over Theresienstadt.

2–3/5: Doenitz forms Government in Ploen and—from 3/5—in Muerwik near Flansburg. Count Schwerin von Krosigk is appointed political adviser and chairman of Doenitz's Cabinet.

3/5: Supreme Command moves with Government from Ploen to Muerwik.

4/5: Field-Marshal Montgomery accepts the capitulation of all German forces in Holland, N.W. Germany and Denmark (approximately 1 million men) in Hecklingen near Lueneberg.

The clergy of Breslau—Pastor Hornig, Dr. Konrad, Bishop Ferche and Canon Kramer—ask the garrison commander, General Niehoff, to surrender the town. Niehoff dismisses them without a definite answer. In the afternoon, Pastor Hornig repeats his demand in an address to the troop commanders. *Gauleiter* Hanke orders General Niehoff not to have any further dealings with the clergy.

5/5: General Blaskowitz surrenders 25th Army in Wageningen (Holland). German troops are disarmed and sent back to the Reich. In Haar, near Munich, the Allied 6th Army Group accepts the capitulation of German Army Group G, consisting of remnants of the German 1st and 19th Armies.

Shortly before the fall of Dresden, *Gauleiter* Mutschmann lets it be known that a large-scale German counter-offensive on all E. fronts is about to be launched. Two days later, Mutschmann is captured by Soviet troops while trying to escape.

Exchange of notes between General Antonov and General Eisenhower. Russians ask Eisenhower to halt the advance of American troops in Czechoslovakia.

5–6/5: *Gauleiter* Hanke flees Breslau by night after hearing of Hitler's death.

6/5: General Niehoff puts up wall placards informing the population that no relief can be expected and that he has started negotiations with the Russians.

Eisenhower orders U.S. 1st Army not to advance beyond Pilsen.

7/5: General Jodl, the German Chief of Staff, signs the unconditional surrender of all German forces in General Eisenhower's H.Q. at Rheims. Fighting stops on all Allied fronts in Europe.

General Hilpert in Courland is ordered by Doenitz to capitulate. He and a member of his staff surrender to the Russians. Three divisions lay down their arms.

The Commander of Breslau capitulates to the 1st Ukrainian Front.

8/5: The world celebrates VE-day.

Field-Marshal Keitel and representatives of the German Navy and Air Force sign the unconditional surrender of the Wehrmacht in Berlin-Karlshorst in the presence of Marshal Zhukov and Air Marshal Tedder. The capitulation takes effect at midnight.

Courland: General Rauser succeeds in obtaining better surrender terms from the Russians.

Troops of the 1st Ukrainian Front occupy Dresden and Olomouc (Olmuetz).

9/5: 90,000 German troops surrender to the Allies. The German garrisons in La Rochelle and La Palisse capitulate to the French. Germans hand over the Channel Islands, St. Nazaire and St. Lorient to British troops.

Soviet commission in Pelei begins interrogation of Staff of German Army in Courland. The round-up of German troops begins. The last German bridgeheads in the Gulf of Danzig capitulate to the 2nd and 3rd White Russian Fronts. The 1st, 4th and 2nd Ukrainian Fronts pursue retreating German troops in Czechoslovakia. In Austria, units of the 1st Ukrainian Front reach Amstetten and Graz and make contact with the Americans. All German resistance in Austria and Czechoslovakia ceases.

Belgrade conference between Field-Marshal Alexander, General Morgan and Marshal Tito on the subject of Trieste.

10/5: Theresienstadt liberated.

11/5: Red Army makes contact with Americans at Chemnitz (Saxony), Pilsen (Czechoslovakia) and Linz (Austria).

20,000 German troops in the Aegean (Rhodes, etc.) capitulate. Konrad Henlein, the leader of the Sudeten Germans, commits suicide.

12/5: In Courland, some 135,000 German troops surrender to the Red Army. The Staff of the Courland Army is taken prisoner and handed over to the NKVD. Some 35,000 German troops capitulate in Hela and the Gulf of Danzig.

German troops on Crete surrender unconditionally.

13/5: Isolated German resistance pockets in Czechoslovakia mopped up by Red Army. Red Army halts all offensives in Europe.

17/5: The total number of German prisoners in the West is reported at 5,000,000.

21/5: Himmler arrested in Bremervoerde.

23/5: Doenitz with members of his government and commanding officers of the Wehrmacht arrested on orders of Allied Supreme Commander. Admiral von Friedeburg commits suicide in protest against the arrest. Himmler commits suicide in Lueneburg.

The round-up of German POW's in Courland completed. Some 180,000 German prisoners are taken to camps in the Valdai Hills.

The victors (from right to left): General de Lattre de Tassigny, General Robertson, Marshal Zhukov, General Patton and General Clay.

German troops stationed abroad
at the time of the capitulation
(9 May 1945)

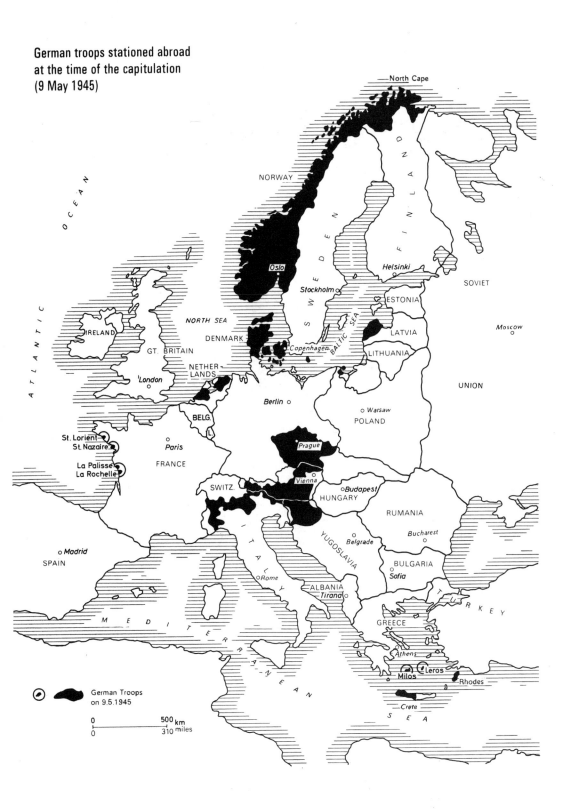

North Cape

ATLANTIC

OCEAN

NORWAY

Oslo

FINLAND

Helsinki

SOVIET

SWEDEN

Stockholm

Moscow

NORTH SEA

DENMARK

ESTONIA

BALTIC SEA

LATVIA

LITHUANIA

UNION

IRELAND

GT. BRITAIN

London

Copenhagen

NETHER-
LANDS

Berlin

Warsaw

POLAND

BELG.

St. Lorient
St. Nazaire

Paris

Prague

La Palisse
La Rochelle

FRANCE

Vienna

SWITZ.

Budapest

HUNGARY

RUMANIA

Madrid

SPAIN

ITALY

YUGOSLAVIA

Belgrade

Bucharest

BULGARIA

Sofia

Rome

ALBANIA

Tirana

TURKEY

MEDITERRANEAN

GREECE

Athens

Milos

Leros

Rhodes

Crete

SEA

German Troops
on 9.5.1945

0   500 km
0   310 miles

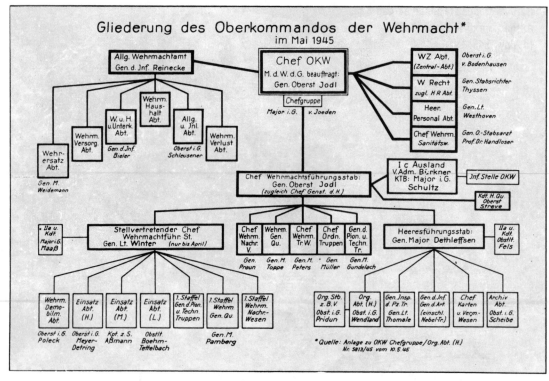

German Supreme Command diagram of Wehrmacht chain of command on 10/5/1945.

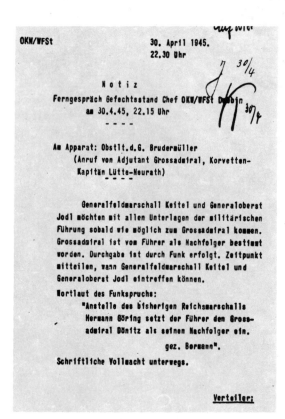

THE DOENITZ GOVERNMENT BEFORE THE CAPITULATION

30 April–4 May 1945

Left: memorandum of telephone conversation between Doenitz's staff and Wehrmacht Command, who wish to see the Fuehrer's successor as soon as possible. Below: Doenitz wires his loyalty to Hitler after the latter's death, on 1 May. "I shall do my utmost to relieve Berlin, and to continue the heroic struggle . . ."

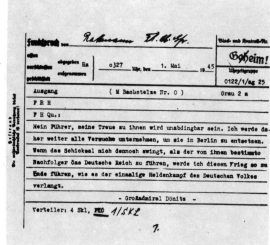

Von Hitler zu Dönitz

Die Persönlichkeit des neuen „Führers" — Die Friedensmission des Grafen Bernadotte

LONDON. — Die Nachricht vom Tode Adolf H i t l e r s ist nicht überraschend gekommen, da man in unterrichteten Kreisen seit Tagen angenommen hat, daß Hitler gestorben sei. Gewisse Kreise wieder zweifeln an der Todesmeldung und betonen, daß man die Ereignisse abwarten müsse, ehe man sich ein Urteil darüber bilden könne, ob Hitler nicht einfach „verschwunden" sei. Zum Nachfolger Hitlers bestimmte sich Großadmiral D ö n i t z. Zugleich halten sich hier auch hartnäckig die Meldungen von Angeboten der b e d i n g u n g s l o s e n K a p i t u l a t i o n, die Deutschland entweder bereits gemacht hat oder zu machen im Begriffe ist.

Die „Mission Bernadotte"

Es wird von offizieller Seite in Washington bestätigt, daß letzte Woche Reichsführer SS Himmler das Ersuchen gestellt hatte, General Eisenhower zu sehen, um mit ihm Unterhandlungen zwecks Übergabe zu pflegen. Das Angebot, das der schwedische Graf Bernadotte weiterleitete, enthielt die bedingungslose Übergabe an die Vereinigten Staaten und Großbritannien. Himmler hoffte, den Kampf im Osten fortsetzen zu können. Präsident Truman setzte sich sofort mit Premierminister Churchill in Verbindung, und beide sandten ein gemeinsames Telegramm an Marschall Stalin. In Übereinstimmung mit Marschall Stalin wurden diese Bedingungen abgelehnt. Graf Bernadotte kehrte nach Deutschland zurück und übergab die Antwort der Alliierten. Er brachte bei seiner Rückkehr aus Deutschland keine weiteren Angebote von dort.

Vom Irrenhaus zur Reichskanzlei

Die Person des Großadmirals D ö n i t z, dem neuen „Führer" von Restdeutschland, ist nur insofern interessant, als Dönitz nicht als ein Vertreter der Flotte oder der Wehrmacht angesehen werden kann, sondern von jeher als ein begeisterter Parteigenosse gegolten hat. Admiral Dönitz selbst kann demgegenüber nicht als ein Vertreter der Berufsarmee oder der Berufsmarine angesehen werden. Er verdankt seine Karriere ganz und gar dem Nationalsozialismus. Sein einziges Bestreben war der bedingungslose U-Boot-Krieg. In der Zeit vor Hitler war es ihm versagt, mit U-Booten zu experimentieren, da Deutschland dem Friedensvertrag gemäß keine U-Boote bauen durfte. Er versprach Hitler, den kommenden Krieg allein mit der Unterseeboot-Waffe zu gewinnen. Hitler gab ihm volle Freiheit in der Erzeugung von U-Booten. Im Weltkrieg war Dönitz britischer Kriegsgefangener. Er war in England während seiner Gefangenschaft in einem Irrenhaus untergebracht, da an seinem Geisteszustand gezweifelt wurde.

Title page of *Kölnischer Kurier* of 5 May 1945, reporting Hitler's death, Bernadotte's negotiations with Himmler, and alleging that Doenitz, Germany's new "Fuehrer", is a fanatical Nazi who was kept under observation in a British mental hospital during the First World War.

The New German Government

From the Memoirs of Admiral Doenitz

These considerations (the bare survival of the German people) which all pointed to the need for the creation of some sort of improvised central government, took shape and form when I was joined by Graf Schwerin-Krosigk. In addition to discharging his duties as Foreign Minister and Minister of Finance, he formed the temporary government we needed and presided over the activities of its cabinet. Although he was restricted in his choice to those men who were in northern Germany, he nevertheless succeeded in forming a workmanlike cabinet of experts.

In overall charge, and directing the business of the Foreign and Finance Ministries: Graf Schwerin-Krosigk. Directing the business of the Ministries of the Interior and Culture: Doctor Stuckart. Directing the business of the Ministries of Industry and Productions: Speer. Directing the business of the Ministries of Food, Agriculture and Forests: Backe. Directing the business of the Ministries of Labour and Social Affairs: Doctor Seldte. Directing the business of the Ministries of Posts and Communications: Doctor Dorpmueller.

We all fully realized that any active government on our part would, for the time being, be impossible. But each member of this improvised government set to work to formulate plans, within his own sphere, by which the central government would be able to cope with the emergency . . .

The picture of the military situation as a whole showed clearly that the war was lost. As there was also no possibility of effecting any improvement in Germany's overall position by political means, the only conclusion to which I, as Head of the State, could come was that the war must be brought to an end as quickly as possible, in order to prevent further bloodshed.

DOENITZ DISMISSES HIMMLER

1 May 1945

"Allow me to become the second man in your State . . ."

From the Memoirs of Admiral Doenitz

At about midnight he arrived, accompanied by six armed SS officers, and was received by my aide-de-camp, Luedde-Neurath. I offered Himmler a chair and myself sat down behind my writing desk, upon which lay, hidden by some papers, a pistol with the safety catch off. I had never done anything of this sort in my life before, but I did not know what the outcome of this meeting might be.

I handed Himmler the telegram containing my appointment. "Please read this," I said. I watched him closely. As he read, an expression of astonishment, indeed of consternation, spread over his face. All hope seemed to collapse within him. He went very pale. Finally he stood up and bowed. "Allow me," he said, "to become the second man in your state." I replied that that was out of the question and that there was no way in which I could make any use of his services.

Thus advised, he left me at about one o'clock in the morning. The showdown had taken place without force, and I felt relieved.

Collapse of Hitler's ''Reich'':
the last operations of Allied troops in the West
and of the Red Army in the East
(April–May 1945)

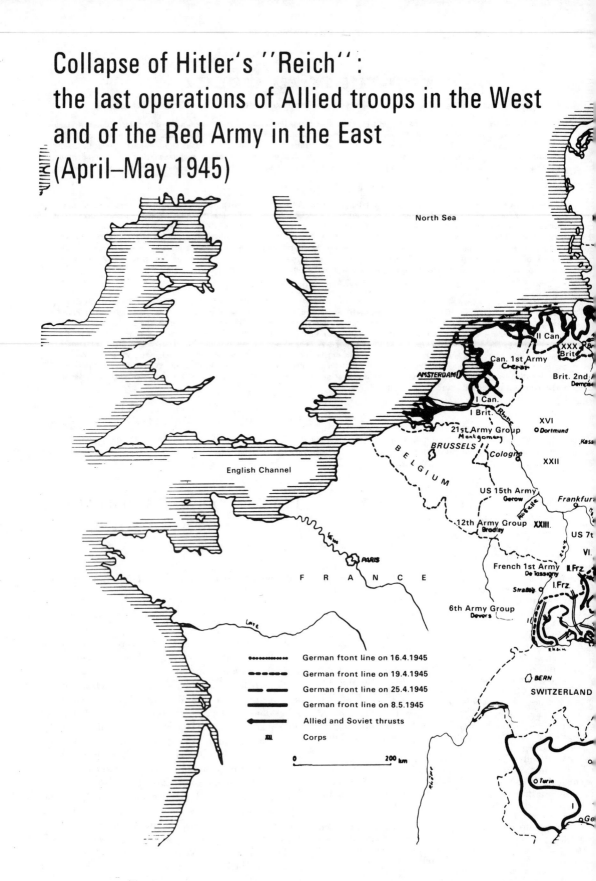

North Sea

II Can.

XXX R
Brit.

Can. 1st Army
Crerar

Brit. 2nd A
Dempse

AMSTERDAM

I Can.

I Brit.

XVI
Dortmund

21st Army Group
Montgomery

Kass

BELGIUM

BRUSSELS

Cologne

XXII

English Channel

US 15th Army
Gerow

Frankfur

12th Army Group
Bradley

XXIII

US 7t

PARIS

VI.

F R A N C E

French 1st Army
De Lassigny

II.Frz.

I.Frz.

Strabb g O

6th Army Group
Devers

Loire

Rhein

BERN

SWITZERLAND

German front line on 16.4.1945

German front line on 19.4.1945

German front line on 25.4.1945

German front line on 8.5.1945

Allied and Soviet thrusts

XII   Corps

0   200 km

Turin

Ge

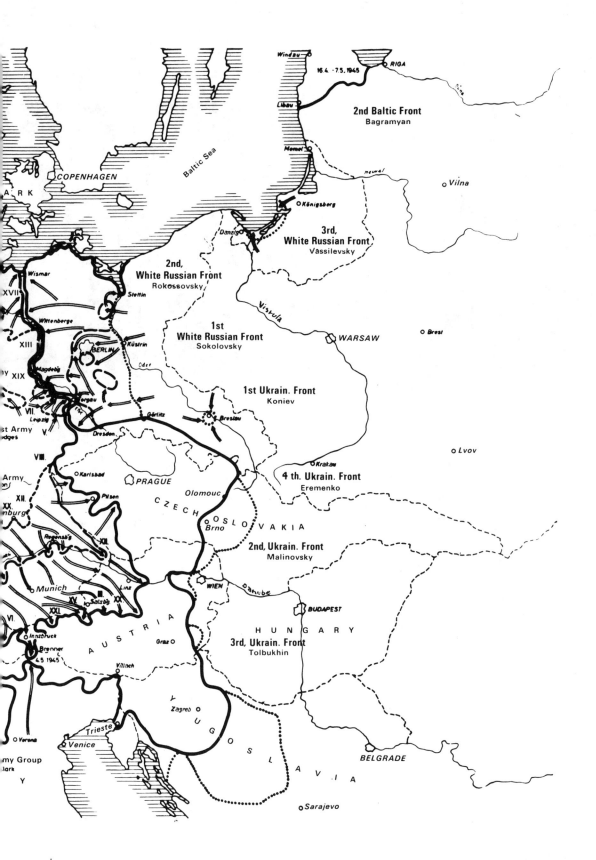

The German surrender delegation led by Admiral von Friedeburg in General Dempsey's H.Q. (left). Right: the Lueneburg delegation in front of Field-Marshal Montgomery's tent.

The instrument of surrender bearing signatures of Field-Marshal Montgomery and the German representatives.

THE GERMAN SURRENDER IN NORTHERN GERMANY, HOLLAND AND DENMARK

4 May 1945

"Who are these men? What do they want?"

From the Memoirs of Field-Marshal Montgomery

They were brought to my caravan site and were drawn up under the Union Jack, which was flying proudly in the breeze. I kept them waiting for a few minutes and then came out of my caravan and walked towards them. They all saluted, under the Union Jack. It was a great moment: I knew the Germans had come to surrender and that the war was over . . .

I said to my interpreter: "Who are these men?" He told me.

I then said, "What do they want?"

Admiral Friedeburg then read me a letter from Field-Marshal Keitel offering to surrender to me the three German armies withdrawing in front of the Russians between Berlin and Rostock. I refused to consider this, saying that these armies should surrender to the Russians. I added that, of course, if any German soldiers came towards my front with their hands up they would automatically be taken prisoner . . .

I was certain von Friedeburg would return with full powers to sign. I therefore decided to see the Press at 5 p.m. . . .

In that tent on Luneburg Heath, publicly in the presence of the Press and other spectators, I read out in English the Instrument of Surrender. I said that unless the German delegation signed this document immediately, and without argument on what would follow their capitulation, I would order the fighting to continue. I then called on each member of the German delegation by name to sign the document, which they did without any discussion. I then signed, on behalf of General Eisenhower.

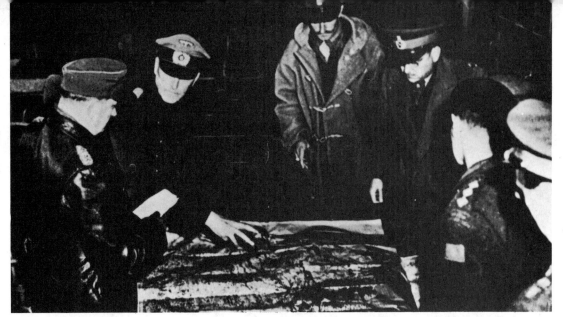

ARMY GROUP H CAPITULATES
IN WAGENINGEN   5 May 1945

On 5 May, General Blaskowitz (second from left) capitu-
lated to General Foulkes (fourth from left) and Prince
Bernhard (extreme right) at the Hotel de Wereld in
Wageningen.

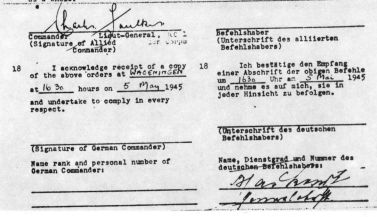

Conclusion of instrument
of surrender signed on 5
May 1945, bearing the signatures of General Foulkes
and General Blaskowitz.

ARMY GROUP G CAPITULATES
AT HAAR   5 May 1945

Lt.-General Foertsch signing the instrument of surrender
at Haar near Munich in the presence of General Devers
(6th Army Group).

THE END OF THE WAR IN AMSTERDAM

5–8 May 1945

Despite the surrender in Lueneburg and Wageningen, German troops fought on in Amsterdam, firing at civilians as late as 7 May.

The German garrison held on until 8 May. In the photograph, the German Commander of Amsterdam is being led off by Dutch Resistance fighters.

Disregarding the capitulation, the *Deutsche Zeitung* proclaimed in banner headlines on 5 May: "No capitulation in Holland".

General Jodl signing the general instrument of surrender in General Eisenhower's H.Q. at Reims on 7 May. Right, Admiral von Friedeburg; left, Soviet General Suzloparov.

THE GERMAN CAPITULATION
AT RHEIMS 7 May 1945

"The representatives of the Allied powers were assembled round a simple table . . ."

The reply (to General Jodl's note) arrived at half-past one o'clock in the morning of 7 May: "Admiral Doenitz authorizes signature of surrender under conditions stated.—Keitel."

The last page of the surrender document signed at Rheims.

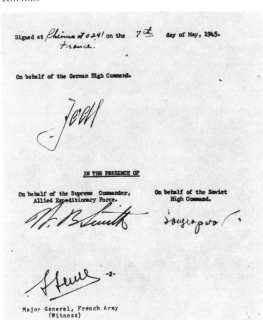

Signed at *Rheims* at 0241 on the 7th day of May, 1945. *France.*

On behalf of the German High Command.

IN THE PRESENCE OF

On behalf of the Supreme Commander, Allied Expeditionary Force.

On behalf of the Soviet High Command.

Major General, French Army (Witness)

-2-

An hour later, Jodl and von Friedeburg entered the room where the surrender document was to be signed. The representatives of the Allied powers were assembled round a simple table. Military maps covered the walls. Four copies of the surrender document, bound in plain grey paper covers, lay on the table.

General Eisenhower wore an expression of aversion if not contempt. Through an interpreter, he asked Jodl whether all points in the document were clear. Jodl replied that they were.

Again through his interpreter, Eisenhower stated:

"You will be held responsible, officially and personally, for any violation of the conditions of this surrender, including the conditions referring to the official surrender before Russia. The German Supreme Commander will appear for the surrender to the Russians at the time and the place that the Russian High Command will designate. That is all."

The four papers were signed with two fountain pens that General Eisenhower had reserved for that purpose ever since his landing in Africa.

Jodl rose. First in English, then continuing in German, he said:

"Sir, with this signature, the German nation and the German Armed Forces are at the mercy of the victors. Through this war, which has lasted for five years, both have performed more, and perhaps suffered more, than any other nation on earth. At this hour, we can only hope that the victors will be generous."

There was no answer. Jodl saluted shortly and left the room.

From Thorwald: *Flight in the Winter*

SECOND GERMAN CAPITULATION IN BERLIN

8 May 1945

At Rheims, General Smith overlooked the existence of an earlier capitulation instrument drafted by the European Advisory Commission. When the Russians protested, and demanded a new surrender document with the original EAC text, the Americans let it be known that the "official capitulation" would take place in Berlin. In the photograph, Keitel is seen leading the Berlin delegation. ▶

The Instrument of Surrender signed at Karlshorst, near Berlin:

1. We, the undersigned, acting by the authority of the German High Command, hereby surrender unconditionally to the Supreme Commander, Allied Expeditionary Force, and simultaneously to the Supreme High Command of the Red Army, all forces on land, at sea, and in the air at this date under German control.

2. The German High Command will at once issue orders to all German military, naval and air authorities and to all forces under German control to cease active operations at 23:01 hours, Central European Time, on May 8, 1945, to remain in the positions occupied at that time, and to disarm completely, handing over their weapons and equipment to the local Allied commanders or officers designated by representatives of Allied Supreme Commands. No ship, vessel or aircraft is to be scuttled, or any damage done to their hulls, machinery or equipment, nor to machines of all kinds, armament, apparatus and all the technical means of prosecution of war in general.

3. The German High Command will at once issue, and ensure the carrying out of, any further orders issued by the Supreme Commander, Allied Expeditionary Force, and by the Supreme Commander of the Red Army.

4. This act of military surrender is without prejudice to, and will be superseded by, any general instrument of surrender imposed by or on behalf of the United Nations and applicable to Germany and the German armed forces as a whole.

5. In the event of the German High Command or any of the forces under their control failing to act in accordance with this act of surrender, the Supreme Commander, Allied Expeditionary Force, and the Supreme Commander of the Red Army will take such punitive or other action as they deem appropriate.

6. This act is drawn up in the English, Russian and German languages. The English and Russian are the authentic texts.

Signed at Berlin, May 8, 1945.

VON FRIEDEBURG   KEITEL   STUMPFF
for the German High Command

In the presence of:

A. W. TEDDER
Representing the Supreme Commander, Allied Expeditionary Force

G. ZHUKOV
On behalf of the Supreme Command of the Red Army

German civilians hearing the news of the capitulation in a village square.

BRESLAU CAPITULATES
7 May 1945

Gauleiter Hanke, Nazi chief of Breslau, who, only a few weeks earlier, had Mayor Dr. Spielhagen publicly shot for "cowardice in the face of the enemy", saw fit to desert his own post during the night of 5 May, when he fled to the West in a small aircraft. Right: Hanke in conversation with Volkssturm men in Breslau. ▶

"Comrades, the war is over . . ."

From the diary of Emil Heinze

May 1945: On Thursday night, we were all called out. The only time we could work now was at night. We started building machine-gun emplacements. The sky over the front was scarlet, as street after street caught fire . . . On the afternoon of 4 May, the Russian loud-speaker told us about a truce offer. That night not a single shot was fired . . . On 5 May, there were supposed to be negotiations with the Russians, but we were called out again during the night. Rumours about the capitulation grew louder on 6 May. I had the afternoon off. When I came back, someone told me the war had ended. I refused to believe him. Towards nightfall, the company leader called us all together and said: "Comrades, the war is over. We have orders to stay where we are until further notice. Things won't be too bad, for all of you have your civvies with you." After that, I put on a suit, packed my bag, and—orders or no orders—made for my home. Many of my comrades refused to disperse like what they called a herd of sheep. I said, everyone must decide for himself. Those who stayed behind were taken prisoner next morning, but I got home all right . . .

To the Town Commander of Breslau,
General Niehoff.

Following your agreement to an honourable surrender of the surrounded Breslau garrison, we propose the following conditions:

(1) All troops under your command will cease acts of hostility at 14:00 hours, Moscow time, on 6 May 1945.

(2) You will surrender your troops, arms, equipment, vehicles, and technical means of prosecuting the war, un-damaged.

(3) We guarantee the lives and maintenance, and will respect the personal property and decorations of yourself and those of your officers and men who lay down their arms, and undertake to repatriate all of you after the war.

(4) All wounded and sick will be given immediate medical assistance.

(5) We guarantee the lives and the restoration of normal conditions to the entire civilian population.

(6) You and all generals under your command will be allowed to retain your personal cars and drivers, and will be treated as captured generals.

Signed: Commander of the 6th Army
of the 1st Ukrainian Front
General Gluzdovski

Chief of Staff
Major-General Panov

6/5/1945

A street in Central Breslau shortly after the capitulation.

THE END OF ARMY GROUP COURLAND

7–8 May 1945

General Hilpert, the last Commander of German Army Group Courland.

"No one knows for sure who has stabbed us in the back . . ."

From the letter of 25-year-old Captain Breuninger in Libau (Courland):

> This letter written on 8 May 1945, from a sector to which the news of Germany's utter collapse had not yet penetrated, affords a glimpse of the fanatical beliefs of many young German officers.

Dear Father,

Now everything is coming to an end. Those of us who will see their homes again will leave Libau tonight and sail for Kiel. I shall give this letter to Hermann Meister, a sergeant of the 11th Infantry Division. I hope you will get it.

Until yesterday we still hoped that all of us would be shipped back to Germany and would keep on fighting the Russians from there. Three days ago we received a secret, oral message from our commander, General Hilpert. It said that Admiral Doenitz had made contact with the Western Powers and would make peace in the west. In the east the war would go on. Army Group Courland would be moved across the Baltic Sea and would go back into action on the Elbe front. On May 6 we were to destroy all excess equipment. An army corps was put in charge of Libau port to cover our transfer to the ships. And the block positions for a gradual withdrawal had been ready since December of last year—in case the Fuehrer should order it.

Some officers claimed that the British would send ships to pick us up. It was even said that English troops would land here and attack the Russian flank together with us.

We had all expected a turn in our fortunes because of the new weapons. Then we received the news of the heroic death of our Fuehrer—it was terrible, bitter disappointment. But then came the secret orders about the withdrawal, and all of us took new hope. We have fought here with all we have against one enemy: Bolshevism. If we fought the English and French and Americans, it was only because they did not want to understand the meaning of our fight in the east. So our hopes were high when we heard about a separate peace in the west—our years of war would have a purpose, even though a whole nation would have been sacrificed.

You can imagine how disappointed we are, now that we have been told that all our forces have surrendered, and that Army Group Courland has joined in the surrender. Russian commissars are expected every day now. They say the English prevented the sailing of the ships that were to come for us. But no one knows for sure who has stabbed us in the back. The Navy has sent some small ships from the Gulf of Danzig. Army Group Reserve, that is the 11th Infantry Division and 14th Tank Division will be evacuated on these ships because they were our "firefighters", always in the thick; they have earned it. And then, each division was allowed to send some officers or an officer and a hundred and twentyfive men on the trip home—mostly family men. And the wounded. You should have seen how the 11th Infantry marched through Libau, fully armed, in perfect order.

Many of the men still do not believe in the surrender. They think they will march from Kiel against the Russians. The port is cordoned by military police, to keep unauthorized personnel from entering the ships. But everything has come off in perfect order, without any panic. Just as the Army fought. We have done our part as German soldiers, if necessary to the bitter end.

We do not know how our Fuehrer died. We do not know what weakness and treason took place at home during the last few weeks. We only know that to this day we have fought Bolshevism, the enemy not of us alone but of all Europe. We have seen Bolshevism in action as no one else has. We have seen the Bolshevist paradise. We know what we fought for . . .

From Thorwald: *Flight in the Winter*

CAPITULATION OF GERMAN BASES IN THE ATLANTIC AND THE AEGEAN

7, 9 and 11 May 1945

On 5 May, Keitel wired: "Grand-Admiral prepared to include garrisons in the Channel and on Channel Islands in truce." On 9 May, Major Engelken (centre of photograph) signed the capitulation on behalf of Major-General Junck, the German commander of St. Nazaire. 28,000 prisoners were taken by the Allies. ▶

The German High Command announced on 8 May that the British had proscribed the Nazi salute, ordering the Wehrmacht to revert to traditional methods of salutation. For the sake of discipline and uniformity, the entire Wehrmacht would therefore observe the following salutation procedure, with immediate effect:

(1) When wearing caps, German soldiers will salute by bringing their right hand up to their cap;

(2) When bare-headed, they will salute by coming to attention;

(3) When reporting, they will use the words: Heil Grenadiers, Engineers, etc.

(4) Women auxiliaries will salute by inclining their head.

*

Allied Mediterranean H.Q. announced on 11 May that all German forces in the Dodecanese and Aegean (some 20,000) had surrendered unconditionally, including the garrisons in Crete, Rhodes, Leros, Milos and Cos.

Kurz-Nachrichten
der Marineflakbrigade

10. Mai 1945 — Feldzeitung der Festung Lorient — Nr. 272

Lorient meldet sich ab!

Durch Funkspruch an die Heimat:
Befehl zur bedingungslosen Übergabe ausgeführt. Übergabe der Festung 10. 5. 1945, 16.00 Uhr.

Melde mich mit meiner standhaften uud unbesiegten Besatzung ab. Wir gedenken unserer schwergeprüften Heimat

Es lebe Deutschland!

Kommandierender General XXV. Armee-Korps
Fahrmbacher, General d. Artillerie.

Soldaten der Festung Lorient!

Der Kampf um die Festung ist zu Ende! Seit über 9 Monaten habt Ihr auf verlorenem Posten, weit entfernt von der Heimat stehend, unter erheblichen moralischen Belastungen und körperlichen Entbehrungen stän-

German Navy Newspaper reporting the surrender of the Lorient garrison.

Capitulation in the port of St. Lorient on 10 May: Colonel Keating (centre) of the U.S. 66th Infantry Division with Colonel Borst (right).

The victorious general returns: Eisenhower's triumphal drive through New York on 18 June 1945.

VE-DAY 8 May 1945

From General Eisenhower's Victory Order of the Day:

It is my special privilege, in the name of all the nations represented in the theatre of war, to commend each of you for the valiant performance of duty . . . Your accomplishments at sea, in the air, on the ground, and in the field of supply have put 5,000,000 of the enemy permanently out of the war. You have taken in stride military tasks so difficult as to be classed by many doubters as impossible. You have confused, defeated, and destroyed your savagely fighting foe . . .

Let us have no part in the profitless quarrels in which other men will inevitably engage as to what country, what service, won the European war. Every man, every woman, of every nation here represented has served according to his or her ability, and the efforts of each have contributed to the outcome. This we shall remember— and in doing so we shall be revering each honoured grave, and be sending comfort to the loved ones of comrades who could not live to see this day.

President Truman's message to Marshal Stalin:

I wish to express to you and through you to your heroic army the appreciation and congratulations of the U.S. Government on its splendid contribution to the cause of civilization and liberty. You have demonstrated what it is possible to accomplish when a free people have superlative leadership and with unfailing courage rises against the forces of barbarism.

From the War Memoirs of General de Gaulle:

At the final act of the German capitulation, the representative of France was a signatory with those of Russia, the United States and Great Britain. Field-Marshal Keitel, exclaiming, "What? The French too?" thereby paid tribute to the *tour de force* which had brought France and her army to such a recovery.

"The war is won. Victory is ours! It is the victory of the United Nations and the victory of France!" I broadcast this announcement on May 8th at three in the afternoon.

From the Diaries of Field-Marshal Viscount Alanbrooke:

May 9th. V.E. 2 Day. I started my diary well by taking a day off and going home! The day was a national holiday. I found you busy putting up wonderful flagstaffs and decorations, and incidentally cutting your hand badly. We had a very happy and peaceful afternoon together looking after goats and chickens.

Soviet troops with captured German flags in Moscow Red Square on VE-day.

LIBERATION OF PROMINENT SOLDIERS AND POLITICAL PRISONERS

Liberated from Koenigstein near Dresden by troops of the U.S. 76th Infantry Division (U.S. 9th Army): General Lousseau (left); General Baurret (centre) and General Condé (right, sitting), former Commander of French 3rd Army. ▶

Other prisoners liberated from German camps (from left to right): General Privalov; Bishop Neuhaeusler of Munich; Colonel von Bonin; Captain S. Payne Best; General A. Paphgos; Captain Liedig (German Navy).

Another batch of prominent prisoners (front row from left to right): M. Kallay, former Prime Minister of Hungary; Baron Shell, Minister of the Interior; Colonel McGrath; Halder (behind McGrath), former Chief of General Staff; Pastor Niemoeller (with pipe); *Frau* Schuschnigg; Prince Friedrich Leopold of Prussia; General Privalov (Red Army); Major Stanek (Czech Army); Czech Minister of Commerce Karoas; and Colonel Brodmikov (Red Army). ▼

THE DOENITZ GOVERNMENT AFTER THE CAPITULATION

9–22 May 1945

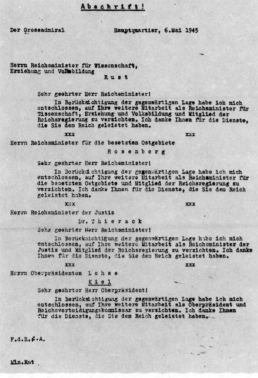

Copy of letter by Doenitz dismissing Rust, Minister of Science and Education; Rosenberg, Minister for the Occupied Eastern Territories; Dr. Thierack, Minister of Justice, and Kiel, Reichs Defence Commissar, from office.

Letter by Jodl requesting that no further news about the release of German POW's be broadcast or published, since such reports are liable to undermine army morale.

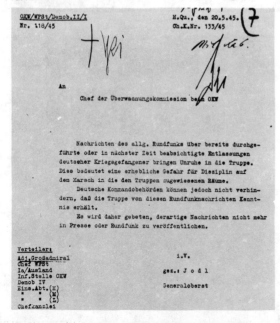

From the broadcast address by Count Schwerin von Krosigk, Doenitz's "Chief Minister" on 7 May 1945:

German men and women!

From the collapse of the past we must preserve and save but one thing: our unity, the idea of a community of brethren that, in the last years of the war found its finest expression in comradeship in the field and selfless devotion at home. We shall need this comradeship and devotion in the coming days of poverty and hunger, as much as ever we needed it in the days of battles and air raids. Only if we preserve our unity, and do not again revert to class and sectional struggles, will we be able to survive the hard times all of us are now facing.

We must make justice the basis of our national life. Let justice become our highest law and guide. We must, moreover, accept justice as the basis of international relationships, as a matter of inner conviction. Respect for our contractual obligations must be as sacrosanct to us as the feeling that we are all members of a European family of nations . . .

Only then can we hope that the atmosphere of hatred that today surrounds Germany will make way for a spirit of reconciliation among the nations, without which no world recovery can even be contemplated . . .

*

From Churchill's world broadcast on 13 May 1945:

On the continent of Europe we have yet to make sure that the simple and honourable purposes for which we entered the war are not brushed aside or overlooked in the months following our success, and that the words "freedom", "democracy", and "liberation" are not distorted from their true meaning as we have understood them. There would be little use in punishing the Hitlerites for their crimes if law and justice did not rule, and if totalitarian or police governments were to take the place of the German invaders. We seek nothing for ourselves. But we must make sure that those causes which we fought for find recognition at the peace table in facts as well as words . . .

*

From a message by Truman to Churchill on 9 May 1945:

I am in agreement with your opinion that a meeting of the three heads of government would be desirable in order to get action on the questions of interest to the three governments . . .

I very much prefer to have the request for such a tripartite meeting originate from Marshal Stalin and not from either of us. Perhaps you have means of some kind with which to endeavour to induce Stalin to suggest or request such a meeting.

In the meantime it is my present intention to adhere to our interpretation of the Yalta agreements . . .

In order to prepare for a possible tripartite meeting in the not distant future, I would be very pleased to have from you a list of the questions that you consider it necessary or desirable for us to bring up for discussion, and also suggestions as to meeting place . . .

SOVIET ATTACKS ON THE "DOENITZ GANG"

"Discussions of the status of the Fascist gang round Doenitz continue . . ."

From an article in Pravda *on 20 May 1945:*

Discussion of the status of the Fascist gang round Doenitz continue. Several prominent Allied circles still deem it necessary to make use of the "services" of Doenitz and his collaborators. In the British Parliament, this gang has been described as the "Doenitz Administration" . . . A reporter of the reactionary Hearst press has called the enlistment of Doenitz "an act of political sagacity". Thus a Fascist scribbler has seen fit to make common cause with Hitler's marauding disciple. At the same time, the Fascist press on both sides of the Atlantic has put it abroad that conditions in Germany will become chaotic if the "Doenitz Administration" is dismissed. In this connection, we must mention the defeat of Germany in 1918, when German Rightists produced similar fairy-tales of impending chaos. Then, the intact German Army units were used for new adventures in the East, immediately after the capitulation. The present campaign has similar objectives. Many reactionary circles among the Allies are opposed to the creation of a new Europe on the basis of the Crimea Conference. These circles consider the preservation of Fascist states and breeding grounds a means of thwarting the democratic aspirations of all freedom-loving nations . . . .

From the official records of the Doenitz Government. Events on 16/5/1945: 10 a.m.—Memorial Service for Captain Lueth; 5 p.m.—Foreign Minister Speer reports on his talks with U.S. General Henderson on the effects of bombing; 5:15 p.m. Speer reports on difficult internal conditions; 5:30 p.m. Speer, Jodl *et al* continue consultations. Disturbing news about conditions in Hitler's concentration camps . . .

On 23 May 1945, British troops entered the buildings of the Doenitz Government in Muerwik.

DOENITZ GOVERNMENT PLACED UNDER ARREST

23 May 1945

Aboard the *Patria* on 23 May 1945: General Rook (standing) tells Jodl, Doenitz and von Friedeburg (right) of Eisenhower's decision to place them under arrest.

After returning to their headquarters in Muerwik, members of the Doenitz Government and of the German Supreme Commander, General Jodl, were placed under arrest.

British soldiers leading off employees and officers in the Doenitz Government.

The unfairness of race discrimination

From the discussion between a British officer (A) and a young German prisoner (B) who had served as a volunteer in the Waffen-SS:

A. Don't you think race discrimination is unfair?

B. Why unfair?

A. Well, why should we discriminate against any human being, simply because he belongs to another race?

B. What if he belongs to a lower race?

A. That's not a fair description. All of us are human.

B. You are wrong there. Surely you don't believe that a Negro is our equal?

A. In many respects he may not be, but not because he is a Negro. He may be less civilized, less intelligent or morally inferior. All the same, he is human.

B. But surely we can't treat everybody alike?

A. Indeed not. But that, as I have been trying to explain, is not a question of race but one of personality. I much prefer a decent Negro to an English scoundrel. I treat everyone according to his moral worth. Maybe the English, who have enjoyed the advantages of an old culture and a good education, include more valuable people than Negroes do. Still, I respect the person of even the most uncivilized Negro, perhaps more so than I do an uncouth Englishman.

B. I can see what you mean. If you look at human beings as individuals, you may find more "valuable" people among the English than among Negroes, but on principle we must not go by race but by the moral development of the individual. I must admit that you are right.

A. You see, if you begin to think, you are bound to realize how unjust and immoral the Nazi tenets are.

B. Yes, but how could I ever have found that out for myself?

After: Second Army Troop News

The interrogation of Himmler

From the Memoirs of Field-Marshal Montgomery:

He left Flensburg on the 9th May under an assumed name, intending to roam the country for some weeks until the tumult of victory had died down. He then hoped to obtain an interview with me so that he could expound his views on the situation. He was, however, arrested by a British patrol on 21st May and taken to an internment camp where he eventually disclosed his identity. He needed no encouragement to speak. He said that before leaving Flensburg he had called off all German resistance movements and that for some time before then he had been urging the conclusion of peace with the Western Allies. His purpose in seeking an interview with me was to stress that sooner or later there would be another war to stop the march of the Asiatic hordes into Western Europe, led by Russia. Now that Germany was beaten, Britain was left alone to face the Asiatic onslaught . . .

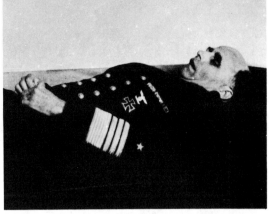

Admiral von Friedeburg committed suicide in protest against what he considered his dishonourable arrest.

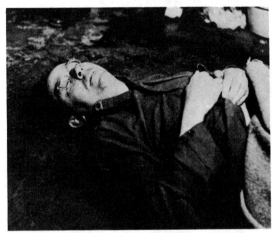

Himmler dead in Lueneburg after swallowing cyanide.

HIMMLER'S ARREST AND SUICIDE

"Take pity on me . . ."

Himmler's leave-taking of his personal physician, Dr. Kersten

It was about 6 a.m. on 21 April 1945, just before dawn. Kersten accompanied Himmler to his car . . . The two men walked in silence. They knew this would be their last meeting. Only when he had reached the car, with his driver holding the door open, did Himmler turn to Kersten: "I don't know how much longer I shall live. But whatever happens, please don't think too badly of me. No doubt, I have committed many grave errors. But Hitler wanted me to take the hard road. Without discipline and obedience there can be no state. With us perishes all that is best in Germany."

Himmler stepped into the car and sat down. Then he took the doctor's hand, clasped it feverishly and said in a choking voice: "Kersten, let me thank you once again for everything . . . Take pity on me . . . I am grieving for my poor family."

In the early light, Kersten could see tears in the eyes of a man who, without the slightest hesitation, had ordered more executions and mass exterminations than any other man in history, and who yet felt so sorry for himself. The car disappeared into the dark.

From Kessel: Medizinalrat Kersten

THE BEGINNING OF POLITICAL TENSION BETWEEN EAST AND WEST

The conflicting political interests of the Allies as reflected at the Potsdam Conference and in the foundation of the United Nations Organization.

CHRONOLOGICAL TABLE:

1945

27/4: Proclamation of Austrian independence. Provisional Government appointed under Dr. Karl Renner.

29/4: "Ulbricht Group" arrives in Germany.

4/5: Provisional Government formed in Denmark.

7/5: General Berzarin appoints Andreas Hermer (formerly Centre Party) food controller for Berlin. Bishop Otto Dibelius confirmed in office by Berzarin.

10/5: U.S. War Department announces the withdrawal from Europe of 3,100,000 American troops.

11–12/5: British troops arrive in Klagenfurt (Austria); Yugoslav partisans arriving three hours later harass the Allied authorities. Truman sends a message to Churchill on Trieste.

12/5: The British Ambassador in Belgrade hands Tito a note demanding the withdrawal of his troops from Austria.

Dr. Arthur Werner appointed Mayor of Berlin.

13/5: The American Government announces the review of its Lend–Lease Programme.

14/5: The independence of Austria proclaimed over the Austrian radio network.

Dr. Emil Hacha, President of the Czechoslovak puppet government is arrested.

15/5: Tito places his troops in Austria under Allied control, and a few days later agrees to their withdrawal.

18/5: America agrees to hand over part of the U.S. Zone of Occupation in Germany to France.

20/5: Pravda denounces the "Doenitz gang".

Yugoslav troops in Austria begin to withdraw across the border.

21/5: U.S. 1st Army under General Hodges begins to withdraw from Europe and prepares to embark for the Pacific.

22/5: Field-Marshal Alexander and General Clark arrive in Trieste. Field-Marshal Montgomery appointed C.-in-C. of British Zone in Germany.

23/5: Julius Streicher captured by Americans.

25/5: Hopkins arrives in Moscow as President Truman's special envoy, to discuss political differences between the Western Allies and the Soviet Union, particularly on the Polish question.

President Benes and Czechoslovak Government in London return to Prague. Ruthenia (Transcarpathian Ukraine) ceded to Soviet Union.

Switzerland expels officials of German Embassy and all German consular staff.

27/5: Field-Marshal Ritter von Greim, Goering's successor as Commander of the Luftwaffe, commits suicide.

28/5: Queen Wilhelmina returns to the Netherlands.

31/5: British Zone of Occupation in Germany to comprise Schleswig-Holstein, Hanover, Westphalia and the Rhineland.

U.N. War Crimes Commission holds inaugural meeting in London.

U.S. Military Government appoints Provisional Government of Bavaria under Fritz Schaeffer.

May: Beginning of expulsion of 2·3 million Sudeten Germans from Czechoslovakia.

5/6: Allied Control Council under Commanders of the four occupying powers set up in Berlin. All decisions of the council must be unanimous. Nazi Party dissolved and all officials declared subject to arrest.

6/6: Soviet newspapers publish maps of the proposed Soviet zone of occupation.

8/6: U.S.A., U.K. and Yugoslavia agree on control of Trieste.

11/6: 9 May officially declared as VE-day.

Proclamation of the newly formed Communist Party of Germany. "Ulbricht Group" ends its activities. Ulbricht becomes a member of the Central Committee of the German Communist Party.

11/6: Re-emergence of various German political parties and trade unions and foundation of Cultural Alliance for the Democratic Restoration of Germany.

16/6: Exchange of telegrams between President Truman and Marshal Stalin on Soviet zone of occupation.

19/6: Four million jubilant Americans give General Eisenhower a hero's welcome.

21/6: General Okulicki, former Commander of Polish Home Army sentenced to 10 years imprisonment in Moscow for alleged sabotage against the Red Army. Ten other Poles given similar sentences. Report of the resettlement of 13,000 Poles from Lodz in Pomerania.

25/6: United Nations Charter unanimously adopted at San Francisco.

1–4/7: American and British troops in the Soviet zone are withdrawn. Greater Berlin garrisoned jointly by four Powers. The regrouping of Allied and Western zones in Austria follows soon afterwards.

Early July: After the withdrawal of American troops from W. Saxony and Thuringia, Ulbricht sets up a new administration with the help of SMAG (Soviet Military Administration in Germany).

2/7: American troops take over Tempelhof airfield in Berlin.

3/7: A British contingent arrives in Berlin.

4/7: Allies recognize independence of Austria and 1937 borders.

5/7: Polish Government of National Unity (with representatives of the London Government-in-exile) recognized at Potsdam Conference.

6/7: British take over their sector in Berlin.

9/7: French troops hand Stuttgart over to the Americans.

On the orders of Soviet Military Government, new Mecklenburg Province will comprise parts of Pomerania and former Mecklenburg.

10/7: Osobka-Morawski, Prime Minister of Poland, announces expulsion of all Germans.

11/7: Allied Control Commission takes charge of the four sectors of Berlin.

13/7: SHAEF dissolved. Victory parade in Berlin.

14/7: Formation of Anti-Fascist Block of Democratic Parties. Ulbricht prepares for land reform. French troops take over their sector in Berlin.

16/7: Potsdam Conference begins.

24/7: Delegation of Polish Provincial Government arrives at Potsdam.

25/7: Churchill leaves Potsdam.

26/7: Overwhelming Labour victory in British general election. Attlee becomes Prime Minister.

Final draft of Four-Power Agreement on the occupation of Germany and Berlin signed at Potsdam. "Potsdam Declaration" to Japan.

28/7: Attlee and Bevin arrive at Potsdam.

27/8: The questionnaire used in the three Western zones of occupation as the basis of de-Nazification, consists of more than 100 personal questions.

7/9: Discord during Victory Parade at Berlin's Brandenburg Gate, when it appears that Soviets have sent more than the agreed contingent.

Zones of Occupation in Germany and Austria at the end of the war

········ Boundary of French zone demanded by General de Gaulle on 12.8.1945

0 ——— 200 km
0 ——— 12 miles

NETHERLANDS
AMSTERDAM
BELGIUM
BRUSSELS
PARIS
FRANCE
L.
SWITZERLAND
BERN
ITALY

Hamburg
Bremen
U.S. Enclave
British
Hanover
Weser
Zone
Dortmund
Cologne
Frankfurt
Worms
French
Stuttgart
Zone
Innsbruck

Stettin
Elbe
Soviet
BERNE (four sectors)
Magdeburg
Oder
Zone
Leipzig
Dresden
Erfurt
PRAGUE
American
Zone
Nuremberg
Munich
Linz
Zone
British
Graz
Zone

POLAND
Breslau
CZECHOSLOVAKIA
Soviet Zone
VIENNA (four sectors)
HUNGARY
BUDAPEST
YUGOSLAVIA

The flight from E. to W. Germany begins. On 12 May 1945, Churchill cabled Truman: "An iron curtain is drawn upon their front. We do not know what is going on behind . . ."

Food was scarce in the early post-war days.

THE FACE OF GERMANY
IMMEDIATELY AFTER THE WAR

The first German POW's returning home.

Young German POW's relearning history from Dr. Hofer.

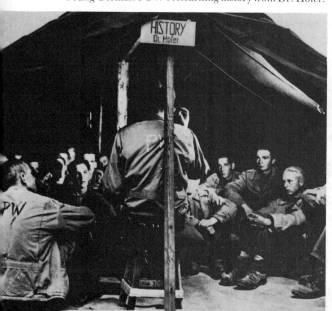

The picket fence becomes a characteristic . . .

. . . of German city-life in 1945: it is the safest and quickest means of communication and marked the re-emergence of commercial activities.

British troops entering Trieste on 18 May 1945.

DISAGREEMENT ON TRIESTE AND ON AUSTRIA'S SOUTHERN BORDERS

British–Yugoslavia differences on the withdrawal of Yugoslav troops from Austria:

On 15 May, troops of the British 8th Army advancing into Carinthia from N. Italy were met by Yugoslav troops who had arrived before them.

On 19 May, the Yugoslav Ministry of the Interior announced that the demarcation line had been discussed by Marshal Tito and Field Marshal Alexander during the latter's visit to Belgrade. The continued presence of Yugoslav troops in Trieste, Istria and the Slovenian coastland was demanded by the entire Yugoslav people and country, and in no way prejudiced the final conclusion of the peace conference . . . (TASS)

On 23 May, the Yugoslav Government informed the British and U.S. Governments that they were prepared to recognize Field Marshal Alexander's authority to the west of the agreed demarcation line, with minor changes . . .

On 25 May, British 8th Army H.Q. announced that the withdrawal of Yugoslav troops from Austria had been completed.

On 22 June 1945, Field Marshal Alexander told a press conference in Milan that the Trieste problem had been solved at the peace conference.

General McCreery arriving at the Trieste Conference on 16 May.

Yugoslav troops evacuating Klagenfurt. ▶

Members of the first Austrian post-war government: Figl, Schaerf, Weinberger with Marshals Koniev and Malinovsky.

MGAF-GO (I)   Appendix „D"   Militär-Regierung Deutschland

General Order No. 1

(Pursuant to Military Government Law No. 52: Blocking and Control of Property)

Allgemeine Vorschrift Nr. 1

(Zur Ausführung des Gesetzes Nr. 52 der Militärregierung: Sperre und Beaufsichtigung von Vermögen)

General Order No. 1 as published by Military Government in all German dailies.

ALLIED CONTROL COUNCIL TAKES OVER IN GERMANY   5 June 1945

The four Military Governors: General Robertson, Marshal Sokolovsky, General Koenig and General Clay.

Control Council Agreement being signed in Marshal Zhukov's H.Q. on 5 June 1945.

American troops taking over their sector in Berlin in early July.

BERLIN BECOMES A FOUR-POWER GARRISON. WESTERN ALLIES WITHDRAW FROM MECKLENBURG, SAXONY AND THURINGIA

1–4 July 1945

German map showing territories evacuated by the Western Allies in July 1945, in accordance with zonal agreements.

Allied MP's patrolling the streets of Berlin.

Zonal control in Linz, Austria.

Europe 1945: Refugees packing railway stations. The Chief of the Allied Liaison Section published the following estimates of displaced persons in the British and American zones: 1·2 million Frenchmen; 200,000 Belgians; 200,000 Dutchmen; 100,000 Luxemburgers; 1·5 million Russians; 600,000 Poles; 100,000 Yugoslavs; 60,000 Czechs; 10,000 Greeks; 10,000 Danes; 10,000 Norwegians and 350,000 Italians.

REFUGEES AND DISPLACED PERSONS IN GERMANY, 1945

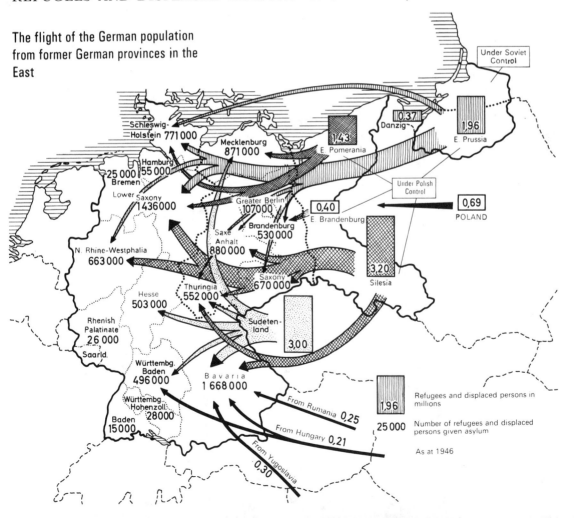

The flight of the German population from former German provinces in the East

Under Soviet Control

Under Polish Control

Schleswig-Holstein 771 000

Mecklenburg 871 000

Danzig 0,37

E. Prussia 1,96

Hamburg 55 000

25 000 Bremen

E. Pomerania 1,43

Lower Saxony 1 436 000

Greater Berlin 107 000

E. Brandenburg 0,40

POLAND 0,69

N. Rhine-Westphalia 663 000

Saxe Anhalt 880 000

Brandenburg 530 000

Silesia 3,20

Hesse 503 000

Thuringia 552 000

Saxony 670 000

Rhenish Palatinate 26 000

Sudetenland 3,00

Saarld.

Württembg. Baden 496 000

Bavaria 1 668 000

Württembg. Hohenzoll. 28 000

Baden 15 000

From Rumania 0,25

From Hungary 0,21

From Yugoslavia 0,30

1,96 Refugees and displaced persons in millions

25 000 Number of refugees and displaced persons given asylum

As at 1946

POTSDAM CONFERENCE: SOVIET ADVANTAGES ARE LEGALIZED

16 July–2 August 1945

Churchill and Eden inspecting the ruins of Berlin.

"Their Quarrel Would Tear the World to Pieces . . ."

Churchill in a letter to Stalin on 28 April 1945:

There is not much comfort in looking into a future where you and the countries you dominate, plus the Communist Parties in many other States, are all drawn up on one side, and those who rally to the English-speaking nations and their associates or Dominions are on the other. It is quite obvious that their quarrel would tear the world to pieces and that all of us leading men on either side who had anything to do with that would be shamed before history.

(from Churchill: *The Second World War*)

The Soviet "People's Democracies"

by Herbert Feis

The determination of the Soviet Union to establish pro-Communist "People's Democracies" and to suppress pro-Western elements in Poland and the smaller states of Central and S.E. Europe, became only too apparent. The Soviet Government ignored all objections to its policy. Western admiration for the courage the Russians had shown in the war was now tempered by fear of Soviet ruthlessness and by the realization that Moscow's disciples in the West would destroy the existing governments wherever they could. The West was also alarmed by the manner in which the Soviet Union, despite incorporating such large areas of Europe, still tried to gain marginal advantages, for instance by trying to coerce

Norway into ceding Spitzbergen, by putting in a claim for an Italian colony in Africa, by demanding control of the Bosphorus, and by using threats in Iran. In the Far East, moreover, the Soviet Union was trying to wrest special privileges from China, with a view to gaining control of Manchuria and Korea.

From Feis: *Zwischen Krieg und Frieden*
(Between War and Peace)

The victor's reparation claims

Allied agreement on reparations from Germany

1. Reparation claims of the U.S.S.R. shall be met by removals from the zone of Germany occupied by the U.S.S.R. and from appropriate German external assets.
2. The U.S.S.R. undertakes to settle the reparation claims of Poland from its own share of reparations.
3. The reparation claims of the United States, the United Kingdom, and other countries entitled to reparations shall be met from the Western zones and from appropriate German external assets.
4. In addition to the reparations to be taken by the U.S.S.R. from its own zone of occupation, the U.S.S.R. shall receive additionally from the Western zones:
   a. 15 per cent of such usable and complete industrial capital equipment, in the first place from the metallurgical, chemical, and machine manufacturing industries, as is unnecessary for the German peace economy and should be removed from the Western zones of Germany in exchange for an equivalent value of food, coal, potash, zinc, timber, clay products, petroleum products, and such other commodities as may be agreed upon.

The "Big Three" after the British elections: Prime Minister Attlee, President Truman and Stalin. Standing behind them are their political advisers: Admiral Leahy, Bevin, Byrnes, and Molotov.

The conference building in Potsdam.

b. 10 per cent of such industrial capital equipment as is unnecessary for the German peace economy and should be removed from the Western zones to be transferred to the Soviet Government on reparation account without payment or exchange of any kind in return.

Removals of equipment as provided in (*a*) and (*b*) above shall be made simultaneously.

5. The amount of equipment to be removed from the Western zones on account of reparations must be determined within 6 months from now at the latest.

6. Removals of industrial capital equipment shall begin as soon as possible and shall be completed within 2 years from the determination specified in Para. 5. The delivery of products covered by Para. 4 (*a*) above shall begin as soon as possible and shall be made by the U.S.S.R. in agreed instalments within 5 years of the date thereof. The determination of the amount and character of the industrial capital equipment unnecessary for the German peace economy, and therefore available for reparation, shall be made by the Control Council under policies fixed by the Allied Commission on Reparations, with the participation of France, subject to the final approval of the Zone Commander in the zone from which the equipment is to be removed.

7. Prior to the fixing of the total amount of equipment subject to removal, advance deliveries shall be made in respect of such equipment as will be determined to be eligible for delivery in accordance with the procedure set forth in the last sentence of Para. 6.

8. The Soviet Government renounces all claims in respect of reparations to shares of German enterprises which are located in the Western zones of occupation in Germany, as well as to German foreign assets in all countries except those specified in Para. 9 below.

9. The Governments of the United Kingdom and the United States renounce their claims in respect of reparations to shares of German enterprises which are located in the Eastern zone of occupation in Germany, as well as to German foreign assets in Bulgaria, Finland, Hungary, Rumania and Eastern Austria.

10. The Soviet Government makes no claims to gold captured by the Allied troops in Germany.

time, France was invited to participate. We accepted—on principle, but without illusions.

It should be said that at this point one matter was settled in a manner which afforded relative satisfaction. In July the London "European Commission", on which France was represented along with Great Britain, the United States and Russia, had established the boundaries of the French zones of occupation. I myself had determined the territories we would control. In Austria, where Béthouart was in command, it was the Tyrol which fell to us, as well as responsibility in Vienna one month out of every four; in Germany, it was the left bank of the Rhine from Cologne to the Swiss frontier and, on the right bank, the state of Baden and a sector of Wurtemberg; we were to be as responsible for the occupation of Berlin as were the other powers. The Allies had subscribed to these conditions save for Cologne, which the British held and insisted on keeping.

CHANGE OF GOVERNMENT IN BRITAIN

26 July 1945

Election Results in Gt. Britain on 26 July 1945

Total votes cast:

	1935	1945
Conservative	10,488,626	8,693,858
Labour	8,325,260	11,935,733
Liberal	1,377,963	2,253,197
Communist	27,117	102,780

Allocation of seats:

Conservative	361	189
Labour	166	393
Liberal	18	22
Communist	1	2

Germany the object of Russo–American rivalry

From the War Memoirs of General de Gaulle

During the final sessions of the Potsdam Conference, Mr. Churchill's replacement by Mr. Attlee, who became Prime Minister, resolved none of the hostile tensions among the Big Three. Settlements concerning Europe and, above all, the Reich, could therefore not be concluded. For my part, I was convinced that this would be the case for a long time. For Germany would henceforth be the object of Russo–American rivalry until, perhaps, it became the stake of their future conflict. For the moment, no arrangement appeared practicable save some sort of *modus vivendi* relative to the occupation and the administration of the national zones, the feeding of the inhabitants and the trials of the war criminals. Before separating, Truman, Stalin and Attlee, admitting their impotence, had arranged for their foreign ministers to convene in London, under less tense circumstances, and attempt to determine the bases of the peace treaties. This

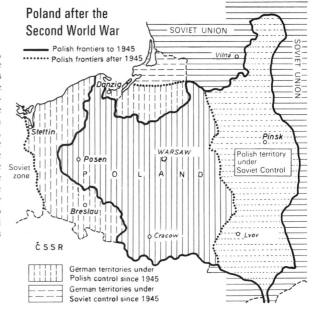

Poland after the Second World War

——— Polish frontiers to 1945
········· Polish frontiers after 1945

German territories under Polish control since 1945

German territories under Soviet control since 1945

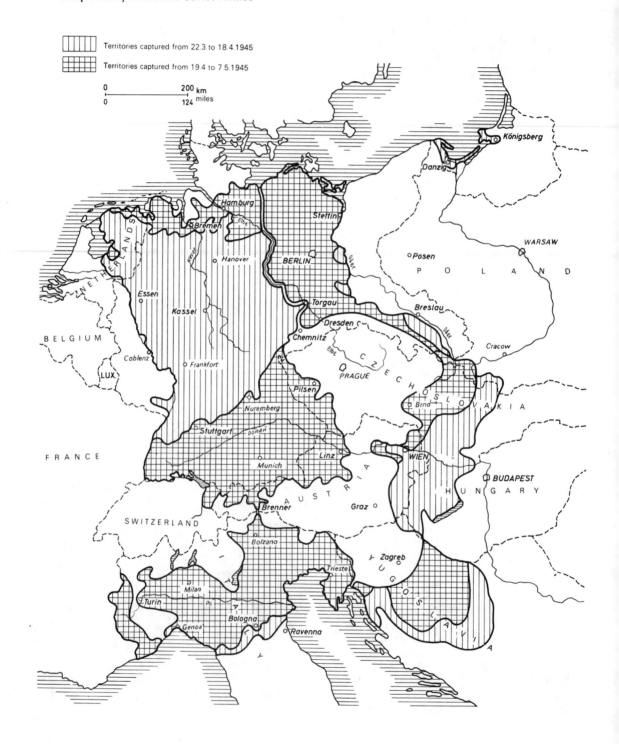

Collapse of "Fortress Europe":
Chronological survey of regions
conquered by Allied and Soviet Armies

Territories captured from 22.3 to 18.4.1945

Territories captured from 19.4 to 7.5.1945

0   200 km
0   124 miles

Königsberg

Danzig

WARSAW

Hamburg
Bremen
Stettin

Hanover
BERLIN
Posen

P O L A N D

NETHERLANDS

Essen
Torgau

Kassel
Breslau

BELGIUM
Dresden
Chemnitz
Cracow

Coblenz
Frankfort
C Z E C H O S L O V A K I A

LUX.
Pilsen
PRAGUE

Nuremberg
Brno

Stuttgart
Donau

FRANCE
Linz
WIEN

Munich
BUDAPEST

H U N G A R Y

Graz

SWITZERLAND
Brenner
A U S T R I A

Bolzano

Zagreb

Trieste
Y U G O S L A V I A

Milan
Po

Turin
Bologna

Genoa
Ravenna

U.S. Secretary of State Stettinius signing the UN Charter.

The San Francisco Conference of the United Nations

The San Francisco Conference was opened in the presence of 850 delegates from the 47 nations who had signed the United Nations Charter by 1 March, with the exception of Poland, which qualified as a United Nation but whose Government of National Unity had not been formed at the time the invitations were issued. The number of participating states was increased to 50 in the course of the Conference, with the admission of Argentina, the Ukrainian and White Russian Soviet Republics and Denmark. Hence the following 51 qualified as founding members of the United Nations: Argentina, Australia, Belgium, Bolivia, Brazil, Canada, Chile, China, Colombia, Costa Rica, Cuba, Czechoslovakia, Denmark, Dominican Republic, Ecuador, Egypt, Ethiopia, France, Great Britain, Greece, Guatemala, Haiti, Honduras, India, Iran, Iraq, Lebanon, Liberia, Luxemburg, Mexico, Netherlands, New Zealand, Nicaragua, Norway, Panama, Paraguay, Peru, Philippine Commonwealth, Poland, El Salvador, Saudi Arabia, Soviet Union, South Africa, Syria, Turkey, Ukraine, Uruguay, U.S.A., Venezuela, Yugoslavia and White Russia.

Chinese delegation signing the United Nations Charter.

THE BIRTH OF THE UNITED NATIONS

San Francisco, 26 June 1945.

Gromyko signing for the Soviet Union.

Manuilski signing for the Ukrainian Soviet Republic.

THE CHARTER OF THE UNITED NATIONS SIGNED ON 26 JUNE 1945

"We, the peoples of the United Nations, determined,

to save succeeding generations from the scourge of war, which twice in our lifetime has brought untold sorrow to mankind;

to reaffirm faith in fundamental human rights, in the dignity and worth of the human person, and in the equal rights of men and women and of nations large and small;

to establish conditions under which justice and respect for obligations arising from treaties and other sources of international law can be maintained;

to promote social progress and better standards of life in larger freedom;

to practice tolerance and live together in peace with one another as good neighbours;

to unite our strength to maintain international peace and security;

to ensure, by the acceptance of principles and the institution of methods, that armed force shall not be used, save in the common interest;

to employ international machinery for the promotion of the economic and social advancement of all peoples;

have resolved to combine our efforts to accomplish these aims, have agreed to the present Charter of the United Nations, and do hereby establish an international organization to be known as the United Nations.

THE RULERS OF EUROPE IN 1945

Albania: Enver Hoxha

Belgium: van Acker

Bulgaria: G. Dimitrov

Czechoslovakia: E. Benesch

Denmark: von Buhl

Germany (Soviet Zone) Zhukov

Germany (American Zone): Eisenhower

Germany (British Zone): Montgomery

Germany (French Zone): Lattre de Tassigny

Finland: Paasikivi

France: De Gaulle

Greece: Archbishop Damaskinos

Great Britain: Attlee

Ireland: S. O'Callaigh

Iceland: S. Björnsson   Italy: Count Sforza   Yugoslavia: Tito   Luxemburg: E. Reuter

etherlands: Prof. Gerbrandy   Norway: Gerhardsen   Austria: L. Figl   Poland: Osobka-Morawski

Portugal: O. Salazar   Rumania: Petru Groza   Sweden: P. A. Hansson   Switzerland: E. von Steiger

Spain: General Franco   Turkey: Ismet Inönü   U.S.S.R.: J. Stalin   Hungary: Z. Tildy

EUROPE AT THE END OF THE SECOND WORLD WAR

The most important political events of 1945

1945

11/1: Truce between British troops (fighting on the side of the Government) and Communist units in Greece.

11/2: In Belgium, Prime Minister Hubert Pierlot (Christ. Soc.) is replaced by Achille van Acker (Soc.).

Greek Government and Central Committee of EAM sign agreement.

23/2: Turkey declares war on the Axis Powers.

February–March: Members of the Szalasi Government in Hungary flee the country. All who are caught are handed over to the new Hungarian Administration for trial and execution.

1/3: Saudi Arabia declares war on Germany.

6/3: National Front (FND) Government under Petru Groza formed in Rumania.

19/3: Soviet Union terminates 1925 Non-Aggression Pact with Turkey with effect from 7 November 1945.

23/3: Iraq, Egypt, Syria, Lebanon, Transjordan, Saudi Arabia and Yemen form an Arab League in Cairo.

27/3: Argentina declares war on the Axis Powers.

2/5: Pierre Laval arrested in Barcelona.

5/5: Finland introduces land reforms in favour of Finnish citizens displaced from ceded territories.

21/5: Switzerland gives in to Allied pressure and signs an agreement on the expropriation of German assets.

2/6: Pope Pius XII broadcasts on the end of the war in Europe and roundly condemns National Socialism.

14/6: Czechoslovak Government lodges claims to German territories.

22/6: Secretary of State Stettinius announces that 14 members of the U.N. Executive would meet in London to plan the first meeting of the Security Council.

25/6: Arrest of Darnand, former Minister of the Interior in the Vichy Government.

26/6: 50 United Nations delegates sign the UN Charter at San Francisco.

June: Formation of political parties and trade-unions in the Soviet-occupied zone of Germany.

14/7: Italy declares war on Japan.

14/7: Prof. Schemerhorn appointed Prime Minister of Dutch "Cabinet of Reconstruction and Rejuvenation".

17/7: German assets blocked in Spain.

19/7: King Leopold III of Belgium informed that his return to the throne is subject to the approval of Parliament. Accusations of friendliness towards collaborators during the Occupation persuade him to remain in Switzerland. His brother, Prince Charles, remains Regent of Belgium.

27/7: Marshal Zhukov orders the setting up of a Central German Administration for the Soviet Zone of Occupation in the former government quarter of Berlin.

14/8: Soviet Union signs pact of friendship with Chiang Kai-Shek.

16/8: Soviet-Polish border agreement signed in Moscow.

27/8: Soviet Military Administration orders registration of all officials and members of the Nazi Party, the SA, SS and Gestapo.

28/8: Soviet Military Administration orders speed-up of production drive in Soviet Zone.

31/8: President Truman asks Attlee to admit 100,000 Jews to Palestine, before any final decision. Arab League reminds America of President Roosevelt's written promise to Ibn Saud not to arrive at a decision without the agreement of both Jews and Arabs.

August: Political parties formed in the American zone of Germany.

Marshal Pétain tried for high treason in Paris (the Marshal is sentenced to death and later reprieved to life imprisonment).

Poland agrees to cede her E. provinces to the Soviet Union.

10/9: Land reforms in the Soviet-occupied zones of Germany (expropriation and distribution of all estates larger than 200 acres).

11/9–2/10: Foreign Ministers confer in London.

23/9: Russians withdraw their entries from international sports meeting in the Olympia Stadium Berlin.

September–December: Soviet troops withdraw from Czechoslovakia.

5/10: Otto Grotewohl and Kurt Schumacher disagree on the overall leadership of the German Social Democratic Party at its first General Conference in Weenigsee, near Hanover.

Spanish troops withdraw from Tangier. Restoration of international status.

21/10: In elections for the French Constituent Assembly, Communist Party obtains the largest number of votes, followed by Socialists and M.R.P. (*Mouvement Républicain Populaire*).

Elections in Luxemburg, following the return of Grand-Duchess Charlotte. Trial of some 10,000 collaborators. Coalition Government formed.

24/10: Ratification of United Nations Charter. Fifty-one nations sign the Charter before the end of the year.

27/10: President Truman announces 12 fundamental points of U.S. foreign policy.

October: Laval tried and sentenced to death for high treason.

Egypt, Iraq, Syria and Lebanon warn that the setting up of a Jewish state in Palestine will be followed by war.

6/11: Hungarian elections lead to the victory of Smallholders' Party over Socialists and Communists.

9/11–21/12: Allied Conference in Paris on German reparations. Allocation of German foreign assets.

10/11: Pro-Communist Popular Front Government under Enver Hoxha formed in Albania, and recognized by the U.S.S.R., Britain and America.

11/11: Almost 90% of the Yugoslav electorate vote for Popular Liberation Front candidates.

13/11: Charles de Gaulle becomes Prime Minister of Provisional Government of France.

16/11: Preparatory Conference of UNESCO (United Nations Educational Scientific and Cultural Organization) in London.

18/11: Salazar Government re-elected in Portugal without any effective opposition. (The autocratic Salazar regime has held power since 1932).

20/11: International Military Tribunal begins trial of war criminals in Nuremberg.

25/11: Coalition Government in Austria between People's Party, Socialists and Communists. Leopold Figl appointed Chancellor. Karl Brenner is the new President.

29/11: Yugoslavia proclaimed a People's Republic. Peter II dethroned. Tito's Government recognized by Big Three.

8/12: Christian Democrats, Social Democrats, Communists and Liberal Democrats form Anti-Fascist Bloc in Berlin.

1–26/12: Moscow Conference: Foreign Ministers of Big Three agree on Peace Treaties with Italy, Rumania, Bulgaria, Hungary and Finland, and on the withdrawal of U.S. and Soviet troops from China. Korea to become an independent state. Commission for Far East and Allied Council for Japan appointed. Trieste to be administered jointly.

21/12: Social Democrats and Communists in the Soviet sector of Berlin agree to unite under certain conditions.

24/12: Curfew lifted in Berlin.

Will Germany be able to save her soul?

By Franz Werfel

It is a terrible trial you are facing, German men and women, a trial without equal in the history of the world. Not in the defeat of your proud armies, not in the ruins of your flourishing cities, not in the millions whom you have driven from their gutted homesteads and who are now wandering homeless through the lands—not in all this suffering, horrible though it is, lies the terrible trial you have to undergo. The same sorrow that now drives you hollow-eyed over your ruined streets, was what you cold-heartedly prepared for others, not even bothering to look back at all the havoc you had caused. The other nations have survived their suffering. You, too, will survive yours, but only on condition that you save your souls. And this is your terrible trial and the great question: Will Germany be able to save her soul?

*

As a precondition, you will have to take a long look at your past and acknowledge your guilt. German men and women, do you know what they did in your name during the "Great Years of Salvation" (1939–1945)—do you know that it was Germans who killed millions and millions of peaceable, harmless and innocent people with methods that would make even the devil blush with shame? Do you know about the ovens and gas chambers of Maidanek, the dung-heap of rotting corpses in Buchenwald, Belsen and hundreds of other hell camps like these? Do you know of the fertilizer and soap factories set up in the vicinity of many a camp, lest human fat and human bones be lost to the German economy? Have you heard about the camp commandant's wife who had a predilection for lampshades made of human skins?

Many of you will pale, turn away and murmur: "What has all that to do with me?" That is just it: it has to do with you, with every least one of you. If ever the course of history has expressed God's judgment, it has done so here and now. Did you not boast of your "national communion", in which the individual was no more than a fanatical atom, unconditionally serving the whole? It was not individual criminals, therefore who committed all these horrors, but your "communion", in which each stood for all, and all for each. The crimes of National Socialism and the unspeakable denigration of German civilization are but the logical outcomes of the devilish exaltation of the rights of the strongest and the claim that right is merely what serves the nation, or rather a few party bosses and swindlers. Nothing can undo the fact that you not only heeded these devilish doctrines, but that you embraced them fervently, defending them with fire, steel and blood. Never before has a less heroic generation boasted a more heroic philosophy. Too late have your eyes been opened to the revolting behaviour of your leaders, bosses, and generals.

*

Comfort ye, comfort ye my people, exclaimed the prophet Isaiah in the Bible, a book to which you may return with profit. Every nation has its comforters, of which no defeat can rob it. They bear true witness to the nation's glory before men and of its destiny before God.

German men and women, in this terrible hour of trial, remember with humility and gratitude your great masters, who will speak for you through all eternity. They alone can wipe out your shame. Before God, who alloweth all things to pass, yea, even this hour.

From *Ruhr Zeitung*, 19 May 1945

THE COLLAPSE OF JAPAN'S "CO-PROSPERITY SPHERE" IN S.E. ASIA

The last hundred days of the
Second World War in Asia

1945

A GOD IS DEFEATED

Rise and Decline of Japan as a Great Power

On 7 December 1941, when Japanese planes swooped down on the U.S. Fleet in Pearl Harbour, and America declared war on the Axis Powers—Germany, Italy and Japan—the Second World War took on a new dimension.

Japan's policies at the time were being moulded on the one hand by extremist groups associated with the Army, and on the other hand by liberal and moderate politicians round the Japanese Navy. The Army aimed at military control of the entire Asiatic mainland, while the Liberals wanted to consolidate Japan's position by diplomatic means. The Army gained the upper hand, by its skilful exploitation of China's internal weakness. This enabled Japan to cut off Manchuria and Jehol Province and, in 1937, to declare war on China. Japan's expansionist policies could not but arouse the suspicions of the United States. At the time, the Japanese Navy was no match for the U.S. Fleet; in particular it was short of oil, which could only be secured by conquests in British S.E. Asia, a fact that did not escape the British Government. When British power in the East was greatly weakened by the conflict with Germany, the balance of power in S.E. Asia shifted radically, the more so as America, too, became increasingly involved in the Atlantic operations. Roosevelt knew that Japan's Achilles' heel was her lack of raw materials, and hoped by economic pressure gradually to ease Japan out of the Axis. Faced with the alternative of having to give in to U.S. pressure or else seizing raw material supplies in S.E. Asia by force, Japanese moderates made a final effort to obtain American recognition of Japan's right to retain the territories she had annexed from China. When America refused to yield, the extremists took over and prepared for immediate war. General Tojo, one of their Party, became head of the Government and, a few weeks later, sent a shower of bombs on Pearl Harbour.

The Japanese advanced with surprising speed, capturing the rich sources of raw material in the south in little more than three months. But instead of consolidating their gains, they scattered their Fleet in far-flung campaigns, while the Americans preferred to concentrate their forces and bide their time. Then, only seven months after Pearl Harbour, the Americans scored their decisive Midway victory, and changed the entire course of the war. America's steadily growing arms potential prevented a Japanese come-back; Japan's plan of conquest was shattered, and America's victory only a question of time.

After the loss of Guadalcanal, where the Japanese had tried to cut the American supply route to Australia, and after fierce battles for the Solomon Islands, the Japanese Imperial H.Q. was forced on 25 March 1943, to go over to the defensive. The Japanese Navy was ordered to hold a line running from the Aleutian Archipelago through Wake, Marshall and Gilbert Islands to the Bismark Archipelago, with the result that Rabaul, the natural harbour in the Bismark Archipelago became a vast Japanese base. In June 1943, the Americans launched their offensive against Japanese bases in the Solomon Islands and on the S.E. and E. coasts of New Guinea. The experiences gained during this long and bloody campaign, during which the Japanese were thrown back step by step, led to a change in strategy towards the end of 1943, when General MacArthur, Allied Commander, S.W. Pacific, decided to by-pass the Japanese bases in Rabaul and New Guinea, and to land to the rear of the Japanese by a series of "island hops". Thence he would blast the Japanese concentrations from the air. Early in 1944, Rabaul was isolated by the occupation of the Admiralty Islands, and the Japanese centres in New Guinea were rendered impotent by American landings and subsequent advances from the N. coast. Towards the end of 1943, the U.S. Fleet had been so greatly augmented with new ships that it was able to launch an independent offensive through the Central Pacific. A trial assault on the Aleutian Islands was followed in November 1943 by an attack on the Gilbert Islands; in January–February, 1944 by an attack on the Marshall Islands and in June–July, 1944 by an attack on the Marianas. In the autumn of 1944, the two U.S. spearheads linked up in a common attack on the Philippines, culminating in the storming of Luzon in January, 1945.

U.S. marines of the 10th Army advancing on Okinawa.

Their landing on Iwo Jima on 19 February 1945, brought the Americans to the gates of the Japanese Home Islands. Okinawa, in the Ryukyu Archipelago, an apparently invincible fortress with a network of underground fortifications, was now Nippon's last bulwark. With its fall (1 April 1945) and Britain's success in opening the Burma road (May, 1945), conditions were ripe for the invasion of Japan (Summer of 1945). Neither the American nor the Japanese troops did, however, have the slightest inkling that the last hundred days of the murderous war in the Pacific had already begun.

Even when Japan's Allies in Europe had lost the war, the Japanese continued to fight with a fanaticism that can only be explained in terms of Japan's history and religion. The tattered Japanese soldier, who emerged from a rock cave in Okinawa, reporting that his superiors had ordered a fight to the last man, and who added laconically that he was just that, was typical of the Japanese attitude. Yet another facet of the Pacific war sprang from this mentality: the fact that the Japanese called their suicide planes Kamikazes (Divine Wind) after the typhoon which destroyed the fleet of Kublai Khan off the coast of Japan in 1281.

After the end of the bloody battle for Okinawa, the Americans intensified their air offensive on the Japanese Home Islands, hoping to break the resistance of the Japanese people with a rain of bombs. The man behind this offensive, General Spaatz, had proved his mettle in the strategic bombardment of German cities. Needless to say, the offensive was also directed against Japanese naval bases and against military and industrial centres.

In S.E. Asia, the Australians had meanwhile landed on Borneo, where they succeeded in driving the Japanese into the jungle. In Burma, the British had pushed the Japanese back to the impassible mountain territory on the borders of Thailand. The threat to the Home Islands, finally, forced the Japanese to withdraw their troops from S. China, with the result that the Chinese, supported by Allied bombers, could continue their advance from Nanning to Kweilin. In the N.E., the Chinese Communist Army was cutting Japanese communications between Manchuria and China; in the S.E., American bombers were pounding the remaining Japanese forces. That, in brief, was the situation at the beginning of August 1945, when Harry S. Truman, the new American President, was placed before the ominous decision of whether or not to use the atomic bomb against Japan. The realization that the Japanese defences were so formidable that tremendous American losses must be expected from a direct assault, and the hope that an atomic bomb might convince the Japanese of the hopelessness of all further resistance, finally decided the President: at 9:15 a.m., on 6 August 1945, the *Enola Gray,* a B-29 Superfortress of the U.S.A.A.F. from Tinian (Mariana Islands) dropped the first atomic bomb on Hiroshima in S. Japan. Before that date, the Americans, British and Chinese had issued an ultimatum to Japan, drafted at the Potsdam Conference, which the Japanese had chosen to ignore.

Despite the shock that the bomb caused in Japan, the Japanese Government refused to agree to an unconditional surrender; even the Soviet declaration of war on 8 August 1945, and the entry of the Red Army under Marshal Vassilevsky into Manchuria and N. Korea on 8 August, failed to alter their resolve. After dropping millions of leaflets to warn the Japanese of further devastating raids, the Americans exploded a second atomic bomb over Nagasaki at 12 noon on 9 August.

At this late stage, the Emperor Hirohito forced the Supreme Council to accept the unconditional surrender terms, after hours of discussion. A telegram, demanding only the continuance of the dynasty, was accordingly dispatched to the Allied Governments via Sweden and Switzerland on 10 August. The Allies replied on 11 August that the Japanese people themselves would have to decide what sort of government they wanted, but that the Allied Supreme Commander in Japan—General MacArthur—reserved the right to have a say in all government decisions. The God had been vanquished at last.

On 2 September 1945, a Japanese delegation headed by Foreign Minister Shigemitsu arrived on board the U.S. battleship *Missouri* to sign the official instrument of surrender before General MacArthur, and in the presence of American, British, Chinese, Soviet, Australian, Canadian, French, Dutch, and New Zealand delegates. In November 1945, the capitulation of all Japanese troops in the Pacific, in S.E. Asia, and on the E. Asiatic mainland was completed.

The year 1945 brought S.E. Asia not only the end of Japanese domination, but also the rise of national movements of independence. Like Europe, Asia, too, changed its face completely after the war. As Raymond Aron put it: "In 1945, all that was left was a diplomatic field of force; it spanned the five continents and was dominated by two giants". Europe had lost her political dominance at last. The consequences were formulated by the leader of the Indian Congress Party, when he said: "The day of Europe is waning; the suns of America and Asia are in the ascendant".

The war in the Pacific at the end of 1944

0 ____ 3000
km
0 ____ 1860 miles

S O V I E T   U N I O N

Alaska

Outer Mongolia

Manchuria

Kamchatka

Aleutian Is.

Sakhalin

Peking

KOREA

Kuril Is.

PACIFIC   OCEAN

T i b e t

Chungking

Tokyo

IA

Ryukyu Arch.

Bonin Is.

Midway-Is.

BURMA

Okinawa

Iwo Is.

Volcano-In.

Marcus-In.

Hawaii-Is.

Hong Kong

TAIWAN
(Formosa)

Marianas Is.

Wake

THAILD

FR.
INDO-CHINA

Manila

PHILIPPINES

Guam

Eniwetok

Marshall-
In.

Sumatra

Java

Singapore

Borneo

Celebes

Timor

New Guinea

Yap

Palau-Is.

Caroline Is.

Truk

Ponape

Gilbert Is.

Equator

Palmyra Is.

Canton Is.

BRIT.-
MALAYA

O   Z   E   A   N

Solomon Is.

New
Hebrides

Samoa-Is.

Fiji Is.

New Caledonia

AUSTRALIA

Sydney

NEW ZEALAND

Under Japanese control in August 1942
Line reached by U.S. and Allied Forces on 31.12.1944
Under Japanese control on 31.12.1945

1943

12/3: Pacific Conference opened in Washington. Operations against Japan decided.

1944

18/6: Resignation of Tojo Cabinet. New Japanese Government formed under General Koiso and Admiral Yonai.
Mid-August: Change of command of U.S. Pacific Fleet: U.S. 5th Fleet becomes 3rd Fleet. Admiral Halsey replaces Admiral Spruance as Commander and prepares next operation in Hawaii.
18/10: President Roosevelt recalls General Stilwell from China.

1945

26/1: Change of command of U.S. Pacific Fleet. 3rd Fleet becomes 5th Fleet. Admiral Spruance returns to former post. Vice-Admiral Mitcher replaces Vice-Admiral McCain as Commander of Fast Carrier Task Force 58 (previously Task Force 38).
January: Japanese transfer 11th, 25th and 27th Divisions and 1st Tank Division from Manchuria to Japan.
11/2: Roosevelt, Stalin and Churchill decide at Yalta—without the knowledge of China—that the Soviet Union is to be given post-war control of E. Chinese and S. Manchurian Railway, and of Japanese-annexed Port Arthur and Dairen on Kwantung Peninsula. Russia's control of Outer Mongolia to continue.
February: Stalin agrees at Yalta to participate in the war against Japan within about 3 months of the termination of hostilities in Europe.
24/3: The Deputy Japanese Minister of War, Lt. General Shibayama, informs the Japanese Diet of the formation of a militia for the defence of the Home Islands.
Late March: Kettsu, the last Japanese operational plan for the defence of the Home Islands, is issued.
3/4: General MacArthur becomes Supreme Commander of U.S. Forces in the Pacific: Admiral Nimitz appointed Commander-in-Chief Pacific Fleet.

5/4: Soviet Union terminates non-aggression pact with Japan.
6/4: General MacArthur's H.Q. (AFPAC) set up in Manila.
9/4: General Wedemeyer meets officers of the U.S. 10th Air Force and of the India–Burma Front, to discuss the transfer of the 10th U.S. Air Force to China.
14/4: Japanese Army Group China is ordered to transfer four divisions from Central to Northern China.
21/4: U.S. Joint Chiefs of Staff plan the capture of Hong Kong.
2/5: General Wedemeyer appoints General Stratemeyer Commander of U.S.A.A.F. in China. Stratemeyer takes command of 10th and 14th Air Forces.
4/5: Admiral Mountbatten proposes a new plan for Malayan campaign to British Chiefs of Staff.
25/5: U.S. Joint Chiefs of Staff plan Operation Olympic, the invasion of the Japanese Home Islands on 1/11/1945.
27/5: Change of command of U.S. Pacific Fleet: 5th Fleet becomes 3rd Fleet. Admiral Halsey and Vice-Admiral McCain replace Admiral Spruance and Vice-Admiral Mitcher (Task Force 58 becomes Task Force 38 again).
30/5: Admiral Mountbatten arrives in Delhi to discuss Operations Zipper and Mailfist (the capture of Malaya and Singapore) with his Staff.
12/6: British Air Ministry announces that 26,000 airmen and women will be used in the war against Japan.
14/6: U.S. Joint Chiefs of Staff ask Generals MacArthur and Arnold and Admiral Nimitz to make arrangements for the occupation of Japan, in case the Japanese Government should suddenly be forced to capitulate.
1/7: Moscow: Negotiations with Chinese Premier Soong on Yalta decisions. Negotiations interrupted on 13 July, when Stalin and Molotov leave for Potsdam.
Early July: Japanese repeat an earlier attempt (February 1945) to end the war through Soviet intermediaries.
23/7: 10th U.S.A.A.F. set up H.Q. in Kunming, China.
26/7: Potsdam Declaration on Japan (unconditional surrender) drafted.
7/8: An advance party of the Staff of U.S. 1st Army arrives in Luzon to plan the invasion of Japan.

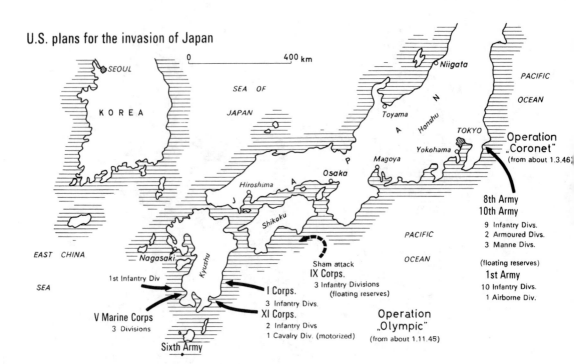

U.S. plans for the invasion of Japan

Chronological Table of the most important military events in the Pacific from 1941 to March 1945

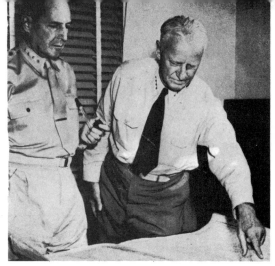

General MacArthur and Admiral Nimitz.

1941

10/12: Japanese land on Luzon and Guam. First attack on Wake I. beaten off.

1942

2/1: Japanese enter Manila.
26/1: Japanese land on Solomon Is.
9/4: Fall of Bataan.
5–6/5: Japanese take Corregidor.
7/8: U.S. 1st Marine Division lands on N. Beach, Guadalcanal.

1943

8/2: Japanese evacuate Guadalcanal.
11/5: U.S. 7th Division lands on Attu (Aleutian Is.).
30/6: U.S. troops land on Rendova (Solomon Is.).
1/11: Americans land on Bougainville, the largest of the Solomon Islands.
20–23/11: U.S. 2nd Marine Division lands on Tarawa, Makin and Abemama (Gilbert Is.).

1944

31/1: Americans land on Kwajalein (Marshall Is.).
17/2: U.S. 2nd Division lands on Eniwetok Atoll (S. of Marshall Is.).
29/2: U.S. invade Admiralty Is. and Bismarck Archipelago.
Early March: Decisive jungle-battle on Bougainville ends in American victory.
12–15/6: U.S. marines land on Saipan (Marianas).
15/9: Americans land on Morotai, S.W. of Mindanao.
20/10: Recapture of Philippines begun with the fall of Leyte.
15/12: Americans land on Mindoro (Philippines).

1945

7/1: U.S. troops land on Luzon (Philippines).
9/1: U.S. 6th Army lands 4 divisions in the Gulf of Lingayan (Luzon).
3/2: Troops of U.S. 6th Army enter Manila and liberate 3,700 Allied prisoners.
16/2: Americans recapture Bataan.
19/2: After launching continued air attacks from carrier bases and a 3-day bombardment by battleships and cruisers, 2 U.S. Marine Divisions land on Iwo Jima, which is captured on 16/3 after very heavy fighting.
28/2: Americans recapture Corregidor.
10/3: Units of U.S. 8th Army land on Zamboanga Peninsula, Mindanao (Philippines).

Japanese troops in Asia on 18 June 1945

Pacific theatre:	approximately
Marshall and Gilbert Islands	35,000
Caroline Is.	100,000
Bonin Is.	20,000
Solomon Is.	80,000
Philippines	90,000
Taiwan (Formosa)	190,000
Ryukyu Is.	100,000
South and East Asia:	
New Guinea	15,000
Timor and Celebes	150,000
Java, Sumatra and Borneo	150,000
Malaya	55,000
Andaman and Nicobar Is.	20,000
Burma	65,000
Thailand	40,000
French Indo-China (Cambodia, Laos, Vietnam)	110,000
S. China	500,000
E. China	160,000
N. China	325,000
Manchuria	650,000
Korea	225,000
Japan	1,415,000
S. Sakhalin	25,000
Kuril Is.	95,000
	4,615,000

These troops were divided into 106 Infantry divisions, 4 armoured divisions, and 19 supply divisions.

Amphibious force off Iwo Jima on 19 February 1945.

The Commanders of the American Forces in the Pacific after May 1945:

Supreme Commander U.S. Forces in the Pacific:
General Douglas MacArthur.

C.-in-C. Pacific Fleet:
Fleet Admiral Chester W. Nimitz:

Commander U.S. Strategic Air Force:
General Carl Spaatz (from 9 July 1945).

Deputy Commander, U.S. Strategic Air Force:
Lt.-General B. McK. Giles.

Commander, U.S. Far East Air Force:
General George C. Kenney.

Commander, U.S. Forces in Central Pacific:
General R. C. Richardson.

Commander, U.S. Forces in W. Pacific:
Lt.-General W. D. Styer.

AMERICA'S ATTACK ON JAPAN'S INNER DEFENCES

The battle for Okinawa and the Philippines

CHRONOLOGICAL TABLE

1945

1/4: U.S. 10th Army lands 4 Divisions on Okinawa. American landing forces subjected to constant Kamikaze attacks. U.S. losses: 11 destroyers and 15 minor vessels.

2/4: XIV Corps of U.S. 6th Army reaches An Pablo on Luzon.

U.S. 10th Army continues advance on Okinawa, capturing Kadena and Yontan airstrips and rendering them operational.

3/4: U.S. 8th Army clears Bolo Ridge on Cebu (Philippines).

U.S. troops on Okinawa advance to Atanniya-Futema-Chi-yunna-Isa line in the west.

4/4: Troops of U.S. 10th Army in W. Okinawa advance into the Uchitomare sector.

7/4: Okinawa: suicide attack by Japanese naval squadron and Kamikaze beaten off by Task Force 58. Japanese battleship *Yamato*, 1 cruiser and 2 destroyers sunk.

U.S. troops complete occupation of Cactus Ridge on Okinawa.

8/4: Troops of U.S. 8th Army in the Philippines occupy Hill 27 on Cebu and hold their positions during severe counter-attacks at night.

9/4: U.S. troops land on Jolo Is., Sulu Sea.

10/4: Troops of U.S. 1st Cavalry Division take Mauban on Luzon, while other American units occupy Atimonan. General Suzuki killed at sea during the Japanese withdrawal from Cebu to Mindanao. Hill 20 on Cebu captured by U.S. troops and Filipino guerillas. Hill 26 captured by U.S. troops.

11/4: Japanese launch two-day air offensive against U.S. ships off Okinawa. Task Force 58, which has to bear the brunt of the attack, decides not to ask for reinforcements.

12/4: Troops of U.S. 10th Army take Kakazu Ridge on Okinawa. After heavy artillery fire, the Japanese launch a series of counter-attacks by night, chiefly against the 96th Division. The American line holds, though some Japanese units succeed in breaking through.

13/4: Units of U.S. 8th Army in the Philippines prepare to land on Mindanao.

15/4: Japanese offer desperate resistance on Motobu Peninsula, Okinawa, and cause heavy casualties among the attacking 6th Marine Division.

16/4: On Cebu, American troops make slow progress in their advance on Cebu City. Japanese effect orderly withdrawal after nightfall.

At 8 a.m., after heavy bombing from the sea and the air, U.S. 77th Division lands on the S. and S.W. coast of Ie, W. of Okinawa, advances rapidly, and captures an airfield.

17/4: U.S. troops on Luzon attack Mt. Mataasna Bundoc, the last Japanese stronghold in the S. of the island.

After heavy bombardment from the sea and the air, units of the 24th Division (U.S. 8th Army) land on Mindanao, meeting little Japanese resistance, and capturing Polloc Harbour.

Jolo Island in U.S. hands, except for Mount Daho.

3rd Amphibian Corps puts an end to organized Japanese resistance on Motobu Peninsula (Okinawa) by occupying Yae Take Ridge.

18/4: On Mindanao, U.S. 24th Division begins to advance on Fort Pikit, a Japanese key position on the road to Kabacan. U.S. troops also capture Cobabato, Tamontaca, and Lomopog. On Palawan Is., U.S. units take Balabac.

19/4: Severe fighting for Kakazu Ridge, Okinawa. Units of the 96th Division advance through Kaniku and take up positions before Nishibaru Ridge.

20/4: U.S. 10th Army makes small progress on Okinawa in the face of obstinate Japanese resistance.

21/4: Fort Pikit on Mindanao taken by U.S. troops after Japanese withdrawal.

On Okinawa, U.S. troops continue to attack Kakazu, N. of Gusukuma, with heavy losses.

22/4: U.S. 10th Corps from Morotai lands on Mindanao in support of 24th Division. Japanese forces on the island are split in two.

U.S. troops overrun Mt. Daho on Jolo Is.

Palawan Is. completely in U.S. hands.

U.S. troops occupy Nishibaru Village on Okinawa.

23/4: Kabacan on Mindanao falls to the Americans. Other U.S. troops reach Fort Pikit.

24/4: The occupation of Ie Shima (Ryukyu Is.) continues. American losses so far: 172 killed, 902 wounded and 46 missing.

27/4: General Eichelberger proposes plan to clear Mindanao of Japanese forces. Japanese withdraw to make a last-ditch stand in the hills N.W. of Davao City.

Japanese launch severe 2-day air attack on U.S. ships off Okinawa.

Little progress is made by U.S. 96th Division on Okinawa, despite tank and flame-thrower support. Japanese continue desperate resistance, particularly on the right flank.

28/4: By occupying Digos, U.S. forces split Japanese on Mindanao in two.

29/4: U.S. troops on Mindanao advance through Coronon and Astorga. Other units reach Guma, N.W. of Digos.

On Okinawa, U.S. troops take Hill 138, overlooking Shuri which is now in their direct line of fire.

30/4: On Mindanao, U.S. troops come to within 4 miles of Davao and capture Daliao airstrip.

3/5: U.S. troops land at Davao (Mindanao) and clear the ruined town.

On Okinawa, Japanese launch their only major counter-offensive in the area by landing troops behind the American lines on the W. and E. coast, with strong artillery and air support. The operation is a costly failure: 800 Japanese are killed, and most of the landing craft are destroyed.

4/5: Troops of U.S. 6th Army take Mt. Haruna on Luzon.

7/5: On Okinawa, U.S. 10th Army takes direct control of operations in the south. Major-General Hodge orders an attack on the Asa-Dakesi-Gaja line, with a view to a co-ordinated offensive against the south.

8/5: On Mindanao, troops of U.S. 8th Army capture bridgeheads on the Talomo River, N. of Mintal.

9/5: On Okinawa, Lt. General Buckner orders a general offensive for 11 May.

10/5: Okinawa: 5th Marine Division launches attack in the Asa estuary at 3 a.m. Despite heavy resistance, U.S. marines advance through Asa and establish a 200-mile bridgehead. Under heavy fire from Shuri, Americans make further progress. Other units reach Zebra Hill and defend it successfully against Japanese night attack.

11/5: General offensive on Okinawa launched after concentrated shelling for half an hour. U.S. troops advance in several places south of Asa and take the precincts of Amike, thus gaining control over nearby Naha, the capital. 5th Marine Division surrounds Japanese forces south of Awacha.

12/5: 6th Marine Division on the west coast, north of Naha, advances on Sugar Loaf Hill, a Japanese key position S.E. of Amike. Japanese repulse the attack.

13/5: U.S. troops reach the edge of Naha.

14/5: U.S. troops capture Naha.
   U.S. carrier *Enterprise* severely damaged by Kamikazes.

15/5: 7th Marine Division halts attack on Wana Ridge, while Japanese positions are softened up by shelling.

17/5: On Mindanao, U.S. troops advance to the N.E. to make contact with local guerilla forces.
   American attack on Wana Ridge (Okinawa) continued without success.

18/5: On Mindanao, U.S. troops complete occupation of Mangima Canyon.
   U.S. troops capture Sugar Loaf Hill on Okinawa.

20/5: U.S. troops occupy Hill 55 on Okinawa. 1st Marine Division captures Wana Ridge after two attacks.

21/5: On Mindanao, U.S. troops advance on Sayre Highway in the N.E. and capture Malaybalay.

22/5: Japanese on Okinawa begin to evacuate supplies and wounded from Shuri.

24/5: During the night, Japanese aircraft make concentrated low-level attacks on airfields on Okinawa and Ie Shima and on U.S. ships. Smaller airborne units land on Yontan airstrip and destroy a number of U.S. planes.

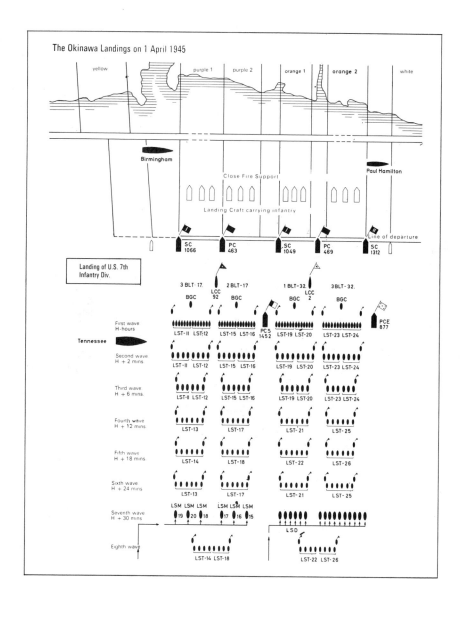

The Okinawa Landings on 1 April 1945

27/5: On Mindanao, U.S. and Filippino troops establish bridge-heads across the Pulangi River, near Sanipon.

On Okinawa, U.S. marines cross the Asato and advance on Naha from the west.

28/5: Last great Japanese air raid on Okinawa. U.S. destroyer *Drexler* is sunk. More than 100 Japanese aircraft are shot down.

29/5: On Luzon, U.S. troops advance on Aritao, while Filippino guerilla forces occupy Cervantes.

On Okinawa, units of U.S. 10th Army cross the canal east of Naha.

30/5: American troops mop up the major part of the north sector of the Yonabaru–Shuri–Naha road on Okinawa.

1/6: After clearing Hill 46 on Okinawa, U.S. 6th Marine Division occupies Shichina and the north bank of the Kokuba. American units occupy Ono-Yama Is. in Naha Bay.

6/6: 6th Marine Division clears the ruined Naha airstrip on Oroku Peninsula.

7/6: Americans storm Mandog on Mindanao.

American units meet stiff Japanese resistance on Oroku Peninsula; other American units take Hill 57.

9/6: U.S. troops on Mindanao breach the last Japanese line of defence and capture Mandog.

10/6: U.S. troops drive Japanese back on Oroku. Some 200 Japanese killed during counter-attacks by night.

12/6: Japanese resistance on Oroku begins to crack. In the south, the Japanese continue to hang on to Yaeju Drake Heights, but the S.E. flank of their defence line has been breached.

13/6: Collapse of Japanese resistance on Oroku. Only 159 Japanese are taken prisoners; the rest have fallen in battle.

15/6: Americans searching the Japanese underground H.Q. on Oroku discover some 200 Japanese dead, including many officers who have committed hara-kiri.

17/6: Final collapse of Japanese 32nd Army on Okinawa. U.S. 7th Division completes occupation of Hills 153 and 115.

18/6: Lt. General Simon B. Buckner, jr., is killed by a Japanese shell, while inspecting an 8th Marine Division advance post.

Major-General Geiger becomes Commander of U.S. 10th Army.

20/6: In the Philippines, U.S. 8th Army concludes Operations Victor I on Panay and Negros, Victor II on Cebu, Boho and Negros, Victor III on Palawan, and Victor IV on Zamboanga.

22/6: U.S. 10th Army completes occupation of Okinawa. Lt. General Mitsuru Ushijima, Commander of Japanese 32nd Army on Okinawa and his Chief of Staff commit hara-kiri. American casualties in the battle for Okinawa: 12,120 killed or missing; 36,631 wounded. Japanese losses: 110,000 killed; 7,400 wounded. During the offensive, 36 American ships were sunk and 368 damaged.

23/6: General Stillwell replaces General Geiger as Commander of U.S. 10th Army on Okinawa. American troops begin systematic mop up of Okinawa.

26/6: U.S. troops reach Pinamola on Mindanao.

Special American units land on Kume Island, in the Okinawa Group.

27/6: Japanese announce Allied landings on Kume. .

28/6: Luzon (Philippines) completely cleared of Japanese.

29/6: Occupation of Kume completed.

30/6: U.S. 10th Army completes occupation of Okinawa.

8/7: Filippino guerillas on Mindanao advance overland from the Gulf of Davao to the Bay. Troops and guerillas of the 116th Infantry Division reach Dadjangasan on the N.W. coast of the Bay, to prepare for the main landing.

12/7: Kiangan (Mindanao) falls to the 6th Division. Japanese continue resistance in the area for a few more days. Americans land on the north coast of Sarangani Bay without meeting resistance.

13/7: Units from Lake Buluan and from Sarangani Bay make contact some 15 miles from the Bay.

15/7: On Mindanao, the landing force makes contact with guerilla units.

25/7: Organized Japanese resistance in Sarangani Bay collapses.

19/8: Japanese delegation arrives in Manila to discuss surrender terms.

U.S. marine watching preparations for Okinawa landing from a troopship.

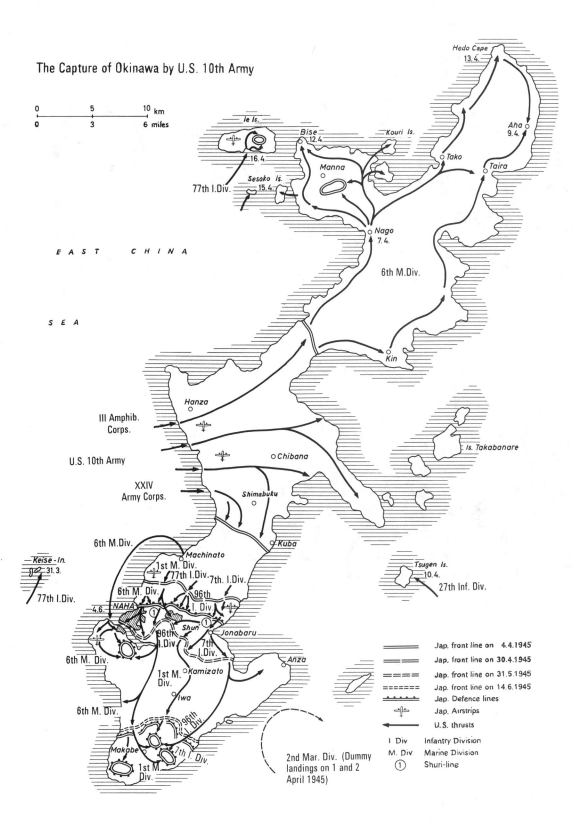

The Capture of Okinawa by U.S. 10th Army

0   5   10 km
0   3   6 miles

E A S T   C H I N A

S E A

Hedo Cape
13.4.

Aha
9.4.

Ie Is.
16.4.

Bise
12.4.

Kouri Is.

Tako

Taira

Manna

Sesoko Is.
15.4.

77th I.Div.

Nago
7.4.

6th M.Div.

Kin

Hanza

III Amphib.
Corps.

U.S. 10th Army

XXIV
Army Corps.

Chibana

Is. Takabanare

Shimabuku

6th M.Div.

Machinato

Kuba

1st M. Div.

77th I.Div. 7th. I.Div.

Keise - In.
31.3.

6th M. Div.

77th I.Div.

96th
I. Div.

Tsugen Is.
10.4.

27th Inf. Div.

NAHA
4.6.

96th
I.Div.

Shuri

Jonabaru

Anza

6th M. Div.

7th
I.Div.

1st M.
Div.

Kamizato

Iwa

6th M. Div.

96th
I. Div.

Makabe

7th I. Div.

1st M.
Div.

2nd Mar. Div. (Dummy
landings on 1 and 2
April 1945)

Jap. front line on 4.4.1945
Jap. front line on 30.4.1945
Jap. front line on 31.5.1945
Jap. front line on 14.6.1945
Jap. Defence lines
Jap. Airstrips
U.S. thrusts

I Div   Infantry Division
M. Div   Marine Division
①   Shuri-line

After preparatory air attacks . . .

. . . and bombardment from warships such as the *Tennessee* (shown here) . . .

. . . Americans launch the largest of all Pacific landing operations.

U.S. 10TH ARMY LANDS IN OKINAWA

8:32 a.m., 1 April 1945

Lt.-General Buckner (right), Commander of U.S. 10th Army on Okinawa with Major-General Hodge, Commander of U.S. XXIV Army Corps.

The U.S. Expeditionary Force

It was Easter Sunday, 1 April 1945. The bombardment ships stood off the beachheads, guns poised and loaded, just waiting for the Japs to make the first move.

Steaming slowly in column formation to the north in support of the Third Amphibious Corps, Major General Roy S. Geiger, commanding, were four old battleships, *West Virginia* (Captain Herbert V. Wiley), *Idaho* (Captain Herbert J. Grassie), *New Mexico* (Captain John M.

Salt Lake City (Captain Edward A. Mitchell), *Portland* (Captain Thomas G. W. Settle), *Pensacola* (Captain Allen P. Mullinix), and *Biloxi* (Captain Paul R. Heineman), and eight speedy destroyers, *Heywood L. Edwards* (Commander Albert L. Shepherd), *Richard P. Leary* (Commander Duncan P. Dixon, Jr.), *Preston* (Commander Goldsborough S. Patrick), *Newcomb* (Commander Ira E. McMillan), *Rooks* (Commander Joseph A. McGoldrick), *Irwin* (Commander Daniel B. Miller), *Callaghan* (Commander Charles M. Bertholf), and *Porterfield* (Commander Don W. Wulzen).

To the south, in much the same formation, were the support ships for the XXIV Army Corps, Lieutenant General John R. Hodge. These ships included three battleships, *Nevada* (Captain Homer L. Grosskopf), *Tennessee* (Captain John B. Hefferman), and *Colorado* (Captain Walter S. Macaulay): four cruisers, *Wichita* (Captain Douglas A. Spencer), *Minneapolis* (Captain Harry B. Slocum), *Birmingham* (Captain Harry D. Power), and *St. Louis* (Captain John B. Griggs).

In general support of the other ships and sprinkled from the beachhead area to the demonstration beachhead along Okinawa's southeastern coast, where a mock landing was to be staged simultaneously with the main landing, were three battleships, *Texas* (Captain Charles A. Baker), *Maryland* (Captain Julian D. Wilson), and *Arkansas* (Captain George M. O'Rear); one cruiser, *Tuscaloosa* (Captain James G. Atkins); and seven destroyers, *Isherwood* (Commander Louis E. Schmidt), *Laffey* (Commander Frederick J. Becton), *Morrison* (Commander James P. Hansen), *Longshaw* (Commander Theodore R. Dogeley), *Zellars* (Commander Leon S. Kintberger), *Wadsworth* (Commander Raymond D. Fusselman), *Laws* (Commander Lester O. Wood), and *Picking* (Commander Benedict J. Semmes, Jr.).

Ships of all sorts; transports, minelayers, gunboats, and so many other sizes and types that the scene more nearly resembled New York Bay than an assault force off Hagushi beachhead, half the world away. Even in their war paint, swishing long lace trains of bubbling wake behind them, the ships seemed literally to be on parade. For the United States Navy there could have been no more impressive Easter pageant.

From *Battle Report*, Vol. V

Okinawa, a Pacific island in the Ryukyu group 325 miles from the Japanese mainland, was intended as a U.S. spring-board for the attack on Japan in the autumn of 1945 and the spring of 1946. U.S. attacking forces numbered some 183,000.

The first U.S. casualties being taken to safety. The resistance of the 120,000 Japanese troops under General Ushijima was slight at first, but stiffened as the Americans advanced to the southern part of the island.

Two million tons of war supplies were brought to Okinawa, partly from the U.S.A. itself. American troops (including 270,000 landed for construction work) came chiefly from bases in Espiritu Santo, Guadalcanal, Saipan and Leyte.

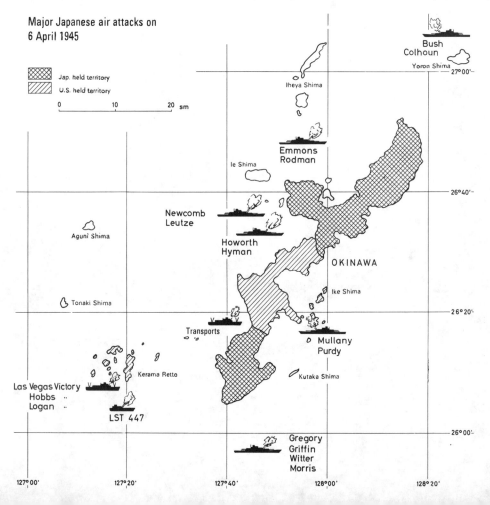

Major Japanese air attacks on 6 April 1945

Jap. held territory

U.S. held territory

0   10   20 sm

Bush
Colhoun
Yoron Shima
27° 00'

Iheya Shima

Emmons
Rodman

le Shima

26° 40'

Newcomb
Leutze

Aguni Shima

Howorth
Hyman

OKINAWA

Ike Shima

Tonaki Shima
26° 20'

Transports

Mullany
Purdy

Kutaka Shima

Las Vegas Victory
Hobbs
Logan

Kerama Retto

LST 447

26° 00'

Gregory
Griffin
Witter
Morris

127° 00'   127° 20'   127° 40'   128° 00'   128° 20'

ADVANCE TO THE INTERIOR
2 April 1945

Japanese Imperial H.Q. announced on 4 April that though American landing forces on Okinawa had suffered heavy casualties in the coastal sector, the enemy had succeeded in expanding his beachhead. Japanese troops in this sector were continuing to engage the enemy in heavy battle.

Japanese troops were also continuing their counter-attacks against the enemy in other parts of the island. The Americans were making strenuous efforts to extend their bridgehead on the west coast of the main island and, under cover of intense naval bombardment, had succeeded in landing more troops.

According to a further communiqué by Imperial H.Q., the Japanese Air Force was keeping up a concentrated attack on enemy vessels in neighbouring waters and had sunk or severely damaged a further thirty-one.

(From *Voelkischer Beobachter*, 5 April 1945)

◄ On 6 April, by which date U.S. troops had already taken Cactus Ridge, Okinawa was raided by a strong U.S. bomber force.

In early May, after beating back a Japanese attack from the rear, U.S. troops reached the Asa–Dakeshi–Gaya line from which they prepared to launch the final offensive.▼

SUICIDE ATTACK BY JAPANESE NAVAL UNIT AND THE SINKING OF THE *YAMATO*

7 April 1945

Vice-Admiral Ho's flagship being blown up.

The loss of the Yamato

On 6 April, the super-battleship *Yamato*, the light cruiser *Yahagi* and 8 Japanese destroyers sailed out to bring relief to the defenders of Okinawa. On 7 April, the *Yahagi* was sunk within two hours of a counter-attack by American carrier-borne planes. The *Yamato*, with Vice-Admiral Ito on board, began to list after several torpedo hits, righted itself after further hits, and was finally attacked by Hellcats and Avengers. Flying just above the water surface, the planes sent at least another five aerial torpedoes into the burning flagship, which slid under completely. 280 of the crew of 2,500 were picked up. Admiral Ito was not among them. Only four Japanese destroyers escaped undamaged.

Close on 400 U.S. carrier-borne aircraft attacked the Japanese naval force off Okinawa.

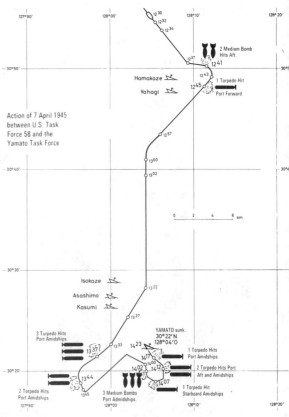

Action of 7 April 1945 between U.S. Task Force 58 and the Yamato Task Force

In their attempt to wipe out the U.S. Fleet off Okinawa, the Japanese sent out 1,900 aircraft but only succeeded in sinking destroyers and minor vessels. In the photograph: a U.S. carrier is hit.

THE JAPANESE AIR AND SEA OFFENSIVE AGAINST THE U.S. FLEET OFF OKINAWA

April–May 1945

Japanese Kamikaze destroys the Mannert L. Abele

But the Kamikazes improved their record by an even wider margin. They sank the destroyer *Mannert L. Abele* (Commander Alton E. Parker) and the LCS 33 (Lieutenant Carroll J. Boone); they solidly smashed into three battleships, *Idaho, New Mexico* (Captain John M. Haines), and *Tennessee* (Captain John B. Hefferman); they seriously damaged six destroyer types, the *Jeffers, Lindsey* (Commander Thomas E. Chambers), *Zellars, Stanly* (Commander John B. Morland), *Purdy* (Commander Frank L. Johnson), and *Cassin Young;* three destroyer escorts, *Rall* (Commander Herman Reich), *Riddle* (Lieutenant Commander Francis P. Steel), and *Whitehurst* (Lieutenant Jack C. Horton), and the LCS 57 (Lieutenant (jg) Harry L. Smith). Nine additional ships suffered minor damage.

The *Mannert L. Abele,* stationed at RP 14, 72 miles northwest of Bolo, was the first ship to be sunk by a "baka"—the humanly piloted glider bomb. She was simultaneously attacked by three diving planes while a dozen more feinted at Commander A. E. Parker's destroyer just out of gun range. The ship was struck by one Kamikaze in the engine room, breaking the keel. As she lay dead in the water, an incredible object winged silently out of the sky, a pudgy, stub-winged thing too small to be an airplane, too big to be a bomb. Only four 20 mm gunners had time to open fire before the Baka's 1,800 pounds of explosives (and 100 pounds of pilot) crashed into the destroyer's side just beneath the forward stack. The ship immediately broke in two and sank, taking 81 of her crew with her.

From *Battle Report,* Vol. V

11 May: U.S. carrier *Bunker Hill* is damaged.

26 U.S. ships were sunk off Okinawa.

On 12 April, the Americans brought down 151 Japanese planes.

THE LAST KAMIKAZE ATTACKS ON OKINAWA

April–May 1945

"The Divine Wind Kept Coming . . ."

By T. Taylor

At the end of each day canvas shrouds slipped into the waters off Okinawa. Death was in the air and on the face of the sea. The Divine Wind blew hot and steady. In April, including both the task force and the invasion forces, a hundred and twenty ships received minor damages, a hundred were damaged severely, and twenty-four were sunk.

. . . (Admiral) Mitcher had come to Okinawa with four task groups. Now there were only enough ships left for three. At 05:00 on 17 April, he disbanded Task Group 58.2, and augmented the other task groups. The Japanese were not winning, but neither were they losing except in equipment and personnel. An average of twenty to thirty *kamikazes* were splashed each day. He sent strikes to Kyushu and raked the fields in desperation, but the Divine Wind kept coming.

From: Flower/Reeves: *The War 1939–1945*

Birth of the Kamikaze

As Admiral Ohnishi spoke, we sensed that he had come here for something more than just to repeat what we already knew was our mission . . . I watched the Admiral's heavily lined face as he spoke again. "In my opinion, there is only one way of assuring that our meagre strength will be effective to a maximum degree. That is to organize suicide attack units composed of Zero fighters armed with 250-kilogramme bombs, with each plane to crash-dive into an enemy carrier . . . What do you think?"

No one spoke for a time, but Admiral Ohnishi's words struck a spark in each of us . . .

*

From the farewell letter of a Kamikaze fighter

Man is only mortal. Death, like life, is a matter of chance. Yet destiny, too, plays a part. I feel confident of my ability in tomorrow's action. Will do my utmost to dive head-on against an enemy warship to fulfil my destiny in defence of the homeland. The time has come when my friend Nakanishi and I must part. There is no remorse whatsoever. Each man is doomed to go his separate way in time . . .

It is my firm belief that tomorrow will be successful. It is my hope that you will share this belief. The time for our departure was set so suddenly that I will not have a chance to write last letters to my relatives and friends. I shall appreciate it if you will write to these people on my behalf, at your convenience, and express my sentiments . . .

From Inoguchi, *The Divine Wind*

◄ A Japanese torpedo-plane leaving its carrier.

On VE-day (8 May) a Japanese Kamikaze fighter dived on the battleship *Missouri*, on which the Japanese later signed the instrument of surrender.

Kamikaze fighters on the alert. During the battle for Okinawa, the Japanese launched some 12 major Kamikaze raids.

American losses in Kamikaze attacks

Thus, as the war against Japan drew to its close, Okinawa became a giant air and naval base which was destined to play a major role in the cold war that followed the war with Japan. For it we paid a heavy price. Thirty naval ships and craft had been sunk, mostly by kamikaze attack, and 368 ships and craft had been damaged. The Fleet lost 763 aircraft. Over 4,900 sailors were killed or missing in action, and an additional 4,824 were wounded. This was by far the heaviest loss incurred in any naval campaign in the war. Tenth Army also suffered heavy casualties: 7,613 killed or missing in action, 31,807 wounded and more than 26,000 non-battle casualties. Sobering thought as it is to record such losses, the sacrifice of these brave men is brightened by the knowledge that the capture of Okinawa helped to bring the Japanese leaders face to face with the inevitable, and that their surrender in August saved many thousands more Americans from suffering flaming death in an assault on the main islands of Japan.

From *Battle Report*, Vol. V

Kamikaze as a counsel of desperation

By Admiral Suzuki

The spirit and the deeds of kamikaze pilots naturally arouse profound admiration. But, considered from the standpoint of strategy, these tactics are a product of defeat.

An able commander would never resort to such extreme measures. The daring attempt to blockade Port Arthur during the Russo–Japanese War was not approved until it was shown that there was a fair chance of rescuing the participants. Their only aim was to sink boats at the entrance to the harbour, but the commanding officer refused his permission for the operation until he was assured that rescue boats would be provided. That is the way of a good commander.

In the midget submarine attack on Pearl Harbour at the outbreak of war we have another example. Admiral Yamamoto would not authorize that part of the operation until it was shown that there was at least some chance of retrieving the small two-man submarines.

Kamikaze attacks, on the other hand, were carried out with no possible hope of return. It is clear evidence of our fear of inevitable defeat that no other chance of turning the tide of war was visualized. The aerial operations which were begun in the Philippines left no possibility of survival. As the able pilots were expended, less experienced pilots had to be used, and finally men who had practically no training were being sent on kamikaze missions.

An Okha bomb (top) being released by a bomber over the target (below).

Admiral Ohnishi's death by hara-kiri

Sometime before daybreak, Admiral Ohnishi's aide was notified that the Admiral had committed hara-kiri. Rushing to the Admiral's residence, the aide found Admiral Ohnishi in the second-floor study where he had disembowelled himself in the traditional manner with a Japanese sword. The abominal cut was cleanly done, but the following attempt by the Admiral to slit his throat was not so successful. When the aide arrived the Admiral was still conscious and said, "Do not try to help me." Thus, refusing both medical aid and a *coup de grâce*, he lingered in agony until six o'clock that evening. His desire to endure this prolonged suffering seemed to be an act of expiation. Alone, after the departure of his staff officers the evening before, Admiral Ohnishi had penned a note which read:

"I wish to express my deep appreciation to the souls of the brave special attackers. They fought and died valiantly with faith in our ultimate victory. In death I wish to atone for my part in the failure to achieve that victory and I apologize to the souls of these dead fliers and their bereaved families.

"I wish the young people of Japan to find a moral in my death. To be reckless is only to aid the enemy. You must abide by the spirit of the Emperor's decision with utmost perseverance. Do not forget your rightful pride in being Japanese.

"You are the treasure of the nation. With all the fervour of spirit of the special attackers, strive for the welfare of Japan and for peace throughout the world."

From Inoguchi: *The Divine Wind*

THE JAPANESE OHKA BOMB

The "Ohka" or "Foolish Bomb"

The *Ohka* ("cherry-blossom"), a small single-seated wooden craft, contained 1,800 kilogrammes of explosives. Carried to within 20,000 metres of the target by a twin-engined bomber, it would then be released to plummet towards its goal, accelerated by blasts of its five rockets. From 6,000 metres altitude it had a range of 30,000 metres. The *Ohka* pilot would ride in the mother bomber until the action area was approached. He would then climb through the bomb bay of the mother plane into the narrow cockpit of the bomb. When enemy targets had been verified and their position made known to the pilot, he would signal his readiness to the crew in the bomber; he would pull the release handle and would be on his way in this missile of destruction, only minutes from the target. Once the release handle was pulled, it became a one-way ride for the *Ohka* pilot. When this weapon became known to the Americans, they gave it the derisive derenive name of "*Baka*" ("foolish") bomb

From Inoguchi: *The Divine Wind*

Aguni Jima, 30 miles west of Okinawa, being taken by U.S. marines on 9 June.

U.S. TROOPS CLEAR THE RYUKYU ISLANDS ROUND OKINAWA

March–June 1945

Tokashiki, one of the Kerama Islands in the Ryukyu group being occupied by U.S. 77th Division. Japanese resistance was quickly crushed.

On 16 April, U.S. marines landed on Ie Shima, one of the largest islands off Okinawa. The photograph shows the burial of fallen Americans (up to 24 April, U.S. casualties on Ie Shima were: 172 killed, 902 wounded, and 46 missing).

THE RECAPTURE OF THE PHILIPPINES

April–June 1945

The main contenders for the Philippines: General Eichelberger, Commander of the U.S. 8th Army and General Yamashita, Commander of the 19th Japanese Army Group.

An American howitzer in action in Cagayan valley, Luzon, the north main island of the Philippines. Landings on Mindanao, the south main island followed on 17 April 1945. ▶

The recapture of the southern Philippine islands in January–15 August 1945

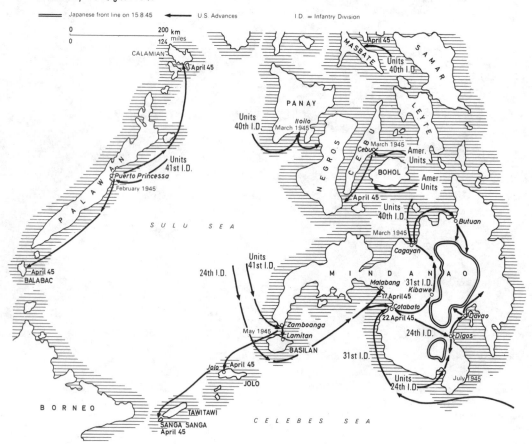

═══ Japanese front line on 15.8.45   ◀— U.S. Advances   I.D. = Infantry Division

0 _____ 200 km
0 _____ 124 miles

CALAMIAN

10 April 45

MASBATE   April 45

SAMAR

Units 40th I.D.

PANAY

Iloilo March 1945

LEYTE

Units 40th I.D.

CEBU   Cebu March 1945   Amer. Units

NEGROS

BOHOL   Amer. Units

Units 41st I.D.

Puerto Princessa

February 1945

PALAWAN

SULU SEA

April 45

Units 40th I.D.   March 1945   Butuan

Cagayan

24th I.D.

Units 41st I.D.

May 1945

MINDANAO   Malabang   31st I.D.   Kibawe   17.April 45   Cotabato   22.April 45   24th I.D.   Davao   Digos

Zamboanga
Lamitan
BASILAN

31st I.D.

Units 24th I.D.   July 1945

April 45   BALABAC

Jolo   April 45   JOLO

BORNEO

SANGA SANGA   April 45   TAWITAWI

CELEBES SEA

The Battle for Luzon
1 March–15th August 1945

======= Jap. front line on 15.3.1945
= = = = Jap. front line on 1.7.1945
‾‾‾‾‾‾‾ Jap. front line on 15.8.1945
◀───── U.S. advances
I.D. = Infantry Division
R.D. = Reconnaissance Division

511th Airborne Btl.
Aparri
Guerilla Unit
Vigan
Tuguegarao
37th I.D.
Bontoc
SOUTH CHINA
6th I.D.
San Fernando
32nd I.D.
Bagabag
Lingayen
Tarlac
Cabanatuan
Calumpit
43rd I.D.
Infanta
38th I.D.
MANILA
1st R.D.
1st R.D.
1st R.D.
Alimonan
2nd Airborne Div.
Lucena
Batangas
1 Btl. 158th Reg.
Naga
1 Btl. 158th Reg.
Legaspi
MINDORO
SAMAR

SEA

PACIFIC OCEAN

0 ———— 200 km
0 ———— 124 miles

With the capture of Callnan on Mindanao on 28 June, all organized Japanese resistance on the island collapsed. On 27 June, General MacArthur announced the complete liberation of Luzon. A few Japanese units persevered until the capitulation. In the photograph: U.S. armour during a halt in the advance on Luzon.

At 3 a.m. on 10 May, the U.S. 6th Marine Division launched an attack across the Asa estuary, reaching the precincts of Amike in the south, and thus gaining control over Naha, the capital.

Major-General Shepherd, Commander of U.S. 6th Marine Division.

U.S. OFFENSIVE ON THE FORTIFIED SOUTH OF OKINAWA

10 May 1945

Preparations for the offensive

On 29 April the 77th Division, fresh and confident after its victories at Kerama Retto and Ie Shima, relieved the riddled and weary 96th Division in the centre. Next day the 1st Marine Division moved into the foxholes and hard-won positions of the 27th Division, now assigned the comparatively restful job of mopping-up in central and northern Okinawa. Both new divisions were assigned to Hodge's XXIV Corps, but for the 1st Marine Division this command setup was to be only temporary. Eight days later the 6th Marine Division was to enter the front line on the right of the 1st Marine Division, and the entire front would be reorganized on a two-corps basis, Hodges XXIV Corps on the left and Geiger's III Amphibious Corps on the right.

From the diary of a Japanese soldier

A Japanese superior private made a final entry in his diary on 23 April: "I am really surprised at the amount of ammunition that the enemy has. When friendly forces fire one round, at least 10 rounds are guaranteed to come back. There is not one of our friendly planes. If some come, I think we can win the fight in a short while. We want planes! We want planes!"

From *Battle Report*, Vol. V

On 13 May, U.S. troops reached the edge of Naha. On the west coast, the U.S. 6th Marine Division advanced on Sugar Loaf Hill, a Japanese key position.

THE FALL OF NAHA, CAPITAL OF OKINAWA   14 May 1945

U.S. troops entering ruined Naha after severe artillery bombardment on 14 May 1945.

"The Japanese aircraft dived through a rain of steel . . ."

THE *ENTERPRISE* BADLY DAMAGED
BY KAMIKAZE OFF OKINAWA
14 May 1945

Kamikaze attack on the *Enterprise*

Eyewitness report by Georges Blond

All the batteries were firing: the 5-inch guns, the 40 mm. and the 20 mm., even the rifles. The Japanese aircraft dived through a rain of steel. It had been hit in several places and seemed to be trailing a banner of flame and smoke, but it came on, clearly visible, hardly moving, the line of its wings as straight as a sword.

The deck was deserted; every man, with the exception of the gunners, was lying flat on his face. Flaming and roaring, the fireball passed in front of the "island" (the funnels, the bridges, the look-outs, which are assembled in a single super-structure) and crashed with a terrible impact just behind the for'ard lift.

The entire vessel was shaken, some forty yards of the flight deck folded up like a banana skin: an enormous piece of the lift, at least a third of the platform, was thrown over three hundred feet into the air. The explosion killed fourteen men . . .

The mortal remains of the pilot had not disappeared. They had been laid out in a corner of the deck, next to the blackened debris of the machine. The entire crew marched past the corpse of the volunteer of death. The men were less interested in his finely modelled features, his wide-open eyes which were now glazed over, than in the buttons of his tunic, which were to become wonderful souvenirs of the war for a few privileged officers of high rank. These buttons, now black, were stamped in relief with the insignia of the kamikaze corps: a cherry blossom with three petals.

From Flower/Reeves: *The War 1939–1945*

". . . all the batteries were firing. The Japanese aircraft crashed with a terrible impact just behind the for'ard lift . . ."

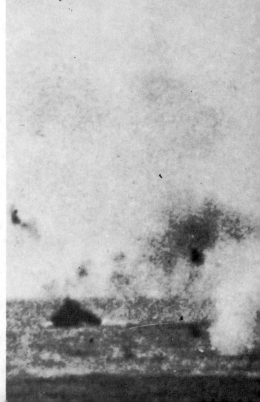

Two days after the fall of Naha, the Japanese 32nd Army withdrew from Shuri Castle, which was occupied by U.S. troops on 29 May.

THE BATTLE FOR SHURI CASTLE, THE HILLS OF KUNISHI AND OROKU PENINSULA

29 May to 20 June 1945

"I'm the last man"

The battle didn't end when Shuri Castle fell. The Japanese divided themselves, like Caesar's Gaul, into three parts. One dug into the knob-shaped Chinen Peninsula on the east, another group defended Oroku Peninsula, across the harbor from Naha, and still another was holed up in Kunishi Ridge to the south.

In this rugged area the Japanese put up their last-ditch stand, knowing it was the end, showing no signs of it in their fighting. Well into June the battle raged, and then resistance slowly faded. The eastern side fell first, to the 7th Infantry Division: the western, defended mostly by naval forces under Admiral Ota, fell next. Ota, true to tradition, stabbed himself just before the final hour.

The end was signaled by one dirty, tattered Japanese Marine, who crawled out of a cave on Oroku Peninsula and walked forward with his hands up.

"Admiral Ota told us to fight to the last man," he told his captors.

"Well?"

"I'm the last man."

The last few days were bitter ones indeed for the 1st Marine Division. On 20 June, Colonel Snedeker's 7th Marines stole a page out of the Japanese book of tactics. They jumped off at night for Kunishi Ridge, and gained the hills without detection.

Daybreak showed the shocked Japanese the Marines in possession of the western slopes. The enemy cut loose with everything to blast the Americans loose. The Marines dug in. They could neither advance nor retreat. Only an occasional tank could bull its way through with supplies and evacuate wounded. Food and ammunition were dropped from the air for six days before the 8th Marines could break through the bullet-swept area, bringing relief.

From: *Battle Report*, Vol. V

Japanese being thrown back after flame-thrower attacks in the hills of Kunishi.

COLLAPSE OF JAPANESE RESISTANCE ON OKINAWA 21 June 1945

Major-General Roy S. Geiger, Commander of III Amphibious Corps, who replaced Lt. General Buckner as Commander of U.S. 10th Army, after the latter's death in action.

The Death of Lieutenant General Buckner

In the early afternoon of 18 June, General Buckner walked, crawled, and climbed up to the front lines to watch the progress of the operation from the newly arrived 8th Marines' command post. Enemy artillery, which had pounded noisily for eighty days, was now silent. It seemed the Japanese had poured out their last round of ammunition. Then one lone enemy gun let go three or four haphazard shots.

The first shot killed General Buckner.

Command of the Tenth Army was immediately passed to General Geiger. A week later, organized Japanese resistance ended.

From: *Battle Report,* Vol. V

The End in Okinawa

From the War-Diary of Admiral Halsey

17 June. Admiral Minoru Ota, Commander Naval Base Force, was found with his throat cut, sitting in a ceremonial pose in a cave in the 4th Marines' zone on the Oruku Peninsula.

18 June. Lieutenant-General S. B. Buckner was killed by enemy shellfire while observing an attack.

19 June. The collapse of Japanese defences was evident across the entire line. At 04:40/1 (Okinawa time) Major-General Roy S. Geiger, U.S.M.C., assumed command *vice* the late General Buckner.

20 June. Civilians surrendered in masses.

21 June. Major-General Geiger announced that organized resistance had ceased.

From: Flower/Reeves: *The War 1939–1945*

Japanese civilians—more than 25,000 in all—hid in the mountains, where they were tended by U.S. troops after the end of the battle.

The Americans lost 11,939 dead and 181 missing during the battle for Okinawa, including 4,907 sailors who fell to Kamikaze attacks.

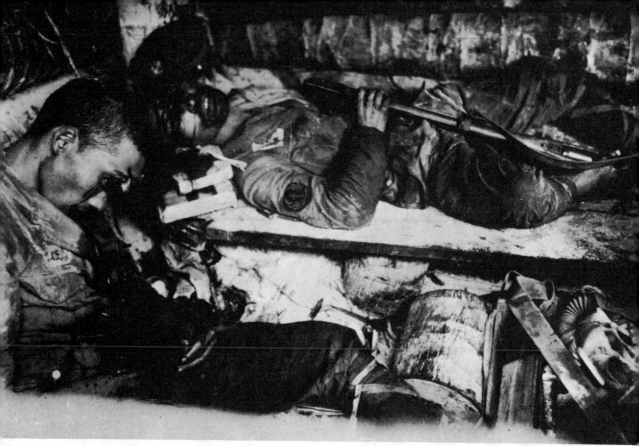

Not all Japanese soldiers committed hara-kiri like the two officers in the photograph. Of the 120,000 Japanese defenders of Okinawa, 111,351 (more than 90%) were killed in action.

Last radio message by the Japanese commander of Okinawa.

More than two months have passed since we engaged the invaders. In complete unity and harmony with the Army, we have made every effort to crush the enemy.

Despite our efforts the battle is going against us. My own troops are at a disadvantage, since all available heavy guns and four crack battalions of naval landing forces were allocated to Army command. Also, enemy equipment is greatly superior to our own.

I tender herewith my deepest apology to the Emperor for my failure to better defend the Empire, the grave task with which I was entrusted.

The troops under my command have fought gallantly, in the finest tradition of the Japanese Navy. Fierce bombing and bombardments may deform the mountains of Okinawa but cannot alter the loyal spirit of our men. We hope and pray for the perpetuation of the Empire and gladly give our lives for that goal.

To the Navy Minister and all my superior officers I tender sincerest appreciation and gratitude for their kindness of many years. At the same time, I earnestly beg you to give thoughtful consideration to the families of my men who fall at this outpost as soldiers of the Emperor.

With my officers and men I give three cheers for the Emperor and pray for the everlasting peace of the Empire.

Though my body decay in remote Okinawa,
My spirit will persist in defence of the homeland.

From Inoguchi: The Divine Wind

The Last Rite of a Japanese General

By a Japanese eye-witness

Four o'clock, the final hour of *hara-kiri;* the Commanding General, dressed in full field uniform, and the Chief of Staff in a white kimono, appeared . . . The Chief of Staff says as he leaves the cave first:

"Well, Commanding General Ushijima, as the way may be dark, I, Cho, will lead the way."

The Commanding General replies: "Please do so, and I'll take along my fan since it is getting warm." Saying this he picked up his Okinawa-made fan and walked out quietly fanning himself . . .

The moon, which had been shining until now, sinks below the waves of the western sea. Dawn has not yet arrived and, at 04:10, the generals appeared at the mouth of the cave. The American forces were only a few metres away.

A sheet of white cloth is placed on a quilt . . . The Commanding General and the Chief of Staff sit down on the quilt . . . bow in reverence to the eastern sky, and Adjutant J— respectfully presents the sword . . .

At this time several grenades were hurled near this solemn scene by the enemy troops who observed movements taking place beneath them. A simultaneous shout and a flash of a sword, then another repeated shout and a flash, and both generals had nobly accomplished their last duty to their Emperor.

From Flower/Reeves: The War 1939–1945

No more than 7,401 Japanese surrendered, the majority of them during the final phase of the battle.

THE RECAPTURE OF JAPANESE-OCCUPIED EAST AND SOUTH-EAST ASIA

Japan's defeat in China, Burma and the Dutch East Indies

CHRONOLOGICAL TABLE

1941

8/12: Japanese advance in S.E. Asia begins with landing of Japanese 25th Army under General Yamashita on Malay Peninsula.
27/12: Hong Kong falls to Japanese.

1942

10/1: Japanese land at Tarakan (Borneo) and on N. Celebes.
22/1: Japanese land on New Ireland and Rabaul (New Britain) in Bismarck Archipelago.
9–15/2: Battle for, and capture of, Singapore by Japanese.
March: Japanese capture most of Burma (Fall of Rangoon on 7 March) together with Sumatra, Java, Celebes, the Lesser Sunda Islands and the Moluccas. Mandalay in Central Burma falls to Japanese.

1943

21/5: Japanese open last phase of their offensive in Central China (to 13/6).
6/9: U.S. and Australian troops land on Lae (New Guinea).
15/12: Americans and Australians land on Arawe (New Britain).

1944

4/2: Japanese launch offensive in Burma.
15/2: New Zealanders land on New Ireland.
8/3: Japanese capture Imphal, on the Indo-Chinese border.
22/4: Americans land on Hollandia (New Guinea).
22/6: Resumption of Allied offensive in Burma.
3/8: Chinese troops capture Myitkyina in Burma.
15/10: N. China Command launches offensive in N. Burma.

Japanese soldiers massacring wounded Indian soldiers.

Part of the re-opened Burma road to China.

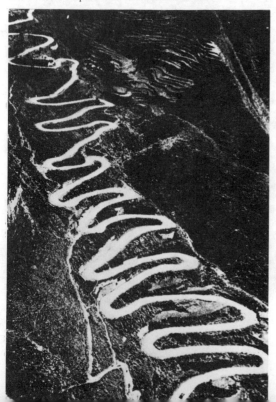

1945

1/1: Indian troops advance in Arakan (Burma).
3/1: Troops of British 14th Army enter Yeo, 68 miles from Mandalay.
5/1: British troops capture Akyab, a Japanese key position in Arakan, and the third-largest harbour in Burma.
21/1: Troops of Indian XV Corps land on Ramree Island, off Burma.
8/2: British troops launch attack on Mandalay.
10/2: British troops in Burma extend their bridgehead on the east bank of the Irrawaddy.
17/2: British troops land on the coast of Arakan, 62 miles south of Akyab. Troops of the 14th Army extend their Irrawaddy bridgehead.
General Wedemeyer warns Marshal Chiang Kai-Shek of possible Japanese attempts to recapture Laohokow and Chihkiang airfields. Changting is now the only airfield in E. China held by 14th U.S.A.A.F.
6/3: British troops cross the Irrawaddy 30 miles from Mandalay.
8/3: The entire Burma Road, from Lashio to Kunming, in Allied hands.
20/3: Mandalay, the key junction on the Burma Road, recaptured by British troops.
2/4: Admiral Mountbatten meets his Staff at Kandy to plan the recapture of Rangoon.
3/4: The battle for Central Burma ends in British victory. General Marshall promises that U.S. forces will not be withdrawn from Burma before 1/6 or the recapture of Rangoon.
7/4: Large Japanese force cut off between Mandalay and Meiktila (Burma).
13/4: Units of Indian 20th Division capture Taungdwingyi in Burma.
Japanese launch major attack on Chihkiang.
20/4: British 14th Army advances to positions 68 miles south of

Meiktila. Units of the British 2nd Division and of the Indian 268th Brigade conclude the encirclement of the Japanese in the Mt. Popa area.

21/4: British 14th Army encircles Pyinmana, 200 miles from Rangoon.

24/4: General Kimura transfers his H.Q. to Moulmein in Burma.

25/4: Japanese continue advance on Chihkiang, routing Chinese 58th Division in Wukang.

1/5: Australian troops land on Tarakan Is., on the N.E. coast of Borneo.

2/5: British troops land by sea and air 20 miles south of Rangoon.

3/5: Indian 26th Division enters Rangoon, while 71st Brigade advances on Syriam across the Rangoon river. Other troops defend the west bank of the river from Thakutpin to Elephant Point.

5/5: Indian 26th Division (XV Corps) completes the recapture of Burma with the occupation of Rangoon.

6/5: General Mountbatten announces end of Burma battle, in which 97,000 Japanese soldiers have been killed.

10/5: British 14th Army in the Arakan hills re-establishes contact with Allied forces west of the Irrawaddy.

11/5: Australian 6th Division occupies Wewak in New Guinea.

14/5: March of U.S. 5332nd Brigade from Burma to China completed. The Americans left Burma exactly 2 months earlier.

15/5: Indian 26th Division, now under the command of British 14th Army, links up with Indian 20th Division from the south, on the Rangoon–Prome road.

18/5: Australians break Japanese resistance on Tarawak and advance 10 miles towards the east coast.

20/5: Japanese re-organize their forces for the defence of the Home Islands. Japanese withdraw from Hochih (Kwangsi Prov.), China, to the borders of Kweiyang.

21/5: Chinese forces recapture the port of Fuchow.

25/5: British troops occupy the port of Bassein, 87 miles west of Rangoon.

26/5: Japanese re-organization continues. Japanese withdraw from Nanning, abandoning the overland route from China to Indo-China.

Chinese re-occupy Nanning.

10/6: While pursuing the retreating Japanese forces towards Liuchow, Chinese troops capture Ishan.

Australian 9th Division lands on Borneo at Brunei Bay, and on the islands of Labuan and Muara, supported by Allied aircraft and the Seventh Fleet.

11/6: Japanese recapture Ishan from the Chinese.

14/6: Chinese recapture Ishan and pursue the Japanese towards Liuchow.

15/6: Labuan and Muara islands cleared of Japanese.

19/6: British and Indian troops in E. Burma advance on Thailand.

20/6: Australian forces make an unexpected landing at Lutong in Sarawak.

22/6: Collapse of organized Japanese resistance on Tarakan. Australians enter Sarawak.

23/6: General Wheeler replaces General Sultan as U.S. Commander in the Indo-Burmese theatre of war.

24/6: Australians advancing from Brunei Bay sandwich the Seria-Miri oilfield region between two strong forces.

25/6: 14th Army patrols clear Japanese from seven Burmese villages south of Prome.

26/6: Chinese forces occupy Liuchow airbase.

30/6: 50 Allied warships and transports appear off Balikpapan (Borneo) one of the richest oil-producing centres in the Dutch East Indies.

1/7: Chinese forces capture Liuchow.

After heavy naval bombardment by U.S. 7th Fleet and intensive air attacks, Australian troops land near Balikpapan. Japanese resistance is slight at first, but increases as Australians advance inland.

2/7: 7th Australian Division captures Balikpapan.

4/7: U.S. officers fly from India to Chungking to establish Army Air Force H.Q. in China.

15/7: Australians capture Japanese key position of Mt. Batochampar near Balikpapan.

18/7: Reports of Japanese withdrawal from their Sittang bridgehead in Burma.

Advancing units of 7th Australian Division capture the oil centre of Samboja (28 miles N.E. of Balikpapan) evacuated by the Japanese without a fight.

21/7: Japanese launch counter-offensive against British forces on Sittang River (Burma).

23/7: 10th U.S.A.A.F. establishes H.Q. at Kunming.

27/7: Chinese troops close in on, and within 3 days capture, the city and airbase of Kweilin, capital of Kwangsi Province.

3/8: Japanese losses in the Pegu Yomas (Burma) are estimated at 8,600 killed or missing.

5/8: Chinese 13th Army captures Tanchuk. Chinese 58th Division recaptures Hsinking.

19/8: General MacArthur, Allied Supreme Commander in Asia, orders that no more landings must take place until instrument of surrender is signed.

30/8: British forces re-enter Hong Kong.

2/9: British troops land at Penang, and also in Sebang (Sumatra).

Troops of British 14th Army passing through Pyawbwe on 11 April 1945.

ADVANCE OF BRITISH 14TH ARMY IN BURMA DURING APRIL 1945

British soldiers clearing Yamethin railway station on 13 April 1945.

South-East Asia Command from May 1945:	
Supreme Allied Commander:	*Admiral Lord Louis Mountbatten (Br.)*
Deputy Supreme Allied Commander:	*Lieut.-General R. A. Wheeler (U.S.A.)*
C.-in-C. British Eastern Fleet:	*Admiral Sir Bruce Fraser (Br.)*
C.-in-C. British East Indies Fleet:	*Admiral Sir Arthur Power (Br.)*
C.-in-C. Eleventh Army Group:	*General Sir George Giffard (Br.)*
C.-in-C. Allied Land Forces:	*Lieut.-General Sir William Slim (Br.)*
C.-in-C. Allied Air Forces:	*Air Marshal Sir Keith Park (Br.)*
Commanding General, U.S. Army Air Forces in the (U.S.) China–Burma–India Theatre:	*Lieut.-General G. E. Stratemeyer (U.S.A.; until June 1945)*

Allied operations in Burma
from 1 January to 18 June 1945

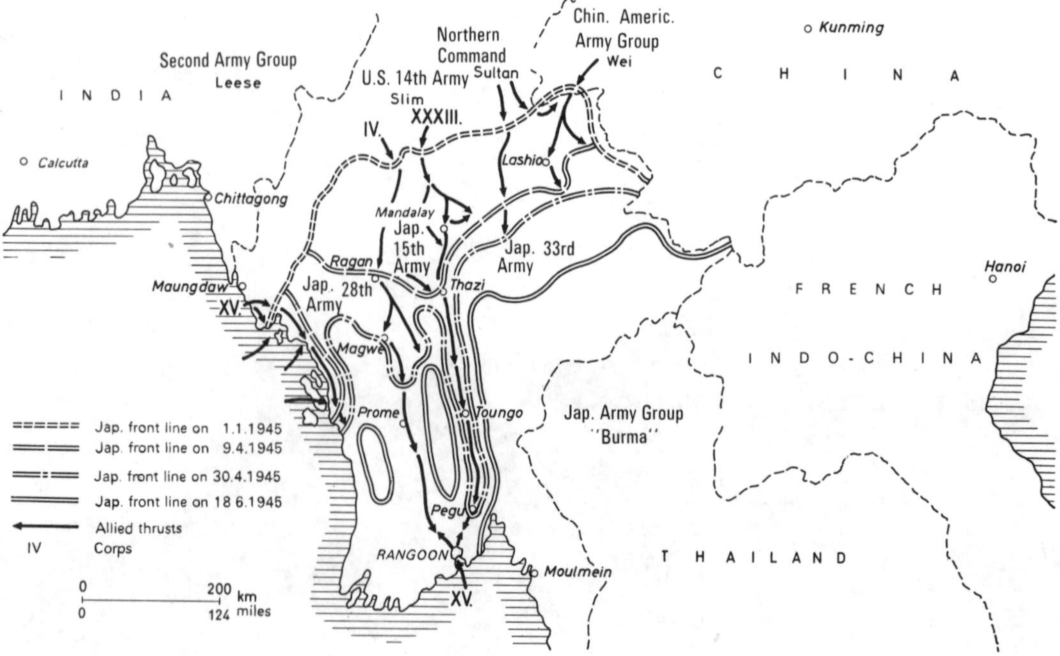

Jap. front line on 1.1.1945
Jap. front line on 9.4.1945
Jap. front line on 30.4.1945
Jap. front line on 18.6.1945
Allied thrusts
IV Corps

0   200 km
0   124 miles

South-East Asia Command (SEAC). From left to right: Lieut.-General Slim, General R. A. Wheeler, Admiral Lord Mountbatten, Admiral Sir A. Power, Air Marshal Sir K. Park and General Browning.

Japanese prisoner being given first-aid. After the British victory in Central Burma (March 1945), Japanese forces under General Kimura made vain attempts to cut off the Allied road to the south.

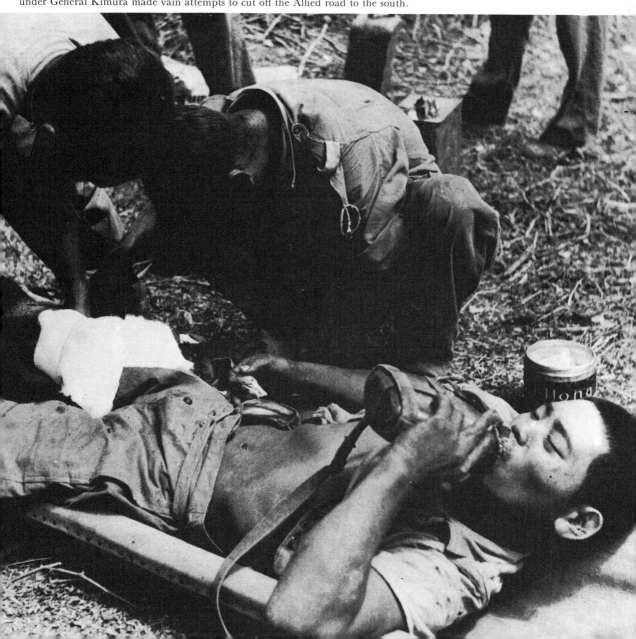

AUSTRALIANS LAND ON TARAKAN, OFF N.E. BORNEO

1 May 1945

Landing craft with members of Australian 26th Brigade.

In the background: burning oil storage tanks.

Allied planes laying a smoke screen before the landing.

While offering little resistance at first, the Japanese dug in on 2 May.

A dead Japanese soldier on the coast of Tarakan.

In the morning of 2 May, the Indian 26th Brigade under Major-General Chambers . . .

RANGOON RETAKEN

3 May 1945

"Japs gone. Exdigitate . . ." *By General Slim*

The overture to the landing was on D-1 Day, 1 May, when a heavy bombing attack was delivered on all located defences on both sides of the Rangoon River. Some hours later, a battalion of 50 Indian Parachute Brigade dropped at Elephant Point. A party of about thirty Japanese, either left for observation or just forgotten, offered resistance to the Gurkha paratroops. One wounded Japanese survived. Early on the same morning a pilot, flying over Rangoon, saw written in large letters on the gaol roof the words, "*Japs gone. Exdigitate.*" The R.A.F. slang was not only evidence of the genuineness of the message, but a gentle hint to speed up operations. However, it was determined, wisely I think, to continue according to plan. Early on the 2nd the weather became worse and there was some doubt whether the small landing craft could face the sea. However, it was decided to risk it and by skilful seamanship all reached and entered Rangoon River. A brigade of 26 Division, under Major-General Chambers, was landed on each bank and the advance began . . .

While 26 Division was thus plodding forward, the pilot of a Mosquito aircraft of 221 Group, flying low over Rangoon and seeing no signs of enemy, decided to land on Mingaladon airfield at the Cantonment, about eight miles north of the city. The strip was in bad repair and he crashed his aircraft on landing, but, undismayed, he walked into Rangoon, visited our prisoners at the gaol, and assured himself that the Japanese had really gone. In the evening, commandeering a *sampan*, he sailed down the river and met the advancing 26 Division . . .

It was not until the evening of 3 May that the brigade on the east bank, struggling through waterlogged country, appeared on the Hlaing River, immediately south of Rangoon. It was ferried over and entered the town.

(From: Flower/Reeves: *The War 1939–1945*)

◄ A captured Japanese sniper.

. . . landed on both banks of the Rangoon River and advanced on Rangoon.

Major-General Chambers, Commander of Indian 26th Division, at the victory parade in Rangoon.

After landing on the north coast of New Guinea in April, Australian troops captured Wewak on 11 May 1945.

AUSTRALIANS ADVANCE IN NEW GUINEA
May–August 1945

Australian gunners in action on New Guinea.

Oil production on Tarakan was resumed on 28 June.

Chinese 6th Army units being transferred from Burma to China in mid-June.

FIGHTING ON THE CHINESE FRONT   May–June 1945

Chinese Army H.Q. announced on 31 May that Chinese troops advancing in Fukien, had captured Lognan, 34 miles north of Fuchow, on 27 May, and had reached the Kiao river on 31 May. Chinese forces also captured Nanning, the capital of Kwangsi Province, on 27 May, and Pinyang (W. Hunan), 58 miles N.E. of Nanning, on 28 May. Japanese forces were reported to be in the process of evacuating the corridor between China and Indo-China.

14 June: 200,000 Japanese in the corridor between Indo-China and W. China were reported cut off.

The re-opening of communications with China—for instance the railway line on the Ledo Road shown here— greatly aided Allied progress in China.   ►

General Sultan (U.S.) and General Wei Li-Huang inspecting troops of the Chinese Expeditionary Corps in Burma, equipped by the United States.

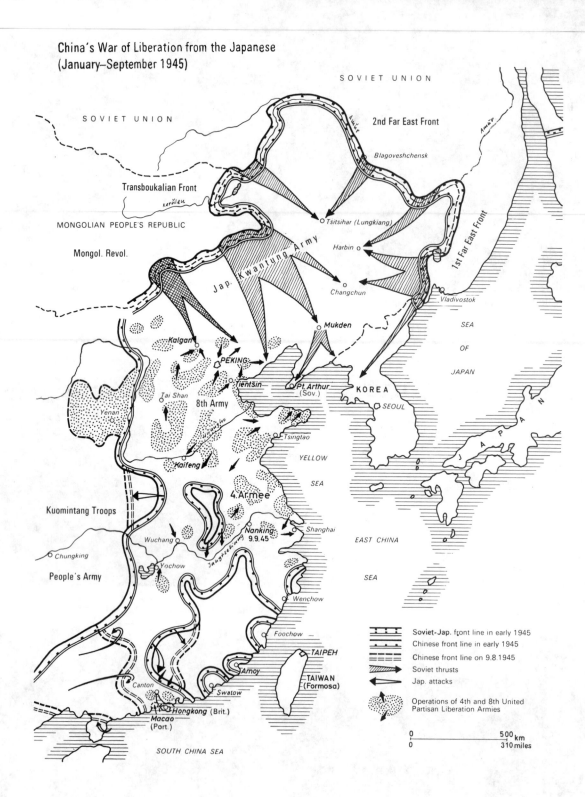

China's War of Liberation from the Japanese
(January–September 1945)

SOVIET UNION

SOVIET UNION

2nd Far East Front

Amur

Blagoveshchensk

Transboukalian Front

kernten

MONGOLIAN PEOPLE'S REPUBLIC

Mongol. Revol.

Tsitsihar (Lungkiang)

Jap. Kwantung Army

Harbin

1st Far East Front

Changchun

Vladivostok

Mukden

SEA

OF

JAPAN

Kalgan

PEKING

Tientsin

Pt. Arthur
(Sov.)

KOREA

Tai Shan

8th Army

SEOUL

Yenan

Hoangho

Tsingtao

YELLOW

Kaifeng

SEA

4. Armee

J   A   P   A   N

Kuomintang Troops

Wuchang

Jangtsekiang

Nanking
9.9.45

Shanghai

EAST CHINA

Chungking

Yochow

SEA

People's Army

Wenchow

Foochow

TAIPEH

Amoy

TAIWAN
(Formosa)

Canton

Swatow

Hongkong (Brit.)

Macao
(Port.)

SOUTH CHINA SEA

	Soviet-Jap. front line in early 1945
	Chinese front line in early 1945
	Chinese front line on 9.8.1945
	Soviet thrusts
	Jap. attacks
	Operations of 4th and 8th United Partisan Liberation Armies

0   500 km
0   310 miles

In June, many Chinese towns changed hands several times.

JAPANESE FORCES WITHDRAW IN N. CHINA June 1945

Chinese troops in pursuit of the retreating Japanese Army.

AUSTRALIAN 9TH DIVISION LANDS AT BRUNEI BAY (N.W. BORNEO) AND ON LABUAN AND MUARA ISLANDS 10 June 1945

Australian armour off Brunei Bay.

Troops of Australian 43rd Infantry Battalion in landing craft off Labuan.

Smoke bombs give the signal for the attack on Muara.

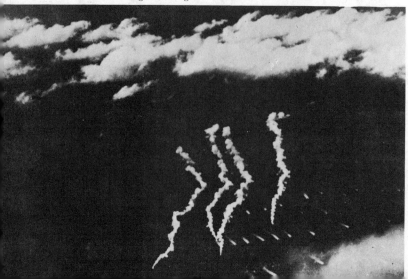

An Australian patrol on Labuan. On 22 June, Field-Admiral Nimitz announced that Labuan was cleared. On 18 June, the Australians had

reached Tutong in N.W. Borneo. On the same day, amphibious forces landed 10 miles S.E. of Brunei; on 19th June, Australian troops had landed at Mempakul, on the N. side of Brunei Bay. On 20 June, finally, came an Australian landing on the coast of Sarawak, at Lutong, some 82 miles from Brunei Bay.

AUSTRALIANS LAND AT BALIKPAPAN (E. BORNEO) AND ADVANCE INTO THE INTERIOR   1 July 1945

U.S. 7th Fleet landing the Australian 7th Division near Balikpapan.

Australian landing craft approaching Balikpapan after a two-hour bombardment.

The further inland the Australians advanced, the stiffer became Japanese resistance.

Australian guns shelling Japanese positions.

Occupation of a Japanese command post.

Advancing from the north, west, and east, Australian and New Zealand troops enclosed the enemy in a ring of steel.

THE LIBERATION OF BURMA
July–August 1945

After the occupation of Rangoon, the British 14th Army advanced to the borders of Thailand. Japanese forces were split up into a series of pockets, and either destroyed or forced to withdraw across the border. In the photograph: British troops clearing a village near Waw on 13 July.

In some sectors, the Japanese continued to offer fierce resistance until July. In the photograph, an Indian patrol is shown mowing down a group of Japanese soldiers with machine guns and incendiary bombs.

Two hungry and sick Japanese soldiers captured in the Penwegon sector on 30 July. In the Pegu sector, 8,600 Japanese were reported killed by 2 August.

The war in China and Burma on 15 August 1945

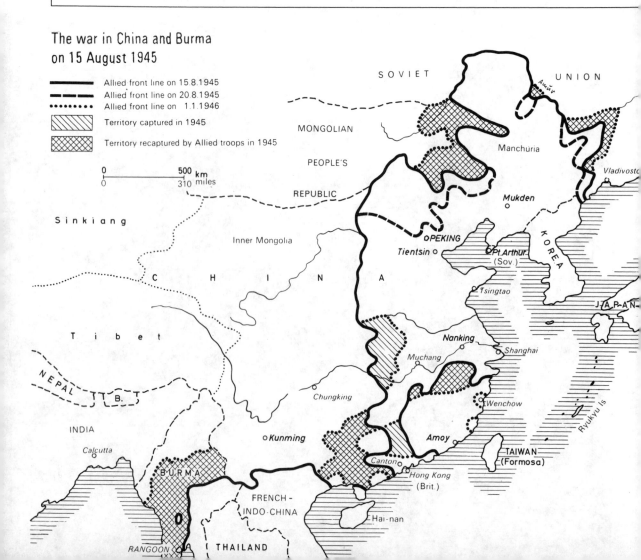

— Allied front line on 15.8.1945
- - - Allied front line on 20.8.1945
••••• Allied front line on 1.1.1946

Territory captured in 1945

Territory recaptured by Allied troops in 1945

0 — 500 km
0 — 310 miles

Chinese and American soldiers in a Sherman tank.

Chinese forces recapturing Kweilin on 5 August.

CHINESE ADVANCE TO KWEILIN

July–August 1945

From a Chinese High Command communiqué:

16 July 1945: Japanese troops are withdrawing from Amoy towards Canton, from Liuchow Peninsula towards the north, and from Kanchow towards Nanchang.

29 July 1945: After many weeks of fierce fighting, Kweilin was occupied by our forces on 27 July, and the nearby airfields on 28 July.

9 August 1945: The Japanese are trying to withdraw their main forces from S. China and to concentrate them north of the Yellow River, in order to fall back on N.E. China and the industrial regions of Manchuria. The Chinese Army, with the support of the USAAF is attempting to tie down the greatest possible number of Japanese forces in the south. To that end, Chinese paratroopers trained in the U.S.A. have been dropped on the Canton–Hankow railway line and on other important centres of communication.

CRUCIAL BATTLES IN THE PACIFIC

The final phase of the naval campaign in the Pacific

CHRONOLOGICAL TABLE: 1941–1945

1941

7/12: Japanese make surprise attack on U.S. Fleet in Pearl Harbour. American losses: 2,117 killed, 960 missing and 876 wounded.

1942

27/2: Naval battle in Java Sea. Americans fail to stop Japanese invasion fleet bound for Java.
18/4: U.S. carrier-borne bombers attack Tokyo and Yokohama.
6–8/5: Naval battle in Coral Sea forces Japanese to abandon attempts to land troops in Port Moresby (New Guinea).
4–7/6: Air–sea battle off Midway Island. First American victory, and decisive turning point in the Pacific war. Japanese losses: 3,500 killed (including 100 of their best pilots). American losses: 307 killed. The Japanese lose 4 carriers, the Americans only 1.
23–25/8: Air–sea battle east of Solomon Islands (outcome indecisive).
26–27/10: Air–sea battle off Santa Cruz. Japanese score a tactical victory.

1943

26/3: Naval battle off Komandorskiye Island.
2/11: Naval battle in Empress Augusta Bay, off Bougainville.
5–11/11: Heavy U.S. raid on Rabaul.

1944

18–20/6: Air–sea battle in the Philippine Sea and off the Marianas with crippling Japanese losses.
23–26/10: Air–sea battle for Leyte.

1945

12–22/1: Task Force 58 makes carrier raid in South China Sea and successfully attacks targets in Indo-China, S. and S.W. China, N. Luzon, Formosa and the Ryukyu Islands.
16–17/2: Task Force 58 makes carrier raid on Tokyo (also on 25–26/2).
18–21/3: Task Force 58 makes raids on Kyushu and Honshu. Counter-attacks by Japanese bombers and Kamikazes. U.S. losses: 5 carriers damaged. First Japanese attempt to use piloted bombs proves unsuccessful.
26/3–25/5: Carrier-borne planes of British Pacific Fleet fly 5,335 sorties and drop nearly 1,000 tons of bombs on Japanese airfields and harbours. British losses: 160 planes, of which about one-third were damaged or destroyed while trying to land on the carriers.
9/4: Admiral Spruance (U.S.) uses carrier-borne aircraft of British Pacific Fleet to raid airfields in N. Formosa, from which Japanese bombers have attacked ships off Okinawa.
4/5–25/5: Admiral Rawlings renews his attacks on Sakishima Gunto by shelling the airfield. His ships are attacked by Kamikazes. The carriers *Formidable* and *Indomitable* are hit, but quickly restore themselves to full activity. Five days later, the *Formidable* is hit again: another Kamikaze flings itself on the *Victorious*. Carrier raids continue until 25/5, despite damage caused by Japanese.
11/5–15/6: Task Force 58 and British carrier-borne planes raid Ryuku Island.
16/5: Japanese cruiser *Haguro* sunk by 4 British destroyers in Malacca Strait.
28/5: Admiral Nimitz announces that, during 1944, U.S. submarines have sunk 2 million tons of Japanese shipping.
2–3/6: U.S. carrier-borne planes raid S. Kyushu.
5/6: Units of U.S. 3rd Fleet surprised by typhoon in the Philippine Sea. 4 aircraft carriers, 4 escort carriers, 4 battleships, 7 cruisers, 14 destroyers and 2 tankers damaged.
10/6: British Pacific Fleet sends special force, including the carrier *Indomitable*, from Manus to attack the Japanese base at Truk in the Carolines, which the Americans had by-passed in their drive across the central Pacific to the Philippines.
20/6: U.S. carrier-borne aircraft raid Wake Island.
10–30/7: Task Force 38 and British carrier-borne aircraft make a series of raids on targets in Hokkaido, Honshu, and shipping in the Inland Sea. Battleships and cruisers bombard the coast. From 24/7 to 28/7, concentrated raids on the Japanese naval base of Kure and on remnants of the Japanese Fleet: 2 carriers, 3 battleships and 4 cruisers destroyed.
14/7: Warships bombard Kamaishi, a harbour some 250 miles north of Tokyo.
22/7: Japanese battleship *Nagato* bombed by Allied planes in Yokosuka: 12 other Japanese ships sunk.
29/7: U.S. cruiser *Indianapolis* sunk by Japanese submarine.
30/7: British midget submarines XE-1 and XE-3, towed in by larger submarines from Brunei, place limpet mines on the bottom of the heavy cruiser *Takao* in Singapore. The Japanese ship subsides on the sea bed. At about the same time, British midget submarines cut Japanese cable communications between Singapore, Saigon and Hong Kong.

U.S. NAVAL COMMANDERS IN THE PACIFIC IN 1945

From left to right: Admiral Nimitz, C.-in-C. U.S. Pacific Fleet and Pacific Ocean Areas; Admiral Spruance, Commander of U.S. Fifth Fleet; Admiral Fletcher, Commander of U.S. N. Pacific Fleet; Admiral Halsey, Commander of U.S. Third Fleet.

THE ROLE OF AMERICA'S PACIFIC FLEET

U.S. carrier *Saratoga* after Kami-kaze attack.

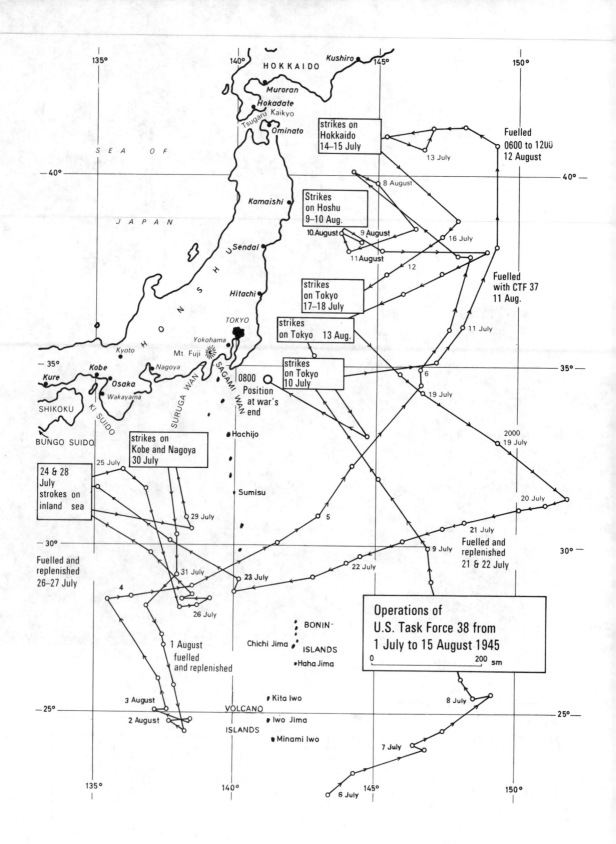

SEA OF JAPAN

HOKKAIDO

Kushiro

Muroran

Hokadate
Tsugaru Kaikyo
Kaikyo

Ominato

strikes on
Hokkaido
14–15 July

Fuelled
0600 to 1200
12 August

13 July

8 August

Kamaishi

Strikes
on Hoshu
9–10 Aug.

10.August   9 August

11 August

16 July

HONSHU

Sendai

12

Fuelled
with CTF 37
11 Aug.

Hitachi

strikes
on Tokyo
17–18 July

11 July

Mt. Fuji   TOKYO
Yokohama

strikes
on Tokyo   13 Aug.

6

Kyoto

Nagoya

SURUGA WAN

SAGAMI WAN

0800
Position
at war's
end

strikes
on Tokyo
10 July

19 July

Kure   Kobe

Osaka
Wakayama

KI SUIDO

Hachijo

2000
19 July

SHIKOKU

BUNGO SUIDO

strikes on
Kobe and Nagoya
30 July

Sumisu

5

20 July

25 July

24 & 28
July
strokes on
inland sea

29 July

21 July

9 July

Fuelled and
replenished
21 & 22 July

22 July

Fuelled and
replenished
26–27 July

31 July

23 July

26 July

4

BONIN-

Chichi Jima   ISLANDS

Haha Jima

Operations of
U.S. Task Force 38 from
1 July to 15 August 1945

0   200   sm

1 August
fuelled
and replenished

Kita Iwo

8 July

3 August

2 August

VOLCANO

ISLANDS

Iwo Jima

Minami Iwo

7 July

6 July

372

DESTRUCTION OF JAPANESE FLEET

10–30 July 1945

The end of the world's third-largest fleet

On 28 July the coup de grace was given to the Japanese Fleet. Once again the fliers from Task Force 38 smashed at what remained of the battered hulks near Kure. Although most of the ships were irreparably damaged, this was not completely evident from the air. Some were partially flooded while others rested upright on the shallow bottom, but from the air they looked as if they might possibly become a nuisance again. Nimitz wanted to make sure that Japan did not have one capital ship that might interfere with the coming operations against the Home Islands.

The attacks were concentrated on the battleship *Haruna*. From eight in the morning till five in the afternoon carrier planes hit her again and again. Far Eastern Air Force B-24s flying from Okinawa fields also added their punches between carrier strikes but unfortunately swung wide. Even the *Haruna's* luck could not hold out against such wrath and the ship settled to the shallow bottom, her turrets just above the water.

The *Ise*, too, received a shower of bombs and settled to the bottom. Again the B-24s tried but missed. They connected, however, with the heavy cruiser *Aoba*, which was already on the bottom, and blew her stern off. The carrier *Amagi*, already leaking from the 24 July raid, had more of her seams ripped and slowly eased to starboard, coming to rest on her side. The *Oyodo*, *Tone* and *Izumo* were polished off. The carrier *Katsuragi* had its flight deck bulged by two 1,000-pound bombs, but her hull fortunately remained undamaged; "fortunately", because she soon had to be used to repatriate Japanese from overseas, a detail to which no one gave a thought at the moment. The only ship not damaged was the carrier *Ryuho*, undiscovered under her camouflage. By the end of the day Japan, once the third largest sea power in the world, barely ranked ahead of Ireland. From: *Battle Report*, Vol. V

Planes of Task Force 38 preparing to attack Japanese naval bases.

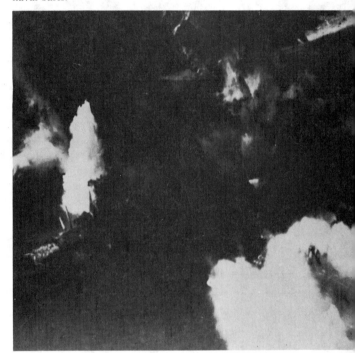

Only a very few Japanese submarines survived to capitulate at the end of the war.

The battleship *Haruna* being sunk by U.S. carrier-borne aircraft in Kure base. ▶

THE ROLE OF THE BRITISH PACIFIC FLEET IN EAST ASIA IN 1945

The most important operations of British Pacific Fleet from May to September 1945

On 1 May the British Fleet was ready to re-enter the fray, and sailed north from Leyte in much the same strength as before. Three days later, Admiral Rawlings reopened his attack on the Sakishima Gunto with a battleship and cruiser bombardment of the airfields, and it was now that the British ships came in for their full share of suicide attacks. On the 4th the *Formidable* and *Indomitable* were both hit but were able to carry on working their aircraft; five days later the *Formidable* was hit again, and another Kamikaze crashed aboard the *Victorious*. Though many aircraft parked on the carriers' flight decks were destroyed, the strikes at the enemy airfields continued until 25th, on which day the fleet set course for Manus . . .

One part of the British Pacific Fleet, including the newly-arrived carrier *Implacable*, left Manus on 10 June to attack the Japanese naval base at Truk in the Carolines —which the Americans had by-passed in their great drive westwards across the central Pacific; and on 28th the main body sailed from Sydney to resume duty with the Third Fleet. When Admiral Rawlings met Admiral Halsey off Japan in mid-July, they discussed the manner in which the British task force should be fitted into the Third Fleet's organization, and how it should be employed during the next phase of the offensive. This was to consist of carrier air attacks and heavy gun bombardments of the Japanese mainland . . .

When the American carrier aircraft had destroyed the last enemy warships in Kure the Third Fleet, including the British contingent, moved north-east up the Japanese coast and continued its air attacks and bombardments against shore targets . . .

On 12 August, the greater part of Admiral Rawlings' force . . . set course for the south, leaving only his flagship the *King George V*, the carrier *Indefatigable* and certain smaller units, including a few from the Australian and New Zealand units, to represent the British Empire at the surrender ceremonies . . .

Meanwhile, in the Indian Ocean, Admiral Mountbatten had ordered that the combined operation against the west coast of Malaya, which had reached an advanced stage of planning, should go ahead; and the whole East Indies Fleet therefore set out across the Bay of Bengal with the object of occupying Penang, and then sweeping the approaches to Singapore. But on 19 August General MacArthur, in his capacity of Supreme Commander, Allied Powers, ordered that no landings were to be made until the instrument of surrender had been signed . . . The fleet and the troop transports had to hang about in very uncomfortable circumstances off the Nicobars; and it was 28 August before they reached Penang. On 2 September we landed forces there and also at Sabang in Sumatra, what time the sweepers were clearing the waters to the south. Next day the Commander-in-Chief, East Indies Fleet, arrived at Singapore . . .

◀ A smashed Japanese Kamikaze (right on photograph) on the deck of a British carrier during the Sakishima Gunto operations.

U.S. battleship *Massachusetts* firing 16-inch shells at Kamaishi on the N.W. coast of Honshu.

"You have brought an implacable, treacherous and barbaric foe to his knees . . ."

From Admiral Halsey's Victory Speech as broadcast to Third Fleet on 15 August 1945, during a Kamikaze attack

Men of the Third Fleet, the war is ended. You, in conjunction with your brothers in arms, of all services and all branches of all services, have contributed inestimably to this final result. You have brought an implacable, treacherous, and barbaric foe to his knees in abject surrender. This is the first time in the recorded history of the misbegotten Japanese race that they as a nation have been forced to submit to this humiliation. I said in 1942 the Nips were no supermen. You have helped write finis on that estimate in 1945 . . .

(Thanks to you) our dear ones at home have not been endangered. Give praise to God Almighty for this and give humble and grateful thanks that He saw fit to use us as His instruments. Victory is not the end—rather it is but the beginning. We must establish a peace—a firm, a just, and an enduring peace. A peace that will enable all decent nations to live without fear and in prosperity. A peace that will glorify the inherent dignity and nobility of mankind. Never again should we permit the enslavement of decent human beings—never again should tyrants be permitted to rise in a civilized world . . .

The present and immediate duty of the Third Fleet is crystal clear. We must in conjunction with all Allied forces so employed—reduce Nippon to military impotence. We must keep them militarily impotent. This should not be a difficult undertaking. Following this, it is imperative that instrumentalities be set up to educate and divorce the Japanese from their barbaric traditions, teachings, and thoughts . . .

There are no words to a sailorman more expressive of the highest commendation than the Navy's "Well Done". With great pride, gratitude and thankfulness, I give to each and every one of you my sincere and heart-felt "Well Done". To our fighting brothers of the British Pacific Fleet, my eternal gratitude for your efficient and generous services . . .

To those of our brothers that have given their all—who have made the supreme sacrifice—Hail, Rest with God. You will never die. Your names and your deeds will rest with and be an inspiration to all decent mankind through all ages. "What greater love hath a man, that he give his life for his country." To your loved ones, my deepest sympathy. May time assuage your grief, and bring a full realization of your dear ones' immortal fame . . .

From: Battle Report, *Vol. V*

U.S. AIR SUPREMACY

Operations of U.S. Strategic Air Force in the Pacific during April–August 1945

CHRONOLOGICAL TABLE: 1942–1945

1942

23/1: Japanese aircraft raid Lae on New Guinea.

1944

24/11: Beginning of U.S. air offensive against Japan from captured air bases in the Marianas.

1945

27/1: U.S. Superfortresses raid Tokyo.
15/2: U.S. raid on Tokyo.
9–10/3: Heavy incendiary-bomb raid on Tokyo. More than 83,000 killed and 40,000 wounded.
14/5: Heavy U.S. air raids on Central and Southern Japan.
21/5: U.S. Superfortresses attack Hamamatsu and Tokyo.
23–25/5: Heavy incendiary-bomb raid on Tokyo.
7/6: U.S. Superfortresses make concentrated attack on Osaka.
9/6: U.S. Superfortresses raid various Japanese cities.
19/6: U.S. Superfortresses make heavy attack on Japanese industrial centres.
22/6: U.S. bombers drop 3,000 tons of high explosives on Japanese arms factories in Kobe, Okayama, Nagoya and Osaka.
26/6: B-29 Superfortresses of XXI U.S. Bomber Command make night raid on Japanese oil refineries.

29/6: American bombers continue to attack Japanese harbours.
2/7: 600 U.S. bombers drop 4,000 tons of incendiary bombs on Japanese cities. Because of incessant attacks, Tokyo evacuated except for 200,000 people.
8/7: U.S. bombers from Iwo Jima attack Japanese airfields for the fourth time in four days. Tokyo and Yokohama raided as well.
10/7: 2,000 Allied aircraft raid Tokyo.
17/7: U.S. bombers raid various Japanese cities.
18/7: U.S. Army Strategic Air Force under General Spaatz sets up H.Q. on Guam.
20/7: U.S. aircraft discover Japanese warships off Yokosuku and attack in the face of concentrated anti-aircraft fire.
24/7: 1,000 U.S. aircraft attack Japanese naval bases.
28/7: Population of eleven Japanese towns warned by leaflets to evacuate their towns, on which major raids are about to be made.
29/7: Incendiary bombs dropped on six Japanese cities.
30/7: Daily raids by USAAF increase in intensity.
5/8: U.S. planes lay mines in coastal waters and complete the blockade of Japan.

A spokesman of the 20th Air Force points out that Japan has less than half the food and raw materials needed for continuing the war.

12/8: Tokyo raided by Allied aircraft, while the world awaits Japan's reply to the Allied capitulation terms.

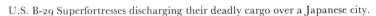

U.S. B-29 Superfortresses discharging their deadly cargo over a Japanese city.

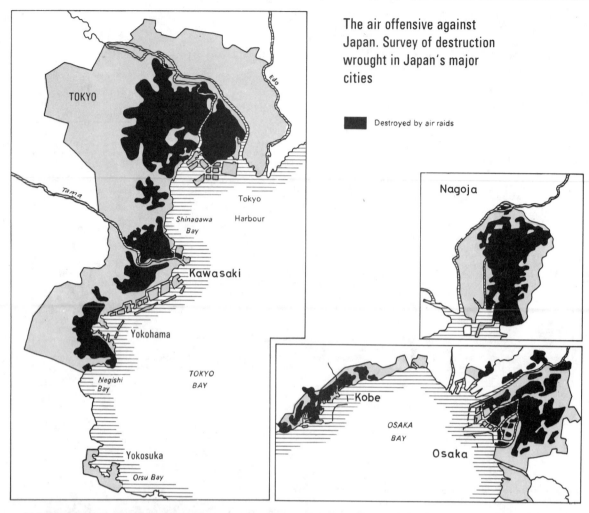

The air offensive against Japan. Survey of destruction wrought in Japan's major cities

■ Destroyed by air raids

TOKYO

Edo

Tama

Tokyo Harbour

Shinagawa Bay

Kawasaki

Yokohama

Negishi Bay

TOKYO BAY

Yokosuka

Orsu Bay

Nagoja

Kobe

OSAKA BAY

Osaka

U.S. B-29 Superfortresses attacking a Japanese base on Formosa.

THE LAST PHASE IN THE STRATEGIC AIR ATTACK ON JAPAN

April–July 1945

> Admiral Nimitz's H.Q. announced on 11 July that the USAAF had gained complete air supremacy over Tokyo. The Japanese air force had ceased to offer significant resistance.

After the victory in Europe, General Spaatz was appointed C.-in-C. U.S. Strategic Air Force in the Pacific.

"Day by day Japan turned into a furnace . . ."

From the memoirs of Mamoru Shigemitsu, the Japanese Foreign Minister

The air-raids were the most frightful experience the Japanese people have ever undergone. On the grounds that Japanese production of munitions was parcelled out among home industries, the raiders systematically burnt out the whole of large and small cities and towns. These were mostly built of wood and it was comparatively easy to set them on fire with oil-incendiaries. These were invented by the Americans and, as they improved, were extremely powerful. Their use was perfected to a fine art. The first wave dropped bombs round a town and set up a circle of fire. Nights of strong wind were chosen and bombs were dropped to windward in great quantity. The area encompassed by a wall of flame then became the target for the next wave which systematically bombed the whole. The area became a sea of flame. Such was carpet-bombing.

Large cities such as Tokyo and Yokohama were attacked by one formation after another throughout the night. For small towns one formation was ample. Picked towns received a baptism of fire; as fire called up wind and wind called up fire, fierce conflagrations arose, in which parks and streams availed nothing as places of refuge. The populace had no means of escape and were burnt to death.

Raids on the low-lying districts of Tokyo in March 1945 killed over 100,000. Sumida River's waters were at one time converted into a Turkish bath covered with burnt corpses. Not even the Great Earthquake could equal the inferno. Over the whole of Japan tens and tens of thousands were burnt to death. Day by day Japan turned into a furnace, from which the voice of a people searching for food rose in anguish. And yet the clarion call was accepted. If the Emperor ordained it, they would leap into the flames. That was the people of Japan.

From Shigemitsu: *Japan and her Destiny*

American B-29 Superfortress over Mt. Fuji.

From November 1944 to July 1945, U.S. Strategic Air Force dropped some 150,000 tons of bombs on Japanese cities.

JAPAN'S CITIES IN FLAMES   June–August 1945

4 June: 500 B-29s attacking Kobe.

B-29s raiding Osaka.

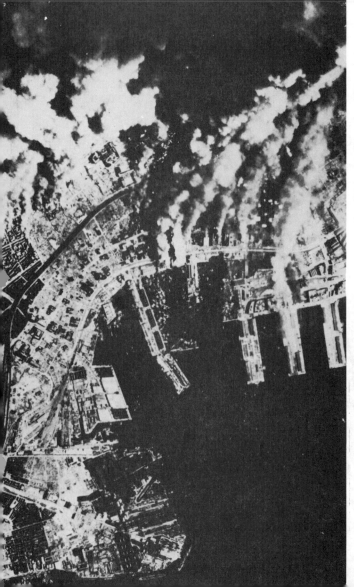

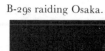

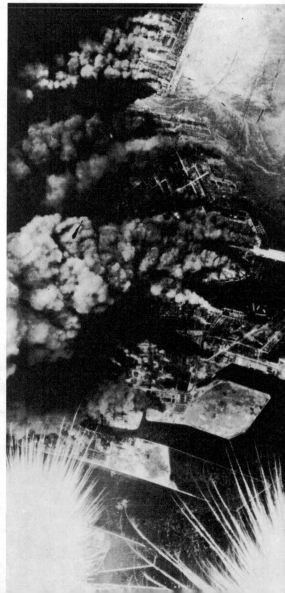

THE FATEFUL DECISION

The history of the atomic bomb and the destruction of Hiroshima and Nagasaki.

CHRONOLOGICAL TABLE: 1939–1945

1939

2/8: Einstein sends letter to President Roosevelt mentioning the possible construction of bombs which, exploded in a port, "might well destroy the whole port together with some surrounding territory".

A team of British scientists, led by George Thomson, studies atomic fission at Oxford, Cambridge, London and Liverpool.

1940

March: R. Peierls and O. R. Frisch inform the British Government that it is possible to construct an atomic bomb by using the isotope U-235.

1941

Spring: British atomic scientists make contact with their American counterparts through Sir John Cockcroft and Ernest O. Lawrence. British scientists will collaborate in the American project.

September: Lawrence reports from Berkeley, that certain new developments now make the construction of atomic bombs a feasible project.

Autumn: President Roosevelt suggests to Churchill that British and American research teams pool their ideas. A group of British physicists arrives in the United States.

6/11: National Academy Committee submits report to Vannevar Bush, Head of the National Defense Research Committee, recommending the speedy construction of an atomic bomb.

27/11: Bush submits the recommendation to President Roosevelt. Vice-President Henry A. Wallace, Secretary of War Henry L. Stimson, Chief of the General Staff George C. Marshall, and James B. Conant of the National Defense Research Committee consider the report.

6/12: Roosevelt votes "a few million dollars" for the project, and promises "enormous resources" in case of success.

7/12: Japanese attack on Pearl Harbour.

1942

17/6: President Roosevelt receives further report on the production of atomic bombs from plutonium or U-235, and instructs General William D. Styer, of the Military Policy Committee, to proceed with the atomic project.

June: Production of atomic bombs entrusted to U.S. Corps of Engineers.

17/9: Brigadier-General Leslie R. Groves chosen by Army to take charge of entire atomic project.

14/11: S-1 Committee meets in Washington.

19/11: Edward Teller, J. R. Oppenheimer, John H. Manley and Robert Serber submit a further "feasibility report".

2/12: Fermi succeeds in producing the first chain reaction in his laboratory in Chicago.

1943

April: Control of entire atomic project now in hands of U.S. Army.

4/11: Experimental reactor at Clinton Labor (Oak Ridge) put into operation.

January: Work of Oppenheimer Group in Los Alamos gradually becomes central part of entire project.

1945

Secretary of War Henry Stimson asks Interim Committee (Members: Stimson himself; George L. Harrison, president of the New York Life Insurance Company; James F. Byrnes, as personal representative of the President; Ralph A. Bard, Under-Secretary of the Navy; William L. Clayton, Assistant Secretary of State; Vannevar Bush; Karl T. Compton; and James B. Conant. Advising Committee: Enrico Fermi, E. O. Lawrence, J. R. Oppenheimer and A. H. Compton) whether and in what manner the bomb should be used. Oppenheimer notes that if the bomb were exploded over a city, some 20,000 people would probably be killed.

June: Lawrence, Fermi, Compton and Oppenheimer suggest the possibility of a non-military demonstration of the bomb, which would convince the Japanese of its deadly effects without actual loss of life. The idea is dropped, since experience has shown that the Japanese will not give up their fanatical struggle until the new weapon has been demonstrated militarily. Stimson: "We see no acceptable alternative to direct military use."

Several petitions for and against the use of the atomic bomb.

Early June: The first trial bomb is built.

16/7: First successful test explosion of an American atomic bomb in Alamogordo (New Mexico) under the direction of R. Oppenheimer. Truman in Berlin (Potsdam Conference) receives the famous message: "Babies satisfactorily born".

17/7: Second telegram from Harrison at Alamogordo to Stimson in Potsdam.

24/7: Truman tells Stalin of intention to use the bomb against Japanese.

26/7: Potsdam: U.S.A., Great Britain and China call for the unconditional surrender of Japan. The alternative is utter destruction of the country.

27/7: Allies drop pamphlets on Japan calling for surrender and warning that eleven Japanese cities will be severely bombed.

28/7: Japan ignores Potsdam ultimatum. Six of the specified cities are bombed.

30/7: Thirty young scientists and technicians from Los Alamos arrive on Tinian (Marianas) to assemble the bomb, sections of which had arrived in the *Indianapolis*, a cruiser sunk by a Japanese submarine a few days later.

6/8: President Truman announces the dropping of the first atomic bomb on Hiroshima. Japan is given 48 hours to capitulate before another bomb is dropped. (The first atomic bomb hit Hiroshima at 9:15 a.m. At 9:20 a.m., those waiting at Tinian received the message: "Mission successful". Losses: 78,150 dead, 13,983 missing and 37,425 wounded. More than half the city destroyed.)

7–9/8: Millions of leaflets calling for surrender dropped over Japan.

8/8: The Soviet Union declares war on Japan with effect from midnight, 9 August.

9/8: Second atomic bomb dropped on Nagasaki at noon. Losses: 36,000 dead, 40,000 wounded, city almost completely destroyed.

Four members of the Los Alamos team of scientists: George B. Kistakowsky, Hans A. Bethe, Edward Teller and Enrico Fermi.

THE ATOM BOMB: ITS EARLY DEVELOPMENT—1939–1942

"This phenomenon will also lead to the construction of bombs . . .

From the letter by Albert Einstein to President Roosevelt on 2 August 1939.

Some recent work by E. Fermi and L. Szilard, which has been communicated to me in manuscript, leads me to expect that the element uranium may be turned into a new and important source of energy in the immediate future.

Certain aspects of the situation which has arisen seem to call for watchfulness and, if necessary, quick action on the part of the Administration. I believe therefore that it is my duty to bring to your attention the following facts and recommendations:

In the course of the last four months it has been made probable—through the work of Joliot as well as Fermi and Szilard, in America—that it may become possible to set up a nuclear chain reaction in a large mass of uranium, by which vast amounts of power and large quantities of new radium-like elements would be generated. Now it appears almost certain that this could be achieved in the immediate future.

This new phenomenon would also lead to the construction of bombs, and it is conceivable—though less certain—that extremely powerful bombs of a new type may thus be constructed. A single bomb of this type, carried by boat and exploded in a port, might very well destroy the whole port together with some of the surrounding territory. However, such bombs might well prove to be too heavy for transportation by air.

The United States has only very poor ores in uranium in moderate quantities. There is some good ore in Canada and the former Czechoslovakia, while the most important source of uranium is the Belgian Congo.

In view of this situation you may think it desirable to have some permanent contact maintained between the Administration and the group of physicists working on chain reactions in America. One possible way of achieving this might be for you to entrust with this task a person who has your confidence and who could perhaps serve in an unofficial capacity. His task might comprise the following:

A—to approach Government departments, keep them informed of the further development, and put forward recommendations for Government action, giving particular attention to the problem of securing a supply of uranium ore for the United States.

B—to speed up the experimental work, which at present is being carried on within the limits of the budgets of university laboratories, by providing funds, if such funds are required, through his contacts with private persons who are willing to make contributions for this cause, and perhaps also by obtaining the co-operation of industrial laboratories which have the necessary equipment.

From Brown/Teller: *The Legacy of Hiroshima*

Vital Stages in the Development of the Atom Bomb

By Arthur H. Compton

Photoflash Bulbs and the Hydrogen Bomb

It was hard for me to believe that using as little material as is present in an atomic bomb the strength of the shock wave would be determined solely by the amount of energy developed. Kistiakowsky knew otherwise. The question is one of straightforward thermodynamics, which I had myself used several years before in calculating for the General Electric Company the forces that cause the bursting of photoflash bulbs. All the tests of atomic explosions have verified Kistiakowsky's point. It is to me a matter of no small interest that the same theoretical formula includes equally a tiny flash bulb and a hydrogen bomb.

". . . a sufficient mass of element U-235 . . ."

At last the report of our Committee of the National Academy of Sciences was ready. In its final form the report stated:

The possibility must be seriously considered that within a few years the use of bombs such as described above, or something similar using uranium fission, may determine military superiority. A fission bomb of superlatively destructive power will result from bringing quickly together a sufficient mass of element U-235. This seems to be as sure as any untried prediction based upon theory and experiment can be . . .

Report by U.S. Academy Committee

That such bombs could be made was only a question of time and cost. These bombs might decide the outcome of the war. The report had the unanimous approval of the committee.

I presented the report personally to Vannevar Bush on 6 November 1941. We spent an hour discussing its contents and what the next action should be. This was less than two months after the crucial meeting in Chicago with Lawrence and Conant. Bush took the report at once to President Roosevelt. A committee at the highest level was ready to consider it. This committee consisted of

President Roosevelt, Vice-President Henry A. Wallace, Secretary of War Henry L. Stimson, Chief of Staff General George C. Marshall, James B. Conant, Chairman of the National Defense Research Committee, and Vannevar Bush, Director of the newly created Office of Scientific Research and Development.

The British Thomson Committee Report

The Thomson Committee report was endorsed by the British Scientific Advisory Committee of the War Cabinet, which created a Consultative Council for its supervision. Sir John Anderson, now Lord Waverly, served as Chairman of this Council, with Sir Edward Appleton, Lord Brabazon, Lord Cherwell, Sir Henry Dale, and Lord Hankey. With the authorization of this Council, Thomson gave a copy of his report to Bush and Conant on 3 October. It was this document that was in Bush's hands when I gave him the final National Academy report. As long as the American atomic program was under the exclusive control of Bush and Conant the co-operation with the British was maintained as closely as possible.

The President acts: If Atomic Bombs can be made we must make them first

Bush had already briefed Mr. Roosevelt and Mr. Wallace on the nature of the American and British reports. Our Academy Committee report was transmitted to the President on 27 November with Bush's comments:

> The present report estimates that the bombs will be somewhat less effective than the British computation showed, although still exceedingly powerful. It predicts a longer interval before production could be started. It also estimates total costs much higher than the British figures.

Action was immediate. Bush called together a small group to hear the President's reply. Present were Conant, Briggs, Lawrence, and myself. Later included in the group were Pegram and Urey, at this moment in England, and Eger V. Murphree, Research Director of the Standard Oil Development Company. We were asked to constitute a new committee, called S-1. Our task would be to recommend to Bush action on fission research and to see that the authorized tasks were done. Our instructions were to do everything possible to find out whether atomic bombs could be made and to report back our findings within six months. If at that time the report was favorable, we should expect authorization to proceed with all the resources that the nation could make available. Out of a fund that Congress had set aside for use at his own discretion, President Roosevelt was supplying the necessary money. This meant a few million dollars, which was not large as war expenditures were going. But it presaged an enormous commitment of time and funds if the program went as expected.

(From Compton: *Atomic Quest*)

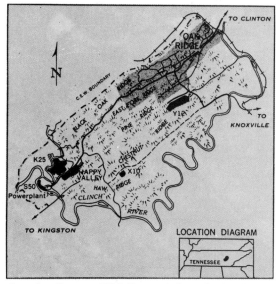

Location diagram of U.S. Research Centre in Oak Ridge.

Left: Leading scientific and technical members of the S-1 Committee in 1942. From left to right: J. R. Oppenheimer, Harold C. Urey, E. O. Lawrence, James B. Conant, Lyman J. Briggs, E. V. Murphree, A. H. Compton, R. L. Thornton and K. D. Nichols.
Right: Tablet commemorating the first man-made chain reaction.

THE FIRST ATOM BOMB TEST IN ALAMOGORDO, NEW MEXICO

16 July 1945

"The pinpoint of light grew and then faded"

Edward Teller reports on the first atom bomb test in Alamogordo

Early on the morning of July 16, 1945, I was one of a group watching the explosion of the world's first atomic bomb. Our observation post was about twenty miles from the Alamogordo test site. We were told to lie down on the sand, turn our faces away from the blast, and bury our heads in our arms. No one complied. We were determined to look the beast in the eye.

But, having practised to expect the impossible, I was cautious. Beneath the welder's glasses provided us, I wore an extra pair of dark glasses. I smeared my face with sun-tan lotion and offered some to the others. I wore a heavy pair of gloves. Holding the welder's glasses securely to my face with both gloved hands, I converted the glasses into goggles.

The test, delayed ninety minutes by a desert rainstorm, was rescheduled for 5:30 a.m. Twenty minutes before, our observation post was tied in with the control center by radio. The count-down began: "It is now minus twenty minutes, nineteen minutes, eighteen minutes, seventeen minutes . . . It now is minus thirty seconds, twenty-five, twenty, fifteen." At ten, the count-down was second by second: "Nine . . . eight . . . seven . . . six . . . five." Then there was silence.

The five seconds of quiet stretched out until I thought the explosion had failed. I was almost ready to take off my protective glasses. But then, through the glasses, I saw a tiny pin-point of light. I was disappointed: "Is this all? Is this what we have worked so hard to develop?"

In a second, I remembered that I was wearing a double thickness of dark glasses. The pin-point of light grew and then faded. I tipped my right hand away from my face to allow a crack of light beneath my glasses. It was like opening the heavy curtains of a darkened room to a flood of sunlight. Then I was impressed.

In a minute, the explosion's noise and pressure wave reached us. William H. Lawrence, the well-known and competent science reporter was alarmed: "What was that?"

I took off both pairs of dark glasses to watch the explosion's remarkable mushroom cloud swell into the atmosphere, stop when it hit a layer of warm air, and then shoot up again.

(From Teller/Brown: *The Legacy of Hiroshima*)

U.S. Secretary of War Stimson with Colonel Kyle.

Babies satisfactorily born . . .

On July 17 world-shaking news had arrived. In the afternoon Stimson called at my abode and laid before me a sheet of paper on which was written, "Babies satisfactorily born." By his manner I saw something extraordinary had happened. "It means," he said, "that the experiment in the Mexican desert has come off. The atomic bomb is a reality."

Next morning the plane arrived with a full description of this tremendous event in human history . . . The bomb, or its equivalent, had been detonated at the top of a pylon 100 feet high. Everyone had been cleared away for ten miles round, and the scientists and their staffs crouched behind massive concrete shields and shelters at about that distance. The blast had been terrific. An enormous column of flame and smoke shot up to the fringe of the atmosphere of our poor earth. Devastation inside a one-mile circle was absolute.

From Churchill: *The Second World War*

President Truman: "The secret of the Atomic bomb"

At Potsdam, as elsewhere, the secret of the atomic bomb was kept closely guarded. We did not extend the very small circle of Americans who knew about it. Churchill naturally knew about the atomic bomb project from its very beginning . . .

On July 24th I casually mentioned to Stalin that we had a new weapon of special destructive force. The Russian Premier showed no unusual interest. All he said was that he was glad to hear it and hoped we would make "good use of it against the Japanese".

Left: Sergeant Lehr carrying the active test material (plutonium). Above: Last preparations before hoisting the bomb.

SHOULD THE BOMB BE USED AGAINST JAPAN?

May to July 1945

Secretary Stimson's Statement on 31 May 1945

"Gentlemen, it is our responsibility to recommend action that may turn the course of civilization. In our hands we expect soon to have a weapon of wholly unprecedented destructive power. Today's prime fact is war. Our great task is to bring this war to a prompt and successful conclusion. We may assume that our new weapon puts in our hands overwhelming power. It is our obligation to use this power with the best wisdom we can command. To us now the matter of first importance is how our use of this new weapon will appear in the long view of history."

This, as accurately as I can recall it, was the statement made by Secretary of War Henry L. Stimson as he presented to the "Interim Committee" the question of what should be done with the atomic bomb. The place was the Secretary's office in Washington. The date was 31 May 1945.

Leo Szilard Opposes the Use of the Bomb

The heart of his argument was this: once they (atom bombs) were introduced as an instrument of war it would be difficult to resist the temptation of putting them to such use . . . Thus a nation which sets the precedent of using these newly liberated forces of nature for purposes of destruction may have to bear the responsibility of opening the door to an era of devastation on an unimaginable scale.

In this form of his petition Szilard found almost no support. His colleagues saw that other factors also needed consideration, among them that thousands of men were daily being killed on both sides . . .

85 Per Cent Agree

The question was asked in the early autumn of 1945: "Did you approve or disapprove of the use of the atomic bomb?" In the United States 85 per cent of those sampled registered approval; in other countries the vote was as follows:

	Canada	Britain	France
Approval	77%	72%	85%
Disapproval	12%	21%	10%
No opinion	11%	7%	5%

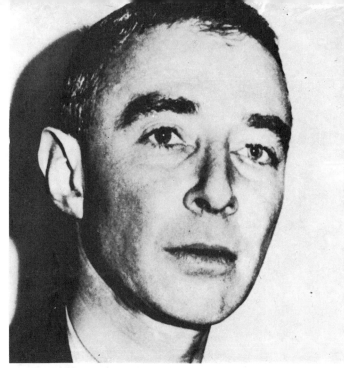

J. R. Oppenheimer: "The physicists have known sin."

The Ultimatum to Japan on 26 July

The ultimatum called for "unconditional surrender", but proceeded to offer conditions according to which the Japanese could end the war with honor. It assured the Japanese of continued sovereignty of the islands of Honshu, Hokkaido, Kyushu, Shikoku, and certain minor islands. It required that the Japanese military forces should be completely disarmed and said that they would be permitted to return to their homes. It stated further that the occupying forces of the Allies would be withdrawn from Japan when certain specific objectives had been accomplished, and when there had been established "in accordance with the freely expressed will of the Japanese people a peacefully inclined and responsible government". The alternative for Japan was given as complete and utter destruction.

From Compton, *Atomic Quest*

Top: "Little Boy", the uranium bomb dropped on Hiroshima (diameter: 29 ins., length: 10 ft.). Below: "Fat Man", the uranium bomb dropped on Nagasaki (diameter: 60 ins., length: 11 ft.).

To: General Carl Spaatz,
Commanding General,
United States Army Strategic Air Force.

24 July 1945

1. The 509 Composite Group, 20th Air Force, will deliver the first special bomb as soon as weather will permit visual bombing after about 3 August 1945 on one of the targets: Hiroshima, Kokura, Niigata and Nagasaki. To carry military and civilian scientific personnel from the War Department to observe and record the effects of the explosion of the bomb, additional aircraft will accompany the airplane carrying the bomb. The observing planes will stay several miles distant from the point of impact of the bomb.

2. Additional bombs will be delivered on the above targets as soon as made ready by the project staff. Further instructions will be issued concerning targets other than those listed above.

3. Dissemination of any and all information concerning the use of the weapon against Japan is reserved to the Secretary of War and the President of the United States. No communiqué on the subject or release of information will be issued by Commanders in the field without specific prior authority. Any news stories will be sent to the War Department for special clearance.

4. The foregoing directive is issued to you by direction and with the approval of the Secretary of War and the Chief of Staff, U.S.A. It is desired that you personally deliver one copy of this directive to General MacArthur and one copy to Admiral Nimitz for their information.

/s/ Thos. T. Hardy,
General, GSC,
Acting Chief of Staff.

HIROSHIMA, 6 AUGUST 1945, 09:15 HOURS

"The crew said, 'My God!'"

By Captain Parsons aboard the bomber Enola Gay

It was 09:15 when we dropped our bomb and we turned the plane broadside to get the best view. Then we made as much distance from the ball of fire as we could.

We were at least ten miles away and there was a visual impact even though every man wore coloured glasses for protection. We had braced ourselves when the bomb was gone for the shock and Tibbets said "close flak" and it was just like that—a close burst of anti-aircraft fire.

The crew said, "My God," and couldn't believe what had happened.

A mountain of smoke was going up in a mushroom with the stem coming down. At the top was white smoke but up to 1,000 feet from the ground there was swirling, boiling dust. Soon afterwards small fires sprang up on the edge of the town, but the town was entirely obscured. We stayed around two or three minutes and by that time the smoke had risen to 40,000 feet. As we watched, the top of the white cloud broke off and another soon formed.

(From Snyder: *The War 1939–1945*)

"Then a tremendous flash of light cut across the sky . . ."

By John Hersey

Then a tremendous flash of light cut across the sky. Mr. Tanimoto has a distinct recollection that it travelled from east to west, from the city towards the hills. It seemed a sheet of sun. Both he and Mr. Matsuo reacted in terror—and both had time to react (for they were 3,500 yards, or two miles, from the centre of the explosion). Mr. Matsuo dashed up the front steps into the house and dived among the bedrolls and buried himself there. Mr. Tanimoto took four or five steps and threw himself between two big rocks in the garden. He bellied up very hard against one of them. As his face was against the stone he did not see what happened. He felt a sudden pressure, and then splinters and pieces of board and fragments of tile fell on him . . .

When he dared, Mr. Tanimoto raised his head and saw that the rayon man's house had collapsed. He thought a bomb had fallen directly on it. Such clouds of dust had risen that there was a sort of twilight around.

In panic, not thinking for the moment of Mr. Matsuo under the ruins, he dashed out into the street. He noticed as he ran that the concrete wall of the estate had fallen over—toward the house rather than away from it. In the street, the first thing he saw was a squad of soldiers who had been burrowing into the hillside opposite, making one of the thousands of dugouts in which the Japanese apparently intended to resist invasion, hill by hill, life for life; the soldiers were coming out of the hole, where they should have been safe, and blood was running from their heads, chests and backs. They were silent and dazed.

Under what seemed to be a local dust cloud, the day grew darker and darker.

*

Outside the gate of the park, Father Kleinsorge found a faucet that still worked—part of the plumbing of a vanished house—and he filled his vessels and returned. When he had given the wounded the water, he made a second trip. This time, the woman by the bridge was dead. On his way back with the water, he got lost on a detour round a fallen tree, and as he looked for his way through the woods, he heard a voice ask from the underbrush, "Have you anything to drink?" He saw a uniform. Thinking there was just one soldier, he approached with the water. When he had penetrated the bushes, he saw there were about twenty men, and they were all in exactly the same nightmarish state: their faces were wholly burned, their eyesockets hollow, the fluid from their melted eyes had run down their cheeks. (They must have had their faces upturned when the bomb went off; perhaps they were anti-aircraft personnel.) Their mouths were mere swollen, pus-covered wounds, which they could not bear to stretch enough to admit the spout of the teapot. So Father Kleinsorge got a large piece of grass and drew out the stem so as to make a straw, and gave them all water to drink that way. One of them said: "I can't see anything." Father Kleinsorge answered as cheerfully as he could, "There's a doctor at the entrance to the park. He's busy now, but he'll come soon and fix your eyes, I hope."

(From Hersey: *Hiroshima*)

After dropping the bomb (left), the Enola Gay, a B-29 bomber, returned to Tinian (below).

Before the White House on 9 November 1945. From left to right: George L. Harrison, General L. R. Groves, James B. Conant, and Vannevar Bush.

"It was an overwhelming success"

That same day President Truman was on the cruiser *Augusta* on the fourth day of his journey home from Potsdam. He was handed an urgent message:

TO THE PRESIDENT
FROM THE SECRETARY OF WAR

Big bomb dropped on Hiroshima August 5 at 7:15 p.m. Washington time. First reports indicate complete success which was even more conspicuous than earlier test.

In a few minutes there came a second message:

Following info regarding Manhattan received. Hiroshima bombed visually with only one tenth cover at 052315A. There was no fighter opposition and no flak. Parsons reports 15 minutes after drop as follows: "Results clear cut successful in all respects. Visible effects greater than in any test. Conditions normal in aircraft following delivery."

The President, accompanied by Secretary of State James F. Byrnes, went to the *Augusta's* ward-room, where the ship's officers were at lunch. In a voice tense with excitement, he said: "Keep your seats, gentlemen, I have an announcement to make to you. We have just dropped a bomb on Japan which has more power than 20,000 tons of T.N.T. It was an overwhelming success."

Warning to Japan after Hiroshima

TO THE JAPANESE PEOPLE

America asks that you take immediate heed of what we say in this leaflet.

We are in possession of the most destructive explosive ever devised by man. A single one of our newly developed atomic bombs is actually the equivalent in explosive power to what 2,000 of our giant B-29s can carry on a single mission. This awful fact is one for you to ponder and we solemnly assure you it is grimly accurate.

We have just begun to use this weapon against your homeland. If you still have any doubt, make inquiry as to what happened to Hiroshima when just one atomic bomb fell on that city.

Before using this bomb to destroy every resource of the military by which they are prolonging this useless war, we ask that you now petition the Emperor to end the war. Our President has outlined for you the thirteen consequences of an honourable surrender. We urge that you accept these consequences and begin the work of building a new, better, and peace-loving Japan.

You should take steps now to cease military resistance. Otherwise, we shall resolutely employ this bomb and all our other superior weapons to promptly and forcefully end the war.

Radio Tokyo reported:

The impact of the bomb is so terrific that practically all living things, humans and animals were seared to death by the tremendous heat and pressure engendered by the blast. All the dead and injured were burned beyond recognition. With houses and buildings crushed, including many emergency medical facilities, authorities are having their hands full in giving every available relief possible under the circumstances. The effect of the bomb is widespread. Those outdoors burned to death, while those indoors were killed by the indescribable pressure and heat.

(From Snyder: *The War 1939–1945*)

62,200 of Hiroshima's 90,000 houses were completely destroyed, and 6,000 more were damaged beyond repair.

Official figures gave 78,150 dead, 13,983 missing and 37,425 wounded in Hiroshima. Captain R. A. Lewis noted in the *Enola Gay* log-book that he would never forget those few minutes even if he lived to be a hundred.

Nagasaki on 9 August 1945

Twenty minutes after the bombing of Nagasaki, Hiro-michi Matsuda, a Japanese industrial worker, took this photograph from a suburb.

NAGASAKI, 9 AUGUST 1945, NOON

The deadly effect of the rays

Dr. Sasaki and his colleagues at the Red Cross Hospital watched the unprecedented disease unfold and at last evolved a theory about its nature. It had, they decided, three stages. The first stage had been all over before the doctors even knew they were dealing with a new sick-ness: it was the direct reaction to the bombardment of the body, at the moment when the bomb went off, by neutrons, beta particles, and gamma rays. The apparently uninjured people who had died so mys-teriously in the first few hours or days had succumbed in this first stage. It killed ninetyfive per cent of the people within a half-mile of the centre, and many thousands who were further away. The doctors realized in retrospect that even though most of these dead had also suffered from burns and blast effects, they had absorbed enough radia-tion to kill them. The rays simply destroyed the body cells—caused their nuclei to degenerate and to break their walls. Many people who did not die right away came down with nausea, headache, diarrhoea, malaise, and fever, which lasted several days. Doctors could not be certain whether some of these symptoms were the result of radiation or nervous shock. The second stage set in ten or fifteen days after the bombing. The main symptom was falling hair. Diarrhoea and fever, which in some cases went as high as 106°, came next. Twentyfive to thirty days after the explosion, blood disorders appeared: gums bled, the white blood-cell count dropped sharply, and *petechiae* appeared on the skin and mucuous membranes. The drop in the number of white blood corpuscles reduced the patient's capacity to resist infection, so open wounds were unusually slow in healing and many of the sick developed sore throats and mouths. The two key symptoms, on which the doctors came to base their prognosis, were fever and the lowered white corpuscle count. If fever remained steady and high, the patient's chances of survival were poor. The white count almost always dropped below four thousand: a patient whose count fell below one thousand had little hope of living. Toward the end of the second stage, if the patient survived, anaemia, or a drop in the red blood count also set in. The third stage was the reaction that came when the body struggled to compensate for its ills—when, for instance, the white count not only returned to normal but increased to much higher than normal levels. In this stage, many patients died of complications, such as infections in the chest cavity. Most burns healed with deep layers of pink, rubbery scar tissue, known as keloid tumours. The duration of the disease varied, depending on the patient's constitution and the amount of radiation he had received.   (From Hersey: *Hiroshima*)

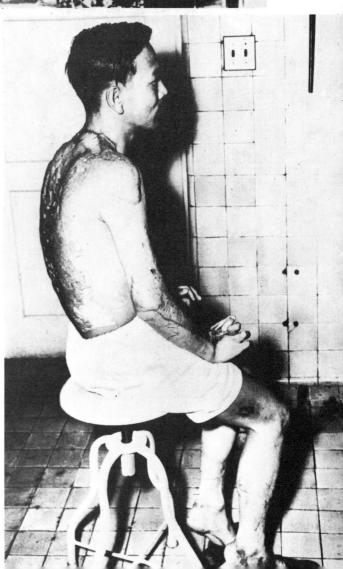

A victim of the Hiroshima bomb during a check-up in an American hospital, two years later. ▶

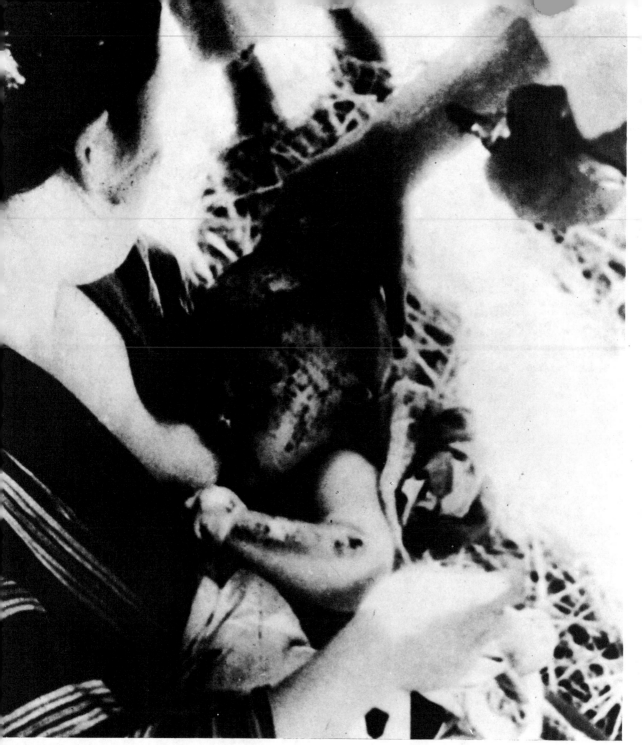

Mother and child—Hiroshima, 1945.

The lesson that men everywhere must learn

By Henry L. Stimson, U.S. Secretary for War.

In this last great action of the Second World War we were given final proof that war is death. War in the twentieth century has grown steadily more barbarous, more destructive, more debased in all its aspects. Now, with the release of atomic energy, man's ability to destroy himself is very nearly complete. The bombs dropped on Hiroshima and Nagasaki ended a war. They also made it wholly clear that we must never have another war. This is the lesson men and leaders everywhere must learn, and I believe that when they learn it they will find a way to lasting peace. There is no other choice.

A GOD IS VANQUISHED

The Soviet entry into the E. Asian theatre of war, the Emperor's capitulation, and the occupation of Japan by U.S. troops.

CHRONOLOGICAL TABLE:

1945

8/8: Soviet Union declares war on Japan.

9/8: Soviet troops enter N. Manchuria.

10/8: Japanese Government announces that it is prepared to accept the Allied ultimatum of 26 July and capitulate provided the sovereignty of the Emperor is maintained.

Malik, the Soviet ambassador, informs Foreign Minister Togo that the Soviet Union has joined the Allies in demanding Japan's unconditional surrender. Togo declares Japan's readiness to capitulate, but repeats stipulation about the Emperor's sovereignty. The offer is sent simultaneously to London and Washington via Sweden and Switzerland.

10–11/8: Molotov tries to delay the Soviet reply to the Japanese note for two days, so as not to jeopardize the advance of the Red Army in Manchuria and subsequent Soviet territorial claims. American ambassador presses for a decision.

11/8: Allied and Soviet reply reaches Tokyo. Emperor's powers to be restricted, Japan to elect its own government which, during the immediate post-war period, will have to be under the control of General MacArthur.

11–14/8: Marshal Vassilievsky appointed Supreme Commander, Red Armies in the Far East. Soviet troops have advanced up to 12 miles into Manchuria.

12/8: Soviet troops march into N. Korea.

13/8: Instrument of surrender approved by President Truman and forwarded to General MacArthur.

14/8: After three days of consultation in the Japanese Council before the throne, Emperor Hirohito demands and obtains agreement to capitulation in terms of the Allied note of 11 August. The end of the war is announced simultaneously in London, Washington, Moscow and Chungking.

15/8: General MacArthur appointed Supreme Commander, Allied Forces in the Pacific.

Japanese Emperor announces capitulation in a personal broadcast address, and orders the termination of hostilities on all fronts.

19/8: Japanese delegation arrives in Manila to make arrangements for the occupation of Japan.

20/8: Japanese delegation leaves Manila with full instructions.

Japanese forces in Manchuria surrender to Red Army, after Prince Takeda, the Emperor's brother, has personally transmitted the Emperor's orders.

21/8: Japanese commander of the remnants of Kwangtung Army in Manchuria capitulates to Red Army in Changchun.

23/8: Despite the Japanese capitulation, the Red Army continues to advance and to occupy all the territory promised to the Soviet Union at Yalta. An Order of the Day by Marshal Stalin then announces the end of hostilities.

27/8: U.S. warships enter Sagami Bay, Tokyo.

28/8: Typhoon delays occupation of Japan for 48 hours.

30/8: U.S. forces occupy Japan. U.S. 11th Airborne Division lands on Atsugi airfield; 6th Marine Division lands at Yokosuka naval base.

Rear-Admiral Harcourt enters Hong Kong harbour with a powerful British naval force.

2/9: Signing of the unconditional surrender of Japan on board the U.S. battleship *Missouri.*

8/9: U.S. troops enter Tokyo.

9/9: Formal surrender of about 100,000 Japanese troops in China signed at a ceremony in Nanking.

12/9: Admiral Mountbatten accepts the official surrender of all Japanese forces in S.E. Asia in the Council' Chamber of the Municipal Buildings in Singapore.

16/9: Official surrender of Hong Kong by the Japanese.

End of September: Admiral Fraser sends a British squadron to Rabaul, to accept the surrender of some 140,000 Japanese troops, which have been cut off for more than a year in New Britain and neighbouring islands.

16/11: Capitulation of all Japanese troops completed.

SOVIET UNION DECLARES WAR ON JAPAN   8 August 1945

The Soviet Information Bureau announces:

In the Far East, Soviet troops have crossed the Manchurian border on a broad front at dawn on 9 August. One Soviet Army, attacking from the Maritime Province, overcame strong initial resistance from the Japanese Kwantung Army, pierced powerful concrete fortifications, crossed the Amur and Ussuri rivers in the Khabarovsk area, and advanced over 9 miles into Manchuria, capturing the town of Fuyuan and other inhabited localities. About 1,000 miles to the west, another Soviet army, striking south and S.E. from Transbaikalia, obtained similar initial success . . .

"The hour of victory is at hand"

The Chinese people heartily welcome the Soviet government's declaration of war on Japan on 8 August. The Soviet Union's action will very much shorten the duration of the war against Japan. The war is already in its last stage and the time has come for us to defeat finally the Japanese invaders and all their jackals . . .

All the people in our country must make efforts to prevent civil war and expedite the formation of a democratic coalition government. A new stage in China's war of national liberation has arrived: all our people should strengthen their solidarity and struggle for the final victory.

From: *Selected Works of Mao Tse-Tung*

◄ Entering Manchuria from Vladivostok, the Red Army forced the Japanese back to Changchun.

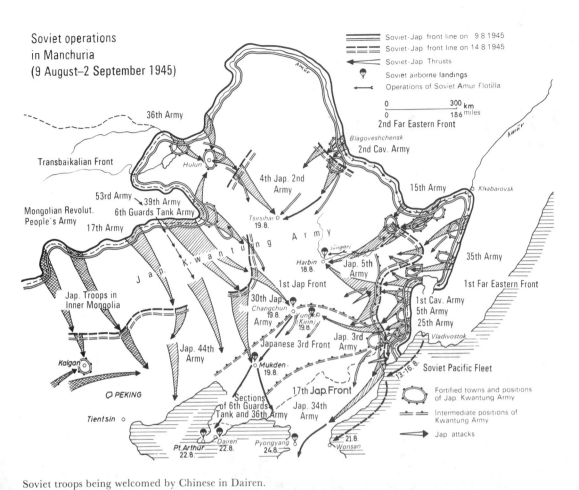

Soviet operations in Manchuria (9 August–2 September 1945)

Soviet-Jap. front line on 9.8.1945
Soviet-Jap. front line on 14.8.1945
Soviet-Jap. Thrusts
Soviet airborne landings
Operations of Soviet Amur Flotilla

| 0 | 300 | km |
| 0 | 186 | miles |

36th Army

Transbaikalian Front

Hulun

2nd Far Eastern Front

Blagoveshchensk
2nd Cav. Army

4th Jap. 2nd Army

15th Army

Khabarovsk

53rd Army
39th Army
6th Guards Tank Army

Tsitsihar 19.8.

Mongolian Revolut. People's Army

17th Army

J a p.   K w a n t u n g   A r m y

Sungari

Harbin 18.8.

Jap. 5th Army

35th Army

1st Far Eastern Front

Jap. Troops in Inner Mongolia

1st Jap Front

30th Jap. Army
Changchun 19.8.

Yungki (Kirin) 19.8.

Japanese 3rd Front

Jap. 3rd Army

1st Cav. Army
5th Army
25th Army

Vladivostok

Kalgan

Jap. 44th Army

Mukden 19.8.

17th Jap. Front

Jap. 34th Army

13.–16.8.

Soviet Pacific Fleet

PEKING

Sections of 6th Guards Tank and 36th Army

Tientsin

Pt. Arthur 22.8.
Dairen 22.8.

Pyongyang 24.8.

21.8. Wonsan

Fortified towns and positions of Jap. Kwantung Army
Intermediate positions of Kwantung Army
Jap. attacks

Soviet troops being welcomed by Chinese in Dairen.

Soviet troops in Port Arthur. The Red Army continued its advance into Manchuria until 23 August 1945.

On 11 August, Marshal Vassilievsky took command of all Soviet troops in the Far East.

Japanese troops surrendering on 20 August.

Stalin's Conditions for Entering the War Against Japan

By Winston S. Churchill

In the most rigid secrecy Stalin informed Roosevelt and myself at the Crimea Conference (on 11 February) of the Soviet Government's willingness to enter the war against Japan two or three months after Germany's surrender, on the conditions stated below:

1. (a) Preservation of the *status quo* in Outer Mongolia.
   (b) Restoration of the Russian rights lost in the year 1904, viz.:
      (i) Recovery of Southern Sakhalin and the islands adjacent to it.
      (ii) Internationalization of the commercial port of Dairen, with safeguards for the pre-eminent interests of the U.S.S.R. and restoration of the lease of Port Arthur as a Soviet naval base.
      (iii) Joint operation by a Soviet–Chinese company of the Chinese Eastern Railway and the South Manchuria Railway, providing an outlet to Dairen, on the understanding that the pre-eminent interest of the U.S.S.R. will be safeguarded and that China will retain full sovereignty in Manchuria.
   (c) Acquisition by the U.S.S.R. of the Kurile Islands.

2. These conditions were embodied in a personal agreement between Roosevelt, Stalin and myself. The agreement recognized that Chiang Kai Shek's concurrence to the conditions would be required, and Roosevelt undertook to obtain this concurrence on advice from Stalin. We all three agreed to see that the Soviet claims were fulfilled without question following the defeat of Japan. The agreement contained nothing else, except an expression of Russian readiness to enter into a treaty of alliance with China with the object of helping the latter to throw off the Japanese yoke.

*

General Antonov, Chief of the Staff of the Red Army, in a broadcast from Moscow on 15 August, declared that the Japanese Emperor's statement (on the capitulation of Japan) was only a general declaration concerning unconditional surrender, and that, as the cease-fire order to the enemy had not yet been given, and the enemy continued to resist as hitherto, the Red Army would continue their Manchurian offensive.

Chinese Communists entering Kalgan, N.W. of Peking.

The Emperor Hirohito touring Tokyo four days before the American occupation.

HIROHITO ACCEPTS HIS COUNTRY'S UNCONDITIONAL SURRENDER

14 August 1945

The Emperor gives his decision

By M. Shigemitsu

The last Council before the Throne was convened on 14 August. In addition to the Supreme War Council the entire Cabinet attended. The Prime Minister recounted in detail the progress of this question of acceptance of the Potsdam Declaration, which he said had resulted in a difference of opinion between the Army and other parties concerned. The meeting was then open to discussion. Army representatives contented themselves with a brief statement of their views, but there was no general debate.

The Emperor then gave his decision. H.I.M. adopted the view of the Minister of Foreign Affairs and announced that the American reply should be accepted.

The final decision was taken to accept the Potsdam Declaration.

On the following day, 15 August, the Emperor himself broadcast to the nation that the war was at an end.

The Suzuki Cabinet then tendered its resignation . . .

From Shigemitsu: Japan and Her Destiny

From the Emperor Hirohito's broadcast to the nation of 14 August 1945

Indeed we declared war on America and Britain out of our sincere desire to ensure Japan's self-preservation and the stabilization of East Asia, it being far from our thought either to infringe upon the sovereignty of other nations or to embark upon territorial aggrandisement. But now the war has lasted for nearly four years. In spite of the best that has been done by everyone — the gallant fighting of the military and naval forces, the diligence and assiduity of our servants of the State, and the devoted service of our 100,000,000 people — the war situation has developed not necessarily to Japan's advantage, while the general trends of the world have all turned against her interests. The enemy, moreover, has begun to employ a new and most cruel bomb, the power of which to do damage is indeed incalculable, taking toll of many innocent lives. Should we continue to fight, it would not only result in the ultimate collapse and obliteration of the Japanese nation but would lead also to the total extinction of human civilization . . .

*

On 16 August, Tokyo transmitted the following radio message to General MacArthur:

H.M. the Emperor has issued an Imperial rescript to the entire armed forces to cease hostilities immediately. It may, however, take some time for this rescript to reach our troops on remote islands or in mountainous regions.

Japanese prisoners on Rota Island, north of Guam.

AMERICANS LAND IN SAGAMI AND TOKYO BAYS 30 August 1945

U.S. 3rd Fleet in Sagami Bay. Mt. Fuji can be seen in the background.

General MacArthur and General Eichelberger, Commander of U.S. 8th Army, on Atsugi airfield, Tokyo.

The occupation of Yokosuka and Atsugi

With hundreds of Hellcats, Corsairs, and Seafires flying triumphantly above, Allied carriers, battleships, and their escorts accompanied by scores of transports and auxiliaries began moving into Japanese coastal waters on 28 August before steaming into Sagami Wan the next day to await and then support the scheduled landings at Yokosuka, Yokohama, and other points along Sagami and Tokyo Bays.

Major occupation forces landed early morning of 30 August with Marines and Army airborne troops hitting Japanese soil almost simultaneously. Under command of Brigadier General William Clements the first Marine unit to land, the 2nd Battalion of the 4th Regiment of the 6th Division, went ashore at Futtsu Cape, on the eastern shore of Tokyo Bay opposite Yokosuka. It was a fitting tribute that the 4th Marines could be the first to land on Japanese soil. It was the old 4th that had fought at Bataan and Corregidor until every man had been killed, wounded, or captured.

At 35 minutes past 9:00 in the morning with all the heavy guns of the anchored fleet trained ashore, 9,000 Marines, 1,200 bluejackets, and 450 British marines and sailors landed at Yokosuka Naval Base, 30 August—using the main seaborne landing. Half an hour later the cruiser *San Diego*, flagship of Rear-Admiral Oscar C. Badger, docked at the Japanese naval base. At 12 minutes past 11:00 a.m. surrender of Yokosuka was accepted by Rear-Admiral Robert B. Carney.

Meanwhile the 11th Airborne Division had established a perimeter around Atsugi airfield and had occupied Yokohama in preparation for the arrival of General MacArthur, who was expected in his personal plane "Bataan" that afternoon. Major-General Joseph M. Swing, Commander of the 11th Airborne, was the first of his division to set foot on Japanese soil. Under cover of Army and Navy fighter squadrons, C-47s and C-54s landed at the rate of 20 planes an hour. Except for a few bursts of anti-aircraft at one of the transport planes, all the landings were made without incident.

Occupation forces spread smoothly and swiftly. Troops from the 11th Airborne took up their stand on the south banks of the Tama River and awaited the official surrender ceremonies before moving into Tokyo. In a driving rain Marines landed at Tateyama Naval Base, at the eastern entrance of Sagami Bay, to prepare for the arrival of the Eighth Army the next day.

(From: *Battle Report*, Vol. V)

At 9:35 a.m. on 30 August, 9,450 Allied marines and 1,200 sailors set foot on Japanese soil at Yokosuka.

Troops of U.S. 8th Army occupying Japan after the official surrender. General MacArthur announced on 21 September that he intended to bring in a total of about 500,000 men. The peaceful occupation of Japan and speedy implementation of all measures would have been impossible without the preservation and support of the dynasty. It was quite untrue that the Japanese had hidden arms or that they did not appreciate the implications of their defeat.

JAPANESE CAPITULATE ON THE PHILIPPINES 25 August 1945

General Yamashita Surrenders

Island by island the Philippines were recovered, but although the battlefront had moved inexorably towards the mainland of Japan, General Yamashita was still in the field at the end of the war. He finally gave in on 25 August 1945 . . .

On 16 August—the Emperor first offered to capitulate on 10 August—the attitude of the Japanese interrogators abruptly changed. The pilot received medical treatment for his parachute-jump injuries and was extended many small courtesies. The next day the American was guided towards the American lines; when the Japanese soldiers had gone as far as they dared, they gave the flier a letter, written by Yamashita himself, which explained the circumstances of the pilot's capture and commended him for his military spirit and devotion to duty.

On 24 August the same pilot flew an L.5 liaison plane over the area in which he had been held, and dropped a message of thanks to General Yamashita and two signals of great visibility. The message, written by General Gill of 32 Division, suggested that if Yamashita were in the mood for surrender negotiations he should display the two signal panels as evidence of his willingness to parley. The following morning another pilot found the panels staked out according to instruction; also on the ground were many cheering, hand-waving Japanese soldiers, who beckoned the plane to land. Instead, a second message was dropped. It suggested that Yamashita send an envoy to the American lines to receive detailed instructions for his surrender.

Late in the afternoon of 26 August a Japanese captain, carrying Yamashita's answer, entered the American lines under a flag of truce. The letter, which was written in English, follows:

Although General MacArthur announced the liberation of the Philippines on 5 July, adding that 23 of the 53 Japanese divisions in the area had been wiped out, the Japanese under General Yamashita continued to resist until 25 August 1945. In the photograph: the Japanese delegation arriving in Manila on 31 August to sign the instrument of surrender.

> General Headquarters,
> Imperial Japanese Army in the Philippines
> 25 August 1945.
>
> To:
> General W. H. Gill,
> Commanding-General Kiangan–Boyombong Area,
> United States Army in the Philippines.
>
> 1. I have the honour to acknowledge receipt of your communication addressed to me, dropped by your aircraft on 24 August as well as your papers dropped on 25 August in response to our ground signals.
>
> 2. I am taking this opportunity to convey to you that order from Imperial Headquarters pertaining to cessation of hostilities was duly received by me on 20 August and that I have immediately issued orders to cease hostilities to all units under my command insofar as communications were possible. I also wish to add to this point the expression of my heartfelt gratitude to you, fully cognizant of the sincere efforts and deep concern you have continuously shown with reference to cessation of hostilities as evidenced by various steps and measures you have taken in this connexion. To date of writing, however, I have failed to receive order from Imperial Headquarters authorizing me to enter into direct negotiations here in the Philippines with the United States Army concerning the carrying out of the order for cessation of hostilities, but I am of the fond belief that upon receipt of this order, negotiations can be immediately entered into. Presenting my compliments and thanking you for your courteous letter. I remain, yours respectfully,
>
> (Signed) T. Yamashita,
> General, Imperial Japanese Army,
> Highest Commander of the Imperial
> Japanese Army in the Philippines.

(From Flower/Reeves: *The War 1939–1945*)

Rear-Admiral Matsubara (Japanese Commander of Marcus Island) surrendering to Rear-Admiral Whiting (U.S. Commander in Saipan) on board the U.S. destroyer *Bagley* on 31 August 1945.

PENANG SURRENDERS—HONG KONG BACK IN BRITISH HANDS

30 August 1945

Penang, Malaya; Japanese signing instrument of surrender on 1 September. Left: Rear-Admiral Walker, R.N.

Four Japanese soldiers surrendering in Hong Kong on 30 August. The official surrender ceremony did not take place until 16 September.

The *Missouri* during the capitulation ceremony.

SHIGEMITSU CONCEDES DEFEAT

2 September 1945

Signal "Well done"

0800 Steaming as before. Position 34°-00-00 North Latitude 142-11-00 East Longitude. 0804 Received news flash that President Truman had announced Japan's surrender. 0840 Early morning strikes returning and landing as directed. 1055 Received orders from Admiral Nimitz to cease offensive operations against Japan; but to continue searches and to beware of treachery. 1110 Broke out *Missouri*'s Battle Flag and Admiral Halsey's Four Star Flag and began sounding ship's whistle and siren. All ships in the task force followed the motion. Admirals Halsey and Carney on the bridge to witness the event. 1113 Admiral Halsey ordered the signal "Well Done" hoisted to fleet. So closes the watch we have been looking forward to, unconditional surrender of Japan, with Admiral Halsey at sea in command of the greatest combined fighting fleet in all history! As he stands on the bridge I can see a gleam in his eye that is unmistakable.

Signed, H. E. Stassen, Commander on board the *Missouri*

Japanese Foreign Minister Shigemutsu signing the instrument of surrender on board the *Missouri* in Tokyo Bay. Left: Lieut.-General Sutherland, Chief of Staff, U.S. Forces in S.W. Pacific.

The Japanese instrument of surrender

We, acting by command of and on behalf of the Emperor of Japan, the Japanese Government and the Japanese Imperial General Headquarters, hereby accept the provisions set forth in the declaration issued by the heads of the Governments of the United States, China and Great Britain on 26 July 1945, at Potsdam, and subsequently adhered to by the Union of Soviet Socialist Republics, which four powers are hereafter referred to as the Allied Powers.

We hereby proclaim the unconditional surrender to the Allied Powers of the Japanese Imperial General Headquarters and of all Japanese armed forces and all armed forces under Japanese control wherever situated.

We hereby command all Japanese forces wherever situated and the Japanese people to cease hostilities forthwith, to preserve and save from damage all ships, aircraft, and military and civil property and to comply with all requirements which may be imposed by the Supreme Commander for the Allied Powers or by agencies of the Japanese Government at his direction.

We hereby command the Japanese Imperial General Headquarters to issue at once orders to the Commanders of all Japanese forces and all forces under Japanese control wherever situated to surrender unconditionally themselves and all forces under their control.

We hereby command all civil, military and naval officials to obey and enforce all proclamations, orders and directives deemed by the Supreme Commander for the Allied Powers to be proper to effectuate this surrender and issued by him or under his authority and we direct all such officials to remain at their posts and to continue to perform their non-combatant duties unless specifically relieved by him or under his authority.

We hereby undertake for the Emperor, the Japanese Government and their successors to carry out the provisions of the Potsdam Declaration in good faith, and to issue whatever orders and take whatever action may be required by the Supreme Commander for the Allied Powers or by any other designated representative of the Allied Powers for the purpose of giving effect to that Declaration.

We hereby command the Japanese Imperial Government and the Japanese Imperial General Headquarters at once to liberate all allied prisoners of war and civilian internees now under Japanese control and to provide for their protection, care, maintenance and immediate transportation to places as directed.

The authority of the Emperor and the Japanese Government to rule the state shall be subject to the Supreme Commander for the Allied Powers who will take such steps as he deems proper to effectuate those terms of surrender.

Signed at *Tokyo Bay, Japan* at *0908* on the *second* day of September 1945.

MAMORU SHIGEMITSU
By Command and on behalf of the
Emperor of Japan and the Japanese Government

YOSHIJIRO UMEZU
By command and on behalf of the
Japanese Imperial General Headquarters

THE IMPERIAL RESCRIPT OF 2 SEPTEMBER 1945

Accepting the terms set forth in Declaration issued by the heads of the Governments of the United States, Great Britain and China on 26 July 1945 at Potsdam and subsequently adhered to by the Union of Soviet Socialist Republics, We have commanded the Japanese Imperial Government and the Japanese Imperial General Headquarters to sign on Our behalf the Instrument of Surrender presented by the Supreme Commander for the Allied Powers and to issue General Orders to the Military and Naval Forces in accordance with the direction of the Supreme Commander for the Allied Powers. We command all Our people forthwith to cease hostilities, to lay down their arms and faithfully to carry out all the provisions of Instrument of Surrender and the General Orders issued by the Japanese Imperial Government and the Japanese Imperial General Headquarters hereunder.

This second day of the ninth month of the twentieth year of Syowa.

Seal of the Emperor	HIROHITO
Naruhiko-o *Prime Minister*	Kenzo Matsumura *Minister of Welfare*
Mamoru Shigemitsu *Minister for Foreign Affairs*	Kotaro Sengoku *Minister of Agriculture and Forestry*
Iwao Yamazaki *Minister for Home Affairs*	Chikuhei Nakajima *Minister of Commerce and Industry*
Juichi Tsushima *Minister of Finance*	Naoto Kobiyama *Minister of Transportation*
Sadamu Shimomura *Minister of War*	Fumimaro Konoe *Minister without Portfolio*
Mitsumasa Yonai *Minister of Navy*	Taketora Ogata *Minister without Portfolio*
Chuzo Iwata *Minister of Justice*	Binshiro Obata *Minister without Portfolio*
Tamon Maeda *Minister of Education*	

From Butow: *Japan's Decision to Surrender*

Holding the Imperial rescript, from left to right: Secretary of War Stimson, Chief of General Staff G. Marshall, President Truman, Admiral of the Fleet King, and Secretary of State Dean Acheson.

Singapore, 4 September 1945: General Itagaki (centre) surrendering Japanese forces in S.E. Asia.

SUPREME COMMANDER
JAPANESE EXPEDITIONARY FORCES,
SOUTHERN REGIONS.

SUPREME ALLIED COMMANDER,
SOUTH EAST ASIA

SURRENDER IN SOUTH-EAST ASIA

12 September 1945

The Vanquished

By Lieutenant-General Slim

In Singapore on 12 September 1945 I sat on the left of the Supreme Commander, Admiral Mountbatten, in the line of his Commanders-in-Chief and principal staff officers, when the formal unconditional surrender of all Japanese forces, land, sea, and air, in South-east Asia was made to him. I looked at the dull impassive masks that were the faces of the Japanese generals and admirals seated opposite. Their plight moved me not at all. For them, I had none of the sympathy of soldier for soldier, that I had felt for Germans, Turks, Italians, or Frenchmen that by the fortune of war I had seen surrender. I knew too well what these men and those under their orders had done to *their* prisoners. They sat there apart from the rest of humanity. If I had no feeling for them, they, it seemed, had no feeling of any sort, until Itagaki, who had replaced Field-Marshal Terauchi, laid low by a stroke, leant forward to affix his seal to the surrender document. As he pressed heavily on the paper, a spasm of rage and despair twisted his face. Then it was gone and his mask was as expressionless as the rest. Outside, the same Union Jack that had been hauled down in surrender in 1942 flew again at the masthead.

The war was over.

(From: Flower/Reeves: *The War 1939–1945*)

◀ The instrument of surrender bearing the signatures of General Itagaki and Admiral Mountbatten.

JAPANESE FORCES CAPITULATE IN RABAUL, NEW BRITAIN, NEW GUINEA, SOLOMON IS. AND BOUGAINVILLE

September 1945

Admiral Kusaka (left) discussing the occupation of Rabaul with Lt.-General Sturdee (Australian 1st Army).

Lt.-General Imamura surrendering Japanese forces in New Britain, New Guinea and the Solomon Is. on board the carrier *Glory*.

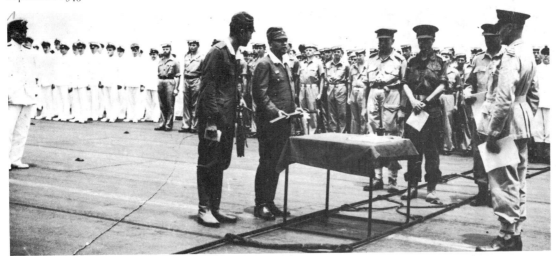

Lt.-General Savage (Austr. 2nd Corps) accepting the capitulation of Bougainville from General Kanda.

General Okamura, Japanese Commander in China, signing the surrender of all Japanese forces in China, Formosa and French Indo-China at Nanking on 8 September.

SURRENDER IN CHINA, SAIGON, MANCHURIA AND BORNEO

September 1945

The French in Saigon

On 12 September, the first French troops, and on the 13th a British unit, arrived in Saigon. Riots broke out in the city on the twentythird, and several Europeans and Americans were killed by fanatics. Nevertheless, Allied forces, including a regiment of French soldiers and officers who had recently been prisoners of war, finally gained the upper hand. Jean Cédile negotiated a truce and on 5 October General Leclerc entered the capital . . .

In Europe, in Africa, in Asia, where France had suffered an unprecedented humiliation, an astonishing recovery and an extraordinary combination of circumstances already offered her the opportunity of playing a role in accordance with her genius. Were these the first rays of a new dawn or the last rays of the setting sun?

(from the War Memoirs of General de Gaulle)

◄ Japanese forces in Harbin surrendering to Major General Shalkov of the Red Army.

Japanese in Borneo surrendering on board the *Burdekin* (Australian Navy).

Japanese capitulation in Saigon.

Jubilation in San Francisco

ALLIED VICTORY IN ASIA

To the President of the United States of America, Harry S. Truman

    Allow me, on the occasion of your signing the instrument of surrender by Japan, to congratulate you, the U.S. Government and the American people on your great victory over Japan.

    I salute the forces of the United States of America on the occasion of their brilliant victory.

J. STALIN

2 September 1945

THE STRUGGLE AGAINST COLONIALISM

Resistance to Japanese colonial rule in 1940–45 and the fight for post-war independence.

INDIA

1940

March: Indian Congress demands complete independence as "only solution".
23/3: Moslem League (under Mohammed Jinnah) calls for the creation of two independent Moslem states in N.W. and I. India ("Pakistan Resolution").
October: Gandhi launches anti-war *satyagraha.*

1942

22/3–12/4: Sir Stafford Cripps leads mission to India: India is promised Dominion status after the war.
June: First "Free India" Congress held in Bangkok (its leader, Subhas Chandra Bose, is still in Europe).
July–August: Gandhi calls on British to quit India. Last non-co-operation campaign.
9/8: Gandhi arrested.

1942–1943

British Government proscribes Congress. Arrest of Congress leaders gives rise to widespread disturbances (318 railway stations burned, 1,945 post offices attacked and 11,285 telephone and telegraph lines cut).

1943

Emergence of "Indian National Army" (from December 1941 under Mahan Sing, dissolved in 1942, and re-organized in 1943 by S. C. Bose to participate in the Japanese spring offensive in Burma.)
21/10: Japanese establish "Provisional Government of Free India" in Singapore under Bose (transferred on 28/4/1943 from a German to a Japanese submarine); Bose declares war on U.S.A. and Gt. Britain.

Mahatma Gandhi (1869–1948).

Pandit Jawaharlal Nehru (1889–1964).

1944

6/5: Gandhi released from prison for health reasons.

1945

20/3: Lord Wavell (Viceroy of India since 20/10/1943) stresses the necessity of handing over power to the Indians in an article in *The Times.*
14/6: New British plan for India. Release of leading Congress members (including Nehru) from prison.
25/6–14/7: Simla Conference to form Executive Council, on which Indian public opinion will be more strongly represented than heretofore. Conference founders due to Moslem conditions.

"Without Truth and Non-Violence: Destruction for Humanity."

From a letter by Gandhi to Nehru on 5 October 1945

"I am convinced that if India is to attain true freedom and through India the world also, then sooner or later the fact must be recognized that people will have to live in villages, not in towns, in huts, not in palaces. Scores of people will never be able to live at peace with each other in towns and palaces. They will then have no recourse but to resort to both violence and untruth. I hold that without truth and non-violence there can be nothing but destruction for humanity. We can realize truth and non-violence only in the simplicity of village life and this simplicity can best be found in the Charka and all that the Charka connotes. I must not fear if the world today is going the wrong way. It may be that India too will go that way and like the proverbial moth burn itself eventually in the flame round which it dances more and more furiously. But it is my bounden duty up to my last breath to try to protect India and through India the entire world from such a doom. The essence of what I have said is that man should rest content with what are his real needs and become self-sufficient. If he does not have this control he cannot save himself. After all the world is made up of individuals just as it is the drops that constitute the ocean. I have said nothing new. This is a well known truth."

bhas Chandra Bose (1897–1945).

47
8: India gains independence (within the British Commonwealth).

EYLON
43
: Keunemann formally establishes Communist Party.

47
lon gains independence (within the British Commonwealth).

URMA
(under British rule since 1885)

41
cember: Emergence of Burma Independence Army under Aung San.

42
7: Japanese dissolve Burma Independence Army.

43
2–20/5: The Chindits (Indian 77th Brigade) under Wingate wage erilla warfare behind the enemy lines.
: National Assembly in Rangoon declares independence of Burma der Ba Maw.
/8: Declaration of war on Allies. Pact with Japan. Formation of w army.
'9: New army becomes Burma National Army.

44
ne: Thakin Soe and Thein Pe (Communists) form anti-Japanese rtisan Army.
8: Burmese Government in exile formed in Simla.

45
'3: After making secret contact with the Allies (beginning in 1gust, 1944), Burmese National Army declares war on Japan.
/8: The anti-Fascist organization becomes Anti-Fascist People's ague for Freedom under U Nu.

1948
4/1: Burma becomes an independent state outside the British Commonwealth.

THAILAND
(independent since 1851)

1941
21/12: Marshal Pibul Songram enters alliance with Japan.

1942
25/1: Declaration of war on U.S.A. and Gt. Britain.

1942–43
Thailand annexes Shan States and Kedah, Kelantan, Perlis and Trengganu (Malaya) with Japanese help. Dictatorship under Marshal Pibul Songram.
  Formation of Free Thai Organization (under Pridi Phanomyong); more than 50,000 guerillas co-operate with the Allies.

1945
Thailand surrenders annexed territories.

1946
Government formed under Pridi Phanomyong.

Religions in S.E. Asia (in per cent)						
Country	Population in Millions	Hindus	Moslems	Christians	Buddhists	Others
Bhutan	0·70			80		
Brunei	0·08		70	20		10
Burma	21·50	4	4	85		
Cambodia	5·00		8	90	2	
Ceylon	10·50	22	7	61	7	
Hong Kong	3·13			40	10	50
India	440·00	85	9·9		2·3	2·8
Indonesia	96·00	2	84	1	4	9
Japan	95·00			58	0·7	Shintoism widespread
Laos	2·40			96	1	3
Macao	0·22		10	10	5*	75 (Confuc.)
Malaysia	10·30	4	57	24	4	11
Malaysian Union	7·30	10	48	35	5	2
N. Borneo	0·45		70	20	1	9
Sarawak	0·85		70	20	1	9
Singapore	1·70	5	40	20	10	25
Nepal	9·41	6		80		14
Pakistan	93·81	12	82		0·7	5·3
Philippines	27·46		7		85*	8
Port. Timor	0·56		10	10	5*	75
Ryukyu Is.	1·00			45		45 (Shinto.)
Sikkim	0·16			85		15
S. Korea	25·00			80	7	13
S. Vietnam	14·20		4	66	15*	15 (Confuc.)
Taiwan	10·05			45	10	45
Thailand	23·00		4	95	0·3	0·7

* Chiefly Catholic.

From: Winkler: *Südostasien*, Berlin, 1964

MALAYA
(Under British rule since 1874)

1942
Autumn: Formation of Communist, anti-Japanese Malaysian People's Army (MPAJA) with 7,000 guerillas.

1943
MPAJA under the Chinese leadership of Chen Ping.

Malaya.

1944
January: Allies supply MPAJA with new weapons, ammunition and explosives.
  Jungle warfare.

1957
31/8: Malayan Union becomes an independent member of the British Commonwealth.

INDONESIA
(Declared an "integral" part of the Netherlands in 1922)

1941
Formation of anti-Japanese Resistance Movement under Nationalist leadership.

1942
29/4: Japanese establish the "Three A's Movement" teaching that the Japanese are the "leaders, protectors and light of Asia".
6/12: Queen Wilhelmina promises Indonesia full partnership in the Kingdom of the Netherlands, and complete internal autonomy.

1943
9/3: Japanese support formation of "Centre of Popular Power" ("Poetara") as a first stage in self-rule.
September: Japanese-trained "Voluntary Army of Defenders of the Fatherland" under Gatot Mangkoepradja.

1944
Dissolution of Poetara and replacement by "Loyal People's Organization".
Summer: Resistance Movement under Soetan Sjahrir. Formation of "Student Union". "Peta-revolt" in Blitar and Indramaju.
October: Japanese Premier promises Indonesia's independence.

1945
1/3: Formation of Investigation Committee to prepare for independence.
1/6: Soekarno outlines the five principles of Pantja Sila: Nationalism — Internationalism — Humanism — Popular Rule and Social Justice — Faith in God. Co-operation with pro-Japanese nationalists.
22/6: Djakarta Charter.
17/8: Hatta and Soekarno proclaim independence of Indonesia.

PHILIPPINES
(Since 1889 under U.S. rule)

1942
23/1: Japanese appoint Philippines Executive Committee under Vargas.
  President Manual Quezon sets up Government-in-exile in Washington.
29/3: Formation of anti-Japanese People's Army ("Huks") under the Communist Taruc.
December: Formation of pro-Japanese Union under Ramos.

1943
14/10: Proclamation of independent republic under President J. Laurel; alliance with Japan.
Autumn: Huks (Hukbalahaps) make contact with General MacArthur's H.Q.

1945
June: Huks form "National Peasant Union".

1946
4/7: Philippines an independent republic under Roxas.

INDOCHINA (VIETNAM)
(Under French rule since 1787)

1940
June: Admiral Dacoux, French Governor-General forced to collaborate with Japanese by Vichy treaty with Japan.

1941
19/5: Formation of Independent Vietnam League under Ho Chi-minh.

1944
28/3: Formation of Provisional Republican Government.
22/12: Formation of Vietnamese Liberation Army under Vo Nguyen-giap (contacts with U.S. Office of Strategic Services).

1944–45
French Resistance group attacks Japanese.

1945
9/3: Japanese troops overrun French garrisons: Emperor Bao Dai proclaims independence; Japanese abolish colonial status of Vietnam.
2/9: Bao Dai abdicates; Ho Chi-minh proclaims Vietnam an independent democratic republic.
10/11: Japanese capitulate in Saigon.

Indonesian slogan on a wall in Batavia (October 1945).

Indonesian propaganda postcard discovered in a Japanese office in Singapore.

CAMBODIA
(Under French rule since 1863)

1941
9–28/1: Attacks by Thailand.
11/3: Treaty signed in Tokyo.

1942
Son Ngoc Thank leads revolt against French rule. Formation of anti-French nationalist movement (Khmer-Issarak).

12/3: King Norodom Shihanouk declares independence with Japanese support.
1/6: Son Ngoc Thank appointed Foreign Minister.

1947
Cambodia becomes a constitutional monarchy.

LAOS
(French protectorate since 1893)

1940
Emergence of anti-French nationalist movement (Issarak—Free Laos).

1943
Collaboration with Allies in Thailand.

1945
April: King Sisavang Vong proclaims independence.
15/9: Prince Phetsarath proclaims independent Kingdom of Laos.

1947
11/5: New constitution.

1954
20/7: Geneva Conference debars Laos from entering into military alliances. Laos is cleared of French and Viet-minh troops.

Anti-Japanese guerillas on Timor.

Indonesia's five principles
From Soekarno's speech of 1 June 1945

". . . the first and best principle on which we must build the state of Indonesia is *nationalism* . . . All of us should strive to construct an Indonesia ranging from Sumatra to Irian . . .

"Beyond constructing a free Indonesian state, we must also strive to join all other nations in a single family. And this is the second principle that I ask you to adopt, and which I propose to call *internationalism* . . .

"The third principle is that of *general consent,* the principle of democratic consultation. The Indonesian state must not be a state of one individual, of a group, of the rich. What we are about to create is a state for all . . .

"This brings me to the fourth principle. It is the *abolition of poverty* in free Indonesia. The people want prosperity. A people that has but recently known what it means to suffer hunger, to go naked, wants to live in a world ruled by justice. If, therefore, we truly understand and love the Indonesian people, and seek their advancement, we must accept the principle of social justice, a principle that means far more than mere political equality.

"Let the fifth principle of our state be *Faith in God,* faith in its noblest sense, faith that goes hand in hand with respect for others. I should be most happy if you agreed with me to make faith in God the Almighty one of the bases on which to build our new state.

"If I reduce all these five principles to a single one, I obtain the truly Indonesian concept of ''gotong rojong'' (mutual aid). Let the state of Indonesia be built on mutual co-operation."

In August 1945, Soviet troops occupied N. Korea down to the 38th parallel.

KOREA

(Since 1910 under Japanese rule)

1919

Provisional government-in-exile under Syngman Rhee in Chungking.

1945

12/8: Soviet troops march into N. Korea.
25/8: Soviet command establishes Korean People's Executive Committee.
2/9: General MacArthur passes Order No. 1 (dated 17/8) stipulating the surrender of all Japanese forces north of the 38th parallel to the Red Army (in accordance with the Yalta and Potsdam agreements).
6/9: Revolutionary Congress in Seoul proclaims the setting up of a Democratic People's Republic on the Communist pattern (not recognized by U.S.).
8/9: U.S. troops land in S. Korea to oppose Communist Partisan Army under Kim Ir Sen.

1946

9/2: Kim Il Sung appointed provisional People's Commissar of N. Korea.

CHINA

1941

15/4: Roosevelt publishes list of materials available to China under Lend-Lease Agreement.
25/4: America and Great Britain sign agreement with China on stabilization of Chinese currency.

1942

3/1: General Chiang Kai-shek takes command of Chinese theatre of war.
1/2: U.S. votes 500 million dollars to stabilize Chinese currency.

1943

9/1: Pro-Japanese Nanking Government under Wang Ching-Wai declares war.
6/9: Eleventh Plenary Session of Kuomintang Government in Chungking. Chiang Kai-shek elected President of National Government.

1944

6/9: Special units of Chinese Expeditionary Force in W. Yunnan link up with Chinese Army on Kaolingkung Pass, N. Burma, establishing the first overland junction between China and S.E. Asia since the Japanese occupation of Burma.
15/9: Communists in Lin Tsu-han call for a national emergency conference: representatives of all anti-Japanese parties form a democratic coalition government.

Estimated population of some countries in S.E. Asia (1945–1958) in 1,000						
Year	Burma	Ceylon	Indonesia	Malayan Union	Singapore	Thailand
1945	17,564	6,650	—	—	—	16,737
1946	17,749	6,854	—	5,250	—	17,041
1947	17,934	7,037	—	4,908	938	17,478
1948	18,119	7,244	73,700	4,987	962	17,808
1949	18,304	7,455	74,800	5,082	981	18,145
1950	18,489	7,678	76,000	5,227	1,015	18,488
1951	18,672	7,876	77,100	5,337	1,042	18,837
1952	18,860	8,074	78,300	5,506	1,077	19,193
1953	19,272	8,290	79,500	5,706	1,121	19,556
1954	19,464	8,520	80,500	5,889	1,165	19,925
1955	19,659	8,723	81,500	6,058	1,211	20,302
1956	19,856	8,929	83,200	6,252	1,262	20,686
1957	20,054	9,165	85,100	6,277	1,474	21,076
1958	20,255	—	86,900	—	—	21,474

From: *Monthly Bulletin of Statistics*, Vol. XIII
No. 3, March 1959

U.S. 1st Marine Division taking control of Tientsin (N. China) on 2 October.

October: U.S. Government recalls General Stilwell, Commanding General, China–Burma–India Theatre.
10/11: Death of Wang Ching-wai; Chen Kiung-po becomes acting President.

1945
3/2: Draft for a conference of Kuomintang, Communist and other anti-Japanese groups presented by Wang Shih-chieh, Nationalist Minister of Information, and by Chou En-lai.
14/8: After the Japanese capitulation, Communist forces rapidly extend their hold, particularly on Manchuria, Shantung, Honan, Hopei and other parts of N. China. Kuomintang forces occupy all the major cities.
28/8: Mao Tse-tung arrives in Chungking.
April–June: Seventh Congress of Chinese Communist Party. Mao Tse-tung reports on coalition government. Communist Party adopts new constitution. Mao elected leader.
October: Clashes between Communist and Nationalist troops throughout China. In a referendum, Mongolian people vote almost unanimously for independence.
28/8–10/10: Chiang Kai-shek and Mao Tse-tung confer on acceptance of Japanese surrender and collaboration between Kuomintang and Communist Party.

November–December: Armed clashes between Government and Communist forces in various provinces. Beginning of civil war. Soviet troops in Manchuria prevent the entry of Government troops.
December: General Marshall arranges conference between both sides in Chungking.

Communist demands to Marshal Chiang Kai-shek

1. The Chinese Communist Army will participate as an equal partner in the disarming of Japan.
2. The Communist Government will participate in all armistice and peace negotiations with Japan.
3. Chiang Kai-shek will renounce party dictatorship in any form.
4. Chungking and Yennan will immediately form a coalition cabinet.

19 August 1945

Japanese soldiers surrendering their arms to a Red Army man. These arms were later used to equip the Chinese Communists.

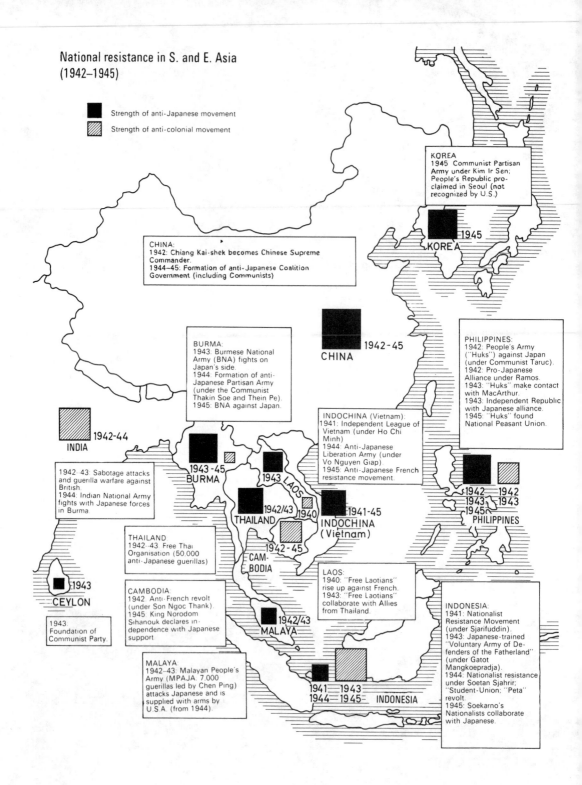

National resistance in S. and E. Asia (1942–1945)

■ Strength of anti-Japanese movement

▨ Strength of anti-colonial movement

KOREA
1945 Communist Partisan Army under Kim Ir Sen; People's Republic proclaimed in Seoul (not recognized by U.S.)

KOREA 1945

CHINA:
1942: Chiang Kai-shek becomes Chinese Supreme Commander.
1944–45: Formation of anti-Japanese Coalition Government (including Communists)

CHINA 1942–45

PHILIPPINES:
1942: People's Army ("Huks") against Japan (under Communist Taruc).
1942: Pro-Japanese Alliance under Ramos.
1943: "Huks" make contact with MacArthur.
1943: Independent Republic with Japanese alliance.
1945: "Huks" found National Peasant Union.

PHILIPPINES 1942 1943 1945

BURMA:
1943: Burmese National Army (BNA) fights on Japan's side.
1944: Formation of anti-Japanese Partisan Army (under the Communist Thakin Soe and Thein Pe).
1945: BNA against Japan.

BURMA 1943–45

INDIA
1942–44

1942–43: Sabotage attacks and guerilla warfare against British.
1944: Indian National Army fights with Japanese forces in Burma.

INDOCHINA (Vietnam):
1941: Independent League of Vietnam (under Ho Chi Minh)
1944: Anti-Japanese Liberation Army (under Vo Nguyen Giap)
1945: Anti-Japanese French resistance movement.

INDOCHINA (Vietnam) 1941–45

LAOS 1943

THAILAND 1942/43

1940

THAILAND:
1942–43: Free Thai Organisation (50.000 anti-Japanese guerillas)

CEYLON 1943

1943: Foundation of Communist Party.

CAMBODIA 1942–45

CAMBODIA:
1942: Anti-French revolt (under Son Ngoc Thank).
1945: King Norodom Sihanouk declares independence with Japanese support.

LAOS:
1940: "Free Laotians" rise up against French.
1943: "Free Laotians" collaborate with Allies from Thailand.

MALAYA 1942/43

MALAYA:
1942–43: Malayan People's Army (MPAJA, 7.000 guerillas led by Chen Ping) attacks Japanese and is supplied with arms by U.S.A. (from 1944).

INDONESIA:
1941: Nationalist Resistance Movement (under Sjarifuddin).
1943: Japanese-trained "Voluntary Army of Defenders of the Fatherland" (under Gatot Mangkoepradja).
1944: Nationalist resistance under Soetan Sjahrir; "Student-Union; "Peta" revolt.
1945: Soekarno's Nationalists collaborate with Japanese.

INDONESIA 1941 1943 1944 1945

CHINA BECOMES COMMUNIST

End of 1945

On the danger of the Hurley policy

By Mao Tse-tung

The danger of the U.S. policy towards China as represented by Hurley consists in its encouraging the reactionary trend of the Kuomintang government and increasing the danger of civil war in China. If Hurley's policy continues, the U.S. government will fall hopelessly into the deep, stinking cesspool of Chinese reaction; it will place itself in opposition to the hundreds of millions of awakened or awakening Chinese people, and become a hindrance to the anti-Japanese War at present and to world peace in the future. Isn't it clear enough that this policy can lead only to such a result?

(From a published comment, 12 July 1945)

"Let China stew in her own juice"

From a report to President Truman by William Bullitt, former U.S. Ambassador in Moscow, published in Life *on 13 October 1947:*

General Marshall reached Chungking, which was then the capital of China, on 22 December 1945 and so great was his prestige that he was able by 10 January 1946 to obtain signature of an armistice by the Chinese government and the Communists . . .

But the Soviet government's objectives were not those of General Marshall. On V-J Day there were no Chinese Communist troops in Manchuria. The Soviet plan was to use the time gained by the armistice to transfer as many Communist troops as possible from North China to Manchuria and there to arm them with the abundant Japanese supplies and equipment which the Russian Red Army had seized when the Japanese army in Manchuria surrendered. To withdraw the Russian Red Army from Manchuria only when it could be replaced by a well-armed Chinese Red Army and to use the Marshall armistice period for this purpose, was the Soviet plan. It worked perfectly . . .

After the failure of General Marshall's mission, American policy toward China fell into a tired apathy, marked by a weary and petulant inclination to "let China stew in her own juice" . . .

The $500 million loan earmarked for China was with-held . . .

Most serious of all, having equipped some Chinese divisions entirely with American artillery, machine guns and rifles, and others partially, and promised to help maintain this armament, we had held up export licences for munitions. In consequence Chinese divisions without ammunition and with worn-out American equipment were facing Communist troops newly equipped in Manchuria by the Soviet Union with abundant supplies of Japanese rifles, machine guns and cannon. Our policy resulted in disarming our friends while the Soviet Union was arming our enemies. By the spring of this year it was evident that unless we changed our policy, China would not "stew in her own juice" but in Soviet juice . . .

The Soviet government, which occupied Manchuria when the Japanese surrendered, began to rush Chinese Communists into Manchuria and to arm them with surrendered Japanese arms. In Manchuria they recruited not only local peasants but also Koreans, and their strength is now close to 350,000. Scattered throughout North China they have now perhaps 400,000 men organized in small armies and guerilla bands.

Chinese Communist troops in Nanking. ▶

ASIA AT THE END OF THE SECOND WORLD WAR

Burma, S.E. Asia: Admiral Lord Mountbatten

India: Lord Wavell

China (Comm.): Mao Tse-tung

Indonesia: Achmed Soekarno

China (Nat.): Chiang Kai-shek

Japan, S. Korea: General MacArthur

THE RULERS OF SOUTH AND EAST ASIA IN 1945

Cambodia:
Norodom
Shihanouk II

USSR, Man-
churia:
Joseph Stalin

Laos: King
Sisavang Vong

USA, Pacific:
Harry S.
Truman

Thailand: Nai
Pridi Phano-
myong

Vietnam:
Ho Chi-Minh

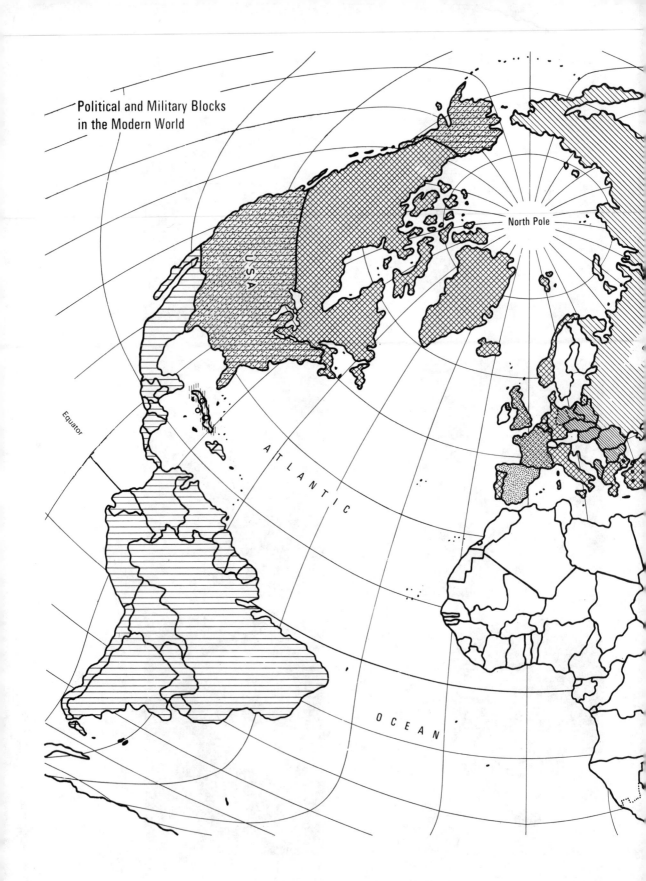

Political and Military Blocks
in the Modern World

North Pole

USA

Equator

ATLANTIC

OCEAN

PACIFIC

OCEAN

SOVIET UNION

CHINA

INDIAN OCEAN

	U.S.A. and North Atlantic Treaty Organization (NATO)
	Central Treaty Organization (Bagdad Pact—CENTO)
	South East Asia Treaty Organization (SEATO)
	Organization of American States (OAS)
	Special treaties with U.S.A.
	Soviet Union and Warsaw Pact
	Chinese People's Republic and Allies
	Friendship pacts with USSR

As at 1 January 1965

THE CONSEQUENCES OF THE SECOND WORLD WAR IN EUROPE AND ASIA *By J. R. von Salis*

The similarity between the post-war fate of Japan and that of Germany is not accidental. Two ambitious industrial and military powers had tried to extend their territory at the expense of others and to establish a new order under their control by methods and programmes that aroused dismay, alarm and finally resistance in the world at large. They entered an alliance for joint world domination. Both lost their conquests, parts of their former territory, and their position as world powers. Both were forced to accept unconditional surrender terms, and had to look on while their country was occupied. The defeat of Germany and Japan proved clearly that relatively small countries, even if they can choose the moment of attack and are better armed than the bigger opponent, must crumble under the latter's onslaught . . .

The belief that force of arms coupled to extreme nationalism is enough to wrest territory from the great powers and to hang on to them indefinitely proved to be a grievous error. The underrating of the force of moral resistance outside, too, was a grave mistake; that force came down heavily on the side of the attacked and persecuted. Much as Hitler's war changed the balance of power in Europe to Germany's disadvantage, so Japan's war changed the balance of power in Asia to hers. Germany pulled down the dams that had kept out Communist Russia since 1920, thus opening up Central and Eastern Europe to the Soviets. By calling up Chinese resistance, Japan helped China to become one of the greatest powers in Asia. Germany's policy forged an alliance between the Anglo–American naval powers and the Soviet Union—an alliance that would never have come about otherwise. Japan's war forced the Kuomintang Government to accept the help of the Soviet Union, thus weakening Chinese opposition to the rising Communist challenge. These historical factors are so clear today, that no one can possibly deny them.

As in Europe, but on a very much larger scale, the political face of Asia changed radically after the war. The conditions were created by the war, but the events themselves took place in the post-war era. Two factors, above all, transformed Asia after the Japanese defeat: the end of colonial rule and the rise of the Communist Party of China. There was one question on which Soviet Russia and America were and are of one mind: the abolition of those vast colonial empires in Asia and Africa that the European powers had built up during the second half of the nineteenth century. Holland lost its island empire in

the South Pacific and Indonesia became an independent state. Great Britain relinquished India and Burma, followed by other territories in the Middle East and Africa. Britain's war effort had so weakened her that she could not halt the onslaught of colonial resistance movements. Instead she tried successfully to gain India, Pakistan and Ceylon—the three independent members of her former Indian realm—as dominions for her Commonwealth, with the result that the latter lost its purely British character. The King of England formally renounced the title of Emperor of India, a title first assumed by his grandmother, Queen Victoria. France continued to fight for her possessions in Indo-China, but lost out in the end. In China, after years of civil war, the Communists took power in 1949. Marshal Chiang Kai-shek's Kuomintang régime had dissipated its strength in the long war against Japan, so much so that it succumbed to internal weakness and corruption. In the face of the victorious Communist advance, the Marshal had no alternative but to withdraw to Formosa, there to place himself under American protection. The emergence of the Chinese People's Republic under Mao Tse-tung and Chou En-lai, joined by the left wing of the Kuomintang under the widow of Sun Yat-sen, was to Asia precisely what the Russian Revolution of 1917 and the Communist victory in the Russian Civil War had been to Europe. The struggle between Communists and anti-Communists was now transferred to Asia, and at the very moment when her people were entering the path of national independence with anti-colonialist fervour . . .

However, after the Second World War, true national independence was no longer a reality, not even in the form of Continental or other alliances. The main problem now was to find a peaceful way of controlling the mutual dependence of nations and Continents, despite national, political and ideological differences. After the atomic revolution, which threatened to turn every war into international suicide, the preservation of mankind became the only worthwhile task, and the only question now was how this could be made consonant with the dignity of man. After 1945, there could be no doubt but that the slightest mistake might unleash a conflict with terrible consequences, more terrible than any war in the near or distant past. The memory of Hiroshima had more influence on government decisions after the Second World War, than peace treaties or political and social considerations.

From J. von Salis: *Weltgeschichte der Neuesten Zeit* (World History of Recent Times), Zurich 1962

THE CATASTROPHE IN FIGURES

POPULATION LOSSES IN EUROPE AND ASIA

Europe

Dead and missing

American	170,000	dead
British	330,000	dead
French	250,000	dead
Belgian	10,000	dead
Dutch	10,000	dead
Norwegian	10,000	dead
German	3,250,000	dead
Italian	330,000	dead
Austrian	230,000	dead
Czech	20,000	dead
Hungarian	120,000	dead
Yugoslav	300,000	dead
Greek	20,000	dead
Bulgarian	10,000	dead
Rumanian	200,000	dead
Polish	120,000	dead
Finnish	90,000	dead
Soviet	13,600,000	dead
	19,070,000	dead

Civilian dead

British	60,000	dead
French	270,000	dead
Belgian	50,000	dead
Dutch	100,000	dead
German	3,640,000	dead
Italian	70,000	dead
Austrian	40,000	dead
Czech	70,000	dead
Hungarian	80,000	dead
Yugoslav	1,300,000	dead
Greek	80,000	dead
Rumanian	40,000	dead
Polish	2,500,000	dead
Lithuanian	170,000	dead
Latvian	120,000	dead
Estonian	140,000	dead
Soviet	6,000,000	dead
	14,730,000	dead

Murdered Jews
(figures after Lesczynski, June 1946, more recent estimates do not differ appreciably)

France	90,000	dead
Belgium	40,000	dead
Holland	90,000	dead
Luxembourg	3,000	dead
Denmark	1,500	dead
Norway	1,500	dead
Germany	170,000	dead
Austria	40,000	dead
Czechoslovakia	260,000	dead
Hungary	200,000	dead
Italy	15,000	dead
Yugoslavia	55,000	dead
Greece	60,000	dead
Rumania	425,000	dead
Bulgaria	7,000	dead
Poland	2,800,000	dead
Soviet Union (including Lithuania, Latvia and Estonia)	1,720,000	dead
	5,978,000	dead

European Totals:

Soldiers	19·0	Millions dead
Civilians	14·7	Millions dead
Jews	5·9	Millions dead
	39·6	Millions dead

Asia and Pacific

Dead and missing soldiers

American	50,000	dead
New Zealand	10,000	dead
Australian	30,000	dead
British	40,000	dead
Chinese	3,500,000	dead
Japanese	1,700,000	dead
	5,330,000	dead

Civilian dead

Chinese	10,000,000	dead
Japanese	360,000	dead
	15,690,000	dead

(From: Putzger: *Historischer Weltatlas*)

Combined losses in Europe and Asia

Europe	39·6	millions dead
Asia	15·7	millions dead
	55·3	millions dead

The death of German Generals	in World War I	in World War II
Killed	60	287
Suicide	3	108
Sentenced to death (by German courts)	—	25
Sentenced to death (by Allied courts)	—	57
Accidental deaths	—	49
Died	103	310
Missing	—	65
	166	901
Total number of generals serving	2,530	3,363

After *Stern*, Hamburg

MATERIAL DAMAGE

Germany

The extent of the damage

The most serious material damage was the destruction of houses, factories, offices and stores, particularly in the larger cities. The extent of this damage is illustrated by the fact that "on average ten Germans now live where only four had lived in 1939; moreover, some of the cellars which they occupy hardly deserve the name of dwellings". The German railway was a heap of rubble. Not a single one of the inland watercourses, which had carried a large proportion of the German goods traffic, was intact. For a short time, food supplies were assured, but the future was uncertain. The livestock—cattle, sheep, pigs and goats—had been severely reduced. The production of grain and potatoes was endangered by the lack of artificial fertilizer; market supplies were reduced by doubts in the stability of the mark. Coal and steel production was at less than 10% of pre-war level. However, an overall survey suggested that only 15%–20% of industrial plant throughout Germany had been destroyed beyond repair.

From Feis: *Zwischen Krieg und Frieden*
(Between War and Peace)

Historical monuments destroyed by air raids

Town	Buildings destroyed
Aachen	Churches of St. Paul, St. Peter, St. Leonard, and Annakirche. 52 secular buildings, castles, courts; Couven Museum.
Ansbach	Dicker Turm, Hundsturm.
Aschaffenburg	Castle. Church of St. Agatha.
Augsburg	Barfuesserkirche and Churches of St. Jacob, St. Leonard; Bakers' Hall, Ropers' Hall, Ambrosius Hochstätter House, Town Hall, Hacob Fugger House, Augustus Fountain.
Bayreuth	Old Castle, Town Hall, Reitzenstein Palace, Equestrian Hall, Hunting Lodge, Old University, Hermitage.
Berlin	Nikolaikirche, Klosterkirche, Hedwigskirche, Böhmische Kirche and Dreifaltigkeitkirche; Royal Palace; Monbijou Palace; Charlottenburg Castle, Schauspielhaus; Old Museum; Crown Prince's Palace, Presidential Palace; Prince Albrecht Palace; William I Palace; Russian Legation; French Legation; British Legation; Leipziger Gate.
Bielefeld	Nikolaikirche and practically all historical timber-fronted houses.
Bonn	Gertrudis-Kirche, Boeselagerer Court.
Braunschweig (Brunswick)	Martinikirche, Katharinenkirche, Andreaskirche, Nikolaikirche; Castle; Old Weighbridge; nine tenths of historical timber-fronted houses.
Bremen	St. Ansquarii, St. Martini, St. Pauli; Trades Hall, Roselius House; Focke Museum, Seefahrt House, most Gothic houses.
Coblenz	Three churches, Elector's Castle, Deutschorden House, Elector's Palace, most old palaces and historical houses.
Cologne	20 churches, Town Hall, Guerzenich, Fish Market, Cooper's Hall, Marcellen Gymnasium, Klarenturm, most historical houses in the Old Town.
Darmstadt	Theatre, Old High School, New Palace, Artists' Hall, Town Hall, White Tower.
Dessau	Holy Spirit Hospital, Equestrian Hall, Market Colonnades, 18 historical houses.
Dortmund	Reinoldikirche, Marienkirche, Petrikirche, Probsteikirche, Town Hall.
Dueren	St. Anna Kirche, Marienkirche, Clothworkers' Hall, Town Hall, Corn Exchange, all old burghers' houses.
Düsseldorf	Karmeliterkirche, Jaegerhof, Town Hall.
Emden	Great Church, Franciscan Monastery, Catholic Church, Klunderburg Town Hall, Old Weighing House, Old High School, all 16th and 17th century brick buildings.
Erfurt	Barfuesserkirche, Ursuline Cloister, Old University, Collegium Majus, Rebstock House, Greifenstein House.
Frankfurt	More than 1,000 historical buildings, including Engeltaler Hof, Landhaus Bethmann, Braunfels House, Fuersteneck House, Solmser Hof, Luthereck House, Dreischinken House, Red House, Wuerzburger Eck, Antwerp House, Gruene Aue House, Hirschgrabenhof, Goethe House, Rothschild House, Schlesinger Eck, Friedberger Gate Houses, Deutschorden House.
Freiburg	Ludwigskirche, Dominican Cloister, Corn Exchange, Grand-Duke's Palace, Old University Library, countless historical houses.
Gera	Castle, Museum.
Giessen	Armoury, Old Town Hall, New Castle, Einhorn Apothecaries' Hall, all valuable historical buildings.
Hagen	14 churches, Old Museum, Home Museum.
Halberstadt	Reform Church, Andreas Chapel, Holy Ghost Hospital, Comitia.
Hamburg	Dreifaltigkeitskirche, St. Katharinen-Kirche, Michaeliskirche, Town Hall on New Wall, Old Orphanage, Sailors' Refuge, Sailors' Widows' Home, 40 particularly valuable old burgher's houses.
Hameln (Hamelin)	Market Church, Old Town Hall, Bakers' Hall.
Hanau	Marienkirche, Dutch Church, St. John's Church, Town Castle, Old Town Hall, New Town Hall, all valuable 16th and 17th century timber-fronted buildings.
Hanover	Aegidienkirche, Johanniskirche, Kreuzkirche, Nikolaikirche, Schlosskirche, Palace, Herrenhausen Castle, Archducal Armoury, Wangenheim Palace, 20 houses scheduled as being of historical interest, including "Fathers' House".
Heilbronn	Franciscan Church, Fleshers' Hall, German House, Town Hall.
Hildesheim	St. Martin's Cathedral, St. Lamberts, St. Jacob's, Town Hall, Knochenhauer Court, 78 valuable houses.
Karlsruhe	Church of St. Peter and St. Paul, Johanneskirche, Old Catholic Church, Protestant Church, Archduke's Castle, Orangery, Festival Hall, Stables, Margrave's Palace, Town Hall, Mint, Artists' Hall, Ministries on Castle Square, School of Art, Buerklin Palace, Provincial Library, Prince Max Palace.
Kassel	Seven Churches, Elisabeth Hospital, French Town Hall, Au Gate, Old Portrait Gallery, Fridericianum Museum, Kuechen Castle, Armoury, Stables, Orangery, many town houses of the Electoral period.
Kiel	Church of the Holy Ghost, Thaulow Museum, Prehist. Museum, Old Town Hall, Persian Houses, Buchwald Court, Castle, Art Gallery.
Luebeck	Countless ancient brick buildings, including particularly the Fleshers' Hall and Fredenshagen Cellar.
Magdeburg	Eight churches, Old Town Hall and 38 historical buildings.
Mainz	16 churches, Rochus Infirmary, Knights' Hall, Armoury, Sexton's Hall, Old University, Kronenberger Court (High School), Dalberger Court (Palace of Justice), 46 ancient houses.
Mannheim	Six churches, Castle, Jesuit College, Armoury, 3 Palaces, 30 ancient houses.
Muenster	Three churches, Electors' College, Natural History Museum, Town Hall, Guild Hall, Old Academy, Wine Hall, 5 ancient palaces and 25 ancient houses.
Munich	Eleven churches, Academy of Science, Ministry of Interior, Neue Pinakothek, Artists's House, 15 ancient houses.
Nordhausen	Four churches, Old Town Hall, Rosenthal House, Riesenhaus and nearly all ancient steps.
Nuremburg	Seven churches, Dominican cloister, Dominican Convent, Zwoelfbruederhaus, Holy Ghost Hospital, Castle Burgpalast, Armouries, Imperial stables, Weizenbracuhaus, Small Weighing House, majority of late-mediaeval houses and stores.
Osnabrueck	Two churches, Collegium Carolinum, Royal Palace, Weighing House, 16 ancient town houses.
Saarbruecken	Castle Church, Friedenskirche, Deutschherrenhaus, Castle, Old Town Hall, Prince's Palace, Lueder Palace, Doeben Palace.
Siegen	Three churches, Upper Castle, Lower Castle.
Soest	The entire timber-fronted town with all the patrician courts and burghers' houses.
Stuttgart	Hospital and St. Eberhard's Churches, Old Castle, New Castle, Stables, Academy, Old Chancellery, Prince's Hall, Provincial House and many ancient town houses.
Trier	Pfarrkirche, Hospital, Electors' Hall, Merchants' Hall, Red House, Kesselstad Palace, Basilica, Law Courts, ten ancient town houses of historical importance.
Ulm	Spitalkirche, Wengenklosterkirche, Old Armoury, Jurors' Hall, Corn exchange, Deutschorden House, Weinhof School, Loewenhaus, Hospital, countless old guild halls and houses in the Old Town.
Weimar	Town Hall, Court Pharmacy, Templars' Hall, Luetzelburg House.
Wismar	St. Mary's Church, St. Mary's Parsonage, Old School, Fuerstenhof, Fleshers' Hall.
Worms	St. Magnus Church, Ancient Provost's House, Town Hall.
Wuerzburg	Eight churches, Bishop's Palace, Convent, the majority of the ancient town courts and houses.

After Rumpf: *Der Hochrote Hahn*, Darmstadt, 1952

Principal warships losses of the German and Italian Navies

	German Navy	Italian Navy
Battleships	2	1
Battle cruisers	2	—
Pocket battleships	3	—
Old battleships	2	—
Aircraft carrier (never completed)	1	—
Cruisers	8	14
Destroyers and torpedo-boats	101	85
Armed merchant cruisers	7	—
Minelayers	25	3
Submarines	785	84
Corvettes and escort vessels	25	5
Minesweepers (M-boats and R-boats)	282	35
Sperrbrecher (mine destructor ships)	64	
S-boats (M.T.B.s called E-boats by British)	.146	about 50
Miscellaneous craft	860	about 72
Naval Ferry barges	500–600	about 60

The Italian losses have been calculated from 10 June 1940 to 8 September 1943

From Roskill: *The Navy at War*

German Refugee Transports sunk in the Baltic Sea

	GRT	Date	Place	Cause	Killed (approx.)
Wilhelm Gustloff	25,484	30/1/45	Stolpebank	Torp.	5,100
Hedwigshuette	2,221	9/2/45	Fehmarn	Mine	43
General v. Steuben	14,660	10/2/45	Stolpebank	Torp.	2,700
Consul Cords	951	19/2/45	off Warnemuende	Mine	103
Andros	2,995	12/3/45	Swinemuende	Bomb. raid	200
Neuwerk	804	10/4/45	Bay of Danzig	Torp.	710
Posen	1,062	11/4/45	Hela	Bomb. raid	1,000
Moltkefels	7,862	11/4/45	Hela	Bomb. raid	
Karlsruhe	897	13/4/45	Pom. coast	Aer. torp.	850
Goya	5,230	16/4/45	Rixhoeft	Torp.	6,500
Emily Sauber	2,475	25/4/45	Hela	Torp.	50
Musketier		3/5/45	W. Baltic	Bomb. raid	800
Deutschland	21,046	3/5/45	Neustadt	Bomb. raid	no figures
Cap Arkona	27,561	3/5/45	Luebeck Bay	Bomb. raid	great losses
Vega		3/5/45	Fehmarn	Bomb. raid	consid. losses
Bolkoburg		3/5/45	Fehmarn	Bomb. raid	consid. losses
					more than 18,056

From Bildlingmayer: *Ostsee-Brueckenkoepfe*, 1945

Great Britain

British merchant shipping losses caused by enemy action

5,150 ships totalling 21,570,720 Gross Registered tons were sunk. Of this total 2,714 ships of 11,455,906 tons were British, and the remainder were Allied and neutral. In 1939 the British Merchant Navy consisted of 9,488 ships of 21,215,261 tons. Thus 28·6 per cent of the original total ships and 54·4 per cent of the original tonnage were sunk. Of the total Allied losses 2,828 ships of 14,687,231 tons were sunk by submarine.

820 ,,	,, 2,889,883 ,,	,, ,, ,, ,, aircraft
534 ,,	,, 1,406,037 ,,	,, ,, ,, ,, mine
104 ,,	,, 498,447 ,,	,, ,, ,, ,, warship raider
133 ,,	,, 829,644 ,,	,, ,, ,, ,, merchant raider
99 ,,	,, 229,676 ,,	,, ,, ,, ,, E-boat
632 ,,	,, 1,029,802 ,,	,, ,, ,, ,, other cause, scuttling, capture, unknown, etc.

From Roskill: *The Navy at War*

Major warship losses of the navies of the British Commonwealth

	R.N.	R.A.N.	R.C.N.	R.I.N.	British ships manned by Allied Navies
Battleships	3	—	—	—	—
Battle cruisers	2	—	—	—	—
Aircraft carriers	5	—	—	—	—
Escort carriers	3	—	—	—	—
Cruisers	28	3	—	—	1
Destroyers	132	4	6	—	7
Submarines	74	—	—	—	3
Monitors	1	—	—	—	—
Sloops	10	2	—	1	—
Cutters	3	—	—	—	—
Frigates	10	—	1	—	—
Corvettes	22	—	10	1	5
Fleet minesweepers	32	3	4	—	—
Fast minelayers	3	—	—	—	—
Other minelayers	5	—	—	—	—
Armed merchant cruisers	15	—	—	—	—
Anti-aircraft ships	6	—	—	—	—
Fighter-catapult ships	2	—	—	—	—
Submarine and Destroyer Depot ships	2	—	—	—	—

In addition, 1,035 auxiliary and minor war vessels of the Royal Navy, including those on loan to the Commonwealth and Allied navies, were lost.

From Roskill: *The Navy at War*

U.S.A.

Major warship losses of U.S. Fleet in the Pacific

Name	Date	Place	Cause
Battleships			
Arizona	7/12/41	Pearl Harbour	Carrier-borne aircraft

A further 4 battleships sunk in Pearl Harbour were raised and—with the exception of the *Oklahoma*—rendered serviceable again. (15 battleships at the beginning of the war were joined by a further 10 and by 2 battle cruisers completed during the war.)

Name	Date	Place	Cause
Large and medium aircraft carriers			
Lexington	8/5/42	Coral Sea	Carrier-borne aircraft
Yorktown	7/6/42	Midway Is.	Carrier-borne aircraft and submarine
Wasp	16/9/42	Solomon Is.	Submarine
Hornet	26/10/42	Santa Cruz Is.	Carrier-borne aircraft
Princeton	24/10/44	Leyte	Aircraft

(7 carriers at the beginning of the war were joined by 32 completed during the war)

Escort carriers

(Of 73 built during the war, 7 were sunk)

Name	Date	Place	Cause
Heavy cruisers			
Houston	1/3/42	Java Sea	Cruiser and destroyer
Astoria	9/8/42	Savo Is.	Cruiser
Quincy	9/8/42	Savo Is.	Cruiser
Vincennes	9/8/42	Savo Is.	Cruiser
Northampton	30/11/42	Tassafaronga	Destroyer
Chicago	30/3/43	S.E. Solomon Is.	Aircraft
Indianapolis	29/7/45	between Guam and Leyte	Submarine

(18 heavy cruisers at the beginning of the war were joined by 12 completed during the war.)

Name	Date	Place	Cause
Light cruisers			
Atlanta	13/11/42	Savo Is.	Battleship and destroyer
Juneau	13/11/42	E. Solomon Is.	Submarine
Helena	6/7/43	Kula Bay	Destroyer

(19 light cruisers at the beginning of the war were joined by 33 completed during the war)

From Ruge: *Entscheidung im Pazifik*

The tragedy of the Japanese Fleet

Name	Date	Place	Cause
Battleships			
Musashi	24/10/44	Leyte	Aircraft
Yamato	7/4/45	Okinawa	Aircraft
Mutsu	8/6/43	Off Hiroshima	Exploded
Hyuga	24/7/45	Inland Sea	Aircraft
Ise	28/7/45	Inland Sea	Aircraft
Yamashiro	25/10/44	Suritao Strait	Naval engagement
Fuso	25/10/44	Suritao Strait	Naval engagement
Kirishima	15/11/42	Guadalcanal	Naval engagement
Haruna	28/7/45	Inland Sea	Aircraft
Kongo	21/11/45	Formosa Str.	Submarine
Hiei	14/11/42	Guadalcanal	Naval engagement and aircraft
Heavy aircraft carriers			
Shinano	11/11/44	Inland Sea	Submarine
Unryu	19/12/44	E. China Sea	Submarine
Taiho	19/6/44	Philippine Sea	Submarine
Shokaku	19/6/44	Philippine Sea	Submarine
Zuikaku	25/10/44	Leyte	Aircraft
Akagi Soryu Kaga Hiryu	4/6/42	Midway	Aircraft
Light aircraft carriers			
Chitose Chiyoda Zuiho	25/10/44	Leyte	Aircraft
Junyo	9/12/44	China Sea	Submarine
Hiyo	20/6/44	Philippine Sea	Aircraft
Ryuho	24/10/44	E. Solomon Is.	Aircraft
Shoho	7/5/42	Coral Sea	Aircraft
(4 escort carriers sunk by submarines, 1 by mines and aircraft)			
Heavy cruisers			
Chikuma	25/10/44	Samar Is.	Aircraft
Tone	24/7/45	Inland Sea	Aircraft
Kumano	25/11/44	W. of Luzon	Aircraft
Suzuya	25/10/44	Samar	Aircraft
Mogami	25/10/44	Suritao Str.	Aircraft
Mikuma	6/6/42	off Midway	Aircraft
Chokai	25/10/44	Samar	Aircraft and destroyer
Maya	23/10/44	Palawan	Submarine
Atago	23/10/44	Palawan	Submarine
Haguro	16/2/44	Malacca Str.	Destroyer
Ashigara	8/6/45	Banka Str.	Submarine
Nachi	5/11/44	Manila	Aircraft
Myoko	10/12/44	off Formosa	Submarine
Aoba	28/7/45	Inland Sea	Aircraft
Kinugasa	14/11/42	Solomon Is.	Aircraft
Furutaka	11/10/42	Cape Esperance	Cruiser and destroyer
Kako	10/8/42	off Kavieng	Submarine
Light cruisers			
Oyodo	28/5/45	Inland Sea	Aircraft
Yahagi	7/4/45	Okinawa	Aircraft
Noshiro	26/10/44	Leyte	Aircraft
Agano	16/2/44	off Truk	Submarine
Kashii	12/1/45	Indo-China	Aircraft
Katori	17/2/44	off Truk	Aircraft and cruiser
Naka	17/2/44	off Truk	Aircraft
Jintsu	13/7/43	Kula Bay	Cruiser and destroyer
Sendai	2/11/43	Augusta Bay	Cruiser and destroyer
Abukuma	26/10/44	off Suritao	Aircraft
Yura	25/10/42	E. of Solomon Is.	Aircraft
Kinu	26/10/44	Samar	Aircraft
Natori	18/8/44	E. Samar	Submarines
Isuzu	7/4/45	Java Sea	Submarine
Nagara	7/8/44	off Nagasaki	Aircraft
Kiso	13/11/44	Manila Bay	Aircraft
Oi	19/7/44	E. China Sea	Submarines
Tama	25/10/44	Leyte	Aircraft and submarine
Kuma	11/1/44	off Penang	Submarine
Yubari	27/4/44	Palau Is.	Submarine
Tenryu	18/12/44	N.E. New Guinea	Submarine
Tatsuta	13/3/44	off Yokosuka	Submarine
Also sunk during the war: 138 destroyers and 149 submarines.			

From Ruge: *Entscheidung im Pazifik*

RESISTANCE VICTIMS IN DENMARK AND NORWAY

Denmark:

According to information supplied by the Danish Ministry for Special Affairs, 112 Danish Patriots were tried by German courts and sentenced to death. Further victims: 115 murdered or dead in concentration camps (this figure is incomplete); 815 killed during acts of sabotage. Suppression of strikes with severe reprisals. 172 killed in clashes prior to the German collapse. 1,802 Danish civilians and soldiers killed during the Occupation, though having no direct connection with the Resistance.

The first executions, still fairly small in number, took place in 1943. The rate increased greatly in 1944, and reached a peak in 1945, during the first four months of which year the Germans shot as many Resistance fighters as during the whole of 1944. The years 1944 and 1945 also witnessed the worst reprisals and shootings of hostages. Many of the victims were less than 25 years old. 4,000 Danish Patriots were sent to prison.

Norway:

According to official figures, Norwegian losses due to the war and the German occupation were 10,166 killed in a total population of some 3 millions. They fell into the following groups:

— approx. 6,000 members of the Resistance, murdered or killed during clashes, in concentration camps, by way of reprisals, etc. Included in this figure are those killed by firing squads (363 men and 3 women) and Patriots who died as a result of ill-treatment, wounds, etc. (844 women and 16 men).

— 89 men and 4 women killed while trying to flee the country (most of them were escaping arrest).

— 610 Jews (out of a total pre-war population of 1,100) deported by the Germans and killed in extermination camps.

— approx. 3,500 soldiers and sailors killed during the German invasion in 1940.

The number of those murdered in reprisals cannot be computed. To give but one example, the Germans arrested the entire population of Televaag (near Bergen) as a reprisal, and sent all 300 of them to a concentration camp. Thirty of them were killed there; all the fields round the village were burned down.

From Malrezzi-Pirelli: *Letzte Briefe zum Tode Verurteilter 1939 bis 1945* (Last letters from people sentenced to death, 1939–1945)

EPILOGUE

Exactly twenty years ago, in January 1945, the Allies made ready to storm Hitler's Third Reich from the west, east and south. This anniversary seemed a good occasion to write an objective history, based on contemporary documents and sources, of the last 100 days of a war that changed not only the face of Germany, but of the entire world as well. The year 1945 saw the birth of a new world, a world dominated by tension between East and West. That is another reason for publishing this book, and for showing how the political currents underlying the tension arose.

When we speak of "the last hundred days of the war", we do not want to be taken literally. In Europe, that phase comprised the last great drive, from the Rhine and Vistula to the Elbe, ending in the German capitulation—in short, the period Janùary–May, 1945. In Asia, "the last hundred days" began with the American onslaught on Okinawa in April 1945, and ended with the Japanese capitulation in September of that year. These events have been represented in two distinct chronological sections. In the first, we follow the dramatic collapse and subsequent division of Germany day by day, first on land, then at sea and finally in the air. In the second, we deal with the collapse of the Japanese "co-prosperity sphere" in S.E. Asia. In addition to the photographs, documents, maps and quotations illustrating the military campaigns, we have thought it proper to give the reader occasional glimpses of the political and strategic ideas and plans behind them. The statistical section dealing with the losses and damage incurred by both sides in 1945, shows just how much human suffering and political chaos has been wrought by the Second World War. The editors were fortunate in being able to draw on photostats of German military and political communiques, just released by Washington, and now kept in the *Militaergeschichtliches Institut* in Freiburg and the *Bundesarchiv* in Coblenz. The photographic material has been compiled from many sources at home and abroad, including a number of private collectors.

I should like to take this opportunity of expressing my sincere thanks for providing and evaluating the photographic and other material, and for their most helpful general advice to the following: Dr. Frankland, Director of the Imperial War Museum, London; Professor L. de Jong; Director of the Instituut voor Oorlogsdocumentatie, Amsterdam; Dr. Juergen Rohwer, Director of the Institut fuer Zeitgeschichte, Munich; Dr. Maurice E. Lee, Information Office, U.S. Legation, Bad Godesberg; Mrs. Johnson, National Archives and Records Service, Washington; Mrs. Daiker, Reference Librarian, Library of Congress, Washington; Mrs. Peterson, Director of the Central and Western European Collection, Hoover Institution on War, Revolution and Peace, Stanford, California; Major McGrath, Director of Australian War Memorial Library, Canberra; M. Ruge, Nationalmuseet, Copenhagen; J. Kovan, Editor-in-Chief Novosti, Moscow; O. Vercak, Director of Photographic Section, CTK, Prague; Mrs. Cabrajéc, Yugoslav Consulate General, Munich; Army Headquarters, Ottawa; Commanding Officers of the U.S. Army, Coast Guard, Navy and Signal Corps, Washington; and Lothar Leser, Karlsruhe, for use of his pamphlet collection.

Munich, January, 1965   The Editor

INDEX

Sources quoted in the text

Abwehrkämpfe am Nordflügel der Ostfront 1944–1945, Vol. 5, Stuttgart 1963: 133.
von Ahlfen-Niehoff, *So kämpfte Breslau*, Munich 1960: 48, 104, 289.
Anschläge—German Placards 1900–1960, ed. by Fritz Arnold, Ebenhausen 1963: 66, 237.
Battle Report, Vol. V: Victory in the Pacific, New York, 1949: 326, 331, 334, 340, 344, 346, 398.
Bekker, C., *Flucht übers Meer*, Oldenburg 1959: 257.
Bernadotte, Count Folke, *The Fall of the Curtain*, London, 1945: 61, 154, 155, 277.
Bidlingmayer, I., *Ostsee-Brückenköpfe 1945*, Neckargemünd, 1962: 255, 423.
Blumenstock, F., *Der Einmarsch der Amerikaner und Franzosen im nördlichen Württemberg im April 1945*, Stuttgart 1957: 125, 129, 153.
Boldt, G., *Die letzten Tage der Reichskanzlei*, Reinbek 1964: 84, 109, 117, 155, 198, 231, 233, 234, 237, 238.
Briefwechsel Stalins mit Churchill, Attlee, Roosevelt und Truman 1941–1945, Berlin 1961: 32, 164, 166, 188, 292, 407.
Bryant, A., *Triumph in the West* (based on the diaries of Viscount Alanbrooke), London 1959: 100, 108, 160, 188, 292.
Butow, R. J. C., *Japan's Decision to surrender*, Stanford 1954: 403.
Churchill, W. S., *The Second World War*, Vol. VI: Triumph and Tragedy, London, 1954: 158, 181, 188, 306.
Churchill, W. S., *War Speeches 1939–45*, London, 1952: 221, 248, 294.
Compton, A. H., *Atomic Quest*, N.Y., 1956: 382–383, 385, 388, 392.
Dedijer, V., *Tito Speaks*, London, 1953: 189, 191, 219.
Der Gocher Jugend—Gedächtnis und Mahnung, Goch: 59.
Die Tragödie Schlesiens 1945–46, ed. by J. Kaps, Munich: 107.
Dieckert-Grossmann, *Der Kampf um Ostpreussen*, Munich, 1960: 36, 37, 111, 156.
Doenitz, K., *10 Jahre und 20 Tage*, Frankfort, 1963 (Eng. Edition: *Memoirs*, London, 1959): 249, 251, 421.
Document Collection of Dr. H. A. Jacobsen: 19, 63, 68 (2), 69, 116, 160–161, 239, 280, 385, 396, 403.
Domarus, M., *Hitler-Reden und Proklamationen*, Vol. II, Wurzburg, 1963: 25, 152, 183, 241.
Ehrman, J., *History of the Second World War*: Grand Strategy, Vol. VI, London, 1956: 108, 176, 368.
Encyclopaedia Britannica, Vol. 23, p. 792 J: 21.
Feis, H., *Zwischen Krieg und Frieden*, Frankfort, 1962: 306, 384, 423.
Flower, D.—Reeves, J., *The War, 1939–1945*, London, 1960: 44, 80, 81, 96, 127, 137, 149, 195, 332, 342, 346, 348, 356, 398, 400, 404.
Frankfurter Rundschau, Frankfort, 1964: 274.
Galland, A., *Die Esten und die Letzten*, Darmstadt, 1953 (Eng. Edition: *The First and the Last*, London, 1955): 263.
de Gaulle, C., *War Memoirs: Salvation, 1944–46*, London, 1960: 75, 125, 149, 153, 161, 166, 292, 307, 406.
Goebbels, Joseph—Das Dritte Reich und seine Propaganda. Documentary gramophone record, edited by Dr. Krummacher, 1964 (Ariola-Athene): 117.
Guderian, H., *Erinnerungen eines Soldaten*, Neckargemünd, 1960: 27.
Hampe, E., *Ziviler Luftschutz im Zweiten Weltkrieg*, Frankfort, 1963: 264, 274, 275, 423.
Haupt, W., *Kurland*, Bad Nauheim, 1959: 290.
Haupt, W., *Berlin 1945—Hitlers Letzte Schlacht*, Rastatt, 1963: 245.
Heinze, Emil: 40, 104, 289.
Henkys, R., *Die NS-Gewaltverbrechen*, Stuttgart, 1964: 422.
Hersey, J., *Hiroshima*, London, 1946: 387, 391.
Inoguchi, R. and Nakajima, T., *The Divine Wind*, London, 1959: 332, 335, 348.

Irving, D. J., *Und Deutschlands Städte starben nicht*, Zurich, 1963: 265, 269.
Irving, D. J., *The Destruction of Dresden*, London, 1963: 268.
Kästner, E., *Notabene 45*, Berlin, 1961: 79, 280.
Keesing's *Contemporary Archives (1943–45)*: 19, 35, 42, 48, 50, 56, 103, 115, 116, 120, 129, 135, 152, 158, 163, 164, 169, 178, 188, 189, 199, 203, 206, 213, 219, 221, 233, 238, 252, 263, 291, 302, 305, 307, 309, 359, 361, 363, 369, 373, 379, 394, 396, 397, 399, 413.
Kessel, J., *Medizinalrat Kersten*, Munich, 1961: 84, 297.
Kesselring, A., *Soldat bis zum letzten Tag*, Frankfort, 1953: 181.
Kissel, H., *Der deutsche Volkssturm, 1944–45*, Berlin, 1962: 65.
Kogon, E., *Der SS-Staat*, Frankfort, 1946: 137.
Koller, K., *Der letzte Monat*, Mannheim, 1949: 181, 234, 261.
Kriegstagebuch des OKW, Vols. 1–5, Frankfort, 1961–1964: 118, 154, 176, 177, 211, 224, 259, 288, 290, 294.
Lasch, O., *So fiel Koenigsberg*, Munich, 1961: 46, 131.
Leithäuser, *Reportagen zur Weltgeschichte*, Stuttgart, 1964: 415.
Letzte Briefe zum Tode Verurteilter aus dem europäischen Widerstand, Ed. by Malvezzi-Pirelli, Zürich, 1961: 222, 425.
Luftkrieg über Deutschland, 1939–1945, Ed. by E. Klöss, Munich, 1963: 265.
Malotka, Wolfgang: 58, 77.
Mao Tse-Tung, *Selected Works*, Vol. 4, London, 1956: 394, 415.
Marienfeld, W., *Konferenzen über Deutschland*, Hanover, 1962: 162, 163, 295, 306, 307.
Montgomery, Field-Marshal, *Memoirs*, London, 1958: 23, 94, 108, 284, 297.
Morison, *Victory in the Pacific, 1945*. History of United States Naval Operations in World War II, Vol. XIV, Boston, 1961: 424.
Murawski, E., *Der deutsche Wehrmachtsbericht 1939–1945*, Schriften des Bundesarchives, Vol. 9, Boppard, 1962: 40, 85, 94, 97, 113, 206, 248, 291.
Mussolini, B., *Il Fascismo*, Rome, 1935: 208.
Nehru, J., *A Bunch of Old Letters*, London, 1960: 408.
Paul, W., . . . *zum Beispiel Dresden*, Frankfort, 1964: 269.
Poliakoff-Wulff, *Das Dritte Reich und seine Diener*, Berlin, 1956: 134.
Propyläen-Weltgeschichte, Edited by G. Mann, Vol. 9: Das Zwanzigste Jahrhundert, Berlin-Frankfort, 1960: 152.
Putzger, *Historischer Weltatlas*, Bielefeld, 1963: 422.
Reitlinger, G., *Die Endlösung*, Berlin, 1960: 138, 143.
Rendulic, L., *Gekämpft, gesiegt, geschlagen*, Wels-Munich, 1957: 181.
Rohwer, J., *U-Boote, Eine Chronik in Bildern*, Oldenburg, 1962: 249, 250.
Roskill, S. W., *The Navy at War, 1939–45*, London, 1960: 375, 423, 424.
Ruge, F., *Entscheidung im Pazifik*, Hamburg, 1951: 330, 424, 425.
Ruge, F., *Der Seekrieg 1939–1945*, Stuttgart, 1954: 371.
v. Salis, J. R., *Weltgeschichte der Neuesten Zeit*, Vol. III, Zurich, 1962: 420.
Sarkisyanz, E., *Südostasien seit 1945*, Munich, 1961: 411, 412.
Schultz, J., *Die letzten 30 Tage*, Stuttgart, 1951: 176, 231, 304.
Shigemitsu, M., *Japan and her Destiny*, London, 1958: 379, 397.
Snyder, L. L., *The War. A Concise History 1939–1945*, New York, 1960: 164, 208, 292, 387, 388.
Spiegel, Der, Hamburg, No. 30/1964: 288.
Stern, Hamburg, 1964: 422.
Südostasien. Von Pakistan bis Korea. Ed. by H. J. Winkler, Berlin, 1964: 409.
Thompson, R. W., *The Battle for the Rhineland*, London, 1958: 50.
Teller, E. and Brown, A., *The legacy of Hiroshima*, London, 1962: 382, 384.
Thorwald, J., *Flight in the Winter*, London, 1953: 38, 64, 171, 231, 232, 242, 256–257, 398.
Truman, H. S., *Year of Decisions, 1945*, London, 1955: 294.
Tully, A., *Berlin, Story of a Battle, April–May 1945*, New York, 1963: 243.
Zentner, K., *Illustr. Geschichte des Zweiten Weltkriegs*, Munich, 1963: 107.
Zierer, O., *Die Abenteuer der vielgeliebten Stadt München*, Vol. II, Munich, 1958: 173.

Photographs and documents reproduced in this book

Argonne National Laboratory: 383 (2).
Army Headquarters, Ottawa: 74.
Associated Press: 18, 51, 53, 63, 80–81, 83, 126, 134, 135, 136, 151, 164, 169, 296, 303, 310–311 (2), 333, 417.
Atlantic Press: 98, 108, 163, 306.
Australian War Memorial Canberra: 355, 358, 362 (2), 363, 365 (3), 405 (2), 406.
Cartier-Bresson, Henri: 415.
CTK-Photo, Prague: 193 (3), 215.
DPA: 24, 25, 45, 55, 56, 62 (2), 81, 82, 85, 87, 91, 99, 109, 126, 151, 159, 162, 166 (2), 172, 179, 198 (2), 201, 225, 248, 256, 266, 288, 291, 303, 305, 306, 309, 310–311 (8), 416 (2), 417 (3).
Engert, Paul: 36, 39, 47, 255.
FPG, New York: 113, 338, 348.
Gräfe & Unzer Verlag, Munich: 30, 104, 133.
Grund, Erich: 255 (2).
Gyldendal Norsk Forlag, Oslo: 220 (2), 222, 223, 224.

Hauptamt für Hochbauwesen, Nürnberg: 267.
Heinze, Emil: 289.
Henrich, Carl: 101, 156 (2).
Hoover Institution, Stanford, Calif.: 90, 197, 230, 287, 407.
Imperial War Museum, London: 23, 27, 33, 34, 40, 42, 44–45, 50, 51, 52, 53, 54 (3), 59, 60–61, 63, 64, 66, 69, 72 (2), 74, 75, 90, 95 (3), 97, 98 (2), 99, 102, 103, 115 (2), 117, 118, 124 (2), 126, 131, 133, 135, 140, 141 (3), 142, 143 (3), 146, 159, 160 (2), 161, 168, 170 (2), 178 (3), 180 (3), 181, 185, 189 (2), 192, 194 (2), 195,.196 (3), 200, 201, 202 (2), 202–203, 204, 205 (3), 206, 207 (2), 209 (3), 210, 211 (2), 213 (3), 216, 217 (3), 224, 226, 233, 249 (3), 250 (3), 251, 253 (2), 258 (2), 259, 260, 262, 264, 265, 269, 271, 273, 276 (2), 277, 284 (3), 288, 293 (2), 295, 296 (2), 297 (2), 302 (3), 310, 317, 321, 324, 326, 327 (2), 330, 332, 336, 340, 341 (2), 342, 344, 345, 346, 347, 349, 350, 351, 352, 353 (2), 354 (3), 355, 356 (2), 357 (2), 358, 359, 362, 364, 366, 367 (2), 369 (2), 373, 374–375, 376, 379, 380, 393, 404 (2), 405, 406, 410, 413, 416, 417.
Interfoto MTI, Budapest: 184 (2), 187.

Jaeger, Hugo: 174, 240 (2), 277.
Keystone: 40, 44, 45, 63, 72, 73, 83, 102, 115, 127, 138, 164, 172, 188, 210 (2), 211, 221, 222, 238 (2), 240, 264, 303, 304, 310–311 (8), 326, 386, 397, 416 (2).
Kindermann, Klaus: 300.
Leser, Lothar, Karlsruhe (Pamphlet Collection): 13, 24, 42, 46, 49, 83, 103, 115, 117 (2), 120, 124, 134, 150, 157, 168, 201, 276, 281, 291, 303.
Los Alamos-Scientific Laboratory: 382 (3), 384 (2), 385 (2).
Malotka, Wolfgang: 39, 58 (2).
Marmulla (Hoffmann): 77, 239, 274.
Military Museum of Yugoslav Army, Photogr. Section; Beograd: 189, 190, 192 (3).
S. Mohn-Verlag, Gütersloh: 269.
Müller-Reinhardt, Eva Gisela: 30.
Müller-Rodenberger, Franz: 268 (2).
National Archives of United States, Washington: 26 (3), 27, 29 (2), 32 (4), 35, 39, 46, 64, 68, 72 (2), 78, 89, 93 (2), 105, 106 (2), 109, 111 (3), 118, 123 (2), 129, 133, 138 (2), 144, 157, 169, 173 (2), 187 (2), 221 (3), 231, 237, 239 (2), 241 (2), 261 (2), 267, 268 (2), 272 (2), 276, 280 (2), 294 (2), 295.
Nationalmuseet, Copenhagen: 223, 227.
Norsk Telegrambyra, Oslo: 223, 227.
Novosti-Press Agency, Moscow: 71, 104, 133, 144, 157, 163, 186, 198, 212, 229, 237, 238, 242, 243, 288, 292, 394, 395, 396 (2), 402, 412, 413, 421.
Paris Match: rear cover.
Politiken, Copenhagen: 227.
Pospischil, Gustav: 33, 48, 73, 90, 97, 100, 105, 106 (2), 207, 302, 304.
Rijksinstituut voor Oorlogsdocumentatie, Amsterdam: 22, 23, 35, 39, 49, 50, 53, 76, 77, 90, 99, 100 (2), 108, 118, 119 (2), 120 (2), 122, 123 (2), 285 (3), 286 (2), 358, 365, 391, 411 (2).
Sadea S.p.A., Florence: 208 (2).

Schaller, Hans: 78 (2), 79, 214 (2), 232, 233, 234, 235, 239, 262, 275, 310, 379
Schlossar, O.: 129
Schürer, Otto: 17, 87, 116, 125, 129 (2), 169, 174.
Soviet Publications: 29, 33, 36, 37 (2), 55 (2), 57, 76 (2), 88, 101, 111, 132, 167, 197, 225, 240–241, 242 (2), 243, 244, 257, 263 (2), 273, 292, 309 (2), 396, inside back cover.
G. Stalling-Verlag, Hamburg: 249.
Süddeutscher Verlag, Bilderdienst: 21, 22, 23, 31, 39, 44, 55, 57, 61, 65, 66, 71, 75, 80, 84, 88, 94, 101, 105, 116, 131, 154, 174, 175, 194, 219, 237, 261, 265, 303, 338, 346, 385, 406, jacket.
Ullstein-Bilderdienst: 21, 30 (2), 31 (2), 56, 57, 59, 67, 84, 85, 89, 93, 144, 149, 155, 171, 183 (2), 187, 190, 194, 198, 224, 232, 240, 259, 261 (2), 270, 271, 272 (2), 273, 278, 291, 300, 301, 303, 304, 309, 310–311 (8), 382, 396, 416, 417.
United Press International: 90, 137, 140, 151, 165, 179, 181, 219, 226, 275, 287, 307, 387, 390, 391, 392.
U.S. Army: 19 (2), 94, 125, 206, 218, 338, 384, 398, 399.
U.S. Atomic Energy Commission, Oak Ridge, Tennessee: 383.
U.S. Coast Guard: 247, 321, 331, 337, 364, 373, 397, 398.
U.S. Navy: 326 (2), 330, 331, 334, 377, 398.
USIS: 20, 73, 86, 87, 96, 97, 114, 128, 139, 147, 148, 157, 171, 172, 181, 216, 218 (2), 252 (3), 272, 286, 292, 293, 300, 311, 331 (2), 335 (2), 336 (2), 339, 340, 342, 343, 344, 347, 350, 359 (2), 361 (2), 370 (4), 371, 373, 378, 380 (2).
Weltkriegsbücherei (Bibliothek für Zeitgeschichte): 21, 104, 154.
Yugoslav Publications: 190 (3).
Zentralbild: 28, 41, 46, 62, 65, 71, 89, 101, 107, 146 (2), 157, 183, 184, 214 (2), 231, 233, 245, 289, inside front cover.
Dr. Zentner Archives: 228, 241.

Selected Bibliography

Europe

Ahlfen, H. v., *Der Kampf um Schlesien*, Munich, 1961.
Army Air Forces in World War II, The, Vols. 1–7, Chicago.
Atlas: A Military History of the World War II, U.S. Department of Military Art and Engineering, 1956.
Atlas Historique de la Guerre de Liberation Nationale de Yougoslavie 1941–1945, Beograd, 1958.
Balfour, M., *The Four-Power Control in Germany and Austria, 1945–46*, London, 1956.
Battaglia, R., *Storia della resistenza italiana*, Torino, 1953.
Bergschicker, H., *Der Zweite Weltkrieg. Eine Chronik in Bildern.*, Berlin, 1963.
Bilanz des Zweiten Weltkrieges, Oldenburg, 1953.
Birkenfeld, W., *Der synthetische Treibstoff 1933–1945*, Göttingen, 1964.
Bosseler, N. and Steich, R., *Livre d'or de la résistance luxembourgeoise de 1940–1945*, Esch-sur-Alzette, 1952.
Bradley, O. N., *A Soldier's Story*, New York, 1951.
Busse, T., *Die letzte Schlacht der 9. Armee* in: Wehrwiss. Rundschau, Jg. 5, 1955.
Canadian Army at War, The, (3 Vols. so far).
Clark, M. W., *Calculated risk*, London, 1951.
Clay, L. D., *Decision in Germany*, London, 1950.
Command Decisions, General ed: Kent Roberts Greenfield, New York, 1959.
De Strijd op Nederlands grodgebied tijdens de Wereldoorlog II, (20 Vols. so far).
Deutsche Briefe des 20. Jahrhunderts, edit. by W. Heynen, Munich, 1962.
Dokumentation der Vertreibung der Deutschen aus Ostmitteleuropa, Edited by T. Schieder, Vols. 1–5, Bonn, 1954–1961.
Dokumente deutscher Kriegsschäden, Vols. 1–2, Bonn, 1958–1960.
Eisenhower, D. D., *Crusade in Europe*, London, 1948.
Festung Breslau, Documenta Obsidionis 1945, Warszawa, 1962.
Forrestal, J., *The Forrestal Diaries, 1944–1949*, New York, 1951.
Fuller, J. F. C., *The Second World War 1939–1945*, London, 1954.
Gisevius, H. B., *Bis zum bitteren Ende*, Vols. 1–2, Hamburg, 1947.
Guilleaume, A., *Warum siegte die Rote Armee?* Baden-Baden, 1949.
Harris, Sir A., *Bomber Offensive*, London, 1947.
Heidelmeyer, W. and Hindrichs, G., *Documents on Berlin 1943–1963*, Munich, 1963.
Hilberg, R., *The Destruction of the European Jews*, Chicago, 1961.
History of the Great Patriotic War of the Soviet Union, (6 vols.), Moscow.
Hubatsch, W., *Flüchtlingstransporte aus dem Osten über See*. Jahrb. d. Ostd. Kulturrates, Vol. IX, Munich, 1962.
Jacobsen, H. and A., *1939–1945 – Der Zweite Weltkrieg in Chronik und Dokumenten*, Darmstadt, 1961.
Jacobsen, H. and A., *Der "Grosse Vaterländische Krieg". Sowjetkommun. Geschichtsschreibung 1945–1961*. In: Aus Politik und Zeitgeschichte, Supplement to "Das Parlament", No. 5, 1962.
Klose, W., *Generation im Gleichschritt. Ein Dokumentarbericht*, Oldenburg, 1964.
Lagebesprechung im Führerhauptquartier, Ed. by H. Heiber, Munich, 1963.
Lattre de Tassigny, J. de, *Histoire de la Première Armée française*, Paris, 1949.

Luedde-Neurath, W., *Regierung Dönitz*, Gottingen, 1951.
Malakhov, M. M., *Ot Balatona do Veny*, Moscow, 1959.
Meinecke, F., *Die deutsche Katastrophe*, Wiesbaden, 1946.
Morison, S. E., *History of the United States Naval Operations in World War II*, Vols. 1–15, Boston, 1947–1962.
Moseley, P. E. Dismemberment of Germany. The Allied Negotiations from Yalta to Potsdam. *Foreign Affairs*, Vol. 28, No. 3, April, 1950, pp. 487–98.
Murphy, R., *Diplomat among warriors*, Garden City, N.Y., 1964.
Norges Krig 1940–1945, Vols. I–III, Oslo, 1950.
Patton, G. S., *War as I knew it*, London, 1948.
Ploetz, *Geschichte des Zweiten Weltkrieges, I–II*, Würzburg, 1960.
Polens Kriegsverluste 1939–1945, Poznan, 1960.
Potsdam 1945, Edit. by F. Deuerlein, Munich, 1963.
Ridgway, M. B., *Soldier*, New York, 1956.
Rodenberger, A., *Der Tod von Dresden*, Frankfort, 1963.
Rohwer, J., *Schiffsverlustlisten*. In: Wehrw. Rundschau, Jg. 5, 1958.
Schellenberg, W., *Memoiren*, Cologne, 1959.
Schmidt, P., *Statist auf diplomatischer Bühne 1923–1945*, Bonn, 1949.
Schmidt-Richberg, E., *Der Endkampf auf dem Balkan*, Heidelberg, 1955.
Schoernberger, G., *Der Gelbe Stern*, Hamburg, 1961.
Schoernberger, G., *Wir haben es gesehen*, Hamburg, 1962.
Schweiz im Zweiten Weltkrieg, Die, Ed. by H. R. Kurz, Thun, 1959.
Senger und Etterlin, F. v., *Krieg in Europa 1940–1945*, Cologne, 1960.
Smith, W. B., *Eisenhower's six great decisions: Europe, 1944–45*, N.Y., 1956.
Spetzler, E., *Luftkrieg und Menschlichkeit*, Göttingen, 1956.
Stalin, J. V., *On the great patriotic war of the Soviet Union*, Moscow, 1946.
Stegemann, W., *Der Neue Weltkrieg*, 6. Band 1944–45, Zurich, 1946.
Stimson, H. L. and Bundy, McG., *On active Service in peace and war*, New York, 1948.
Tagebuch aus Pommern 1945–46. K. v. Normann, Munich, 1962.
Telpuchovskij, B. S., *Die sowjetische Geschichte des Grossen Vaterlländischen Krieges*, Frankfort, 1961.
Trevor-Roper, H. R., *Last days of Hitler*, London, 1947.
U.S. Army in World War II, The, (56 Vols. so far.)
Vertreibungsverluste, Die deutschen, Bevölkerungsbilanzen für die dtsch. Vertreibungsgebiete 1939–50, Stuttgart, 1958.
Wagener, C., *Kampf und Ende der Heeresgruppe B im Ruhrkessel 22 March bis 17 April 1945*. In: Wehrwiss. Rundschau, Jg. 7, 1957.
Wagenführ, R., *Die deutsche Industrie im Kriege 1939–1945*, Berlin, 1963.
War and Revolution of the peoples of Jugoslavia 1941–1945, The, Beograd.
War and the neutrals, The, London, 1956.
Warlimont, W., *Im Hauptquartier der deutschen wehrmacht 1939 bis 1945*, Frankfort, 1962.
Wedemeyer, A. C., *Der verwaltete Krieg*, Gütersloh, 1960.
Widerstandsbewegung in Europa während des Zweiten Weltkrieges, Die antifaschistische, Moscow, 1962.

Williams, M. H., *Chronology 1941–1945*, Washington, 1960. (Office of the Chief of Milit. History (U.S. Army in World War II). Special Studies, Vol. 4).

Willis, F. R., *The French in Germany 1945–1949*, Stanford, Calif., 1962.

Winkel, L. E., *De ondergrondse pers 1940–1945*, s'-Gravenhage, 1954.

Za Svobodu Československa, (3 vols. so far).

Zweite Weltkrieg in Bildern und Dokumenten, Der, Ed. by H. and A. Jacobsen and H. Dollinger, Vols. I–III, Munich, 1962.

Asia

Australia in the War of 1939–1945, (16 vols. so far).

Albas, A. d', *Death of a navy*, New York, 1957.

Anderson, B. R. O'G., *Some Aspects of Indonesian Politics under the Japanese Occupation: 1944–1945*, New York, 1961, Department of Far Eastern Studies, Cornell Univ. Ithaca.

Brennecke, J., *Haie im Paradies, Der deutsche U-Boot-Krieg in Asiens Gewässern 1943–1945*, Preetz/Holst, 1961.

Buchanan, A. R., *The United States and World War II*. Vols. 1–2, New York, 1964.

Chiang Kai-shek, *Soviet Russia in China*, London, 1957.

Clark, R. W., *The Birth of the bomb*, London, 1961.

Eichelberger, R. L., *Our Jungle Road to Tokyo*, New York, 1950.

Hewlett, R. G., and Anderson, O. E., jr., *A History of the U.S. Atomic Energy Commission*, Vol. 1: The new World, 1939–1946, University Park, Va., 1962.

Inoguchi, R. and Nakajima, T., *The Divine Wind*, London, 1959.

Jmai, J., *Japan's Luftwaffen-Flugzeuge im 2. Weltkrieg*, Munich, 1961.

Sherrod, R. and Nakano, G., *A Concise History of the Pacific War*, Vols. 1–2, Tokyo, 1956.

Slim, Sir W., *Defeat into victory*, London, 1958.

Togo, S., *Japan im Zweiten Weltkrieg*, Bonn, 1958.

Yoshida, S., Japan im Wiederaufstieg, Düsseldorf, 1963.

(See also p. 430).